THE DUCHESS OF MALFI,
THE WHITE DEVIL,
THE BROKEN HEART AND
'TIS PITY SHE'S A WHORE

JOHN WEBSTER was born in about 1578 in the parish of St Sepulchre-without-Newgate, London, the eldest son of a prosperous coachmaker. He probably attended Merchant Taylors' School, before studying law at the Middle Temple, where he developed the rhetorical skills needed for a life in the theatre. His writing career was mainly collaborative, beginning with a tragedy, *Caesar's Fall* (*c.* 1602, now lost), in which Anthony Munday, Thomas Middleton and Michael Drayton all had a hand, and ranging across a number of genres, including popular history (*Lady Jane I* and *II*, 1602), city comedy (*Westward Ho*, 1604), tragicomedy (*The Devil's Law-Case*, *c.* 1618) and civic pageantry (*Monuments of Honour*, 1624). Yet it was his two solo-authored tragedies, *The White Devil* (1612) and *The Duchess of Malfi* (1614), which sealed his reputation. There are no records of theatrical output between 1605 and 1612, though we know that in 1606 he married Sara Peniall, who was seven months pregnant, and they had at least four children. It may be that during this time Webster was labouring over his two greatest plays. He was clearly aggrieved at the negative reaction to *The White Devil* when it was first performed at the Red Bull Theatre by the Queen Anne's Men to an unenthusiastic audience. However, *The Duchess of Malfi*, performed by the King's Men at the Blackfriars Theatre two years later, was an instant success. Despite this new fame, Webster continued to collaborate with all the major dramatists of the time and to work in genres other than tragedy until his death in the 1630s.

JOHN FORD was born in April 1586 in Ilsington, Devon, the second son of a wealthy landowner. We know very little about his life. He may have attended Exeter College, Oxford, before studying law at the Middle Temple in London, an association he seems to have continued throughout his life. His first published work was an elegy entitled *Fame's Memorial* (1606) and his early career was wholly concerned with poetry and philosophical works. It was not until the 1620s that he began writing for the stage, collaborating with the more experienced dramatist Thomas Dekker on plays including *The Witch of Edmonton* (1621) and a masque, *The Sun's Darling* (1624), and developing his connection with the King's Men by completing John Fletcher's *The Fair Maid of the Inn* (1626) with Webster and Philip Massinger. In the late 1620s Ford began writing alone, producing the eight plays on which his reputation is based. The precise dating of these works remains unknown, but the first three were probably *The Lover's Melancholy* (*c.* 1628), *The Broken Heart* (*c.* 1629) and *Beauty in a Trance* (*c.* 1630, now lost), performed by the King's Men at the Blackfriars Theatre. Ford then changed his allegiance to the Queen Henrietta's Men at the Cockpit Theatre, Drury Lane, for whom he wrote *'Tis Pity She's a Whore* (*c.* 1630), *Love's Sacrifice* (*c.* 1632), *Perkin Warbeck* (*c.* 1633) and *The Fancies, Chaste and Noble* (*c.* 1635). What looks like Ford's last play, *The Lady's Trial* (1638), was performed at the Cockpit by Beeston's Boys, after which nothing more of him is known.

JANE KINGSLEY-SMITH studied English at Oriel College, Oxford, and completed her PhD at the Shakespeare Institute, Stratford-upon-Avon. She is the author of two monographs: *Shakespeare's Drama of Exile* (Palgrave, 2003) and *Cupid in Early Modern Literature and Culture* (Cambridge, 2010), and is currently editing *Love's Labour's Lost* for the new Norton Shakespeare. She is a Reader at Roehampton University, London, and a regular guest speaker at Shakespeare's Globe.

JOHN WEBSTER
and JOHN FORD

The Duchess of Malfi, The White Devil, The Broken Heart *and* 'Tis Pity She's a Whore

Edited and introduced by
JANE KINGSLEY-SMITH

PENGUIN BOOKS

PENGUIN CLASSICS

Published by the Penguin Group
Penguin Books Ltd, 80 Strand, London WC2R ORL, England
Penguin Group (USA) Inc., 375 Hudson Street, New York, New York 10014, USA
Penguin Group (Canada), 90 Eglinton Avenue East, Suite 700, Toronto, Ontario, Canada M4P 2Y3 (a division of Pearson Penguin Canada Inc.)
Penguin Ireland, 25 St Stephen's Green, Dublin 2, Ireland (a division of Penguin Books Ltd)
Penguin Group (Australia), 707 Collins Street, Melbourne, Victoria 3008, Australia (a division of Pearson Australia Group Pty Ltd)
Penguin Books India Pvt Ltd, 11 Community Centre, Panchsheel Park, New Delhi – 110 017, India
Penguin Group (NZ), 67 Apollo Drive, Rosedale, Auckland 0632, New Zealand (a division of Pearson New Zealand Ltd)
Penguin Books (South Africa) (Pty) Ltd, Block D, Rosebank Office Park, 181 Jan Smuts Avenue, Parktown North, Gauteng 2193, South Africa

Penguin Books Ltd, Registered Offices: 80 Strand, London WC2R ORL, England

www.penguin.com

First published in Great Britain by Penguin Classics 2014

013

Editorial material copyright © Jane Kingsley-Smith, 2014
All rights reserved

The moral right of the editor has been asserted

Set in 10.25/12.25pt Postscript Adobe Sabon
Typeset by Jouve (UK), Milton Keynes
Printed in Great Britain by Clays Ltd, Elcograf S.p.A.

Except in the United States of America, this book is sold subject to the condition that it shall not, by way of trade or otherwise, be lent, re-sold, hired out, or otherwise circulated without the publisher's prior consent in any form of binding or cover other than that in which it is published and without a similar condition including this condition being imposed on the subsequent purchaser

ISBN: 978-0-141-39223-3

www.greenpenguin.co.uk

Penguin Books is committed to a sustainable future for our business, our readers and our planet. This book is made from Forest Stewardship Council™ certified paper.

Contents

Chronology

c. 1578 John Webster born in Smithfield, London, the first son of John Webster Snr.

1586 John Ford baptized on 12 April at Ilsington, Devon, second son of Thomas Ford and Elizabeth Popham.

1598 Webster admitted to the Middle Temple, London, to study law.

1601 Ford matriculates at Exeter College, Oxford.

c. 1602 Webster collaborates on *Caesar's Fall* (with Anthony Munday, Thomas Middleton and Michael Drayton), *Lady Jane I* and *II* (with Thomas Dekker) and *Christmas Comes but Once a Year* (with Thomas Heywood), all lost.

Webster contributes a commendatory poem to Munday's translation of *Palmerin of England*, Part III.

Ford admitted to the Middle Temple, London, to study law.

1603 Death of Elizabeth I; accession of James I.

1604 Webster writes the Induction and other additions for a revised version of John Marston's *The Malcontent*, performed by the King's Men at the Blackfriars Theatre.

Westward Ho by Webster and Dekker first performed by Paul's Boys.

Webster contributes a commendatory poem to Stephen Harrison's *Arches of Triumph*.

1605 *Northward Ho* by Webster and Dekker first performed by Paul's Boys.

Ford suspended from the Middle Temple for failure to pay his buttery bill.

1606 In March Webster marries Sara Peniall, aged seventeen and pregnant with their first child, John Webster Jnr, born in May 1606.

Ford publishes *Fame's Memorial*, an elegy for Charles Blount, Lord Mountjoy, dedicated to his widow, Penelope, *née* Devereux.

Ford publishes *Honour Triumphant*, a prose pamphlet dedicated to the Countesses of Pembroke and Montgomery.

1607 Publication of Webster and Dekker's *Westward Ho*, *Northward Ho* and *Sir Thomas Wyatt* (based on *Lady Jane*).

1608 Ford readmitted to the Middle Temple.

1610 Death of Ford's father; he inherits £10.

1612 Webster's *The White Devil* performed by the Queen Anne's Men at the Red Bull Theatre in Clerkenwell and published the same year.

Webster contributes prefatory poems to Heywood's *An Apology for Actors*.

Death of Henry, Prince of Wales. Webster publishes an elegy for him entitled *A Monumental Column*.

1613 Ford publishes a Stoic tract, *The Golden Mean*, dedicated to the imprisoned Earl of Northumberland.

Ford publishes the long poem *Christ's Bloody Sweat*, dedicated to the Earl of Pembroke.

Ford's comedy *An Ill Beginning Has a Good End* (now lost) performed at the Cockpit Theatre.

1614 Webster's *The Duchess of Malfi* performed by the King's Men at the Blackfriars Theatre and the Globe Theatre.

Webster writes *The Guise* (now lost).

Death of Webster's father.

1615 Webster contributes thirty-two characters to the sixth edition of Sir Thomas Overbury's *Characters*.

Webster claims membership of the Merchant Taylors' Company.

Ford's work (perhaps an elegy or pamphlet) *Sir Thomas Overbury's Ghost* (now lost) entered into the Stationers' Register.

1616 Death of William Shakespeare.

Death of Francis Beaumont.

Death of Ford's elder brother Henry, leaving Ford with an annuity of £20.

Ford contributes an elegy to the new edition of *Sir Thomas Overbury His Wife*.

1617 Ford reprimanded by the Middle Temple for demonstrating against wearing lawyers' caps in hall.

1618 Webster's *The Duchess of Malfi* performed at court, before the Venetian ambassador, Orazio Busino.

Webster's *The Devil's Law-Case* perhaps first performed by the Queen Anne's Men, probably at the Cockpit Theatre.

Execution of Sir Walter Raleigh.

1620 Ford publishes a neo-Stoic pamphlet, *A Line of Life*, dedicated to Sir James Hay, the son-in-law of the Earl of Northumberland.

1621 Webster collaborates with Middleton on *Anything for a Quiet Life*.

The Witch of Edmonton, a tragedy by Ford, Dekker and William Rowley, first performed.

1623 Publication of Webster's *The Duchess of Malfi*, with a commendatory verse by Ford, and *The Devil's Law-Case*.

The Spanish Gipsy by Ford, Middleton and Rowley first performed.

The Welsh Ambassador by Ford and Dekker first performed.

The Laws of Candy by Ford and John Fletcher first performed.

Webster and Ford contribute commendatory verses to Henry Cockeram's *English Dictionary*.

1624 Webster collaborates with Ford, Dekker and Rowley on *The Late Murder of the Son upon the Mother, or Keep the Widow Waking* (now lost).

Ford's *The London Merchant* (now lost) first performed.

Ford and Dekker's *The Bristol Merchant* and *The Fairy Knight* (both now lost) first performed.

Ford and Dekker's *The Sun's Darling*, a masque (now lost) first performed at the Cockpit Theatre.

Webster writes the pageant *Monuments of Honour* for the inauguration of Lord Mayor, Sir John Gore, of the Merchant Taylors' Company.

1625 Death of James I; accession of Charles I.

Webster and Rowley collaborate on *A Cure for a Cuckold.*

Death of Fletcher. His *The Fair Maid of the Inn* completed by Webster, Ford and Philip Massinger.

1627 Webster collaborates with Heywood on the tragedy *Appius and Virginia.*

1628 Ford's *The Lover's Melancholy* first performed at the Blackfriars and Globe theatres by the King's Men.

Ford publishes commendatory verses to Shirley's *The Wedding* and Massinger's *The Roman Actor.*

1629 Publication of Ford's *The Lover's Melancholy*, his first surviving independent play.

Ford's *The Broken Heart* probably first performed by the King's Men at the Blackfriars Theatre.

1630 Ford's *'Tis Pity She's a Whore* perhaps first performed by Queen Henrietta's Men at the Cockpit Theatre in Drury Lane.

Ford's *Beauty in a Trance* (now lost) perhaps first performed.

Webster's *The Duchess of Malfi* revived by the King's Men for performance in theatres and at court.

1632 Ford's *Love's Sacrifice* perhaps first performed.

Ford publishes commendatory verses to Richard Brome's *The Northern Lass.*

1633 Publication of Ford's *The Broken Heart*, *Love's Sacrifice* and *'Tis Pity She's a Whore.*

Ford's *Perkin Warbeck* perhaps first performed.

c. 1634 Death of Webster, in his mid-fifties.

Publication of Ford's *Perkin Warbeck.*

1635 Ford's *The Fancies, Chaste and Noble* perhaps first performed.

1636 Publication of Ford's commendatory verses to Massinger's *The Great Duke of Florence* and Charles Saltonstall's *The Navigator.*

1637 Death of Ben Jonson.

1638 Publication of Ford's *The Fancies, Chaste and Noble.*

Ford's *The Lady's Trial* first performed by Beeston's Boys at the Cockpit Theatre.

Ford publishes a tribute to Ben Jonson in the collection *Jonsonus Virbius.*

1639 Death of Massinger.

Publication of Ford's *The Lady's Trial.* Nothing more is heard of Ford.

1640 Webster's *The Duchess of Malfi* published again.

1642 English Civil War begins. Closure of the London theatres.

1649 Execution of Charles I.

1653 Anonymous publication of Ford's *The Queen.*

Introduction

In the first printed edition of John Webster's *The Duchess of Malfi* (1623) we find a brief eulogy by his fellow dramatist John Ford, praising it as a 'masterpiece'. Ford makes no mention of having seen the play in performance, nor does he imply any personal relationship with Webster – no account of the dramatists' meeting survives. Yet their professional careers and, perhaps less advantageously, their critical reputations would thereafter be intertwined.

In 1624 Webster and Ford worked on a play with Thomas Dekker and William Rowley, entitled *The Late Murder of the Son upon the Mother, or Keep the Widow Waking*. Perhaps they collaborated in person, though they may equally have written their parts of the manuscript alone. A curious hybrid of comedy and tragedy, the play (now lost) exemplifies both Webster's and Ford's interest in making sensational drama out of real events – here, the abduction and forced marriage of sixty-two-year-old widow Anne Elsdon, and the matricide committed by Nathaniel Tindall, both of which occurred just a few months before the play was performed. So painfully recent was the memory, that Anne's son-in-law tried to prosecute the dramatists for libel.[1] In the following year, Webster and Ford worked together again on John Fletcher's tragicomedy *The Fair Maid of the Inn* – another lost (though less controversial) play. But a subtler kind of collaboration, about which we have more detail, is the influence on Ford's dramatic work of Webster's two great single-authored tragedies, *The White Devil* and *The Duchess of Malfi*. Ford's *Love's Sacrifice* opens with the same shocked response to banishment as *The White Devil*; Orgilus in Ford's

The Broken Heart dies quoting Webster's Flaminio: 'A mist hangs o'er mine eyes' (5.2); and there may be an allusion to *The Duchess of Malfi* in Giovanni's presentation of a dagger to his sister in *'Tis Pity She's a Whore.* As one critic has observed, 'in both contexts the giving of an unsheathed weapon signals the dangerous and unhealthy implications of a sexual relation between siblings and ironically foreshadows the violent cruelty to come'.[2] But if there are intriguing verbal and thematic links between Webster and Ford, perhaps their most enduring association has been created by their detractors.

Since the early nineteenth century both dramatists have been accused of the same crimes, most notably plagiarism, amorality and technical incompetence. Webster and Ford wrote for the King's Men, Shakespeare's company, at a time when its most celebrated playwright was either reducing his theatrical output or dead (see *The Duchess of Malfi* and *The Broken Heart* respectively), but Shakespeare remained a tyrannical presence, compelling his successors to remember and revisit his works. Hence, *The White Devil* borrows from *Antony and Cleopatra*, with additional scenes from *Hamlet* and *King Lear*, and *'Tis Pity* rewrites *Romeo and Juliet.* For subsequent critics, this created the impression that Webster and Ford were decadent (i.e., operating after the great age of tragedy) and imaginatively defunct. More damaging than the charge of plagiarism has been that of amorality. In 1856 the novelist Charles Kingsley complained of all Jacobean tragedians (excluding only Shakespeare, Ben Jonson and Philip Massinger) that 'Revenge, hatred, villainy, incest and murder upon murder are their constant themes . . . and they handle these horrors with little or no moral purpose, save that of exciting and amusing the audience.'[3] Not only are Webster and Ford frequently blamed for being too sympathetic to their protagonists ('He draws this hero and heroine as if he loved them'),[4] but they also notoriously fail to uphold the illusion of a moral universe or to reach any clear moral conclusions, creating 'a world in which no set of values is shown to be the "right" one, no attitude as intrinsically better than any other'.[5] For an earlier generation of critics, these omissions were not just socially irresponsible, but potentially anarchic.[6] Ford's reputation has suffered particularly through his being made to represent the 'decadent' Caroline theatre, whose moral and political disengagement was considered one of the factors that led to the English Civil War (1642–9).[7] Finally, both playwrights are found wanting in terms of dramatic structure and characterization. Charles R. Forker observes that *The White Devil* is 'crammed with incidents that seem discontinuous, interruptive, tonally inconsistent with each other, even functionally gratuitous';[8] and both playwrights seem to struggle with Act Five, in which the piling-up of corpses after a protagonist's death in Act Four (see *The Duchess of Malfi* and *The Broken Heart*) has felt, to some critics, disappointingly random and chaotic.[9] Of a piece with this is the sense that characters are fragmented, inconsistent and unconvincing. When George Bernard Shaw described Webster as the 'Tussaud laureate',[10] he was not only condemning the dramatist's amoral sensationalism (typified by the wax figures in *The Duchess of Malfi*), but also criticizing the lifelessness of his characters. Similarly, Ford's protagonists have been seen to possess 'a certain ethereal indistinctness as of figures passing in mist',[11] and the dearth of soliloquies in his plays has been attributed to his lack of interest in psychology.

In the last fifty years the renewed popularity of Webster and Ford in the theatre has been complemented by a critical re-evaluation. Their reworking of Shakespeare is now more often attributed to a creative ingenuity, which challenges audience expectations, rather than to mere slavish devotion. For example, Ford invokes the innocent lovers destroyed by fate from *Romeo and Juliet* in order to raise questions about the moral guilt or innocence of the incestuous couple in *'Tis Pity She's a Whore*. The dramatists' reputations for amorality have also been revised. Having claimed that Webster and Ford 'do not think on moral issues', David L. Frost argues in their defence that neither dramatist intended to write 'moral tragedy'. At the same time, he perceives them as 'oppressed by the hopeless complication and ambiguity of moral issues', exploring with visceral terror 'the impermanence and fluidity of things'.[12] The defence of Webster's and Ford's bloody and horrifying visual images – such as Annabella's heart on a dagger or the waxworks in *The Duchess of Malfi* – has also proved crucial to this re-evaluation. No longer deemed simply gratuitous, they are understood within a moral and philosophical framework, familiar to an early modern audience with a taste for reading emblems. As Richard Madelaine has shown, '[Ford's] stage images are usually carefully prepared for in terms of theme, character and verbal and visual imagery . . . he is never at *heart* a mere sensationalist.'[13] Finally, 'flaws' in structure and characterization tend now to be perceived as deliberate artistic choices. Rather than deplore the absence of a linear plot, Christina Luckyj identifies in Webster's work a concentric structure, created by patterns of repetition, which de-emphasizes causation and deepens tragic effect: 'a single idea is turned over and over, gaining in intensity and clarity as it is repeated and expanded.'[14] Inconsistencies in characterization reflect the economic and social pressures on the early modern individual (particularly the effects of patriarchy on women), which prevented them from achieving a stable sense of self. As Martin Wiggins observes: '[Webster's] tragedies deal with people who cannot direct their own lives, cannot make their own choices. His theme is, so to speak, the "subjectivity of the subjected".'[15] Hence, the elusiveness of Vittoria in *The White Devil* – a character who never reveals 'a "real", inner self'[16] – is partly explained by the hostile, misogynist world in which she lives.

This edition groups together the four major tragedies of John Webster and John Ford – *The White Devil*, *The Duchess of Malfi*, *The Broken Heart* and *'Tis Pity She's a Whore* – in the belief that, despite being written in the Jacobean and Caroline periods respectively, when read side by side they illuminate one another. Three out of four of these plays are based on true events in sixteenth-century Italy, although viewed from a distinctly Reformation perspective, hence the casting of cardinals and friars as villains and a morbid fascination with confession.[17] They also exploit English assumptions about Italian vices – defined as violent sexual jealousy, ingenuity in murder and political hypocrisy or Machiavellianism[18] – although both dramatists also refer satirically to contemporary English politics. Webster's plays, for example, are fascinated by the moral and fiscal corruption of the court of James I (1603–25) and by the disappointments of a new class of university-educated men, denied the opportunities for social advancement which humanism had promised.[19]

All four plays are indebted to Elizabethan revenge tragedy, in which a terrible crime must be avenged, despite the fact that the perpetrator is a powerful figure whose punishment will 'fall on th'inventors' heads' (*Hamlet*, 5.2.328). But while they deploy some revenge tragedy conventions, these later plays also stand sceptically and even mockingly apart from them. We might compare Shakespeare's Hamlet – a self-conscious but deeply troubled revenger – with Webster's witty Francisco, who declares: 'My tragedy must have some idle mirth in't, / Else it will never pass' (4.1.116–7). If the revenger here has lost interest in his own dilemma, this is partly because the focus has shifted to the female protagonist. Both Webster and Ford are deeply invested in the tragic potential of women – something that Webster helped to define for Ford – moving away from the spectacle of patient suffering to a more dynamic and morally ambiguous female agency.[20]

Finally, three out of these four tragedies approach, with fascinated prurience, the possibility of incest between brother and sister. This finds its fullest (and most sympathetic) treatment in *'Tis Pity She's a Whore*, but a sister's sexual rebellion also drives her brother to insanity in *The Duchess of Malfi*; and in *The Broken Heart* the accusation of incest between Penthea and Ithocles, although unfounded, might explain the motive for Ithocles's disastrous intervention in his sister's betrothal. While incest is partly an expression of the sexual vice habitually deplored in Jacobean and Caroline tragedy – *The Broken Heart*'s Bassanes declares that all kinds of incest are fashionable ''mongst youths of mettle' (2.2.124) – the brother-sister relationship is viewed as particularly susceptible to abuse, given that, in the absence of the father, a brother may be placed as guardian over his sister's chastity. Bassanes's assumption that 'Brothers and sisters are but flesh and blood' (2.2.117) emphasizes the bodily possessiveness and the lack of differentiation that defines all of these relationships, not least because the siblings are also twins.

Having identified these areas of shared interest, we need now to consider the individual plays in more detail, for each one raises a particular set of questions and possesses its own unique dramatic power.

The White Devil

The White Devil was first performed by the Queen Anne's Men in 1612 at the Red Bull Theatre in Clerkenwell. It was the achievement of a long and focused effort. Webster seems not to have written anything else between 1605 and 1612, and he must have been ambitious for its success. However, the tragedy found little favour in performance and was published that same year – often a sign that its theatrical life was thought to be over. In the preface, Webster complains that the 'uncapable multitude' simply didn't understand it, and it may have been ill-suited to the unsophisticated tastes of the Red Bull crowd. Yet *The White Devil* seems always to have provoked and unsettled its audiences.

The play is based on contemporary accounts of an affair between Paulo Giordano, Duke of Bracciano, and Vittoria Accoramboni, in Rome and Padua in the 1580s, which led to the murder of their spouses and their own deaths through retribution. Yet, as J. R. Mulryne observes, 'Webster's restless, mocking intelligence is . . . continually modifying the great and passionate events his narrative offered him.'[21] At first glance, the material obviously lends itself to revenge tragedy: in the first half of Webster's play two murders are committed; in the second, these are avenged by four more deaths. Yet *The White Devil* does not allow the audience access to either the moral conviction or sympathetic engagement usually evoked by this genre. For a start, where the initial crime was expected to be of some magnitude in order to generate horror, and to justify the taking of unlawful revenge, Isabella's death by kissing a picture and Camillo's by vaulting horse are too 'quaintly done' (2.2.38) not to inspire admiration and even amusement. Pathos is deadened by how little we know of the victims and by the distancing effect of dumbshows, accompanied by music and perhaps applause, as Bracciano responds to his wife's tragedy: 'Excellent, then she's dead' (2.2.24). Other revenge conventions are similarly undermined. 'It harrows me with fear and wonder,' says Horatio of the ghost of Hamlet's father (1.1.42), whereas Francisco finds Isabella's mournful spirit a hindrance to his revenge and contemptuously banishes it from the stage (4.1.109–10). Moreover, the villains – Bracciano, Vittoria and Flaminio – seem to have displaced the righteous avenger in the audience's sympathies; Francisco is 'the ultimate horror – the spirit of carefully nurtured hatred, inhumanly Machiavellian and bloodlessly disengaged',[22] who yet survives them all.

The White Devil is similarly problematic as love tragedy, for its erotic embraces are not only fatal but repulsive. Thus, Francisco curses Bracciano and Vittoria: 'Let him cleave to her and both rot together' (2.1.397), while Bracciano shrugs off Isabella's kisses: 'Oh, your breath! / Out upon sweetmeats and continued physic – / The plague is in them!' (2.1.165–7). Here, her excessive consumption of sweets disguises a voracious sexual appetite or it conceals actual bodily decay, both of which threaten to infect him with venereal disease. And yet *The White Devil*'s distrust of *eros* is not simply attributable to man's terror of mortality, for which woman acts as a scapegoat.[23] Rather, the play's compulsive horror of suffocation – whether it be Flaminio's account of 'the fellow was smothered in roses' (1.2.148), Vittoria's nightmare of being buried alive (1.2.235) or Bracciano's strangling by a 'true-love knot' (5.3.169) – implies a deeper fear of erotic self-loss that afflicts both men and women. Whereas love tragedy offers a transcendent vision of the couple becoming one through sex and death, *The White Devil*'s lovers remain stubbornly separate and apart, and it is this, as much as their adulterous, murderous appetites, that inhibits the play's romantic effect. Not only do Bracciano and Vittoria never have a scene alone together, but Vittoria's emotional investment in her lover remains uncertain. She fails to mention him in her dying speech and by implication regrets ever having met him: 'Oh, happy they that never saw the court, / Nor ever knew great man but by report' (5.6.259–60).

The dangers of intimacy with great men extend beyond Vittoria to her siblings, Flaminio and Marcello, to their mother, Cornelia, and even to the audience. Flaminio is Bracciano's secretary, a role defined by the production of written correspondence, but also the keeping of secrets. As Angel Day suggests in *The English Secretary* (1586, repr. 1599), it was often imagined spatially:

> The *Closet* in everie house, as it is a reposement of secrets, so it is onelie . . . at the owners, and no others commaundement. The *Secretorie*, as hee is a *keeper and conserver of secrets*: so is hee by his Lorde or Maister, and by none other to bee directed. To a *Closet*, there belongeth properlie a *doore*, a *locke*, and a *key*: to a *Secretorie*, there appertaineth incidentlie, *Honestie*, *Care* and *Fidelitie*.[24]

Flaminio controls the space of the closet when he has Bracciano hide in one in 1.2, and when he attends secret talks there in 5.1. His fall from power is signalled by his being barred from the new Duke's presence 'and all rooms / That owe him reverence' (5.4.30–31). In fact, Flaminio's machinations have from the start been inspired by displacement: he explains early on that his father sold all his land in order to finance an extravagant lifestyle, thereby destroying not only the family's income but the foundation of its gentrified status (1.2.306–8).[25] When socially sanctioned methods of advancement fail, Flaminio, Marcello and Vittoria are lured into the morally corrupt world of the court, with its opportunities to become pimp, murderer and whore. Moreover, by becoming the repository or closet for the great man's secrets, Flaminio exposes himself to corruption from within. This is made particularly clear in *The Duchess of Malfi*, where the Cardinal warns Julia, his would-be 'secretary' (5.2.227), not to seek the cause of his melancholy: ''Tis a secret / That, like a ling'ring poison, may chance lie / Spread in thy veins, and kill thee seven year hence' (5.2.260–62). In fact, the Cardinal will not wait nearly so long – the only safe secretary is a dead secretary.

Intimacy with great men may also pose a threat to the audience. As Dena Goldberg has argued, we are cast in the roles of eavesdropper and voyeur: '*attendants*, who lurk in corridors waiting to be summoned, are dismissed when private interviews are to take place and sometimes . . . find [ourselves], perhaps inadvertently, behind the arras.'[26] While the audience experiences no physical danger (unlike Polonius behind the arras), we may find ourselves morally compromised through taking pleasure in the spectacle of murder without being sympathetically engaged with the victim. When the murderer, Flaminio, draws a curtain to watch Cornelia winding his brother's corpse he finds a 'tragic entertainment distilled (for his and our aesthetic delectation) from human suffering'.[27] The theatre's potential to arouse moral feeling ('I have a strange thing in me, to th'which / I cannot give a name, without it be / Compassion', 5.4.108–10) comes to nothing in the thrilling climax when Flaminio prepares to force his reward from Vittoria with a brace of pistols.

But if *The White Devil* does little to justify claims by early modern apologists that theatre inculcates virtue and warns against vice, it also comes closest to its own definition of virtue through the role-playing of its protagonists. In 'The Arraignment of Vittoria' – a scene so significant that Webster separated it off with this title in his manuscript – Vittoria's compelling performance in the part of slandered chastity makes us question what we have believed about her guilt, perhaps reinforcing suspicions of the play's amorality, and questioning the capacity of the stage to present truth.[28] Yet it also works to expose the hypocrisy of her accuser, Monticelso, and his pose of moral righteousness. We may well applaud Vittoria's courage in taking on a corrupt judge and challenging the assumption that female sexual appetite is a more serious crime than murder. Similarly, Flaminio's performance as tragic hero in the final scene wins our admiration, though such an accolade is almost entirely undeserved. Denied the possibility of redemption by his guilt and despair, Flaminio faces extinction unconsoled. Only the theatrical ability to fashion his own end seems to give him comfort, and when he utters the memorable lines, 'We cease to grieve, cease to be Fortune's slaves, / Nay, cease to die by dying' (5.6.250–1) he borrows some of the glamour of the suicidal tragic hero, even though he has done everything he can to avoid death, including faking it. The act of self-assertion alone attains some kind of moral stature, in a nihilistic universe where not only Flaminio but all of Webster's characters must live and die 'in a mist' (5.6.258).

The Duchess of Malfi

Webster's next tragedy, *The Duchess of Malfi* (1614), may have overlapped with his composition of *The White Devil* or it might represent a revisiting of that play, for there are obvious similarities in terms of plotting and characterization. Once again we encounter two brothers in conflict with their sexually adventurous sister, and an ambitious malcontent who murders in the hope of a preferment that never comes. Only with *The Duchess of Malfi*, however, did Webster find immediate admiration and acclaim. The play was first acted at the Blackfriars, an indoor theatre whose intimate atmosphere may have been more suited to Webster's style, and by Shakespeare's celebrated company, the King's Men. That they did justice to Webster's most haunting protagonist is attested to by Thomas Middleton, who claims that not just this play, but this one character, has secured the playwright's immortality: 'Thy epitaph only the title be, / Write "Duchess" – that will fetch a tear for thee' (Quarto 1623).

The real-life tragedy of the Duchess Giovanna d'Ancona (d. 1512) had been retold in a number of Italian *novelle* and translated into English by William Painter in his *Palace of Pleasure*, vol. 2 (1567), before Webster turned to it as a source for his play. As its title suggests – 'The Infortunate mariage of a Gentleman, called *Antonie Bologna*, with the Duchesse of *Malfi*, and the pitifull death of them both' – the focus is on Antonio, who 'ought to have contented himself with that degree and honor that hee had acquired by his deedes and glory of his vertues'.[29] Webster rewrites the narrative from a female perspective, building upon the heroic agency with which he had imbued Vittoria in *The White Devil*. But where the latter's claim to luminosity – 'Through darkness diamonds spread their richest light' (3.2.292) – finds few supporters, the Duchess's virtue does indeed shine brightly, to such an extent that Ferdinand cannot bear to look upon her corpse: 'Mine eyes dazzle' (4.2.252). This moral investment in the female protagonist results in a tragedy of sharper ethical distinctions, without compromising the complexity of the Duchess's character or the tensions she creates.

The Duchess 'is caught between classes, between sexes, between tenses; as a young widow, she has a past and seeks a future; as an aristocrat who is also royal, she is independent, politically central, a ruler; but as a woman she is marginal, subordinate, dependent'.[30] Critics disagree over the extent to which Webster intended audiences to blame the widowed Duchess for her secret marriage to a social inferior. Though widely practised, the remarriage of widows was much criticized in Jacobean England. Not only did it represent a slight to the memory of the first husband (if the wife could be unfaithful after his death she might have been unfaithful before it – see *Hamlet*), it was also viewed as having a deleterious effect on her children, who might lose or be forced to share their inheritance (again, see *Hamlet*). Given these disadvantages, the widow's motivation could only be sexual desire; as Ferdinand states: 'They are most luxurious / Will wed twice' (1.2.209–10). What makes the Duchess's situation worse is that her choice of second husband will impact upon her noble family and her kingdom. The fact that she marries a steward represents an assault on the class distinctions which define her own social status (her only given name is 'Duchess of Malfi'); and suggests a more visceral contamination, not only through the mingling of bloods associated with intercourse, but through the mixed-class, 'bastard' children conceived outside Church-sanctified wedlock.[31] Though she confines Antonio's rule to the bedchamber, the Duchess is also guilty of a dereliction of political duty in raising such a man to power – the play's tentative arguments in favour of meritocracy fail to convince: 'The clandestine marriage is too brief, marked by adulterous shame, fertile but socially and affectively undeveloped, politically unregenerative, and always exploitative of Antonio, the alienated nocturnal sex worker who furtively exits before morning.'[32] As this latter description implies, the Duchess is often perceived as an excessively sensual woman whose greedy devouring of apricots, nurtured in dung, indicates her selfish and base desires.

But although these attitudes are all represented in the play – by Bosola, the Cardinal, Ferdinand and the Duchess's gentlewoman, Cariola – we also find powerful counter-arguments. Despite recycling much of *The White Devil*'s misogynist invective, the play invests both the Duchess's pregnancy and the sexuality it manifests with transcendent value. For all the queasiness it provokes in Bosola, the Duchess's pregnant body is a positive symbol of authority: 'Her wholeness, equanimity and fecundity in contrast to her brothers' mental and physical dysfunction suggests that she is the most able ruler among her siblings.'[33] The fact that her son with Antonio will be raised to the throne 'In's mother's right' (5.5.116) implies the triumph of matrilineal succession. At the same time, the play supports the Duchess's commitment to private, domestic life, casting a roseate glow around the marital bedchamber and deepening the pathos of her death scene through the promptings of maternal love: 'look thou giv'st my little boy / Some syrup for his cold, and let the girl / Say her prayers ere she sleep' (4.2.193–5). Perhaps most remarkable is the play's validation of the Duchess's declared right to sexual fulfilment, and her refusal to be rendered cold, chaste (and effectively dead) by the tyranny of her brothers: 'This is flesh and blood, sir; / 'Tis not the figure, cut in alabaster, / Kneels at my husband's tomb' (1.2.362–4). She becomes a 'hero of desire',[34] making political sacrifices and even risking her life for the sake of private pleasure.

Fundamental to the Duchess's inscription as a heroine are the villains who seek to destroy her, namely her brother Ferdinand and her servant Bosola. Although Ferdinand justifies his fascination with his sister's chastity in moral and political terms, it is disturbingly intrusive – he does not merely wish to know the secrets of her bedchamber, he physically appears there, having procured his own key. While this prurience exposes patriarchal assumptions about the need to supervise and control women's bodies, it also hints at Ferdinand's incestuous desire. Showing her their father's dagger as a warning against sexual transgression, he invites the Duchess to die upon its point (3.2.292), 'die' being a common term for orgasm. He later offers her a hand and a ring to kiss, pretending that these are his own 'love-token[s]' (4.1.46), before 'revealing' them to be the possessions of her husband, Antonio, in whose place he compulsively imagines himself. Finally, his affliction with lycanthropy, a disease brought on by lovesickness, sees him once again in darkness, digging up graves to discover not just the buried secret of his sister's murder but his own shocking motives for that murder. As the Duchess's twin, Ferdinand is her dark double. His violent erotic fantasies contrast with the Duchess's innocent marital flirtations; his Grand Guignol deceptions cast into relief her petty lies.

Where Ferdinand acts as an inverted image of the Duchess and must remain so, Bosola is profoundly altered by her death. Like Flaminio, Bosola is an intelligent man, disappointed in hopes to use his skills as a university graduate and soldier in the service of a worthy administration. Instead, he becomes a spy and assassin for not one but two corrupt princes. Too late he discovers that his quest for someone deserving of his loyalty should have been directed to the Duchess – the spectacle of her dead body being 'As direful to my soul as is the sword / Unto a wretch hath slain his father' (4.2.354–5). His ill-starred attempt to rescue Antonio expresses his desire to fulfil the Duchess's wishes posthumously. Yet the spectacle of her death also has a powerful emotional and spiritual effect. She becomes an object of rapturous and implicitly erotic adoration when he offers to add colour to her pale lips with his heart's blood. She is also a saintly, intercessionary figure when she briefly comes to life: 'Her eye opes / And heaven in it seems to ope, that late was shut, / To take me up to mercy' (4.2.334–6). Bosola's sense of being haunted by the Duchess prompts a range of emotions to which he had appeared invulnerable: pity, compassion, love and penitence.[35] It is this capacity to feel which qualifies him to deliver the play's final maxim – so conspicuously missing from *The White Devil*. Thus, he urges: 'Let worthy minds ne'er stagger in distrust/To suffer death or shame for what is just' (5.5.106–8), even as he acknowledges that for him the revelation comes too late.

The Broken Heart

To read Ford's *The Broken Heart* after Websterian tragedy is to experience the shock of virtue. As T. J. B. Spencer has observed: 'There are no villains in *The Broken Heart.*'[36] Rather, we find characters trying to resist the promptings of desire, hatred and revenge, in an effort which ironically proves as destructive as no resistance at all.

The play, first performed *c.* 1629 by the King's Men at the Blackfriars, might be considered Ford's most sophisticated and stylized work. The action centres on King Amyclas's court, where the courtiers speak a measured, ceremonial language (the play is entirely in verse, unusual for Ford). They also perform carefully choreographed gestures, often accompanied by music or elaborated into dance, suggesting the influence of the court masque. The mood is sombre – Amyclas twice observes that there should be more vivacity in his court – and the sense of action unfolding in 'slow motion',[37] not least through the use of onstage tableaux, expresses the 'ideas of freezing, of immobility and of lifelessness',[38] which lie at the heart of this tragedy.

Ford pointedly locates the action in ancient Sparta, a culture much admired in the seventeenth century not only for the valour of its warriors but for its Stoic values, which included implacability in the face of misfortune and a repudiation of affectionate ties.[39] Self-control was highly valued, as was heroic constancy to a particular ideal of the self. In a situation in which one might be forced to act in contradiction of this self or in which control over the emotions was no longer possible, suicide was not only a noble but a necessary choice.[40] Thus, Ford has fashioned an intensely repressive world, in which outbursts of passionate feeling and violence are ideologically shocking. But this is also the setting for a kind of 'problem play'[41] that questions the value of subduing passion.

The crime which impels this revenge tragedy has no political ramifications, but is a private matter of the heart: the forced separation of the betrothed couple, Penthea and Orgilus, and the former's marriage to a man she cannot love. The prologue hints at a historical source: 'What may be here thought a fiction, when Time's youth / Wanted some riper years was known *A Truth*' – perhaps the enforced marriage between Lady Penelope Devereux (most famous as Sir Philip Sidney's Stella) and Lord Rich in 1581.[42] But where Penelope subsequently defied convention by conducting an adulterous relationship with Charles Blount, Lord Mountjoy,[43] by whom she had at least four children, *The Broken Heart*'s Penthea is ruinously faithful to her vows, both to her husband, Bassanes, and to her previously contracted lord, Orgilus, provoking a catastrophic self-division: 'For she that's wife to Orgilus, and lives / In known adultery with Bassanes, / Is at the best a whore' (3.2.74–6). Vying with Calantha to be the broken heart of the title, Penthea descends into madness and starves herself to death. And yet, despite being 'in appearance the most pathetic of seventeenth-century stage women, Penthea is simultaneously the most ruthless'.[44] She punishes Bassanes by withholding her affection and aggressively performing the role of chaste and passive wife; she angrily spurns Orgilus, misrepresenting their entire romantic history as lust when he presses his claim; and she takes a sadistic pleasure in Ithocles's frustrated love, urging heaven not to let his heart break until 'some wild fires' have 'Scorch[ed], not consume[d], it' (3.2.48–9). Orgilus's abject cry: 'I tell 'ee you grow wanton in my sufferance' (2.3.108) identifies the only kind of wantonness in which Penthea will take any pleasure.

Much of the play is spent in denial of revenge. Orgilus repeatedly insists that he has no violent or passionate impulses when eyed with suspicion by the older generation, despite the fact that his name means 'Angry'. What looks like the beginning of a revenge plot, when he puts on the disguise of a scholar/malcontent, comes to nothing. It is only the spectacle of Penthea's madness and the revelation of her own vengefulness ('[*Pointing again at* ITHOCLES] That's he, and still 'tis he'. 4.2.122),[45] that finally releases Orgilus from stasis. But even then, his plotting of revenge is curiously silent and subdued. Brian Morris has observed: 'I know no other Jacobean play[46] in which the figure of the revenger is presented with this degree of self-sufficiency. The audience is never permitted to share Orgilus' reasons; his thoughts are always his own.'[47] Perhaps Ford was too keenly aware of his belatedness: it was nearly fifty years since Hieronimo had appeared on stage debating the ethics of revenge in Thomas Kyd's *The Spanish Tragedy*, the play which had inaugurated the fashion for revenge tragedy and defined all of Shakespeare's works in this genre. It may be that Ford, even more than Webster, felt that the 'will he, won't he?' tension of revenge tragedy had been finally exhausted. But it is also true that *The Broken Heart*'s interests lie more with the dull attrition of despair than with the adrenaline rush of bloody revenge. It is more concerned with the morality of a self-denial that causes suffering, than with the ethics of a revenge which claims to end it.

In general, the play praises those who control their emotions or at least hide them behind masks of implacability. Bassanes redeems himself under the influence of Stoic philosophy, changing from a ludicrously jealous husband to a more sober figure, worthy to be Sparta's marshal. Calantha's extraordinary repression of grief in the dance scene, where she continues as though unaffected after each tragic announcement, is also commended as admirably masculine behaviour and what is required of a monarch. Yet these characters are arguably diminished by their inhuman self-control. Indeed, Penthea's and Calantha's inability to keep up these poses without sustaining fatal internal injuries may be something of a relief to the audience, otherwise denied the extreme emotion which is one of tragedy's chief pleasures.

Perhaps the most fascinating instance of *The Broken Heart*'s ambivalence about passion is the way in which it shapes the play's four major death scenes. Ford imitates Webster in viewing death as a theatrical opportunity for characters to achieve the idealized and stable identities which have eluded them in life: they strike poses and utter speeches, often in elaborate settings they have designed themselves, with accompanying music.[48] But if dying in *The Broken Heart* demonstrates the characters' Stoic heroism and consistency, it also acknowledges their victimization by and submission to passionate feeling. For example, Orgilus's decision to bleed to death, standing on the stage and grasping two posts (unlike his enemy who dies sitting down), expresses his commitment to Stoic values. Yet his bloodletting is also purgative: 'opening a vein too full, too lively' (5.2.123) was a recommended cure for those oppressed by excessive anger or lust. Similarly, having placed a ring on his corpse's finger, Calantha manifests Stoic consistency in wishing to follow her husband, Ithocles, into death, but also a kind of emotional incontinence in being unable to live after he is gone. This is perfectly expressed through the ambiguity of her suicide in which she wills her heart to break. The cry of 'Crack, crack' as uttered by Olivia Williams in the 1994 RSC production was described by Peter Holland as 'one of the most extraordinary and appalling sounds I have ever heard in the theatre'.[49] To what extent this appallingness lies in the self-destructive will of the heroine or in the repression which brought it about remains for the audience to decide.

'Tis Pity She's a Whore

With *'Tis Pity She's a Whore* – performed *c.* 1630 by Queen Henrietta's Men at the Cockpit Theatre – Ford develops further his interest in romantic 'misalliance' and the denial of the heart's desires for the sake of social convention.[50] Yet here he is much more daring, urging audiences to care for a brother and sister who give themselves up to incestuous lust.

Ford appears to have had no single source for his play, but to have drawn upon a number of incest narratives,[51] perhaps inspired by a theatrical fascination which is hinted at in *The Duchess of Malfi*, but brought out into the open by Beaumont and Fletcher's *A King and No King* (1611), Thomas Middleton's *Women Beware Women* (1621) and Richard Brome's *The Lovesick Court* (1638). The incest theme has often been thought to exemplify the worst excesses of Jacobean and Caroline sensationalism. Yet it could produce a variety of effects, dependent on a basic division between innocent and knowing lovers, and between those who consummate the union and those who resist it. As Lois E. Bueler observes:

> Unwitting incest plays tend to be plays about virtue, in which the triumph of good or at least good luck is actually aided by the aborted threat of incest. Witting incest plays, on the other hand, are about evil, the evil of an aggravated selfishness which takes that portion of one's own which is intended for others and reserves it for oneself.[52]

Part of the fascination of Ford's treatment of incest in *'Tis Pity She's a Whore* is the way in which it confuses these categories, with the lovers fully cognizant of their blood relationship and the sinfulness of incest as they consummate their union, yet maintaining an appearance of romantic heroism and even virtue. Although Giovanni's final appearance – soaked in blood, with the heart of Annabella on a dagger – is that of a 'frantic madman' (5.6.40), Ford's representation of incest at other points is surprisingly non-judgemental.

While incest was condemned from the early modern pulpit as a monstrous sin, it may also have been comparatively common. In a sermon given in 1628 Arthur Lake, Bishop of Bath and Wells, pointed out that if God had not created sexual aversion between close relatives, incest would be hard to avoid for 'the necessarie cohabitation of Parents and Children, Brethren and Sisters would yeeld too much opportunitie, and be too strong an incentive unto this unlawfull coniunction'.[53] Equally, the fact that brothers and sisters were often raised and educated apart (Giovanni has been at university; Annabella remained at home) created the conditions for what we might now identify as Genetic Sexual Attraction (GSA), where family members long separated, perhaps by the process of adoption, find themselves sexually compelled to one another when reunited. Not only was incest probably more common, it was leniently punished. Until 1650, along with fornication, adultery and drunkenness, incest was prosecuted by the ecclesiastical rather than the secular courts. The offender would be made to stand in the parish church, dressed in penitential white, with a placard bearing the words 'FOR INCEST', before confessing their sin and asking for forgiveness.[54] Though humiliating, this was far preferable to the physical punishments given out by the secular justice system, which included whipping and branding for prostitutes, and death by hanging for thieves. In fact, there were very few prosecutions for incest in the late sixteenth and early seventeenth centuries in England. This may be because it occurred only rarely or because it remained secret or because it was a crime that did not unduly trouble local authorities.

In *'Tis Pity She's a Whore* incest repeatedly disappears from view, either reinvented as an ennobling passion or displaced by the crime of adultery. For example, the fact that Annabella's suitors are so flawed throws into relief the virtues of Giovanni,[55] whose love is free from any financial motive and is expressed in the play's most lyrical language. He invokes Petrarchan and Neoplatonic terms to praise Annabella's beauty: 'View well her face, and in that little round, / You may observe a world of variety: / For colour, lips; for sweet perfumes, her breath . . .' (2.5.49–51), thereby casting incestuous love in an irresistibly romantic mould. This perverse idealization is reinforced by the play's allusions to *Romeo and Juliet*.[56] By providing Giovanni with the Friar as confidant, and Annabella with the Nurse-like Puttana, Ford establishes the couple as a pair of vulnerable, star-crossed lovers. Moreover, Annabella's infatuation begins as she unknowingly glimpses her brother from the balcony. Her dismay on discovering his identity is rendered more acceptable through its echoes of Shakespeare's Juliet: 'My only love sprung from my only hate! / Too early seen unknown, and known too late!' (1.5.135–6). We might afford Ford's lovers more pity, given that their tragedy is not enmity between their families, but too great an affinity because they are one family.

A further distraction from incest is the limelight-stealing role given to adultery. Where the former is quietly domestic, contained within Florio's household and not named as such until 3.6, adultery repeatedly breaks out into scenes of violence and confusion. Hippolita, the spurned mistress, attempts to poison Soranzo at his wedding feast, while her husband bungles a revenge plot to dispatch his rival, thereby causing the death of Bergetto. Soranzo and Giovanni are partly motivated to kill Annabella through their self-identification as the cuckolded husband (Ford had a career-long fascination with *Othello*), rather than any moral outrage relating to incestuous love.[57] Finally, the Cardinal apparently overlooks incest in favour of adultery when he delivers his famous summation of the tragedy: ''Tis pity she's a whore,' (5.6.156) with 'whore' being a term to describe female infidelity. This shifting of blame on to the unchaste and adulterous Annabella may have been a feature of the play's reception. In his commendatory poem, Thomas Ellice refers to Giovanni as 'unblamed' and focuses on Annabella: 'With admiration I beheld this whore . . .'[58]

By comparison with its overt condemnation of adultery, the play's interrogation of incest is both marginal – pushed to the edges of the play in the dialogues between Giovanni and the Friar (1.1, 2.5 and 5.3) – and surprisingly complex. Giovanni's scholarly defence is blasphemous: the biblical prohibition carries no weight with him, and rather prompts him to deny divine providence and the existence of heaven and hell. Like Marlowe's Dr Faustus, he is arguably directed by 'a fatal intellectual pride', both men 'provid[ing] spectacular examples of the catastrophe attendant upon the misuse of the divinely given powers of reason'.[59] And yet, both of these rebellious thinkers have also inspired sympathy as they challenge old orthodoxies, responding to the new spirit of intellectual and personal ambition which defined the Renaissance world.[60] More specifically, Giovanni's rejection of the incest taboo as 'a peevish sound, / A customary form' (1.1.24–5) may have gained credibility through its echoes of the nominalist philosophy of Pietro Pomponazzi (1462–1525) – like Giovanni, an alumnus of the University of Bologna – which questioned the existence of universal laws, and re-examined what was natural and unnatural.[61] Remarkably, even the Friar admits that if one ignores divine law, the prohibition on incest will not hold (2.5.29–32).

Giovanni's shocking appearance in 5.6, drenched in his sister's blood and wielding her heart upon his dagger, represents a final judgement which seems to brook no further argument. It destroys the romantic illusions/allusions which have built up around the relationship by casting Giovanni as a sadistic Cupid, torturing the beloved. Moreover, the martyrological significance of the pierced heart finds Giovanni guilty of blasphemy and of idolatry,[62] without the desire for self-immolation that partly redeems Romeo and Juliet's erotic passion (it is not clear whether Giovanni would commit suicide after Annabella's death, if given the chance to live). At the same time, this scene offers the clearest condemnation of incest as socially (and therefore psychologically) damaging. Giovanni's claustrophobic image of Annabella's heart as one 'in which mine is entombed' (5.6.25) echoes the anthropological basis for the taboo on incest, the latter defined as 'A refusal of social obligations, a withdrawal from "the formation and maintenance of suprafamilial bonds on which major economic, political and religious functions of the society are dependent"'.[63] Giovanni is physically isolated for most of the play, usually in private dialogue with the Friar or Annabella, and he is awkwardly integrated into larger social gatherings. Incest exacerbates his withdrawal far more than it does in the case of Annabella, who remains 'half in her brother's world of sexual self-indulgence but also, crucially, half out of it, placed in a wider social world and subject to the moderating demands of its conventional sexual morality'.[64] Thus, Giovanni's presentation of her heart on a dagger emblematizes a dangerously introverted, claustrophobic desire. But, equally, what started as a heavily romanticized passion, defined against the lovelessness of the play's other marriage arrangements, has been bled dry. R. J. Kaufmann argues that 'Giovanni's tragedy . . . rests on the most terrible sacrifice of love – not of the object of love only, but of one's ability to give and receive love.'[65]

It is this act of self-mutilation that we find resonating throughout the tragedies of Webster and Ford. Where *The White Devil* and *The Duchess of Malfi* explore a new susceptibility to emotion experienced by the ruthless Flaminio and Bosola, Ford's tragedies dramatize this process in reverse, examining the consequences of a love that hardens into unfeeling (although in *The Broken Heart* this is only ever an illusion and the heart literally cracks under the strain). By reading all four plays together in this way, we may be further inclined to reject the notion of Webster and Ford as amoral sensationalists, committed to horror. Rather, they appear deeply engaged not only with the destruction of virtuous, life-giving characters, such as the Duchess and Annabella, but with villains whose capacity for love, compassion and remorse is awoken just at the moment when their lives must end. In these tragedies of wasted potential, Webster and Ford show a keen moral awareness, and a desire to extend the pity and compassion, not just of their protagonists, but of the audience as well.

NOTES

1. For further discussion, see Charles J. Sisson, *Lost Plays of Shakespeare's Age* (Cambridge: Cambridge University Press, 1936, reprint 1970), pp. 80–110.
2. Charles R. Forker, *The Skull Beneath the Skin: The Achievement of John Webster* (Cardondale: Southern Illinois University Press, 1986), p. 496. On other possible echoes, see pp. 493–6.
3. Charles Kingsley, 'Plays and Puritans' (1856), reprinted in *Plays and Puritans and Other Historical Essays* (London, 1873), pp. 1–80, 18.
4. S. P. Sherman, discussing *'Tis Pity*'s Giovanni and Annabella, in 'Forde's Contribution to the Decadence of the Drama' in *John Fordes Dramatische Werke*, ed. W. Bang (Louvain and London: David Nutt, 1908), pp. vii–xix, xii.
5. J. R. Mulryne on Webster in '*The White Devil* and *The Duchess of Malfi*', *Stratford-upon-Avon Studies* 1 (London: Edward Arnold, 1960), pp. 201–25, 204.
6. Kingsley concludes that 'We should call him a madman who allowed his daughters or his servants to see such representations,' 'Plays and Puritans', pp. 25–6.
7. See Sherman's discussion of *'Tis Pity* in 'Forde's Contribution', pp. xii–xiii. For a thorough rebuttal of this argument, see Martin Butler, *Theatre and Crisis 1632–1642* (Cambridge: Cambridge University Press, 1984), and Julie Sanders, *Caroline Drama: The Plays of Massinger, Ford, Shirley and Brome* (Plymouth: Northcote House, 1999).

8. Forker, *The Skull Beneath the Skin*, p. 288.
9. George Saintsbury remarked of the fifth act in *The Duchess of Malfi*: '[it] is a kind of gratuitous appendix of horrors stuck on without art or reason', *A History of Elizabethan Literature* (London: Macmillan, 1887), p. 278.
10. George Bernard Shaw, *Our Theatres in the Nineties*, 3 vols, (London: Constable, 1932), vol. 3, p. 317.
11. Sherman, 'Forde's Contribution', p. xviii.
12. David L. Frost, *The School of Shakespeare: The Influence of Shakespeare on English Drama 1600–42* (Cambridge: Cambridge University Press, 1968), pp. 122–3, 120, 131.
13. Richard Madelaine, 'Sensationalism and Melodrama in Ford's Plays' in *John Ford: Critical Re-Visions*, ed. Michael Neill (Cambridge: Cambridge University Press, 1988), pp. 29–54, 47, 51.
14. Christina Luckyj, *A Winter's Snake: Dramatic Form in the Tragedies of John Webster* (Athens and London: University of Georgia Press, 1989), p. 150.
15. Martin Wiggins, *Journeymen in Murder: The Assassin in English Renaissance Drama* (Oxford: Clarendon Press, 1991), p. 165.
16. See Christina Luckyj (ed.), *The White Devil* (London: A & C Black, 1996, rev. 2008), p. xx.
17. On the tradition of anti-Catholicism in revenge tragedy see Alison Shell, *Catholicism, Controversy and the English Literary Imagination, 1558–1660* (Cambridge: Cambridge University Press, 1999), pp. 23–55. On Ford's greater sympathy with Catholicism, see Lisa Hopkins, *John Ford's Political Theatre* (Manchester: Manchester University Press, 1994), and Gillian Woods, 'The Confessional Identities of *'Tis Pity She's a Whore*' in *'Tis Pity She's a Whore: A Critical Guide*, ed. Lisa Hopkins (London and New York: Continuum, 2010), pp. 114–35.
18. On ideas of Italy in early modern England, see *Shakespeare's Italy: Functions of Italian Locations in Renaissance Drama*, ed. Michele Marrapodi (Manchester: Manchester University Press, 1997).
19. On Webster and Ford as court satirists, see Albert H. Tricomi, *Anti-Court Drama in England, 1603–1642* (Charlottesville and London: University Press of Virginia, 1989), pp. 110–20.
20. See Lisa Hopkins, *The Female Hero in English Renaissance Tragedy* (Houndmills and New York: Palgrave, 2002), p. 2, and Naomi Conn Liebler (ed.), *The Female Tragic Hero in English Renaissance Drama* (Houndmills and New York: Palgrave, 2002).

21. Mulryne, '*The White Devil* and *The Duchess of Malfi*', p. 211.
22. Forker, *The Skull Beneath the Skin*, p. 264.
23. See Laure A. Finke, 'Painting Women: Images of Femininity in Jacobean Tragedy', *Theatre Journal* 35 (1984), pp. 357–70, 357.
24. Angel Day, *The English Secretary; or, Methode of writing epistles and letters* (London: C. Burbie, 1599), Part 2, p. 103. For further discussion of the eroticism of the closet and the secretary role, see Alan Stewart, 'The Early Modern Closet Discovered', *Representations* 50 (Spring 1995), pp. 76–100.
25. On the way in which Flaminio's experience of disinheritance and disappointment echoes that of many young Jacobeans, see Tricomi, *Anti-Court Drama*, pp. 110–20.
26. Dena Goldberg, '"By Report": The Spectator as Voyeur in Webster's *The White Devil*', *English Literary Renaissance* 17 (1987), pp. 67–84, 71.
27. Ibid., p. 75.
28. See Christina Luckyj, 'Gender, Rhetoric and Performance in John Webster's *The White Devil*' in *Enacting Gender on the English Renaissance Stage,* ed. Viviana Comensoli and Anne Russell (Urbana and Chicago: University of Illinois Press, 1999), pp. 218–32, 226.
29. William Painter, *The second tome of the Palace of Pleasure* (London: Henry Bynneman and Nicholas England, 1567).
30. Mary Beth Rose, *The Expense of Spirit: Love and Sexuality in English Renaissance Drama* (Ithaca and London: Cornell University Press, 1988), pp. 159–60.
31. The *de praesenti* marriage that the Duchess performs in Act one would have constituted a legal union, indissoluble once the couple had consummated it. However, it still needed to be performed in church to be fully legitimate.
32. Barbara Correll here summarizes the position of, for example, Frank Whigham and Theodora A. Jankowski, in 'Malvolio at Malfi: Managing Desire in Shakespeare and Webster', *Shakespeare Quarterly* 58 (2007), pp. 65–92, 72.
33. Sid Ray, '"So Troubled with the Mother": The Politics of Pregnancy in *The Duchess of Malfi*' in *Performing Maternity in Early Modern England*, ed. Kathryn M. Moncrief and Kathryn R. McPherson (Aldershot: Ashgate, 2007), pp. 17–28, 22.
34. See Linda Woodbridge, 'Queen of Apricots: The Duchess of Malfi, Hero of Desire' in *The Female Tragic Hero in English Renaissance Drama*, pp. 161–84, 162.

35. This haunting extends to the play itself. Not only is the Duchess reanimated through the 'ECHO *from the Duchess's grave*' and the 'face folded in sorrow' experienced by Antonio in 5.3, but in some productions she reappears on stage as a ghostly figure to oversee her own revenge. Moreover, in Lewis Theobald's 1733 adaptation, *The Fatal Secret: A Tragedy* (pub. 1735), the Duchess is not actually dead, but lives on to be reconciled with Antonio.
36. T. J. B. Spencer (ed.), *The Broken Heart* (Manchester: Manchester University Press, 1980), p. 36.
37. Marion Lomax, *'Tis Pity She's a Whore and Other Plays* (Oxford: Oxford University Press, 1995), p. xiii.
38. Hopkins, *John Ford's Political Theatre*, p. 162.
39. Ford's interest in Neo-Stoic ideas is evident in his two early prose works, *The Golden Mean* (1613) and *A Line of Life* (1620).
40. For further discussion, see Gilles D. Monsarrat, *Light from the Porch: Stoicism and English Renaissance Literature* (Paris: Didier Erudition, 1984).
41. This term is used by Sherman in 'Forde's Contribution', p. xi. For further discussion of the play's moral ambiguity, see Harriet Hawkins, 'Mortality, Morality and Modernity in *The Broken Heart*: Some Dramatic and Critical Counter-Arguments' in *John Ford: Critical Re-Visions*, pp. 129–52.
42. See S. P. Sherman, 'Stella and the *Broken Heart*', *PMLA* 24 (1909), pp. 274–85, and Giovanni M. Carsaniga, '"The Truth" in John Ford's *The Broken Heart*', *Comparative Literature* 10 (Autumn, 1958), pp. 344–8. A further allegorical level may be the identification of Calantha and Ithocles with Elizabeth and Essex, and of Nearchus's peaceful succession to the throne with that of James I. See Verna Ann Foster and Stephen Foster, 'Structure and History in *The Broken Heart*: Sparta, England and the "Truth"', *English Literary Renaissance* 18.2 (Spring, 1988), pp. 305–28.
43. Ford's first published work, *Fame's Memorial* (1606), was an elegy for Blount, dedicated to Penelope.
44. Clifford Leech, *John Ford* (Harlow: Longman, 1964), p. 27.
45. See Roberta Barker, 'Death and the Married Maiden: Performing Gender in *The Broken Heart*', *English Studies in Canada* 30.2 (June 2004), pp. 67–89, on Penthea's influence, particularly in Michael Boyd's 1994 production for the Royal Shakespeare Company.

46. The slip here is revealing: *The Broken Heart* is a Caroline rather than a Jacobean play, but its strong links with the earlier period, not least through its debts to Webster, explain the mistake.
47. Brian Morris (ed.), *The Broken Heart* (London: A & C Black, 1994), pp. xx–xxi.
48. Michael Neill describes the dramatists' 'self-perfecting aesthetic of death' in *Issues of Death: Mortality and Identity in English Renaissance Tragedy* (Oxford: Clarendon Press, 1997), pp. 355, 363. See also his discussion of *The Duchess of Malfi*, pp. 328–53.
49. Peter Holland, 'Modality Ford's Strange Journeys', *Times Literary Supplement* (28 October 1994), p. 41.
50. See R. J. Kaufmann's use of this term in 'Ford's Tragic Perspective', in *Elizabethan Drama: Modern Essays in Criticism*, ed. Kaufmann (New York: Oxford University Press, 1961), pp. 356–72, 357.
51. Possible sources include Canace and Macareo in Ovid's *Heroides*, translated in Thomas Heywood's *Gunaikeion* (1624); and Doralice and her twin Lyzaran in Francois de Rosset's *Histoires Tragiques de Notre Temps* (1615).
52. Lois E. Bueler, 'The Structural Uses of Incest in English Renaissance Drama', *Renaissance Drama* 15 (1984), pp. 115–45, 127.
53. Arthur Lake, *Sermons with Some Religious and Divine Meditations* (London: Nathaniel Butter, 1629), pp. 21–2.
54. See Martin Ingram, *Church Courts, Sex and Marriage in England, 1570–1640* (Cambridge: Cambridge University Press, 1987), pp. 245–9.
55. Some critics find Parma fulfilling the same role, with Corinne S. Abate even identifying the city as the 'whore' of the play's title, 'Identifying the Real Whore of Parma' in *'Tis Pity She's a Whore: A Critical Guide*, pp. 94–113. See also Sonia Massai's discussion of the fallen city in *'Tis Pity She's a Whore* (London: Methuen, 2011), pp. 6–20.
56. For further discussion, see Robert Smallwood, '*'Tis Pity* and *Romeo and Juliet*', *Cahiers Elisabéthains* 20 (1981), pp. 49–70.
57. See Raymond Powell, 'The Adaptation of a Shakespearean Genre: *Othello* and Ford's *'Tis Pity She's a Whore*', *Renaissance Quarterly* 48 (1995), pp. 582–92.
58. This point is made by Sonia Massai, who argues that 'What is staggeringly radical about Ford's play is not its decadence, but its profoundly moral concern about the level of disorder unleashed by the extreme passions signified by Annabella as "whore"', *'Tis Pity She's a Whore*, p. 36.

59. Cyrus Hoy, "Ignorance in Knowledge" Marlowe's Faustus and Ford's Giovanni', *Modern Philology* 57 (1959–60), pp. 145–54, 146.
60. See John S. Wilks, *The Idea of Conscience in Renaissance Tragedy* (London and New York: Routledge, 1990), p. 264.
61. See Richard McCabe, *Incest, Drama and Nature's Law 1550–1700* (Cambridge: Cambridge University Press, 1993), p. 216; and Massai, *'Tis Pity She's a Whore*, p. 12.
62. The fullest discussion of these meanings is given by Michael Neill, '"What Strange Riddle's This?": Deciphering *'Tis Pity She's a Whore*' in *John Ford: Critical Re-Visions*, pp. 153–80.
63. McCabe, quoting the French anthropologist Claude Lévi-Strauss, in *Incest, Drama and Nature's Law*, p. 18.
64. Martin Wiggins (ed.), *'Tis Pity She's a Whore* (London: A & C Black, 2003), p. 19.
65. R. J. Kaufmann, 'Ford's Tragic Perspective' in *Elizabethan Drama*, p. 370.

Further Reading

JOHN WEBSTER

Berry, Ralph, *The Art of John Webster* (Oxford: Clarendon Press, 1972)

Bliss, Lee, *The World's Perspective: John Webster and the Jacobean Drama* (New Brunswick, NJ: Rutgers University Press, 1983)

Bogard, Travis, *The Tragic Satire of John Webster* (Berkeley and Cambridge: California University Press and Cambridge University Press, 1955)

Boklund, Gunnar, *The Sources of The White Devil* (New York: Haskell House, 1966)

——, *The Duchess of Malfi: Sources, Themes, Characters* (Cambridge, Mass.: Harvard University Press, 1962)

Bradbrook, M. C., *John Webster: Citizen and Dramatist* (London: Weidenfeld & Nicolson, 1980)

Bromley, Laura, 'The Rhetoric of Feminine Identity in *The White Devil*' in *In Another Country: Feminist Perspectives on Renaissance Drama*, ed. Dorothea Kehler and Susan Barker (Metuchen, NJ and London: Scarecrow Press, 1991)

Callaghan, Dympna, *Woman and Gender in Renaissance Tragedy: A Study of King Lear, Othello, The Duchess of Malfi and The White Devil* (New York and London: Harvester Wheatsheaf, 1989)

Correll, Barbara, 'Malvolio at Malfi: Managing Desire in Shakespeare and Webster', *Shakespeare Quarterly* 58 (2007), pp. 65–92

Forker, Charles R., *The Skull Beneath the Skin: The Achievement of John Webster* (Carbondale: Southern Illinois University Press, 1986)

Goldberg, Dena, *Between Worlds: A Study of the Plays of John Webster* (Ontario: Wilfred Laurier University Press, 1987)

——, '"By Report": The Spectator as Voyeur in Webster's *The White Devil*', *English Literary Renaissance* 17 (1987), pp. 67–84

Hopkins, Lisa, *The Female Hero in English Renaissance Tragedy* (Houndmills and New York: Palgrave, 2002)

Leech, Clifford, *Webster: The Duchess of Malfi* (London: Edward Arnold, 1963)

Lord, Joan M., '*The Duchess of Malfi*: The Spirit of Greatness and of Woman', *Studies in English Literature* 16 (1976), pp. 305–17

Luckyj, Christina, 'Gender, Rhetoric and Performance in John Webster's *The White Devil*' in *Enacting Gender on the English Renaissance Stage*, ed. Viviana Comensoli and Anne Russell (Urbana and Chicago: University of Illinois Press, 1999), pp. 218–32

——, *A Winter's Snake: Dramatic Form in the Tragedies of John Webster* (Athens and London: University of Georgia Press, 1989)

——, '"Great Women of Pleasure": Main Plot and Subplot in *The Duchess of Malfi*', *Studies in English Literature* 27 (1987), pp. 267–83

Mulryne, J. R., 'Webster and the Uses of Tragicomedy' in *John Webster*, ed. Brian Morris (London: Ernest Benn, 1970), pp. 133–55

——, '*The White Devil* and *The Duchess of Malfi*', *Stratford-upon-Avon Studies* 1 (London: Edward Arnold, 1960), pp. 201–25

Neill, Michael, *Issues of Death: Mortality and Identity in English Renaissance Tragedy* (Oxford: Clarendon Press, 1997)

Ray, Sid, '"So Troubled with the Mother": The Politics of Pregnancy in *The Duchess of Malfi*' in *Performing Maternity in Early Modern England*, ed. Kathryn M. Moncrief and Kathryn R. McPherson (Aldershot: Ashgate, 2007), pp. 17–28

Rose, Mary Beth, *The Expense of Spirit: Love and Sexuality in English Renaissance Drama* (Ithaca and London: Cornell University Press, 1988)

Whigham, Frank, 'Sexual and Social Mobility in *The Duchess of Malfi*', *PMLA* 100.2 (March 1985), pp. 167–86

Wiggins, Martin, *Journeymen in Murder: The Assassin in English Renaissance Drama* (Oxford: Clarendon Press, 1991)

Woodbridge, Linda, 'Queen of Apricots: The Duchess of Malfi, Hero of Desire' in *The Female Tragic Hero in English Renaissance Drama*, ed. Naomi Conn Liebler (Houndmills and New York: Palgrave, 2002), pp. 161–84

Wymer, Rowland, *Webster and Ford* (Houndmills and London: St Martin's Press, 1995)

JOHN FORD

Barker, Roberta, 'Death and the Married Maiden: Performing Gender in *The Broken Heart*', *English Studies in Canada* 30.2 (June 2004), pp. 67–89

Barton, Anne, 'Oxymoron and the Structure of Ford's *The Broken Heart*', *Essays and Studies* 33 (1980), pp. 70–94

Blayney, G. L., 'Convention, Plot and Structure in *The Broken Heart*', *Modern Philology* (1958), pp. 1–9

Bueler, Lois E., 'The Structural Uses of Incest in English Renaissance Drama', *Renaissance Drama* 15 (1984), pp. 115–45

Carsaniga, Giovanni M., '"The Truth" in John Ford's *The Broken Heart*', *Comparative Literature* 10 (1958), pp. 344–8

Champion, Larry S., ''*Tis Pity* and the Jacobean Tragic Perspective', *Renaissance Quarterly* 90 (1975), pp. 78–87

Clerrico, Terri, 'The Politics of Blood: John Ford's *'Tis Pity She's a Whore*', *English Literary Renaissance* 22 (1992), pp. 405–34

Crouch, Kristin, '"The Silent Griefs which cut the Heart Strings": John Ford's *The Broken Heart* in Performance' in Edward J. Esche (ed.), *Shakespeare and His Contemporaries in Performance* (Aldershot: Ashgate, 2000), pp. 261–74

Farr, Dorothy, *John Ford and the Caroline Theatre* (London: Macmillan, 1979)

Foster, Verna, '*'Tis Pity She's a Whore* as City Tragedy' in *John Ford: Critical Re-Visions*, ed. Michael Neill (Cambridge: Cambridge University Press, 1988), pp. 181–200

Foster, Verna Ann and Stephen Foster, 'Structure and History in *The Broken Heart*: Sparta, England and the "Truth"', *English Literary Renaissance* 18.2 (Spring, 1988), pp. 305–28

Frost, David L., *The School of Shakespeare: The Influence of Shakespeare on English Drama 1600–42* (Cambridge: Cambridge University Press, 1968)

Hawkins, Harriet, 'Mortality, Morality and Modernity in *The Broken Heart*: Some Dramatic and Critical Counter-Arguments' in *John Ford: Critical Re-Visions*, ed. Michael Neill (Cambridge: Cambridge University Press, 1988), pp. 129–52

Hopkins, Lisa, *John Ford's Political Theatre* (Manchester: Manchester University Press, 1994)

—— (ed.), *'Tis Pity She's a Whore: A Critical Guide* (London: Continuum, 2010)

Hoy, Cyrus, '"Ignorance in Knowledge": Marlowe's Faustus and Ford's Giovanni', *Modern Philology* 57 (1959–60), pp. 145–54

Huebert, Ronald, *John Ford: Baroque English Dramatist* (Montreal and London: McGill-Queens University Press, 1977)

Ide, Richard S., 'Ford's *'Tis Pity She's a Whore* and the Benefits of Belatedness' in '*Concord in Discord*': *The Plays of John Ford, 1586–1986*, ed. Donald K. Anderson (New York: AMS Press, 1986), pp. 61–86

Kaufmann, R. J. (ed.), 'Ford's Tragic Perspective' in *Elizabethan Drama: Modern Essays in Criticism* (New York: Oxford University Press, 1961), pp. 356–72

Leech, Clifford, *John Ford* (Harlow: Longman, 1964)

——, *John Ford and the Drama of his Time* (London: Chatto & Windus, 1957)

Madelaine, Richard, 'Sensationalism and Melodrama in Ford's Plays', *John Ford: Critical Re-Visions*, ed. Michael Neill (Cambridge: Cambridge University Press, 1988), pp. 29–54

McCabe, Richard A., *Incest, Drama and Nature's Law 1550–1700* (Cambridge: Cambridge University Press, 1993)

McMaster, Juliet, 'Love, Lust, and Sham: Structural Pattern in the Plays of John Ford', *Renaissance Drama* 2 (1969), pp. 157–66

Neill, Michael, *Issues of Death: Mortality and Identity in English Renaissance Tragedy* (Oxford: Clarendon Press, 1997)

——, '"What Strange Riddle's This?": Deciphering *'Tis Pity She's a Whore*' in *John Ford: Critical Re-Visions* (Cambridge: Cambridge University Press, 1988), pp. 153–80

Powell, Raymond, 'The Adaptation of a Shakespearean Genre: *Othello* and Ford's *'Tis Pity She's a Whore*', *Renaissance Quarterly* 48.3 (1995), pp. 582–92

——, 'Ford's Unbroken Art: The Moral Design of *The Broken Heart*', *Modern Language Review* 75 (1980), pp. 249–68

Rosen, Carol C., 'The Language of Cruelty in Ford's *'Tis Pity*', *Comparative Drama* 8 (1974), pp. 356–68

Sanders, Julie, *Caroline Drama: The Plays of Massinger, Ford, Shirley and Brome* (Plymouth: Northcote House, 1999)

Sherman, S. P., 'Stella and the *Broken Heart*', *PMLA* 24 (1909), pp. 274–85

Smallwood, Robert, '*'Tis Pity* and *Romeo and Juliet*', *Cahiers Elisabéthains* 20 (1981), pp. 49–70

Stavig, Mark, *John Ford and the Traditional Moral Order* (Madison: University of Wisconsin Press, 1968)

Wiseman, Susan, '*'Tis Pity She's a Whore*: Representing the Incestuous Body' in *Renaissance Bodies: The Human Figure in English Culture c. 1540–1660*, ed. Lucy Gent and Nigel Llewellyn (London: Reaktion Books, 1990), pp. 180–97

Wymer, Rowland, *Webster and Ford* (London: Macmillan, 1995)

Note on the Texts

All four plays have been edited from the earliest quartos, in consultation with modern editions. Spelling and punctuation have been modernized throughout, with any significant changes (for example, where the spelling of characters' names differs from editorial tradition) indicated in the notes. Where the quarto includes massed entries (a notable feature of Webster's plays) these have been divided up, with the originals available for consultation in the Textual Variants. Act and scene divisions have been imposed as consistent with editorial tradition. All additional stage directions are indicated by square brackets.

The White Devil was prepared from the 1612 Quarto in the Bodleian Library, STC 25178, in consultation with *John Webster: Three Plays*, ed. D. C. Gunby (Harmondsworth: Penguin, 1972, repr. 1987); *The Works of John Webster*, 3 vols, ed. David Gunby, David Carnegie and MacDonald P. Jackson (Cambridge: Cambridge University Press, 2007–8); Christina Luckyj (ed.), *The White Devil* (London: A & C Black, 1996, rev. 2008); René Weis (ed.), *The Duchess of Malfi and Other Plays* (Oxford: Oxford University Press, 2009); and Martin Wiggins, 'Notes on Editing Webster', *Notes and Queries* 240 (1995), pp. 369–77.

The Duchess of Malfi was edited from the 1623 Quarto, British Library copy, STC 25176, in consultation with *John Webster: Three Plays*, ed. D. C. Gunby (Harmondsworth: Penguin, 1972, repr. 1987); Brian Gibbons (ed.), *The Duchess of Malfi* (London: A & C Black, 1964, repr. 2001); *The Works of John Webster*, 3 vols, ed. David Gunby, David Carnegie and MacDonald P. Jackson (Cambridge: Cambridge University Press, 2007–8); René Weis (ed.), *The Duchess of Malfi and*

Other Plays (Oxford: Oxford University Press, 2009); and Martin Wiggins, 'Notes on Editing Webster', *Notes and Queries* 240 (1995), pp. 369–77.

The Broken Heart is based on the 1633 Quarto, STC 11156, British Library copy, and has been checked against the 1652 *Comedies, Tragi-Comedies and Tragedies* by John Ford, Wing (2nd ed.)/F1466A, National Library of Scotland. Modern texts consulted are Brian Morris (ed.), *The Broken Heart* (London: A & C Black, 1994); T. J. B. Spencer (ed.), *The Broken Heart* (Manchester: Manchester University Press, 1980); and Marion Lomax (ed.), *'Tis Pity She's a Whore and Other Plays* (Oxford: Oxford University Press, 1995).

'Tis Pity She's a Whore was edited from the 1633 Quarto, STC 11165, Huntingdon Library, and has been checked against the 1652 *Comedies, Tragi-Comedies and Tragedies* by John Ford, Wing (2nd ed.)/F1466A, National Library of Scotland. It is also indebted to Brian Gibbons (ed.), *'Tis Pity She's a Whore* (London: A & C Black, 1968); Marion Lomax (ed.), *'Tis Pity She's a Whore and Other Plays* (Oxford: Oxford University Press, 1995); Martin Wiggins (ed.), *'Tis Pity She's a Whore* (London: A & C Black, 2003); and Sonia Massai (ed.), *'Tis Pity She's a Whore* (London: Methuen, 2011).

JOHN WEBSTER

THE WHITE DEVIL

LIST OF CHARACTERS

VITTORIA COROMBONA *wife of Camillo; later married to Bracciano*
Duke of BRACCIANO, *Paulo Giordano Orsini, husband of Isabella; later married to Vittoria*
FLAMINIO[1] *secretary to Bracciano, brother to Vittoria and Marcello*
CORNELIA *mother of Vittoria, Flaminio and Marcello*
MARCELLO *soldier and follower of Francisco, brother of Vittoria and Flaminio*
ZANCHE *a Moor, servant to Vittoria*

MONTICELSO, *Lorenzo de, a Cardinal, later Pope Paul IV*
CAMILLO *husband of Vittoria, nephew of Monticelso*

FRANCISCO *de Medici, Duke of Florence, brother of Isabella, later disguised as Mulinassar, a Moor*
ISABELLA *sister of Francisco, wife of Bracciano*
GIOVANNI *son of Bracciano and Isabella*
JAQUES* *a Moor, page to Giovanni*
GUID-ANTONIO* *attendant or steward of Isabella*

LODOVICO[2] *an Italian count, later disguised as a Capuchin*
GASPARO *follower of Lodovico, later disguised as a Capuchin*
ANTONELLI *follower of Lodovico*
CARLO *and* PEDRO *attendants of Bracciano, secretly in league with Francisco*

1 *FLAMINIO*: spelled FLAMINEO in the Quarto; however, the current spelling is the accurate Italian version, found in Webster's source, and also offers a better guide to pronunciation
2 *LODOVICO*: spelled LODOWICKE in the Quarto

DOCTOR *Julio, a physician and conjurer*
CHRISTOPHERO* *Doctor Julio's associate*
CONJURER

HORTENSIO *attendant of Bracciano*
YOUNG LORD *attendant of Bracciano*
FERNEZE* *servant of Bracciano*
PAGE *attendant on Cornelia*
COURTIER *attendant on Giovanni*

MATRON *of the House of Convertites*
SAVOY AMBASSADOR
Two FRENCH AMBASSADORS
ENGLISH AMBASSADOR
SPANISH AMBASSADOR
Maltese AMBASSADOR
LAWYER

Cardinal of ARAGON
ARMOURER
Two PHYSICIANS

*Senators, four Captains, Chancellor, Register, Officers, Guards, Attendants, Servants, Cardinals, Ladies**

*non-speaking parts

TO THE READER

In publishing this tragedy, I do but challenge to[1] myself that liberty which other men have ta'en before me. Not that I affect praise by it, for *nos haec novimus esse nihil*;[2] only since it was acted in so dull a time of winter, presented in so open and black a theatre,[3] that it wanted that which is the only grace and setting out of a tragedy – a full and understanding auditory; and that, since that time, I have noted, most of the people that come to that playhouse resemble those ignorant asses who, visiting stationers' shops, their use is not to enquire for good books but new books, I present it to the general view with this confidence:

Nec rhoncos metues, maligniorum,
Nec scombris tunicas, dabis molestas.[4]

If it be objected this is no true dramatic poem, I shall easily confess it; *non potes in nugas dicere plura meas ipse ego quam dixi.*[5] Willingly, and not ignorantly, in this kind have I faulted; for should a man present to such an auditory the most sententious[6] tragedy that ever was written, observing all the critical laws, as height of style and gravity of person, enrich it with the sententious *Chorus*, and, as it were, 'liven death[7] in the passionate and weighty *Nuntius*,[8] yet, after all this divine

1 *challenge to*: claim for
2 *nos . . . nihil*: 'We know these efforts of ours to be worth nothing' (Martial, *Epigrams*, 13.2)
3 *theatre*: the Red Bull at Clerkenwell, a large, open-air theatre
4 *Nec . . . molestas*: 'You [the poet's book] will not fear the sneers of the malicious, nor supply wrappers for mackerel' (Martial, *Epigrams*, 4.86)
5 *non . . . dixi*: 'You cannot say more against these trifles of mine than I have said myself' (Martial, *Epigrams*, 13.2)
6 *sententious*: full of maxims, characteristic of Seneca
7 *'liven death*: make death come alive
8 *Nuntius*: messenger of classical tragedy who often described acts of offstage violence

rapture – O *dura messorum ilia*[1] – the breath that comes from the uncapable multitude is able to poison it, and ere it be acted, let the author resolve to fix to every scene, this of Horace:

Haec hodie porcis comedenda relinques.[2]

To those who report I was a long time in finishing this tragedy,[3] I confess I do not write with a goose-quill, winged with two feathers; and if they will needs make it my fault, I must answer them with that of Euripides to Alcestides,[4] a tragic writer: Alcestides objecting that Euripides had only in three days composed three verses, whereas himself had written three hundred: 'Thou tell'st truth,' quoth he, 'but here's the difference: thine shall only be read for three days, whereas mine shall continue three ages.'

Detraction is the sworn friend to ignorance. For mine own part, I have ever truly cherished my good opinion of other men's worthy labours, especially of that full and heightened style of Master Chapman; the laboured and understanding[5] works of Master Jonson; the no less worthy composures of the both worthily excellent Master Beaumont and Master Fletcher; and lastly (without wrong last to be named) the right happy and copious industry of Master Shakespeare, Master Dekker and Master Heywood, wishing what I write may be read by their light; protesting that, in the strength of mine own judgement, I know them so worthy, that though I rest silent in my own work, yet to most of theirs I dare, without flattery, fix that of Martial:

non norunt, haec monumenta mori.[6]

1 *O . . . ilia*: 'O strong stomachs of harvesters' (Horace, *Epodes*, 3.4), referring to their love of garlic

2 *Haec . . . relinques*: 'What you leave will today become food for pigs' (Horace, *Epistles*, 1.7.19)

3 *long time . . . tragedy*: there is no record of Webster writing anything between 1605 and 1612

4 *Alcestides*: Webster's misspelling of 'Alcestis', an otherwise unknown classical poet mentioned in Jonson's *Discoveries* (pub. 1641)

5 *understanding*: intellectual

6 *non . . . mori*: 'These monuments know not death' (Martial, *Epigrams*, 10.2)

ACT 1

Scene 1

Enter Count LODOVICO, ANTONELLI *and* GASPARO.

LODOVICO
Banished?

ANTONELLI
It grieved me much to hear the sentence.

LODOVICO
Ha, ha! O Democritus,[1] thy gods
That govern the whole world: courtly reward
And punishment. Fortune's a right whore;
If she give aught, she deals it in small parcels,[2]
That she may take away all at one swoop.
This 'tis to have great enemies, God 'quite them.
Your wolf no longer seems to be a wolf
Than when she's hungry.[3]

GASPARO
You term those 'enemies'
Are men of princely rank.

LODOVICO
Oh, I pray for them.
The violent thunder is adored by those
Are pashed[4] in pieces by it.

1 *Democritus*: Ancient Greek philosopher and scientist, recorded in Antonio de Guevera's *Diall of Princes* (trans. 1557) as stating that the gods of reward and punishment ruled the world

2 *parcels*: portions

3 *wolf . . . hungry*: wolves no longer appear wolvish once their appetites are satisfied

4 *pashed*: smashed

ANTONELLI

Come, my lord,
You are justly doomed. Look but a little back
Into your former life. You have in three years
Ruined the noblest earldom.

GASPARO

Your followers
Have swallowed you like mummia,[1] and being sick
With such unnatural and horrid physic
Vomit you up i'the kennel.[2]

ANTONELLI

All the damnable degrees
Of drinkings have you staggered through. One citizen,
Is lord of two fair manors, called you master
Only for caviar.

GASPARO

Those noblemen
Which were invited to your prodigal feasts –
Wherein the phoenix[3] scarce could 'scape your throats –
Laugh at your misery, as fore-deeming you
An idle[4] meteor which drawn forth the earth
Would be soon lost i'th' air –

ANTONELLI

Jest upon you,
And say you were begotten in an earthquake,
You have ruined such fair lordships.

1 *mummia*: medicine ('physic') prepared from mummified (usually human) flesh, proverbially difficult to swallow
2 *kennel*: gutter
3 *phoenix*: this mythical Arabian bird lived for 500 to 600 years, then consumed itself in flames and rose again from its own ashes
4 *idle*: worthless

LODOVICO [*Aside*]

Very good.
This well goes with two buckets;[1] I must tend[2]
The pouring out of either.

GASPARO

Worse than these,
You have acted certain murders here in Rome,
Bloody and full of horror.

LODOVICO

'Las, they were flea-bitings.
Why took they not my head then?

GASPARO

O my lord,
The law doth sometimes mediate; thinks it good
Not ever to steep violent sins in blood.
This gentle penance[3] may both end your crimes,
And in the example better these bad times.

LODOVICO

So – but I wonder, then, some great men 'scape
This banishment. There's Paulo Giordano Orsini,
The Duke of Bracciano, now lives in Rome,
And by close[4] panderism seeks to prostitute
The honour of Vittoria Corombona:
Vittoria – she that might have got my pardon
For one kiss to the Duke!

ANTONELLI

Have a full man within you.[5]
We see that trees bear no such pleasant fruit
There where they grew first, as where they are new set.
Perfumes the more they are chafed, the more they render

1 *This . . . buckets*: both men (perhaps one on each side of Lodovico) draw from the same 'well' of truisms

2 *tend*: attend, listen to 3 *gentle penance*: i.e., banishment

4 *close*: secret 5 *Have . . . you*: be self-sufficient

Their pleasing scents; and so affliction
Expresseth virtue fully, whether true
Or else adulterate.[1]

LODOVICO

Leave your painted[2] comforts!
I'll make Italian cut-works[3] in their guts
If ever I return.

GASPARO

O sir!

LODOVICO

I am patient.
I have seen some ready to be executed
Give pleasant looks and money, and grown familiar
With the knave hangman; so do I, I thank them,
And would account them nobly merciful
Would they dispatch me quickly.

ANTONELLI

Fare you well.
We shall find time, I doubt not, to repeal
Your banishment.

Enter SENATE [*who pass over the stage and exeunt*].

LODOVICO

I am ever bound to you.
[*He gives them money.*]
This is the world's alms – pray, make use of it.
Great men sell sheep thus to be cut in pieces,
When first they have shorn them bare and sold their
fleeces. *Exeunt.*

1 *adulterate*: fake, with a pun on 'adulterous'
2 *painted*: artificial
3 *Italian cut-works*: a popular kind of embroidery in which holes were cut into the cloth and stitched round

ACT 1

Scene 2

Enter BRACCIANO, CAMILLO, FLAMINIO, VITTORIA COROMBONA [*and* ATTENDANTS *with torches*].

BRACCIANO [*to* VITTORIA]
Your best of rest.

VITTORIA
Unto my lord the Duke,
The best of welcome. [*To* ATTENDANTS] More lights, attend the Duke!

[*Exeunt* VITTORIA *and* CAMILLO.]

BRACCIANO
Flaminio –

FLAMINIO
My lord.

BRACCIANO
Quite lost, Flaminio!

FLAMINIO
Pursue your noble wishes; I am prompt
As lightning to your service. (*Whispers*) O my lord!
The fair Vittoria, my happy sister,
Shall give you present audience. [*To* ATTENDANTS] Gentlemen,
Let the caroche[1] go on, and 'tis his pleasure
You put out all your torches and depart.

[*Exeunt* ATTENDANTS.]

BRACCIANO
Are we so happy?

FLAMINIO
Can't[2] be otherwise?
Observed you not tonight, my honoured lord,
Which way so e'er you went she threw her eyes?
I have dealt already with her chamber-maid,

1 *caroche*: luxurious coach, used in town 2 *Can't*: can it?

Zanche the Moor, and she is wondrous proud
To be the agent for so high a spirit.

BRACCIANO

We are happy above thought, because 'bove merit.

FLAMINIO

'Bove merit? – we may now talk freely – 'bove merit? What is't you doubt? Her coyness? That's but the superficies[1] of lust most women have. Yet why should ladies blush to hear that named which they do not fear to handle? Oh, they are politic. They know our desire is increased by the difficulty of enjoying, whereas satiety is a blunt, weary and drowsy passion. If the buttery-hatch[2] at court stood continually open there would be nothing so passionate crowding, nor hot suit after the beverage.[3]

BRACCIANO

Oh, but her jealous husband!

FLAMINIO

Hang him! A gilder[4] that hath his brains perished with quicksilver is not more cold in the liver.[5] The great Barriers[6] moulted not more feathers than he hath shed hairs,[7] by the confession of his doctor. An Irish gamester that will play himself naked, and then wage all downward at hazard,[8] is not more venturous. So unable to please a woman that, like a Dutch doublet,[9] all his back is shrunk into his breeches.

1 *superficies*: external covering

2 *buttery-hatch*: a half-door to the buttery (where provisions were stored) over which food and drink were served

3 *beverage*: usually ale

4 *gilder*: one who gilds objects for a living; gilders might suffer mercury ('quicksilver') poisoning, symptoms of which were tremors and insanity

5 *liver*: thought to be the origin of passion in the body

6 *Barriers*: a jousting competition conducted on either side of a low railing; Flaminio may be recalling the festivities of Christmas 1609 when Prince Henry, the future Prince of Wales, displayed his military prowess

7 *moulted . . . hairs*: feathers may have fallen off the barriers or the competitors' helmets; hair loss is a symptom of syphilis

8 *wage . . . hazard*: he will wager even his genitals, rendering himself impotent

9 *Dutch doublet*: close-fitting, worn with wide breeches, suggesting the shrinking of Camillo's penis and the enlargement of his buttocks, perhaps an allusion to sodomy

Shroud you within this closet,[1] good my lord.
Some trick now must be thought on to divide
My brother-in-law from his fair bed-fellow.

BRACCIANO

Oh, should she fail to come –

FLAMINIO

I must not have your lordship thus unwisely amorous. I myself have loved a lady and pursued her with a great deal of under-age protestation,[2] whom some three or four gallants that have enjoyed would, with all their hearts, have been glad to have been rid of. 'Tis just like a summer bird-cage in a garden: the birds that are without despair to get in, and the birds that are within despair and are in a consumption for fear they shall never get out. Away, away, my lord!

[BRACCIANO *withdraws from sight.*]

Enter CAMILLO.

See, here he comes. This fellow by his apparel
Some men would judge a politician,[3]
But call his wit in question, you shall find it
Merely an ass in's foot-cloth.[4] [*To* CAMILLO] How now, brother,
What, travelling to bed to your kind wife?

CAMILLO

I assure you, brother, no. My voyage lies
More northerly, in a far colder clime.
I do not well remember, I protest,
When I last lay with her.

FLAMINIO

Strange you should lose your count.[5]

CAMILLO

We never lay together but ere morning
There grew a flaw[6] between us.

1 *closet*: small, private room, its entrance sometimes hidden from view
2 *under-age protestation*: immature wooing
3 *politician*: crafty person; Camillo is presumably wearing long robes
4 *foot-cloth*: a richly decorated cloth covering the back of a horse
5 *count*: a variant spelling of 'cunt', may have been pronounced alike
6 *flaw*: disagreement, with a pun on female genitalia

FLAMINIO

'Thad been your part
To have made up that flaw.

CAMILLO

True, but she loathes
I should be seen in't.

FLAMINIO

Why, sir, what's the matter?

CAMILLO

The Duke your master visits me. I thank him,
And I perceive how like an earnest bowler
He very passionately leans that way
He should have his bowl run.

FLAMINIO

I hope you do not think –

CAMILLO

That noblemen bowl booty?[1] 'Faith, his cheek
Hath a most excellent bias: it would fain
Jump with my mistress.[2]

FLAMINIO

Will you be an ass
Despite your Aristotle,[3] or a cuckold
Contrary to your ephemerides,[4]
Which shows you under what a smiling planet
You were first swaddled?

CAMILLO

Pew wew, sir, tell not me
Of planets nor of ephemerides.
A man may be made cuckold in the day-time
When the stars' eyes are out.

1 *bowl booty*: cheat at bowls by ganging up on another player, i.e., Flaminio and Bracciano against Camillo

2 *his cheek . . . mistress*: Bracciano's cheek/buttock, like the weighted bowling ball, curves towards the white target, the 'mistress'; 'jump with', to have sex with

3 *Aristotle*: synonymous with logic

4 *ephemerides*: tables depicting the position of the planets on a particular day

FLAMINIO

Sir, God boy you.[1]
I do commit you to your pitiful pillow
Stuffed with horn-shavings.[2]

CAMILLO

Brother –

FLAMINIO

God refuse me,[3]
Might I advise you now, your only course
Were to lock up your wife.

CAMILLO

'Twere very good.

FLAMINIO

Bar her the sight of revels.

CAMILLO

Excellent!

FLAMINIO

Let her not go to church, but like a hound
In lyam[4] at your heels.

CAMILLO

'Twere for her honour.

FLAMINIO

And so you should be certain in one fortnight,
Despite her chastity or innocence,
To be cuckolded, which yet is in suspense.
This is my counsel and I ask no fee for't.

CAMILLO

Come, you know not where my nightcap wrings[5] me.

FLAMINIO

Wear it i'th' old fashion: let your large ears[6] come through; it will be more easy. Nay, I will be bitter. Bar your wife of her

1 *God boy you*: contracted version of 'God be with you'
2 *horn-shavings*: the cuckold was imagined to possess a pair of horns on his forehead
3 *God refuse me*: an oath 4 *In lyam*: on a leash
5 *wrings*: pinches, because of his cuckold's horns
6 *large ears*: implying that he is an ass

entertainment; women are more willingly and more gloriously chaste when they are least restrained of their liberty. It seems you would be a fine, capricious, mathematically-jealous coxcomb; take the height of your own horns with a Jacob's staff[1] afore they are up. These politic enclosures for paltry mutton[2] makes more rebellion in the flesh than all the provocative electuaries[3] doctors have uttered[4] since last Jubilee.[5]

CAMILLO

This doth not physic me.

FLAMINIO

It seems you are jealous. I'll show you the error of it by a familiar example. I have seen a pair of spectacles fashioned with such perspective art that, lay down but one twelve pence o'th' board, 'twill appear as if there were twenty. Now should you wear a pair of these spectacles and see your wife tying her shoe, you would imagine twenty hands were taking up of your wife's clothes, and this would put you into a horrible, causeless fury.

CAMILLO

The fault there, sir, is not in the eyesight.

FLAMINIO

True, but they that have the yellow jaundice think all objects they look on to be yellow. Jealousy is worser: her fits present to a man, like so many bubbles in a basin of water, twenty several crabbed faces; many times makes his own shadow his cuckold-maker.

Enter [VITTORIA] COROMBONA.

See, she comes. What reason have you to be jealous of this creature? What an ignorant ass or flattering knave might he be counted that should write sonnets to her eyes, or call her

1 *Jacob's staff*: instrument for measuring height and distance

2 *enclosures . . . mutton*: enclosures for sheep-farming were notoriously detrimental to the poor and inspired riots ('rebellion'); 'mutton' is also slang for a promiscuous woman

3 *provocative electuaries*: aphrodisiacs 4 *uttered*: issued

5 *Jubilee*: a year instituted by the Roman Catholic Church in which the penal consequences of sin were avoided by various kinds of penance; it occurred every twenty-five years, with the most recent being 1600

brow the snow of Ida,[1] or ivory of Corinth,[2] or compare her hair to the blackbird's bill when 'tis liker the blackbird's feather![3] This is all. Be wise; I will make you friends[4] and you shall go to bed together. Marry, look you, it shall not be your seeking, do you stand[5] upon that by any means. Walk you aloof; I would not have you seen in't.

[CAMILLO *stands apart.*]

Sister, [*aside*] my lord attends you in the banqueting-house. [*Aloud*] Your husband is wondrous discontented.

VITTORIA

I did nothing to displease him; I carved to him[6] at supper-time.

FLAMINIO [*Aside*]

You need not have carved him, in faith: they say he is a capon[7] already. I must now seemingly fall out with you. [*Aloud*] Shall a gentleman so well descended as Camillo – [*aside*] a lousy slave that within this twenty years rode with the black-guard[8] in the Duke's carriage 'mongst spits and dripping-pans –

CAMILLO

Now he begins to tickle her.

FLAMINIO [*Aloud*]

An excellent scholar – [*aside*] one that hath a head filled with calves' brains[9] without any sage in them – [*aloud*] come crouching in the hams[10] to you for a night's lodging? – [*aside*] that hath an itch in's hams[11] which, like the fire at the

1 *Ida*: sacred mountain in Crete or Phrygia, near Troy
2 *Corinth*: a city famous for its luxury, also slang for a brothel
3 *blackbird's bill . . . feather*: yellow hair was judged the ideal of beauty, rather than Vittoria's black
4 *friends*: lovers 5 *stand*: insist
6 *carved to him*: served him or showed him great courtesy
7 *capon*: a castrated cock
8 *black-guard*: the lowest kitchen servants, in charge of kitchen utensils when a nobleman moved residences
9 *calves' brains*: foolishness; to be unseasoned with 'sage' implies the brain unimproved by knowledge
10 *crouching in the hams*: bending servilely
11 *itch in's hams*: venereal disease or unfulfilled sexual desire

glass-house,[1] hath not gone out this seven years. [*Aloud*] Is he not a courtly gentleman? – [*aside*] when he wears white satin one would take him by his black muzzle to be no other creature than a maggot. [*Aloud*] You are a goodly foil,[2] I confess, well set-out – [*aside*] but covered with a false stone, yon counterfeit diamond.

CAMILLO

He will make her know what is in me.

FLAMINIO

Come, my lord attends you. Thou shalt go to bed to my lord –

CAMILLO

Now he comes to't.

FLAMINIO

– with a relish as curious as a vintner going to taste new wine. I am opening your case[3] hard.

CAMILLO

A virtuous brother, o'my credit.

FLAMINIO

He will give thee a ring with a philosopher's stone[4] in it.

CAMILLO

Indeed, I am studying alchemy.

FLAMINIO

Thou shalt lie in a bed stuffed with turtles'[5] feathers, swoon in perfumed linen like the fellow was smothered in roses. So perfect shall be thy happiness that, as men at sea think land and trees and ships go that way they go, so both heaven and earth shall seem to go your voyage. Shalt meet him – 'tis fixed with nails of diamonds to inevitable necessity.

VITTORIA [*Aside to* FLAMINIO]

How shall's rid him hence?

1 *fire . . . glass-house*: the glass factory near the Blackfriars Theatre kept its furnace constantly burning

2 *foil*: setting for a precious stone 3 *case*: legal case, female genitalia

4 *philosopher's stone*: thought by alchemists to turn base materials into gold, prolong life and cure disease, with a pun on 'stone' as testicle

5 *turtles*: turtle doves, associated with faithful love

FLAMINIO [*Aside*]

I will put breeze[1] in's tail; set him gadding[2] presently.

[*He approaches* CAMILLO.]

I have almost wrought her to it; I find her coming.[3] But might I advise you now, for this night I would not lie with her. I would cross her humour to make her more humble.

CAMILLO

Shall I, shall I?

FLAMINIO

It will show in you a supremacy of judgement.

CAMILLO

True, and a mind differing from the tumultuary[4] opinion, for *quae negata grata*.[5]

FLAMINIO

Right, you are the adamant[6] shall draw her to you, though you keep distance off.

CAMILLO

A philosophical reason.

FLAMINIO

Walk by her i'the nobleman's fashion, and tell her you will lie with her at the end of the progress.[7]

CAMILLO [*coming forward*]

Vittoria, I cannot be induced, or, as a man would say, incited –

VITTORIA

To do what, sir?

CAMILLO

To lie with you tonight. Your silkworm useth to fast every third day, and the next following spins the better. Tomorrow, at night, I am for you.

1 *breeze*: gadflies 2 *gadding*: wandering
3 *coming*: receptive 4 *tumultuary*: confused
5 *quae negata grata*: 'Whatever is denied is desired' 6 *adamant*: magnet
7 *progress*: procession, taken by royal or other noble person, defined by its flamboyant self-display

VITTORIA

You'll spin a fair thread,[1] trust to't.

[*She stands apart.*]

FLAMINIO

But do you hear, I shall have you steal to her chamber about midnight.

CAMILLO

Do you think so? Why, look you, brother, because you shall not think I'll gull[2] you, take the key, lock me into the chamber, and say you shall be sure of me.

FLAMINIO

In troth, I will. I'll be your jailer once. But have you ne'er a false door?

CAMILLO

A pox on't, as I am a Christian. Tell me tomorrow how scurvily[3] she takes my unkind parting.

FLAMINIO

I will.

CAMILLO

Didst thou not mark the jest of the silkworm? Good night. In faith, I will use this trick often.

FLAMINIO

Do, do, do. *Exit* CAMILLO.

So, now you are safe. Ha, ha, ha! Thou entanglest thyself in thine own work like a silkworm.

Enter BRACCIANO.

Come, sister, darkness hides your blush. Women are like curst[4] dogs: civility keeps them tied all daytime, but they are let loose at midnight. Then they do most good or most mischief. My lord, my lord –

BRACCIANO [*To* VITTORIA]

Give credit,[5] I could wish time would stand still
And never end this interview, this hour,
But all delight doth itself soon'st devour.

1 *thread*: with a pun on 'semen' 2 *gull*: trick
3 *scurvily*: rudely, crossly 4 *curst*: vicious, bad-tempered
5 *Give credit*: believe me

ZANCHE *brings out a carpet, spreads it and lays on it two fair cushions.* [BRACCIANO *and* VITTORIA *sit.*]
Enter CORNELIA [*who watches them*].

Let me into your bosom, happy lady,
Pour out instead of eloquence my vows.
Loose[1] me not, madam, for if you forgo me
I am lost eternally.

VITTORIA

Sir, in the way of pity
I wish you heart-whole.

BRACCIANO

You are a sweet physician.

VITTORIA

Sure, sir, a loathèd cruelty in ladies
Is as to doctors many funerals:
It takes away their credit.

BRACCIANO

Excellent creature!
We call the cruel 'fair'; what name for you
That are so merciful?
[*He kisses her.*]

ZANCHE [*Aside*]

See, now they close.[2]

FLAMINIO [*Aside*]

Most happy union!

CORNELIA [*Aside*]

My fears are fall'n upon me. O my heart!
My son the pander! Now I find our house
Sinking to ruin. Earthquakes leave behind,
Where they have tyrannized, iron or lead or stone,
But, woe to ruin, violent lust leaves none.

BRACCIANO

What value is this jewel?
[*He examines her ring.*]

1 *Loose*: release, abandon 2 *close*: come together

VITTORIA

'Tis the ornament
Of a weak fortune.

BRACCIANO

In sooth, I'll have it. Nay, I will but change
My jewel for your jewel.[1]
[*He takes her ring and gives her a pendant.*]

FLAMINIO [*Aside*]

Excellent!
His jewel for her jewel – well put in,[2] Duke!

BRACCIANO

Nay, let me see you wear it.

VITTORIA

Here, sir?
[*She holds it against her bosom.*]

BRACCIANO

Nay, lower; you shall wear my jewel lower.
[*She pins it at the lowest point of her bodice.*][3]

FLAMINIO [*Aside*]

That's better; she must wear his jewel lower.

VITTORIA

To pass away the time I'll tell your grace
A dream I had last night.

BRACCIANO

Most wishedly.

VITTORIA

A foolish idle dream.
Methought I walked, about the mid of night,
Into a church-yard, where a goodly yew-tree
Spread her large root in ground. Under that yew,
As I sat sadly leaning on a grave[4]
Chequered with 'crostics,[5] there came stealing in
Your Duchess and my husband. One of them
A pick-axe bore, th'other a rusty spade,

1 *jewel*: often used to describe a woman's marital chastity or virginity
2 *put in*: demanded, with a sexual pun
3 *lowest . . . bodice*: i.e., over her vagina 4 *grave*: gravestone
5 *'crostics*: acrostics, which often appeared on memorial stones

And in rough terms they 'gan to challenge me
About this yew.

BRACCIANO

That tree?

VITTORIA

This harmless yew.[1]
They told me my intent was to root up
That well-grown yew, and plant i'th' stead of it
A withered blackthorn, and for that they vowed
To bury me alive. My husband straight
With pick-axe 'gan to dig, and your fell[2] Duchess
With shovel, like a fury,[3] voided out
The earth and scattered bones. Lord, how methought
I trembled, and yet for all this terror
I could not pray.

FLAMINIO [*Aside*]

No, the devil was in your dream.

VITTORIA

When to my rescue there arose, methought,
A whirlwind, which let fall a massy[4] arm
From that strong plant,
And both were struck dead by that sacred yew
In that base, shallow grave that was their due.

FLAMINIO [*Aside*]

Excellent devil!
She hath taught him in a dream
To make away his Duchess and her husband.

BRACCIANO [*Embracing* VITTORIA]

Sweetly shall I interpret this your dream:
You are lodged within his arms who shall protect you
From all the fevers of a jealous husband,
From the poor envy of our phlegmatic[5] Duchess.
I'll seat you above law and above scandal;

1 *yew*: tree associated with death, also pun on 'you' 2 *fell*: fierce, cruel
3 *fury*: the three Furies were figures of female revenge in classical mythology, often depicted with snakes for hair
4 *massy*: weighty 5 *phlegmatic*: not easily impassioned

Give to your thoughts the invention of delight
And the fruition. Nor shall government[1]
Divide me from you longer than a care
To keep you great. You shall to me at once
Be dukedom, health, wife, children, friends and all.

CORNELIA [*Coming forward*]
Woe to light hearts! They still forerun our fall.

FLAMINIO
What fury raised thee up? [*Aside to* ZANCHE] Away, away![2]
Exit ZANCHE.

CORNELIA
What make you here, my lord, this dead of night?
Never dropped mildew on a flower here
Till now.

FLAMINIO
I pray, will you go to bed then,
Lest you be blasted?[3]

CORNELIA
Oh, that this fair garden
Had with all poisoned herbs of Thessaly[4]
At first been planted, made a nursery
For witchcraft, rather than a burial plot
For both your honours.

VITTORIA
Dearest mother, hear me.

CORNELIA
Oh, thou dost make my brow bend to the earth
Sooner than nature. See the curse of children!
In life they keep us frequently in tears,
And in the cold grave leave us in pale fears.

BRACCIANO
Come, come, I will not hear you.

1 *government*: the act of governing

2 *Exit* ZANCHE: perhaps suggesting Flaminio is already involved with Zanche, against his mother's wishes

3 *blasted*: blighted, withered

4 *Thessaly*: district of northern Greece associated with the vengeful Medea and with poisonous plants

VITTORIA

Dear my lord –

CORNELIA

Where is thy Duchess now, adulterous Duke?
Thou little dreamed'st this night she is come to Rome.

FLAMINIO

How? Come to Rome?

VITTORIA

The Duchess?

BRACCIANO

She had been better –

CORNELIA

The lives of princes should like dials[1] move,
Whose regular example is so strong,
They make the times by them go right or wrong.

FLAMINIO

So, have you done?

CORNELIA

Unfortunate Camillo!

VITTORIA [*kneeling*]

I do protest, if any chaste denial,
If anything but blood[2] could have allayed
His long suit to me –

CORNELIA [*kneeling*]

I will join with thee,
To the most woeful end e'er mother kneeled.
If thou dishonour thus thy husband's bed,
Be thy life short as are the funeral tears
In great men's.

BRACCIANO

Fie, fie, the woman's mad!

1 *princes* ... *dials*: an allusion to one of Webster's sources for the play, Guevara's *The Dial of Princes*

2 *blood*: bloodshed, but also reciprocal sexual desire

CORNELIA
Be thy act Judas-like: betray in kissing.
May'st thou be envied during his short breath,
And pitied like a wretch after his death.
VITTORIA
O me, accursed! *Exit* VITTORIA.
FLAMINIO [*To* CORNELIA]
Are you out of your wits? [*To* BRACCIANO] My lord,
I'll fetch her back again.
BRACCIANO
No, I'll to bed.
Send Doctor Julio to me presently.
Uncharitable woman, thy rash tongue
Hath raised a fearful and prodigious storm.
Be thou the cause of all ensuing harm. *Exit* BRACCIANO.
FLAMINIO
Now, you that stand so much upon your honour,
Is this a fitting time o'night, think you,
To send a duke home without e'er a man?
I would fain know where lies the mass of wealth
Which you have hoarded for my maintenance,
That I may bear my beard out of the level
Of my lord's stirrup.[1]
CORNELIA
What, because we are poor
Shall we be vicious?
FLAMINIO
Pray, what means have you
To keep me from the galleys or the gallows?
My father proved himself a gentleman:
Sold all's land, and, like a fortunate fellow,
Died ere the money was spent. You brought me up
At Padua, I confess, where, I protest,
For want of means – the university judge me –
I have been fain to heel[2] my tutor's stockings

1 *bear . . . stirrup*: get a promotion above the role of unmounted footman
2 *fain to heel*: obliged to mend

At least seven years. Conspiring with a beard[1]
Made me a graduate; then to this Duke's service
I visited the court, whence I returned
More courteous, more lecherous by far,
But not a suit the richer; and shall I,
Having a path so open and so free
To my preferment, still retain your milk
In my pale forehead? No, this face of mine
I'll arm and fortify with lusty wine
'Gainst shame and blushing.

CORNELIA

Oh, that I ne'er had borne thee!

FLAMINIO

So would I;
I would the common'st courtesan in Rome
Had been my mother rather than thyself.
Nature is very pitiful to whores
To give them but few children, yet those children
Plurality of fathers; they are sure
They shall not want. Go, go,
Complain unto my great lord Cardinal;
Yet maybe he will justify the act.
Lycurgus[2] wondered much men would provide
Good stallions for their mares, and yet would suffer
Their fair wives to be barren.

CORNELIA

Misery of miseries! *Exit* CORNELIA.

FLAMINIO

The Duchess come to court? I like not that.
We are engaged to mischief and must on.
As rivers, to find out the ocean,

1 *Conspiring with a beard*: insinuating himself into the affections of an older man, perhaps sexually; 'beard' might also be a misprint for 'beadle', the university official who collected fees

2 *Lycurgus*: Spartan lawgiver, described in Plutarch's *Lives of the Noble Grecians and Romans* as urging men to share their wives with other worthy men in order to produce the best children

Flow with crook[1] bendings beneath forcèd[2] banks,
Or as we see, to aspire some mountain's top,
The way ascends not straight, but imitates
The subtle foldings of a winter's snake,[3]
So who knows Policy and her true aspect
Shall find her ways winding and indirect. *Exit.*

ACT 2

Scene 1

Enter FRANCISCO *de Medici, Cardinal* MONTICELSO, MARCELLO, ISABELLA, *young* GIOVANNI, *with little* JAQUES *the Moor.*

FRANCISCO
Have you not seen your husband since you arrived?

ISABELLA
Not yet, sir.

FRANCISCO
Surely, he is wondrous kind.
If I had such a dove-house as Camillo's,
I would set fire on't, were't but to destroy
The pole-cats[4] that haunt to't. [*To* GIOVANNI] My sweet cousin[5] –

GIOVANNI
Lord uncle, you did promise me a horse
And armour.

FRANCISCO
That I did, my pretty cousin.
Marcello, see it fitted.

1 *crook*: crooked 2 *forcèd*: man-made
3 *subtle ... snake*: coiled up whilst hibernating, possibly alluding to the mythical, two-headed snake amphisbaena, which sought out cold temperatures
4 *pole-cats*: foul-smelling, predatory mammals, also term for a prostitute
5 *cousin*: used also to describe a nephew or niece

MARCELLO

My lord, the Duke is here.

FRANCISCO

Sister, away! You must not yet be seen.

ISABELLA

I do beseech you,
Entreat him mildly; let not your rough tongue
Set us at louder variance. All my wrongs
Are freely pardoned, and I do not doubt,
As men to try the precious unicorn's horn
Make of the powder a preservative circle
And in it put a spider,[1] so these arms
Shall charm his poison, force it to obeying,
And keep him chaste from an infected straying.

FRANCISCO

I wish it may. Be gone. *Exit* [ISABELLA].

Enter BRACCIANO *and* FLAMINIO.

Void[2] the chamber.

[*Exeunt* FLAMINIO, MARCELLO, GIOVANNI *and* JAQUES.]

You are welcome; will you sit? [*To* MONTICELSO] I pray, my lord,
Be you my orator. My heart's too full;
I'll second you anon.

MONTICELSO

Ere I begin,
Let me entreat your grace forgo all passion
Which may be raised by my free discourse.

1 *unicorn's horn . . . spider*: powdered unicorn's horn was thought to offer protection against poison, the test for which was to place a spider inside a circle of powder and if it remained there the remedy was effective

2 *Void*: clear

BRACCIANO
As silent as i'th' church – you may proceed.
MONTICELSO
It is a wonder to your noble friends
That you that have, as 'twere, entered the world
With a free sceptre in your able hand,
And have to th'use of nature well applied
High gifts of learning, should in your prime age
Neglect your awful[1] throne for the soft down
Of an insatiate bed. O my lord,
The drunkard after all his lavish cups
Is dry, and then is sober; so at length,
When you awake from this lascivious dream,
Repentance then will follow, like the sting
Placed in the adder's tail. Wretched are princes
When fortune blasteth but a petty flower[2]
Of their unwieldy crowns, or ravisheth
But one pearl from their sceptre; but, alas!
When they to wilful shipwreck loose[3] good fame
All princely titles perish with their name.[4]
BRACCIANO
You have said, my lord –
MONTICELSO
Enough to give you taste
How far I am from flattering your greatness.
BRACCIANO [*To* FRANCISCO]
Now you that are his second, what say you?
Do not, like young hawks, fetch a course about;[5]
Your game flies fair and for you.
FRANCISCO
Do not fear it.
I'll answer you in your own hawking phrase:
Some eagles that should gaze upon the sun
Seldom soar high, but take their lustful ease,

1 *awful*: awe-inspiring, magnificent
2 *flower*: another name for a jewel in a crown 3 *loose*: lose
4 *name*: reputation 5 *fetch . . . about*: change direction

Since they from dunghill birds[1] their prey can seize.
You know Vittoria?

BRACCIANO

Yes.

FRANCISCO

You shift[2] your shirt there
When you retire from tennis?

BRACCIANO

Happily.[3]

FRANCISCO

Her husband is lord of a poor fortune,
Yet she wears cloth of tissue.[4]

BRACCIANO

What of this?
Will you urge that, my good lord Cardinal,
As part of her confession at next shrift,
And know from whence it sails?

FRANCISCO

She is your strumpet.

BRACCIANO

Uncivil sir, there's hemlock in thy breath
And that black slander. Were she a whore of mine,
All thy loud cannons and thy borrowed Switzers,[5]
Thy galleys, nor thy sworn confederates
Durst not supplant her.

FRANCISCO

Let's not talk on thunder.
Thou hast a wife, our sister – would I had given
Both her white hands to death, bound and locked fast
In her last winding-sheet, when I gave thee
But one.

1 *dunghill birds*: carrion birds, i.e., Camillo
2 *shift*: change 3 *Happily*: perhaps, with a pun on 'gladly'
4 *tissue*: cloth interwoven with gold or silver, only to be worn by women of high birth
5 *Switzers*: Swiss mercenaries, used at many European courts for protection

BRACCIANO
Thou hadst given a soul to God then.
FRANCISCO
True;
Thy ghostly[1] father, with all's absolution,
Shall ne'er do so by thee.
BRACCIANO
Spit thy poison.
FRANCISCO
I shall not need; Lust carries her sharp whip
At her own girdle. Look to't, for our anger
Is making thunderbolts.
BRACCIANO
Thunder? In faith,
They are but crackers.[2]
FRANCISCO
We'll end this with the cannon.
BRACCIANO
Thou'lt get nought by it but iron in thy wounds,
And gunpowder in thy nostrils.
FRANCISCO
Better that
Than change perfumes for plasters.[3]
BRACCIANO
Pity on thee,
'Twere good you'd show your slaves or men condemned
Your new-ploughed[4] forehead. Defiance – and I'll meet thee,
Even in a thicket of thy ablest men.
MONTICELSO
My lords, you shall not word it[5] any further
Without a milder limit.
FRANCISCO
Willingly.

1 *ghostly*: spiritual, i.e., his confessor
2 *crackers*: fireworks 3 *plasters*: to cover the sores of venereal disease
4 *new-ploughed*: furrowed with rage 5 *word it*: argue

BRACCIANO

Have you proclaimed a triumph that you bait
A lion thus?[1]

MONTICELSO

My lord!

BRACCIANO

I am tame, I am tame, sir.

FRANCISCO

We send unto the Duke for conference
'Bout levies 'gainst the pirates; my lord Duke
Is not at home. We come ourself in person;
Still my lord Duke is busied. But we fear
When Tiber to each prowling passenger[2]
Discovers flocks of wild ducks,[3] then, my lord –
'Bout moulting-time,[4] I mean – we shall be certain
To find you, sure enough, and speak with you.

BRACCIANO

Ha?

FRANCISCO

A mere tale of a tub;[5] my words are idle.
But to express the sonnet by natural reason,
When stags grow melancholic[6] you'll find the season.

Enter GIOVANNI [*wearing armour, and* JAQUES].

MONTICELSO

No more, my lord. Here comes a champion
Shall end the difference between you both,
Your son, the prince Giovanni. See, my lords,

1 *triumph . . . thus*: in 1604 James I experimented with lion-baiting at the Tower of London, a few days before his triumphal entry into the city (see Stow's *Annals*, 1605); the lion killed the dogs that were set upon it
2 *passenger*: abbreviation of passenger (peregrine) falcon
3 *wild ducks*: also a term for prostitutes
4 *moulting-time*: i.e., when Bracciano's hair starts to fall out he will realize that Vittoria is no better than a prostitute
5 *tale of a tub*: cock and bull story, also an allusion to the sweating tubs used to cure venereal disease
6 *stags . . . melancholic*: stags (horned like the cuckold) supposedly went off to lie alone after mating, i.e., after Bracciano has finished with Vittoria he will find time ('the season') to meet with them

What hopes you store in him; this is a casket
For both your crowns, and should be held like dear.
Now is he apt for knowledge; therefore know,
It is a more direct and even way
To train to virtue those of princely blood
By examples than by precepts. If by examples,
Whom should he rather strive to imitate
Than his own father? Be his pattern, then.
Leave him a stock of virtue that may last,
Should fortune rend his sails and split his mast.

BRACCIANO
Your hand, boy. [*Shakes his hand*] Growing to soldier?

GIOVANNI
Give me a pike.
[JAQUES *hands him a weapon.*]

FRANCISCO
What, practising your pike so young, fair coz?

GIOVANNI
Suppose me one of Homer's frogs,[1] my lord,
Tossing my bulrush thus. Pray, sir, tell me:
Might not a child of good discretion
Be leader to an army?

FRANCISCO
Yes, cousin, a young prince
Of good discretion[2] might.

GIOVANNI
Say you so?
Indeed, I have heard 'tis fit a general
Should not endanger his own person oft,
So that he make a noise when he's o'horseback
Like a Dansk[3] drummer. Oh, 'tis excellent!
He need not fight – methinks his horse as well
Might lead an army for him. If I live,

1 *Homer's frogs*: in *The Battle of Frogs and Mice*, a burlesque poem attributed to Homer, the frogs carry bulrushes as pikes
2 *discretion*: judgement 3 *Dansk*: Danish, famous for their military music

I'll charge the French foe in the very front
Of all my troops, the foremost man –

FRANCISCO
What, what?

GIOVANNI
And will not bid my soldiers up and follow,
But bid them follow me.

BRACCIANO
Forward lapwing![1]
He flies with the shell on's head.

FRANCISCO
Pretty cousin!

GIOVANNI
The first year, uncle, that I go to war,
All prisoners that I take I will set free
Without their ransom.

FRANCISCO
Ha, without their ransom?
How then will you reward your soldiers
That took those prisoners for you?

GIOVANNI
Thus, my lord:
I'll marry them to all the wealthy widows
That falls that year.

FRANCISCO
Why then, the next year following
You'll have no men to go with you to war.

GIOVANNI
Why then, I'll press the women to the war,
And then the men will follow.

MONTICELSO
Witty prince!

1 *lapwing*: a proverbially precocious bird, thought to run as soon as it is hatched

FRANCISCO
See, a good habit[1] makes a child a man,
Whereas a bad one makes a man a beast.
Come, you and I are friends.

BRACCIANO
Most wishedly,
Like bones which broke in sunder and wellset
Knit the more strongly.

FRANCISCO [*To* ATTENDANT *offstage*]
Call Camillo hither.
You have received the rumour how Count Lodovic
Is turned a pirate?

BRACCIANO
Yes.

FRANCISCO
We are now preparing
Some ships to fetch him in.
[*Enter* ISABELLA.]
Behold your Duchess.
We now will leave you, and expect from you
Nothing but kind entreaty.

BRACCIANO
You have charmed me.

Exeunt FRANCISCO, MONTICELSO, GIOVANNI [*and* JAQUES].

You are in health we see.

ISABELLA
And above health
To see my lord well.

BRACCIANO
So – I wonder much
What amorous whirlwind hurried you to Rome.

ISABELLA
Devotion, my lord.

1 *habit*: costume, but also behaviour

BRACCIANO

Devotion?[1]
Is your soul charged with any grievous sin?

ISABELLA

'Tis burdened with too many, and I think
The oft'ner that we cast our reck'nings up,[2]
Our sleeps will be the sounder.

BRACCIANO

Take your chamber.[3]

ISABELLA

Nay, my dear lord, I will not have you angry.
Doth not my absence from you two months
Merit one kiss?

BRACCIANO

I do not use to kiss.
If that will dispossess your jealousy,
I'll swear it to you.

ISABELLA

O my lovèd lord,
I do not come to chide. My jealousy?
I am to learn what that Italian[4] means.
You are as welcome to these longing arms
As I to you a virgin.
[*She kisses him.*]

BRACCIANO

Oh, your breath!
Out upon sweetmeats and continued physic –
The plague is in them!

1 *Devotion*: Isabella means marital devotion, but Bracciano chooses to misunderstand her meaning as religious duty

2 *cast . . . up*: tally our sins and good deeds

3 *Take your chamber*: go to your room

4 *that Italian*: Italians were notoriously jealous; Isabella claims that this emotion is so unnatural to her it is a foreign word (even though she was historically Italian)

ISABELLA

You have oft, for these two lips,
Neglected cassia[1] or the natural sweets
Of the spring violet; they are not yet much withered.
My lord, I should be merry. These your frowns
Show in a helmet lovely, but on me,
In such a peaceful interview, methinks
They are too, too roughly knit.

BRACCIANO

O dissemblance!
Do you bandy factions[2] 'gainst me? Have you learnt
The trick of impudent baseness to complain
Unto your kindred?

ISABELLA

Never, my dear lord.

BRACCIANO

Must I be haunted out,[3] or was't your trick
To meet some amorous gallant here in Rome[4]
That must supply our discontinuance?

ISABELLA

I pray, sir, burst my heart, and in my death
Turn to your ancient pity, though not love.

BRACCIANO

Because your brother is the corpulent Duke,
That is the Great Duke – S'death, I shall not shortly
Racket away five hundred crowns at tennis,
But it shall rest upon record! I scorn him
Like a shaved Polack;[5] all his reverent wit
Lies in his wardrobe. He's a discreet fellow
When he's made up in his robes of state.
Your brother, the Great Duke, because h'as galleys,

1 *cassia*: a kind of cinnamon, renowned for its sweet smell
2 *bandy factions*: conspire 3 *haunted out*: pursued, followed
4 *To meet . . . Rome*: in the historical source, Isabella did have a lover
5 *Polack*: Polish men famously shaved their heads except for the forehead; a worthless person

And now and then ransacks a Turkish fly-boat[1] –
Now all the hellish furies take his soul! –
First made this match. Accursèd be the priest
That sang the wedding mass, and even my issue!

ISABELLA

Oh, too, too far you have cursed.

BRACCIANO

Your hand I'll kiss:
This is the latest[2] ceremony of my love.
Henceforth I'll never lie with thee. By this,
This wedding-ring [*removing the ring*], I'll ne'er more lie
with thee;
And this divorce shall be as truly kept
As if the judge had doomed it. Fare you well;
Our sleeps are severed.

ISABELLA

Forbid it, the sweet union
Of all things blessed! Why, the saints in heaven
Will knit their brows at that.

BRACCIANO

Let not thy love
Make thee an unbeliever. This my vow
Shall never, on my soul, be satisfied
With my repentance. Let thy brother rage
Beyond a horrid tempest or sea-fight,
My vow is fixed.

ISABELLA

O my winding-sheet,
Now shall I need thee shortly! Dear my lord,
Let me hear once more what I would not hear:
Never?

BRACCIANO

Never.

ISABELLA

O my unkind lord, may your sins find mercy,
As I upon a woeful, widowed bed

1 *fly-boat*: a pinnace or fast sailing boat 2 *latest*: last

Shall pray for you, if not to turn your eyes
Upon your wretched wife and hopeful son,
Yet that in time you'll fix them upon heaven.

BRACCIANO
No more. Go, go complain to the Great Duke.

ISABELLA
No, my dear lord, you shall have present witness
How I'll work peace between you. I will make
Myself the author of your cursèd vow;
I have some cause to do it, you have none.
Conceal it, I beseech you, for the weal[1]
Of both your dukedoms, that you wrought the means
Of such a separation. Let the fault
Remain with my supposèd jealousy,
And think with what a piteous and rent heart
I shall perform this sad, ensuing part.

Enter FRANCISCO, FLAMINIO, MONTICELSO, MARCELLO.

BRACCIANO
Well, take your course [*turning away from* ISABELLA, *who weeps*]. – My honourable brother –

FRANCISCO
Sister? This is not well, my lord. Why, sister!
She merits not this welcome.

BRACCIANO
Welcome, say?
She hath given a sharp welcome.

FRANCISCO [*To* ISABELLA]
Are you foolish?
Come, dry your tears. Is this a modest course:
To better what is naught,[2] to rail and weep?
Grow to a reconcilement, or, by heaven,
I'll ne'er more deal between you.

1 *weal*: good
2 *To better what is naught*: to exceed what is immoral, i.e., Isabella's upbraiding her husband is worse than his infidelity

ISABELLA

Sir, you shall not;
No, though Vittoria upon that condition
Would become honest.[1]

FRANCISCO

Was your husband loud
Since we departed?

ISABELLA

By my life, sir, no;
I swear by that I do not care to lose.
Are all these ruins of my former beauty
Laid out for a whore's triumph?

FRANCISCO

Do you hear?
Look upon other women, with what patience
They suffer these slight wrongs, with what justice
They study to requite them. Take that course.

ISABELLA

Oh, that I were a man, or that I had power
To execute my apprehended wishes,
I would whip some with scorpions.

FRANCISCO

What, turned fury?

ISABELLA

To dig the strumpet's eyes out, let her lie
Some twenty months a-dying, to cut off
Her nose and lips, pull out her rotten teeth,
Preserve her flesh like mummia, for trophies
Of my just anger. Hell to my affliction
Is mere snow-water. [*To* BRACCIANO] By your favour, sir –
Brother, draw near, and my lord Cardinal –
[*To* BRACCIANO] Sir, let me borrow of you but one kiss.
[*She kisses him.*]
Henceforth I'll never lie with you, by this,
This wedding ring.
[*She removes her ring.*]

1 *honest*: chaste

FRANCISCO

How? Ne'er more lie with him?

ISABELLA

And this divorce shall be as truly kept
As if in throngèd court a thousand ears[1]
Had heard it, and a thousand lawyers' hands
Sealed to the separation.

BRACCIANO

Ne'er lie with me?

ISABELLA

Let not my former dotage
Make thee an unbeliever. This my vow
Shall never, on my soul, be satisfied
With my repentance: *manet alta mente repostum.*[2]

FRANCISCO

Now, by my birth, you are a foolish, mad
And jealous woman!

BRACCIANO

You see 'tis not my seeking.

FRANCISCO

Was this your circle of pure unicorn's horn
You said should charm your lord? Now horns upon thee,
For jealousy deserves them. Keep your vow
And take your chamber.

ISABELLA

No, sir, I'll presently to Padua;
I will not stay a minute.

MONTICELSO

O good madam –

1 *a thousand ears*: i.e., the theatre audience

2 *manet . . . repostum*: 'It shall be treasured up in the depths of my mind' (Virgil, *Aeneid* 1.26); the line expresses Juno's anger at being passed over by Paris in favour of Venus; unlike Juno, whose revenge contributed to the Trojan wars, Isabella feigns anger to prevent war

BRACCIANO

'Twere best to let her have her humour.
Some half-day's journey will bring down her stomach,[1]
And then she'll turn in post.[2]

FRANCISCO

To see her come
To my lord Cardinal for a dispensation
Of her rash vow will beget excellent laughter.

ISABELLA [*Aside*]

Unkindness, do thy office: poor heart, break.
Those are the killing griefs which dare not speak.[3] *Exit.*

Enter CAMILLO.

MARCELLO

Camillo's come, my lord.

FRANCISCO

Where's the commission?

MARCELLO

'Tis here.

FRANCISCO

Give me the signet.
[*They confer apart.*]

FLAMINIO [*To* BRACCIANO]

My lord, do you mark their whispering? I will compound a medicine out of their two heads, stronger than garlic, deadlier than stibium.[4] The cantharides,[5] which are scarce seen to stick upon the flesh when they work to the heart, shall not do it with more silence or invisible cunning.

BRACCIANO

About the murder –

1 *stomach*: pride, vexation 2 *turn in post*: return post-haste
3 *Those . . . speak*: a common proverb, found in Seneca's *Phaedra*, 607
4 *stibium*: metallic antimony, used as an emetic or poison
5 *cantharides*: Spanish fly, applied to create blisters, but poisonous when ingested in large quantities

FLAMINIO

They are sending him to Naples, but I'll send him to Candy.[1]

Enter DOCTOR [*Julio*].

Here's another property[2] too.

BRACCIANO

Oh, the doctor.

FLAMINIO

A poor, quack-salving[3] knave, my lord, one that should have been lashed for's lechery, but that he confessed a judgement, had an execution laid upon him, and so put the whip to a *non plus*.[4]

DOCTOR

And was cozened, my lord, by an arranter knave than myself, and made pay all the colourable execution.[5]

FLAMINIO

He will shoot pills into a man's guts, shall make them have more ventages than a cornet[6] or a lamprey.[7] He will poison a kiss, and was once minded for his masterpiece, because Ireland breeds no poison,[8] to have prepared a deadly vapour in a Spaniard's fart[9] that should have poisoned all Dublin.

BRACCIANO

Oh, Saint Anthony's fire![10]

DOCTOR

Your secretary is merry, my lord.

1 *Candy*: Crete, whose inhabitants were supposed to eat poisonous snakes, i.e., death

2 *property*: a tool, with allusion to a stage prop

3 *quack-salving*: peddling fake medicines

4 *confessed . . . non plus*: acknowledged a previous prosecution for debt, was taken into custody and so escaped whipping

5 *cozened . . . execution*: tricked by someone pretending to be his creditor and forced to pay all that was supposedly owed

6 *cornet*: wind instrument

7 *lamprey*: eel-like fish with holes on the side of its head

8 *Ireland . . . poison*: according to myth, St Patrick banished all poisonous animals from Ireland

9 *Spaniard's fart*: a Spaniard called Don Diego was famous for farting in St Paul's Cathedral

10 *Saint Anthony's fire*: a skin disease or possibly slang for flatulence

FLAMINIO

O thou cursed antipathy to nature! Look, his eye's bloodshed[1] like a needle a chirurgeon[2] stitcheth a wound with. Let me embrace thee, toad, and love thee. O thou abominable, loathsome gargarism,[3] that will fetch up lungs, lights,[4] heart and liver by scruples![5]

BRACCIANO

No more. I must employ thee, honest doctor;
You must to Padua and by the way
Use some of your skill for us.

DOCTOR

Sir, I shall.

BRACCIANO

But for Camillo?

FLAMINIO

He dies this night by such a politic strain[6]
Men shall suppose him by's own engine[7] slain.
But for your Duchess's death –

DOCTOR

I'll make her sure.

BRACCIANO

Small mischiefs are by greater made secure.

FLAMINIO

Remember this, you slave: when knaves come to preferment they rise as gallows are raised i'th' Low Countries – one upon another's shoulders.[8]

Exeunt [BRACCIANO, FLAMINIO AND DOCTOR].

1 *bloodshed*: bloodshot 2 *chirurgeon*: surgeon
3 *gargarism*: gargle or mouth-wash 4 *lights*: lungs
5 *by scruples*: in small quantities
6 *politic strain*: a cunning device, with a pun on 'strain' meaning strong muscular effort, alluding to his attempt at vaulting
7 *engine*: means
8 *one . . . shoulders*: rather than use a wooden platform, one man would lift another up to the noose; Flaminio may be insinuating that Bracciano will similarly dispatch the Doctor when he has made use of him

MONTICELSO

Here is an emblem,[1] nephew. Pray, peruse it.
'Twas thrown in at your window.
[*He hands* CAMILLO *a paper.*]

CAMILLO

At my window?
Here is a stag, my lord, hath shed his horns,
And for the loss of them the poor beast weeps;
The word:[2] '*Inopem me copia fecit*'.[3]

MONTICELSO

That is,
'Plenty of horns hath made him poor of horns'.[4]

CAMILLO

What should this mean?

MONTICELSO

I'll tell you. 'Tis given out
You are a cuckold.

CAMILLO

Is it given out so?
I had rather such report as that, my lord,
Should keep within doors.

FRANCISCO

Have you any children?

CAMILLO

None, my lord.

FRANCISCO

You are the happier.
I'll tell you a tale.

CAMILLO

Pray, my lord –

1 *emblem*: moral allegory in the form of an illustration and explanatory text
2 *word*: motto
3 '*Inopem . . . fecit*': 'Abundance has rendered me poor' (Ovid, *Metamorphoses*, 3.466)
4 '*Plenty . . . horns*': i.e., by being made a cuckold many times over Camillo has lost his own sexual potency, or referring to Bracciano as the stag whose sexual activity has resulted in venereal disease and impotence

FRANCISCO

An old tale.[1]

Upon a time, Phoebus, the god of light,
Or him we call the sun, would needs be married.
The gods gave their consent, and Mercury
Was sent to voice it to the general world.
But what a piteous cry there straight arose
Amongst smiths and felt-makers, brewers and cooks,
Reapers and butter-women, amongst fishmongers
And thousand other trades, which are annoyed
By his excessive heat; 'twas lamentable!
They came to Jupiter, all in a sweat,
And do forbid the banns.[2] A great fat cook
Was made their speaker, who entreats of Jove
That Phoebus might be gelded, for if now,
When there was but one sun, so many men
Were like to perish by his violent heat,
What should they do if he were married
And should beget more, and those children
Make fireworks like their father? So say I,
Only I will apply it to your wife:
Her issue, should not providence prevent it,
Would make both nature, time, and man repent it.

MONTICELSO

Look you, cousin,
Go change the air,[3] for shame. See if your absence
Will blast your cornucopia.[4] Marcello
Is chosen with you joint commissioner
For the relieving our Italian coast
From pirates.

MARCELLO

I am much honoured in't.

1 *old tale*: taken from *The Fables of Esop in English* (1596)
2 *banns*: public notice given in church of an intended marriage
3 *change the air*: leave this place
4 *cornucopia*: horn of plenty, a symbol of fertility, here meaning his cuckold's horns

CAMILLO

But, sir,
Ere I return the stag's horns may be sprouted
Greater than these are shed.

MONTICELSO

Do not fear it;
I'll be your ranger.[1]

CAMILLO

You must watch i'th' nights;
Then's the most danger.

FRANCISCO

Farewell, good Marcello.
All the best fortunes of a soldier's wish
Bring you o'ship-board.

CAMILLO

Were I not best, now I am turned soldier,
Ere that I leave my wife, sell all she hath
And then take leave of her?

MONTICELSO

I expect good from you,
Your parting is so merry.

CAMILLO

Merry, my lord? O'th' captain's humour right;
I am resolvèd to be drunk this night.

Exeunt [CAMILLO *and* MARCELLO].

FRANCISCO

So, 'twas well fitted. Now shall we discern
How his wished absence will give violent way
To Duke Bracciano's lust.

MONTICELSO

Why, that was it;
To what scorned purpose else should we make choice
Of him for a sea-captain? And besides,
Count Lodovic, which was rumoured for a pirate,
Is now in Padua.

1 *ranger*: gamekeeper

FRANCISCO

Is't true?

MONTICELSO

Most certain.
I have letters from him which are suppliant
To work his quick repeal from banishment.
He means to address himself for pension
Unto our sister[1] Duchess.

FRANCISCO

Oh, 'twas well.
We shall not want[2] his absence past six days.
I fain would have the Duke Bracciano run
Into notorious scandal, for there's naught
In such cursed dotage to repair his name,
Only the deep sense of some deathless shame.

MONTICELSO

It may be objected I am dishonourable
To play thus with my kinsman, but I answer:
For my revenge I'd stake a brother's life,
That being wronged durst not avenge himself.

FRANCISCO

Come to observe this strumpet.

MONTICELSO

Curse of greatness!
Sure, he'll not leave her.

FRANCISCO

There's small pity in't.
Like mistletoe on sere[3] elms spent by weather,
Let him cleave to her and both rot together. *Exeunt.*

1 *sister*: either used here as a courtesy title or indicating that Webster has confused Monticelso with Isabella's real-life brother, who was also a cardinal
2 *want*: lack 3 *sere*: dry, withered

ACT 2

Scene 2

Enter BRACCIANO *with one in the habit of a* CONJURER.

BRACCIANO

Now, sir, I claim your promise. 'Tis dead midnight,
The time prefixed to show me, by your art,
How the intended murder of Camillo
And our loathèd Duchess grow to action.

CONJURER

You have won me by your bounty to a deed
I do not often practise. Some there are,
Which by sophistic tricks aspire that name –
Which I would gladly lose – of necromancer;[1]
As some that use to juggle[2] upon cards,
Seeming to conjure when indeed they cheat;
Others that raise up their confederate spirits
'Bout windmills,[3] and endanger their own necks
For making of a squib;[4] and some there are
Will keep a curtal[5] to show juggling tricks
And give out 'tis a spirit. Besides these,
Such a whole ream[6] of almanac-makers, figure-flingers,[7]
Fellows, indeed, that only live by stealth,
Since they do merely lie about stol'n goods,[8]
They'd make men think the devil were fast and loose,[9]
With speaking fustian[10] Latin. Pray, sit down.
Put on this nightcap, sir; 'tis charmed.
[BRACCIANO *puts on a nightcap.*]

1 *necromancer*: magician, conjurer
2 *juggle*: play tricks 3 *windmills*: fanciful schemes
4 *squib*: firework
5 *curtal*: a horse with its tail docked; a horse called Morocco was famous in 1590s London for its tricks, including counting money and playing dead
6 *ream*: realm, and quantity of paper 7 *figure-flingers*: horoscope-casters
8 *lie . . . goods*: horoscopes were sometimes consulted to locate property
9 *fast and loose*: unscrupulous 10 *fustian*: invented, i.e., gibberish

And now
I'll show you by my strong, commanding art
The circumstance that breaks your Duchess's heart.

A Dumb Show.

[Music sounds.] Enter, suspiciously,[1] [DOCTOR] *Julio and* CHRISTOPHERO. *They draw a curtain where* BRACCIANO*'s picture is. They put on spectacles of glass which cover their eyes and noses, and then burn perfumes afore the picture, and wash the lips of the picture. That done, quenching the fire and putting off their spectacles, they depart, laughing.*
Enter ISABELLA, *in her nightgown, as to bed-ward, with lights after her; Count* LODOVICO, GIOVANNI, GUID-ANTONIO *and others waiting on her. She kneels down as to prayers, then draws the curtain of the picture, does three reverences to it, and kisses it thrice. She faints and will not suffer them to come near it; dies. Sorrow expressed in* GIOVANNI *and in Count* LODOVICO. *She's conveyed out solemnly.*

BRACCIANO
Excellent, then she's dead.

CONJURER
She's poisoned
By the fumed picture. 'Twas her custom nightly,
Before she went to bed, to go and visit
Your picture, and to feed her eyes and lips
On the dead shadow.[2] Doctor Julio,
Observing this, infects it with an oil
And other poisoned stuff, which presently
Did suffocate her spirits.

BRACCIANO
Methought I saw
Count Lodovic there.

1 *suspiciously*: in a manner arousing suspicion
2 *dead shadow*: lifeless image

CONJURER

He was, and by my art
I find he did most passionately dote
Upon your Duchess. Now turn another way
And view Camillo's far more politic fate.
Strike louder music from this charmèd ground,[1]
To yield, as fits the act, a tragic sound.

The Second Dumb Show.

[*Music sounds.*] *Enter* FLAMINIO, MARCELLO, CAMILLO, *with four more as* CAPTAINS. *They drink healths and dance. A vaulting-horse is brought into the room.* MARCELLO *and two more whispered out of the room, while* FLAMINIO *and* CAMILLO *strip themselves into their shirts, as to vault; compliment who shall begin. As* CAMILLO *is about to vault,* FLAMINIO *pitcheth him upon his neck, and, with the help of the rest, writhes his neck about; seems to see if it be broke, and lays him folded double as 'twere under the horse; makes shows to call for help.* MARCELLO *comes in, laments, sends for the Cardinal* [MONTICELSO], *and Duke* [FRANCISCO], *who comes forth with armed men; wonder at the act;* [FRANCISCO] *commands the body to be carried home, apprehends* FLAMINIO, MARCELLO *and the rest, and go as 'twere to apprehend* VITTORIA.

BRACCIANO

'Twas quaintly[2] done; but yet each circumstance
I taste not fully.

CONJURER

Oh, 'twas most apparent.
You saw them enter, charged with their deep healths
To their boon[3] voyage, and, to second that,
Flaminio calls to have a vaulting-horse
Maintain their sport. The virtuous Marcello
Is innocently plotted forth the room,

1 *Strike . . . ground*: the music was probably heard from under the stage
2 *quaintly*: skilfully 3 *boon*: prosperous

Whilst your eye saw the rest and can inform you
The engine of all.

BRACCIANO

It seems Marcello and Flaminio
Are both committed.

CONJURER

Yes, you saw them guarded,
And now they are come with purpose to apprehend
Your mistress, fair Vittoria. We are now
Beneath her roof; 'twere fit we instantly
Make out by some back postern.[1]

BRACCIANO

Noble friend,
You bind me ever to you. [*Shakes his hand*] This shall stand
As the firm seal annexèd to my hand.[2]
It shall enforce a payment.

CONJURER

Sir, I thank you.

Exit BRACCIANO.

Both flowers and weeds spring when the sun is warm,
And great men do great good or else great harm.

Exit CONJURER.

ACT 3

Scene 1

Enter FRANCISCO *and* MONTICELSO, *their* CHANCELLOR *and* REGISTER.

FRANCISCO

You have dealt discreetly to obtain the presence
Of all the grave, lieger[3] ambassadors
To hear Vittoria's trial.

1 *postern*: entrance 2 *hand*: signature 3 *lieger*: resident

MONTICELSO

'Twas not ill;
For, sir, you know we have nought but circumstances
To charge her with about her husband's death.
Their approbation, therefore, to the proofs
Of her black lust shall make her infamous
To all our neighbouring kingdoms. I wonder
If Bracciano will be here.

FRANCISCO

Oh fie!
'Twere impudence too palpable. [*Exeunt all.*]

Enter FLAMINIO *and* MARCELLO *guarded, and a* LAWYER.

LAWYER

What, are you in by the week?[1] So, I will try now whether thy wit be close prisoner. Methinks none should sit upon[2] thy sister but old whoremasters.

FLAMINIO

Or cuckolds, for your cuckold is your most terrible tickler[3] of lechery. Whoremasters would serve, for none are judges at tilting[4] but those that have been old tilters.

LAWYER

My lord Duke and she have been very private.[5]

FLAMINIO

You are a dull ass; 'tis threatened they have been very public.[6]

LAWYER

If it can be proved they have but kissed one another –

FLAMINIO

What then?

LAWYER

My lord Cardinal will ferret[7] them.

1 *in . . . week*: caught 2 *sit upon*: judge, with sexual pun
3 *tickler*: chastiser, provoker
4 *tilting*: a form of jousting, but also sexual intercourse
5 *private*: secret, intimate 6 *public*: open, promiscuous
7 *ferret them*: hunt them down, ferrets being used to catch rabbits

FLAMINIO
A cardinal, I hope, will not catch conies.[1]

LAWYER
For to sow kisses – mark what I say – to sow kisses is to reap lechery, and I am sure a woman that will endure kissing is half won.

FLAMINIO
True, her upper part by that rule; if you will win her nether part too, you know what follows.
[*Sennet sounds.*]

LAWYER
Hark! The ambassadors are lighted.

FLAMINIO [*Aside*]
I do put on this feignèd garb of mirth
To gull suspicion.

MARCELLO
O my unfortunate sister!
I would my dagger's point had cleft her heart
When she first saw Bracciano. You, 'tis said,
Were made his engine and his stalking-horse
To undo my sister.

FLAMINIO
I made a kind of path
To her and mine own preferment.

MARCELLO
Your ruin!

FLAMINIO
Hum! Thou art a soldier,
Followest the Great Duke, feedest his victories
As witches do their serviceable spirits,[2]
Even with thy prodigal[3] blood. What hast got,
But, like the wealth of captains, a poor handful,

1 *conies*: rabbits; to catch 'conies' also meant to trick fools out of money or have sex with women
2 *witches . . . spirits*: witches were thought to feed their familiars with their own milk or blood
3 *prodigal*: wastefully spent

Which in thy palm thou bear'st, as men hold water:
Seeking to gripe it fast, the frail reward
Steals through thy fingers.

MARCELLO

Sir –

FLAMINIO

Thou hast scarce maintenance
To keep thee in fresh chamois – [1]

MARCELLO

Brother!

FLAMINIO

Hear me –
And thus when we have even poured ourselves
Into great fights, for their ambition
Or idle spleen, how shall we find reward?
But as we seldom find the mistletoe,
Sacred to physic, on the builder[2] oak
Without a mandrake[3] by it, so in our quest of gain.
Alas, the poorest of their forced dislikes
At a limb proffers, but at heart it strikes.[4]
This is lamented doctrine.

MARCELLO

Come, come!

FLAMINIO

When age shall turn thee
White as a blooming hawthorn –

MARCELLO

I'll interrupt you.
For love of virtue, bear an honest heart
And stride over every politic respect,
Which where they most advance they most infect.
Were I your father, as I am your brother,

1 *chamois*: leather jerkins worn under armour 2 *builder*: used for building
3 *mandrake*: a medicinal plant that supposedly shrieked when it was pulled from the earth, the sound inducing madness in the hearer
4 *the poorest . . . strikes*: the least of their dislikes appears to injure superficially, but does mortal harm

I should not be ambitious to leave you
A better patrimony.

Enter SAVOY [AMBASSADOR].

FLAMINIO

I'll think on't.
The lord ambassadors!

Here there is a passage of the lieger Ambassadors over the stage severally.

Enter FRENCH AMBASSADORS.

LAWYER

O my sprightly Frenchman! Do you know him? He's an admirable tilter.

FLAMINIO

I saw him at last tilting; he showed like a pewter candlestick fashioned like a man in armour, holding a tilting-staff in his hand little bigger than a candle of twelve i'th' pound.

LAWYER

Oh, but he's an excellent horseman.

FLAMINIO

A lame[1] one in his lofty tricks. He sleeps o'horseback like a poulter.[2]

Enter ENGLISH *and* SPANISH [AMBASSADORS].

LAWYER

Lo, you, my Spaniard!

FLAMINIO

He carries his face in's ruff, as I have seen a serving-man carry glasses in a cypress hat-band: monstrous steady for fear of breaking. He looks like the claw of a blackbird,[3] first salted and then broiled in a candle. *Exeunt.*

1 *lame*: also implying impotence

2 *poulter*: traders in poultry, who went to market early in the morning and so were associated with falling asleep on horseback, also with a sexual connotation

3 *He looks . . . blackbird*: an allusion to the wide Spanish ruff

ACT 3

Scene 2

The Arraignment of Vittoria.

Enter FRANCISCO, MONTICELSO, *the six lieger* AMBASSADORS, BRACCIANO, VITTORIA [ZANCHE, FLAMINIO, MARCELLO], LAWYER *and a* GUARD [*with* ATTENDANTS].

MONTICELSO

Forbear, my lord. Here is no place assigned you.
This business by his Holiness is left
To our examination.

BRACCIANO

May it thrive with you.

[*He*] *lays a rich gown under him.*

FRANCISCO

A chair there for his lordship!

BRACCIANO

Forbear your kindness. An unbidden guest
Should travel as Dutchwomen go to church:
Bear their stools with them.

MONTICELSO

At your pleasure, sir.
Stand to the table, gentlewomen. Now, signor,
Fall to your plea.

LAWYER

Domine Judex converte oculos in hanc pestem mulierum corruptissimam.[1]

VITTORIA

What's he?

FRANCISCO

A lawyer that pleads against you.

1 *Domine . . . corruptissimam*: 'Lord Judge, turn your eyes upon this plague, the most corrupt of women'

VITTORIA
Pray, my lord, let him speak his usual tongue.
I'll make no answer else.

FRANCISCO
Why? You understand Latin.

VITTORIA
I do, sir, but amongst this auditory[1]
Which come to hear my cause, the half or more
May be ignorant in't.

MONTICELSO
Go on, sir.

VITTORIA
By your favour,
I will not have my accusation clouded
In a strange tongue. All this assembly
Shall hear what you can charge me with.

FRANCISCO
Signor,
You need not stand on't much. Pray, change your language.

MONTICELSO
Oh, for God's sake. Gentlewoman, your credit[2]
Shall be more famous by it.

LAWYER
Well then, have at you.

VITTORIA
I am at the mark, sir; I'll give aim to you,[3]
And tell you how near you shoot.

LAWYER
Most literated judges, please your lordships
So to connive[4] your judgements to the view
Of this debauched and diversivolent[5] woman,

1 *auditory*: audience, includes spectators at the Red Bull Theatre, some of whom may have been sitting on the stage
2 *credit*: reputation
3 *give aim*: in archery, to let the shooter know how near the target they are
4 *connive*: direct, but also 'to be complicit with', casting suspicion on the judges' impartiality
5 *diversivolent*: strife-wishing, a nonce word

Who such a black concatenation[1]
Of mischief hath effected, that to extirp
The memory of't must be the consummation
Of her and her projections.[2]

VITTORIA

What's all this?

LAWYER

Hold your peace!
Exorbitant sins must have exulceration.[3]

VITTORIA

Surely, my lords, this lawyer here hath swallowed
Some 'pothecary's bills[4] or proclamations,[5]
And now the hard and undigestable words
Come up[6] like stones we use give hawks for physic.[7]
Why, this is Welsh[8] to Latin.

LAWYER

My lords, the woman
Knows not her tropes nor figures, nor is perfect
In the academic derivation
Of grammatical elocution.

FRANCISCO

Sir, your pains
Shall be well spared, and your deep eloquence
Be worthily applauded amongst those
Which understand you.

LAWYER

My good lord –

1 *concatenation*: plot 2 *projections*: schemes
3 *exulceration*: punishment; literally, the lancing of an ulcer
4 *bills*: prescriptions, often included a long list of difficult words
5 *proclamations*: royal commands, often expressed in high-flown terms
6 *Come up*: are vomited
7 *like stones . . . physic*: overheated birds were thought to be cured by eating stones
8 *Welsh*: often assumed to be an incomprehensible language

FRANCISCO (*speaks this as in scorn*)

Sir,
Put up your papers in your fustian[1] bag –
Cry mercy, sir, 'tis buckram[2] – and accept
My notion of your learn'd verbosity.

LAWYER

I most graduatically[3] thank your lordship.
I shall have use for them elsewhere. [*Exit*.]

MONTICELSO

I shall be plainer with you, and paint out
Your follies in more natural red and white
Than that upon your cheek.

VITTORIA

Oh, you mistake.
You raise a blood as noble in this cheek
As ever was your mother's.

MONTICELSO

I must spare you, till proof cry 'whore' to that.
Observe this creature here, my honoured lords,
A woman of a most prodigious spirit
In her effected –

VITTORIA

Honourable my lord,
It doth not suit a reverend cardinal
To play the lawyer thus.

MONTICELSO

Oh, your trade instructs your language!
You see, my lords, what goodly fruit she seems.
Yet like those apples travellers report
To grow where Sodom and Gomorrah[4] stood,
I will but touch her and you straight shall see
She'll fall to soot and ashes.

1 *fustian*: coarse cloth, also inflated language
2 *buckram*: coarse linen used for lawyers' bags
3 *graduatically*: like a graduate, a nonce word
4 *Sodom and Gomorrah*: biblical cities destroyed by flame as punishment for the inhabitants' sins, particularly unlawful sexual practices; the image of fruit made of ashes derives from Deuteronomy 32:32

VITTORIA

Your envenomed
'Pothecary should do't.

MONTICELSO

I am resolved,
Were there a second paradise to lose
This devil would betray it.

VITTORIA

O poor charity,
Thou art seldom found in scarlet.[1]

MONTICELSO

Who knows not how, when several night by night
Her gates were choked with coaches, and her rooms
Outbraved the stars with several kind of lights;
When she did counterfeit a prince's court
In music, banquets and most riotous surfeits,
This whore, forsooth, was holy.

VITTORIA

Ha? 'Whore'? What's that?

MONTICELSO

Shall I expound 'whore' to you? Sure, I shall;
I'll give their perfect character.[2] They are first
Sweetmeats which rot the eater; in man's nostril
Poisoned perfumes. They are coz'ning[3] alchemy,
Shipwrecks in calmest weather. What are whores?
Cold Russian winters that appear so barren,
As if that nature had forgot the spring.
They are the true material fire of hell,
Worse than those tributes[4] i'th' Low Countries paid –
Exactions upon meat, drink, garments, sleep;
Ay, even on man's perdition, his sin.
They are those brittle evidences of law
Which forfeit all a wretched man's estate

1 *scarlet*: colour of clerical and legal robes
2 *character*: a formal description of a character type; Webster contributed several to an edition of Sir Thomas Overbury's *Characters* (1615)
3 *coz'ning*: deceiving 4 *tributes*: taxes

For leaving out one syllable. What are whores?
They are those flattering bells have all one tune
At weddings and at funerals; your rich whores
Are only treasuries by extortion filled,
And emptied by cursed riot. They are worse,
Worse than dead bodies which are begged at gallows
And wrought upon by surgeons,[1] to teach man
Wherein he is imperfect. What's a whore?
She's like the guilty,[2] counterfeited coin
Which, whosoe'er first stamps it, brings in trouble
All that receive it.

VITTORIA
This character 'scapes me.

MONTICELSO
You, gentlewoman –
Take from all beasts and from all minerals
Their deadly poison –

VITTORIA
Well, what then?

MONTICELSO
I'll tell thee;
I'll find in thee a 'pothecary's shop
To sample[3] them all.

FRENCH AMBASSADOR [*Aside*]
She hath lived ill.

ENGLISH AMBASSADOR [*Aside*]
True, but the Cardinal's too bitter.

MONTICELSO
You know what whore is: next the devil, Adult'ry,
Enters the devil, Murder.

FRANCISCO
Your unhappy husband
Is dead –

1 *surgeons*: the barber-surgeons were legally allowed the bodies of four executed criminals per year on which to demonstrate anatomy; they may have 'begged' more

2 *guilty*: with a pun on 'gilt', golden 3 *sample*: stand as a parallel or match

VITTORIA

Oh, he's a happy husband;
Now he owes nature nothing.

FRANCISCO

And by a vaulting-engine.

MONTICELSO

An active plot:
He jumped into his grave.

FRANCISCO

What a prodigy[1] was't
That from some two yards' height a slender man
Should break his neck!

MONTICELSO

I'th' rushes.[2]

FRANCISCO

And what's more,
Upon the instant lose all use of speech,
All vital motion, like a man had lain
Wound up[3] three days. Now mark each circumstance.

MONTICELSO

And look upon this creature was his wife.
She comes not like a widow; she comes armed
With scorn and impudence. Is this a mourning habit?

VITTORIA

Had I foreknown his death, as you suggest,
I would have bespoke[4] my mourning.

MONTICELSO

Oh, you are cunning.

VITTORIA

You shame your wit and judgement
To call it so. What, is my just defence
By him that is my judge called impudence?

1 *prodigy*: strange occurrence
2 *rushes*: leaves used as a floor covering in private houses and on the stage
3 *Wound up*: corpses were usually wrapped in a winding sheet
4 *bespoke*: ordered

Let me appeal then from this Christian court
To the uncivil Tartar![1]

MONTICELSO

See, my lords,
She scandals[2] our proceedings.

VITTORIA [*kneeling*]

Humbly thus,
Thus low, to the most worthy and respected
Lieger ambassadors, my modesty
And womanhood I tender; but withal
So entangled in a cursèd accusation
That my defence, of force,[3] like Perseus,[4]
Must personate masculine virtue to the point.[5]
Find me but guilty: sever head from body;
We'll part good friends. I scorn to hold my life
At yours or any man's entreaty, sir.

ENGLISH AMBASSADOR

She hath a brave spirit.

MONTICELSO

Well, well, such counterfeit jewels
Make true ones oft suspected.

VITTORIA

You are deceived;
For know, that all your strict-combinèd[6] heads,
Which strike against this mine of diamonds,
Shall prove but glassen hammers: they shall break.
These are but feignèd shadows of my evils.
Terrify babes, my lord, with painted devils;
I am past such needless palsy.[7] For your names
Of 'whore' and 'murd'ress', they proceed from you;

1 *Tartar*: synonymous with cruelty and barbarism 2 *scandals*: disgraces

3 *of force*: of necessity

4 *Perseus*: in classical mythology Perseus saved Andromeda from a sea monster and cut off the head of Medusa; synonymous with masculine courage and virtue in Jonson's *Masque of Queens* (1609)

5 *to the point*: in every detail, with a pun on the point of a sword

6 *strict-combinèd*: closely allied 7 *palsy*: trembling

As if a man should spit against the wind,
The filth returns in's face.

MONTICELSO
Pray you, mistress, satisfy me one question:
Who lodged beneath your roof that fatal night
Your husband brake his neck?

BRACCIANO
That question
Enforceth me break silence. I was there.

MONTICELSO
Your business?

BRACCIANO
Why, I came to comfort her
And take some course for settling her estate,
Because I heard her husband was in debt
To you, my lord.

MONTICELSO
He was.

BRACCIANO
And 'twas strangely feared
That you would cozen[1] her.

MONTICELSO
Who made you overseer?

BRACCIANO
Why, my charity, my charity, which should flow
From every generous and noble spirit
To orphans and to widows.

MONTICELSO
Your lust!

BRACCIANO
Cowardly dogs bark loudest. Sirrah priest,
I'll talk with you hereafter. Do you hear?
The sword[2] you frame of such an excellent temper[3]
I'll sheathe in your own bowels.

1 *cozen*: cheat 2 *sword*: the sword of Justice
3 *temper*: Monticelso's anger, and the process of tempering metal to make a sword

There are a number of thy coat[1] resemble
Your common post-boys.[2]

MONTICELSO

Ha?

BRACCIANO

Your mercenary post-boys;
Your letters carry truth, but 'tis your guise
To fill your mouths with gross and impudent lies.
[*He makes to leave.*]

SERVANT

My lord, your gown –
[*He offers it to* BRACCIANO.]

BRACCIANO

Thou liest, 'twas my stool.
Bestow't upon thy master that will challenge[3]
The rest o'th' household-stuff; for Bracciano
Was ne'er so beggarly to take a stool
Out of another's lodging. Let him make
Valance for his bed on't, or a demi-footcloth
For his most reverend moil.[4] Monticelso,
Nemo me impune lacessit.[5] *Exit* BRACCIANO.

MONTICELSO

Your champion's gone.

VITTORIA

The wolf may prey the better.

FRANCISCO

My lord, there's great suspicion of the murder,
But no sound proof who did it. For my part,
I do not think she hath a soul so black
To act a deed so bloody. If she have,
As in cold countries husbandmen plant vines,
And with warm blood manure them, even so
One summer she will bear unsavoury fruit,
And ere next spring wither both branch and root.

1 *coat*: i.e., his profession of cleric 2 *post-boys*: letter-carriers
3 *challenge*: lay claim to 4 *moil*: mule
5 *Nemo . . . lacessit*: 'No one injures me with impunity'

The act of blood let pass; only descend
To matter of incontinence.

VITTORIA

I discern poison
Under your gilded pills.[1]

MONTICELSO [*bringing out a letter*]

Now the Duke's gone, I will produce a letter,
Wherein 'twas plotted he and you should meet
At an apothecary's summer-house,
Down by the river Tiber – view't, my lords –
[*He passes the letter to the* AMBASSADORS.]
Where, after wanton bathing and the heat
Of a lascivious banquet – I pray, read it.
I shame to speak the rest.

VITTORIA

Grant I was tempted;
Temptation to lust proves not the act;
Casta est quam nemo rogavit.[2]
You read his hot love to me, but you want[3]
My frosty answer.

MONTICELSO

Frost i'th' dog-days?[4] Strange!

VITTORIA

Condemn you me for that the Duke did love me?
So may you blame some fair and crystal river
For that some melancholic, distracted man
Hath drowned himself in't.

MONTICELSO

Truly drowned, indeed.

1 *gilded pills*: apothecaries sometimes covered their pills in gold to justify a higher price
2 *Casta . . . rogavit*: 'She is chaste whom no one has solicited' (Ovid, *Amores* 1.8.43), though originally used to persuade a woman to take many lovers
3 *want*: lack
4 *dog-days*: characterized by oppressive heat; a time when lust and other malignant influences dominate

VITTORIA

Sum up my faults, I pray, and you shall find
That beauty and gay clothes, a merry heart
And a good stomach to a feast are all,
All the poor crimes that you can charge me with.
In faith, my lord, you might go pistol[1] flies –
The sport would be more noble.

MONTICELSO

Very good.

VITTORIA

But take you your course. It seems you have beggared me first,
And now would fain undo me. I have houses,
Jewels and a poor remnant of crusadoes;[2]
Would those would make you charitable.

MONTICELSO

If the devil
Did ever take good shape, behold his picture.

VITTORIA

You have one virtue left:
You will not flatter me.

FRANCISCO

Who brought this letter?

VITTORIA

I am not compelled to tell you.

MONTICELSO

My lord Duke sent to you a thousand ducats
The twelfth of August.

VITTORIA

'Twas to keep your cousin
From prison; I paid use[3] for't.

MONTICELSO

I rather think
'Twas interest for his lust.

1 *pistol*: fire a pistol at
2 *crusadoes*: Portuguese coins, stamped with a crown
3 *use*: interest

VITTORIA

Who says so but yourself? If you be my accuser,
Pray cease to be my judge. Come from the bench,
Give in your evidence 'gainst me, and let these
Be moderators. My lord Cardinal,
Were your intelligencing ears[1] as long
As to my thoughts, had you an honest tongue,
I would not care though you proclaimed them all.

MONTICELSO

Go to, go to.
After your goodly and vainglorious banquet,
I'll give you a choke-pear.[2]

VITTORIA

O'your own grafting?

MONTICELSO

You were born in Venice,[3] honourably descended
From the Vitelli. 'Twas my cousin's fate –
Ill may I name the hour – to marry you;
He bought you of your father.

VITTORIA

Ha?

MONTICELSO

He spent there in six months
Twelve thousand ducats, and to my acquaintance
Received in dowry with you not one julio.[4]
'Twas a hard penny-worth, the ware being so light.[5]
I yet but draw the curtain; now to your picture:
You came from thence a most notorious strumpet,
And so you have continued.

VITTORIA

My lord!

1 *intelligencing ears*: i.e., those of an informer or spy

2 *choke-pear*: unpalatable pear, rebuke

3 *Venice*: the historical Vittoria was born in Gubbio; Webster may have chosen Venice because of its reputation for courtesans

4 *julio*: silver Italian coin, with a possible pun on 'Doctor Julio', who arranged Camillo's death

5 *ware . . . light*: the goods being so worthless, unchaste

MONTICELSO

Nay, hear me.
You shall have time to prate. My Lord Bracciano –
Alas, I make but repetition
Of what is ordinary and Rialto talk,
And balladed,[1] and would be played o'th' stage,
But that vice many times finds such loud friends
That preachers are charmed silent.
You gentlemen, Flaminio and Marcello,
The court hath nothing now to charge you with;
Only you must remain upon your sureties[2]
For your appearance.

FRANCISCO

I stand for Marcello.

FLAMINIO

And my lord Duke for me.

MONTICELSO

For you, Vittoria, your public fault,
Joined to th'condition of the present time,
Takes from you all the fruits of noble pity.
Such a corrupted trial have you made,
Both of your life and beauty, and been styled
No less in ominous fate than blazing stars
To princes.[3] Here's your sentence: you are confined
Unto a house of convertites,[4] and your bawd –

FLAMINIO [*Aside*]

Who I?

MONTICELSO

– the Moor.

FLAMINIO [*Aside*]

Oh, I am a sound man again.

VITTORIA

A house of convertites? What's that?

1 *balladed*: popularized in a ballad
2 *sureties*: those who make themselves liable for another's appearance at court
3 *blazing . . . princes*: comets were thought to portend the fall of princes
4 *house of convertites*: institution for reformed prostitutes, like Bridewell in London

MONTICELSO

A house

Of penitent whores.

VITTORIA

Do the noblemen in Rome

Erect it for their wives, that I am sent
To lodge there?

FRANCISCO

You must have patience.

VITTORIA

I must first have vengeance.

I fain would know if you have your salvation
By patent,[1] that you proceed thus.

MONTICELSO

Away with her!

Take her hence.

[GUARDS *lead* VITTORIA *and* ZANCHE *away.*]

VITTORIA

A rape, a rape!

MONTICELSO

How?

VITTORIA

Yes, you have ravished Justice,
Forced her to do your pleasure.

MONTICELSO

Fie, she's mad!

VITTORIA

Die with these pills in your most cursèd maw[2]
Should bring you health, or while you sit o'th' bench
Let your own spittle choke you –

MONTICELSO

She's turned fury.

1 *By patent*: the patent or monopolies system granted individuals the control of a particular trade; it was notoriously used by James I to raise funds
2 *maw*: throat

VITTORIA

– That the last day of judgement may so find you,
And leave you the same devil you were before.
Instruct me, some good horse-leech,[1] to speak treason;
For since you cannot take my life for deeds,
Take it for words. Oh, woman's poor revenge
Which dwells but in the tongue! I will not weep;
No, I do scorn to call up one poor tear
To fawn on your injustice. Bear me hence
Unto this house of – what's your mitigating title?

MONTICELSO

Of convertites.

VITTORIA

It shall not be a house of convertites.
My mind shall make it honester to me
Than the Pope's palace, and more peaceable
Than thy soul, though thou art a cardinal.
Know this, and let it somewhat raise your spite:
Through darkness diamonds spread their richest light.

Exeunt VITTORIA [*and* ZANCHE, *with* GUARDS].
Enter BRACCIANO.

BRACCIANO

Now you and I are friends, sir, we'll shake hands
In a friends' grave together – a fit place,
Being the emblem of soft peace t'atone our hatred.

FRANCISCO

Sir, what's the matter?

BRACCIANO

I will not chase more blood from that loved cheek;
You have lost too much already. Fare you well. [*Exit.*]

FRANCISCO

How strange these words sound. What's the interpretation?

FLAMINIO [*Aside*]

Good, this is a preface to the discovery of the Duchess's death. He carries it well. Because now I cannot counterfeit a whining passion for the death of my lady, I will feign a mad

1 *horse-leech*: thought to have two tongues, synonymous with the rhetorician

humour for the disgrace of my sister, and that will keep off idle questions. Treason's tongue hath a villainous palsy[1] in't; I will talk to any man, hear no man, and for a time appear a politic madman. [*Exit.*]

Enter GIOVANNI [*and*] *Count* LODOVICO [*both in mourning*].

FRANCISCO
How now, my noble cousin. What, in black?

GIOVANNI
Yes, uncle, I was taught to imitate you
In virtue, and you must imitate me
In colours for your garments. My sweet mother
Is –

FRANCISCO
How? Where?

GIOVANNI
– is there. No, yonder – indeed, sir, I'll not tell you,
For I shall make you weep.

FRANCISCO
Is dead?

GIOVANNI
Do not blame me now.
I did not tell you so.

LODOVICO
She's dead, my lord.

FRANCISCO
Dead?

MONTICELSO
Blessèd lady, thou art now above thy woes.
Wilt please your lordships to withdraw a little?
[*Exeunt* AMBASSADORS.]

GIOVANNI
What do the dead do, uncle? Do they eat,
Hear music, go a-hunting and be merry,
As we that live?

FRANCISCO
No, coz, they sleep.

1 *palsy*: trembling

GIOVANNI

Lord, Lord, that I were dead!
I have not slept these six nights. When do they wake?

FRANCISCO

When God shall please.

GIOVANNI

Good God, let her sleep ever!
For I have known her wake an hundred nights,
When all the pillow, where she laid her head,
Was brine-wet with her tears. I am to complain to you, sir.
I'll tell you how they have used her, now she's dead:
They wrapped her in a cruel fold of lead,
And would not let me kiss her.

FRANCISCO

Thou didst love her.

GIOVANNI

I have often heard her say she gave me suck;
And it should seem by that she dearly loved me,
Since princes seldom do it.[1]

FRANCISCO

Oh, all of my poor sister that remains!
Take him away, for God's sake.

[*Exeunt* GIOVANNI *and* ATTENDANTS.]

MONTICELSO

How now, my lord?

FRANCISCO

Believe me, I am nothing but her grave,
And I shall keep her blessèd memory
Longer than thousand epitaphs. [*Exeunt.*]

1 *gave me suck*: breastfed me; the nobility generally used wet nurses, though there was a growing demand in conduct literature that mothers nurse their own children

ACT 3

Scene 3

Enter FLAMINIO *as distracted*[1] [*with* MARCELLO, *and* LODOVICO, *who observes unseen*].

FLAMINIO

We endure the strokes like anvils or hard steel,
Till pain itself make us no pain to feel.

Who shall do me right now? Is this the end of service? I'd rather go weed garlic; travel through France, and be mine own ostler;[2] wear sheepskin linings,[3] or shoes that stink of blacking; be entered into the list of the forty thousand pedlars in Poland.[4]

Enter SAVOY [AMBASSADOR].

Would I had rotted in some surgeon's house at Venice, built upon the pox as well as on piles,[5] ere I had served Bracciano.

SAVOY AMBASSADOR

You must have comfort.

FLAMINIO

Your comfortable words are like honey. They relish well in your mouth that's whole, but in mine that's wounded they go down as if the sting of the bee were in them. Oh, they have wrought their purpose cunningly, as if they would not seem to do it of malice. In this a politician imitates the devil, as the devil imitates a cannon: wheresoever he comes to do mischief, he comes with his backside towards you.

Enter the FRENCH [AMBASSADORS].

FRENCH AMBASSADOR

The proofs are evident.

1 *as distracted*: the stage conventions of madness included disordered dress and speech
2 *ostler*: groom, stable boy
3 *linings*: underclothes
4 *forty . . . Poland*: Poles were famously poor
5 *piles*: haemorrhoids, the treatment of which is the basis for the doctor's wealth, and the wooden foundations of the Venetian house

FLAMINIO

Proof? 'Twas corruption. O gold, what a god art thou! And O man, what a devil art thou to be tempted by that cursed mineral! Yon diversivolent[1] lawyer, mark him. Knaves turn informers as maggots turn to flies; you may catch gudgeons[2] with either. A cardinal? I would he would hear me. There's nothing so holy but money will corrupt and putrify it, like victual under the line.[3]

Enter ENGLISH AMBASSADOR.

You are happy in England, my lord; here they sell justice with those weights they press men to death with. O horrible salary![4]

ENGLISH AMBASSADOR

Fie, fie, Flaminio!

FLAMINIO

Bells ne'er ring well, till they are at their full pitch;[5] and I hope yon cardinal shall never have the grace to pray well, till he come to the scaffold.

[*Exeunt* AMBASSADORS.]

If they were racked now to know the confederacy! But your noblemen are privileged from the rack, and well may,[6] for a little thing would pull some of them i'pieces afore they came to their arraignment. Religion! Oh, how it is commeddled[7] with policy.[8] The first bloodshed[9] in the world happened about religion. Would I were a Jew!

MARCELLO

Oh, there are too many.

1 *diversivolent*: strife-wishing; Flaminio uses the Lawyer's own word against him

2 *gudgeons*: small fish

3 *under the line*: at the equator

4 *salary*: reward

5 *full pitch*: highest point in the bell-tower

6 *well may*: with good reason

7 *commeddled*: mixed together, contaminated

8 *policy*: intrigue

9 *first bloodshed*: i.e., Cain's killing of Abel, anticipating Flaminio's murder of his brother

FLAMINIO
You are deceived. There are not Jews enough, priests enough, nor gentlemen enough.

MARCELLO
How?

FLAMINIO
I'll prove it. For if there were Jews enough, so many Christians would not turn usurers; if priests enough, one should not have six benefices; and if gentlemen enough, so many early mushrooms,[1] whose best growth sprang from a dunghill, should not aspire to gentility. Farewell. Let others live by begging. Be thou one of them. Practise the art of Wolner[2] in England to swallow all's given thee; and yet let one purgation make thee as hungry again as fellows that work in a sawpit. I'll go hear the screech-owl.[3] *Exit.*

LODOVICO [*Aside*]
This was Bracciano's pander, and 'tis strange
That in such open and apparent guilt
Of his adulterous sister he dare utter
So scandalous a passion. I must wind[4] him.

Enter FLAMINIO.

FLAMINIO [*Aside*]
How dares this banished count return to Rome,
His pardon not yet purchased?[5] I have heard
The deceased Duchess gave him pension,
And that he came along from Padua
I'th' train of the young prince. There's somewhat in't.
Physicians that cure poisons still do work
With counter-poisons.

MARCELLO [*Aside*]
Mark this strange encounter!

1 *mushrooms*: young upstarts
2 *Wolner*: a famous glutton who died from eating raw eel
3 *screech-owl*: a bird of ill-omen 4 *wind*: find out about
5 *purchased*: obtained

FLAMINIO [*To* LODOVICO]
The god of melancholy turn thy gall to poison,
And let the stigmatic[1] wrinkles in thy face,
Like to the boisterous waves in a rough tide,
One still overtake another.

LODOVICO
I do thank thee,
And I do wish ingeniously[2] for thy sake
The dog-days all year long.

FLAMINIO
How croaks the raven?[3]
Is our good Duchess dead?

LODOVICO
Dead.

FLAMINIO
O fate!
Misfortune comes like the crowner's[4] business,
Huddle upon huddle.

LODOVICO
Shalt thou and I join housekeeping?

FLAMINIO
Yes, content.
Let's be unsociably sociable.

LODOVICO
Sit some three days together and discourse.

FLAMINIO
Only with making faces. Lie in our clothes –

LODOVICO
With faggots[5] for our pillows.

FLAMINIO
And be lousy.[6]

1 *stigmatic*: ignominious, suggesting villainy
2 *ingeniously*: often used to mean 'ingenuously'
3 *raven*: another bird associated with death
4 *crowner's*: coroner's
5 *faggots*: bundles of sticks 6 *lousy*: infested with lice

LODOVICO

In taffeta linings – that's gentle[1] melancholy –
Sleep all day.

FLAMINIO

Yes, and like your melancholic hare
Feed after midnight.[2]

Enter ANTONELLI [*and* GASPARO, *both laughing*].

We are observed: see how yon couple grieve.

LODOVICO

What a strange creature is a laughing fool,
As if man were created to no use
But only to show his teeth.

FLAMINIO

I'll tell thee what,
It would do well, instead of looking-glasses,
To set one's face each morning by a saucer
Of a witch's congealèd blood.[3]

LODOVICO

Precious rogue,
We'll never part.

FLAMINIO

Never, till the beggary of courtiers,
The discontent of churchmen, want of soldiers,
And all the creatures that hang manacled,
Worse than strappadoed,[4] on the lowest felly[5]
Of fortune's wheel be taught, in our two lives,
To scorn that world which life of means deprives.

ANTONELLI

My lord, I bring good news. The Pope on's death-bed,
At th'earnest suit of the great Duke of Florence,
Hath signed your pardon, and restored unto you –

1 *gentle*: fit for a gentleman

2 *melancholic … midnight*: hares were believed to be cold-blooded, and therefore melancholic, and to sleep all day and feed at night

3 *witch's … blood*: witches were also believed to be melancholic

4 *strappadoed*: a form of torture, being lifted from the ground by one's hands when they were tied behind one's back

5 *felly*: part of a wheel rim

LODOVICO
I thank you for your news. [*Laughing*] Look up again,
Flaminio, see my pardon!
FLAMINIO
Why do you laugh?
There was no such condition in our covenant.
LODOVICO
Why?
FLAMINIO
You shall not seem a happier man than I.
You know our vow, sir; if you will be merry,
Do it i'th' like posture, as if some great man
Sat while his enemy were executed.
Though it be very lechery unto thee,
Do't with a crabbèd politician's face.
LODOVICO
Your sister is a damnable whore.
FLAMINIO
Ha?
LODOVICO
Look you, I spake that laughing.
FLAMINIO
Dost ever think to speak again?
LODOVICO
Do you hear?
Wilt sell me forty ounces of her blood
To water a mandrake?
FLAMINIO
Poor lord, you did vow
To live a lousy creature.
LODOVICO
Yes.
FLAMINIO
Like one
That had forever forfeited the daylight
By being in debt.[1]

1 *forfeited . . . debt*: i.e., in prison

LODOVICO

Ha, ha!

FLAMINIO

I do not greatly wonder you do break;[1]
Your lordship learnt long since. But I'll tell you –

LODOVICO

What?

FLAMINIO

And't shall stick by you[2] –

LODOVICO

I long for it.

FLAMINIO

This laughter scurvily becomes your face.
If you will not be melancholy, be angry.

Strikes him.

See, now I laugh too.

MARCELLO

You are to blame. I'll force you hence.

Exeunt MARCELLO *and* FLAMINIO.

[ANTONELLI *and* GASPARO *restrain* LODOVICO.]

LODOVICO

Unhand me!
That e'er I should be forced to right myself
Upon a pander!

ANTONELLI

My lord!

LODOVICO

H' had been as good met with his fist a thunderbolt.

GASPARO

How this shows!

LODOVICO

Ud's death,[3] how did my sword miss him?
These rogues that are most weary of their lives
Still 'scape the greatest dangers.

1 *break*: break your promise, go bankrupt
2 *stick by you*: remain in your memory
3 *Ud's death*: by God's death – an oath

A pox upon him! All his reputation –
Nay, all the goodness of his family –
Is not worth half this earthquake.
I learnt it of no fencer to shake thus.
Come, I'll forget him, and go drink some wine. *Exeunt.*

ACT 4

Scene 1

Enter FRANCISCO *and* MONTICELSO.

MONTICELSO
Come, come, my lord, untie your folded thoughts,
And let them dangle loose as a bride's hair.
Your sister's poisoned.

FRANCISCO
Far be it from my thoughts
To seek revenge.

MONTICELSO
What, are you turned all marble?

FRANCISCO
Shall I defy him, and impose a war
Most burdensome on my poor subjects' necks,
Which at my will I have not power to end?
You know, for all the murders, rapes and thefts,
Committed in the horrid lust of war,
He that unjustly caused it first proceed
Shall find it in his grave and in his seed.

MONTICELSO
That's not the course I'd wish you. Pray, observe me:
We see that undermining[1] more prevails
Than doth the cannon. Bear your wrongs concealed,
And, patient as the tortoise, let this camel
Stalk o'er your back unbruised. Sleep with the lion,
And let this brood of secure, foolish mice

1 *undermining*: laying mines as a military strategy

Play with your nostrils, till the time be ripe
For th'bloody audit and the fatal gripe.
Aim like a cunning fowler:[1] close one eye,
That you the better may your game espy.

FRANCISCO

Free me, my innocence, from treacherous acts.
I know there's thunder yonder, and I'll stand
Like a safe valley, which low bends the knee
To some aspiring mountain, since I know
Treason, like spiders weaving nets for flies,
By her foul work is found, and in it dies.
To pass away these thoughts, my honoured lord,
It is reported you possess a book
Wherein you have quoted,[2] by intelligence,[3]
The names of all notorious offenders
Lurking about the city.

MONTICELSO

Sir, I do;
And some there are which call it my 'black book' –
Well may the title hold. For though it teach not
The art of conjuring, yet in it lurk
The names of many devils.

FRANCISCO

Pray, let's see it.

MONTICELSO

I'll fetch it to your lordship. *Exit* MONTICELSO.

FRANCISCO

Monticelso,
I will not trust thee, but in all my plots
I'll rest as jealous[4] as a town besieged.
Thou canst not reach what I intend to act.
Your flax soon kindles, soon is out again,
But gold slow heats, and long will hot remain.

1 *fowler*: a hunter of fowl 2 *quoted*: set down
3 *intelligence*: information gained by spies 4 *jealous*: vigilant

Enter MONTICELSO [*who*] *presents* FRANCISCO *with a book.*[1]

MONTICELSO
'Tis here, my lord.

FRANCISCO
First, your intelligencers – pray, let's see.

MONTICELSO [*turning the pages*]
Their number rises strangely, and some of them
You'd take for honest men. Next are panders.
These are your pirates; and these following leaves
For base rogues that undo young gentlemen
By taking up commodities;[2] for politic bankrupts;[3]
For fellows that are bawds to their own wives,
Only to put off[4] horses and slight jewels,
Clocks, defaced plate and such commodities,
At birth of their first children –

FRANCISCO
Are there such?

MONTICELSO
These are for impudent bawds
That go in men's apparel; for usurers
That share with scriveners[5] for their good reportage;
For lawyers that will antedate their writs;
And some divines you might find folded there,
But that I slip them o'er for conscience' sake.
Here is a general catalogue of knaves.
A man might study all the prisons o'er,
Yet never attain this knowledge.

1 *presents . . . book*: since he proceeds to turn the pages, Monticelso may show Francisco the book, but not yet hand it over to him

2 *taking up commodities*: to avoid the prohibitions on high interest rates 'rogues' lend cheap goods at a highly inflated price

3 *politic bankrupts*: men who feign bankruptcy to avoid creditors

4 *put off*: pay for

5 *scriveners*: notaries, also brought moneylenders and clients together

FRANCISCO [*reads*]

'Murderers'.

Fold down the leaf, I pray.
Good my lord, let me borrow this strange doctrine.

MONTICELSO

Pray, use't, my lord.

[*He gives him the book.*]

FRANCISCO

I do assure your lordship,
You are a worthy member of the state,
And have done infinite good in your discovery
Of these offenders.

MONTICELSO

Somewhat, sir.

FRANCISCO

O God,
Better than tribute of wolves paid in England![1]
'Twill hang their skins o'th' hedge.

MONTICELSO

I must make bold
To leave your lordship.

FRANCISCO

Dearly, sir, I thank you.
If any ask for me at court, report
You have left me in the company of knaves.

Exit MONTICELSO.

I gather now by this some cunning fellow
That's my lord's officer – one that lately skipped
From a clerk's desk up to a justice' chair –
Hath made this knavish summons, and intends,
As th'Irish rebels wont were to sell heads,[2]
So to make prize of these. And thus it happens:
Your poor rogues pay for't, which have not the means

1 *tribute . . . England*: in the tenth century the Welsh were ordered by King Edgar to pay a tribute of three hundred wolves per year to the English
2 *Irish . . . heads*: Elizabeth's officers paid a bounty for heads in the Irish rebellions

To present bribe in fist; the rest o'th' band
Are razed out of the knaves' record, or else
My lord he winks at them with easy will.
His man grows rich, the knaves are the knaves still.
But to the use I'll make of it: it shall serve
To point me out a list of murderers,
Agents for any villainy. Did I want
Ten leash[1] of courtesans, it would furnish me;
Nay, laundress[2] three armies. That in so little paper
Should lie th'undoing of so many men!
'Tis not so big as twenty declarations.[3]
See the corrupted use some make of books!
Divinity, wrested[4] by some factious blood,
Draws swords, swells battles, and o'erthrows all good.
To fashion my revenge more seriously,
Let me remember my dead sister's face.
Call for her picture – no, I'll close mine eyes,
And in a melancholic thought I'll frame
Her figure 'fore me.

Enter ISABELLA*'s* GHOST.

Now I ha't – how strong
Imagination works! How she can frame
Things which are not! Methinks she stands afore me,
And by the quick[5] idea of my mind,
Were my skill pregnant,[6] I could draw her picture.
Thought, as a subtle juggler,[7] makes us deem
Things supernatural which have cause
Common as sickness. 'Tis my melancholy.
[*To* GHOST] How cam'st thou by thy death? – How idle am I
To question mine own idleness![8] Did ever
Man dream awake till now? Remove this object;
Out of my brain with't! What have I to do

1 *leash*: equivalent to three, used in hunting
2 *laundress*: provide laundry workers for the army, synonymous with prostitution
3 *declarations*: official proclamations
4 *wrested*: stirred 5 *quick*: lively, agile 6 *pregnant*: fertile
7 *juggler*: conjurer, magician 8 *idleness*: delusion

With tombs or death-beds, funerals or tears,
That have to meditate upon revenge? [*Exit* GHOST.]
So now 'tis ended, like an old wives' story.
Statesmen think often they see stranger sights
Than madmen. Come, to this weighty business.
My tragedy must have some idle mirth in't,
Else it will never pass. I am in love,
In love with Corombona, and my suit
Thus halts to her in verse –

He writes.

I have done it rarely. Oh, the fate of princes!
I am so used to frequent flattery
That, being alone, I now flatter myself;
But it will serve; 'tis sealed.

Enter SERVANT.

Bear this
To th'house of convertites [*giving him the letter*]; and watch your leisure
To give it to the hands of Corombona,
Or to the matron, when some followers
Of Bracciano may be by. Away! *Exit* SERVANT.
He that deals all by strength, his wit is shallow;
When a man's head goes through, each limb will follow.
The engine for my business: bold Count Lodovic.
'Tis gold must such an instrument procure,
With empty fist no man doth falcons lure.
Bracciano, I am now fit for thy encounter.
Like the wild Irish[1] I'll ne'er think thee dead,
Till I can play at football with thy head.
Flectere sine queo superos, Acheronta movebo.[2]

Exit MONTICELSO.

1 *Irish*: notoriously bloodthirsty
2 *Flectere . . . movebo*: 'If I cannot change the will of heaven, I shall release hell' (Virgil, *Aeneid*, 7.312)

ACT 4

Scene 2

Enter the MATRON *and* FLAMINIO.

MATRON
Should it be known the Duke hath such recourse
To your imprisoned sister, I were like
T'incur much damage by it.

FLAMINIO
Not a scruple.[1]
The Pope lies on his death-bed, and their heads
Are troubled now with other business
Than guarding of a lady.

Enter SERVANT.

SERVANT [*Aside*]
Yonder's Flaminio in conference
With the Matrona.
[FLAMINIO *withdraws.* SERVANT *approaches the* MATRON.]
Let me speak with you.
I would entreat you to deliver for me
This letter to the fair Vittoria.

MATRON
I shall, sir.

Enter BRACCIANO.

SERVANT
– With all care and secrecy.
Hereafter you shall know me, and receive
Thanks for this courtesy. [*Exit* SERVANT.]

FLAMINIO
How now, what's that?

MATRON
A letter.

1 *scruple*: jot, thought that troubles the conscience

FLAMINIO
To my sister? [*Taking the letter*] I'll see't delivered.
[*Exit* MATRON.]

BRACCIANO
What's that you read, Flaminio?

FLAMINIO
Look.

BRACCIANO
Ha? [*Reads*] 'To the most unfortunate, his best respected Vittoria.'
Who was the messenger?

FLAMINIO
I know not.

BRACCIANO
No? Who sent it?

FLAMINIO
Ud's foot,[1] you speak as if a man
Should know what fowl is coffined[2] in a baked meat
Afore you cut it up.

BRACCIANO
I'll open't, were't her heart! What's here subscribed?
'Florence'? This juggling[3] is gross and palpable.
I have found out the conveyance.[4] Read it, read it!

FLAMINIO (*Reads the letter*)
'Your tears I'll turn to triumphs, be but mine.
Your prop is fall'n. I pity that a vine
Which princes heretofore have longed to gather,
Wanting supporters, now should fade and wither.'
Wine, i'faith, my lord, with lees[5] would serve his turn.
[*Reads*] 'Your sad imprisonment I'll soon uncharm,
And with a princely, uncontrollèd[6] arm
Lead you to Florence, where my love and care

1 *Ud's foot*: by God's foot – an oath
2 *coffined*: enclosed
3 *juggling*: deception
4 *conveyance*: means of communication, but also a document by which property (i.e., Vittoria) was transferred
5 *lees*: dregs 6 *uncontrollèd*: not under anyone else's authority

Shall hang your wishes in my silver hair.'
A halter[1] on his strange equivocation!
[*Reads*] 'Nor for my years return me the sad willow.[2]
Who prefer blossoms before fruit that's mellow?'
Rotten, on my knowledge, with lying too long i'th' bed-straw![3]
[*Reads*] 'And all the lines of age this line convinces:[4]
The gods never wax old, no more do princes.'
A pox on't! Tear it! Let's have no more atheists,[5] for
God's sake.

BRACCIANO

Ud's death, I'll cut her into atomies,[6]
And let th'irregular[7] north wind sweep her up
And blow her int' his nostrils! Where's this whore?

FLAMINIO

That – ? What do you call her?

BRACCIANO

Oh, I could be mad –
Prevent the cursed disease[8] she'll bring me to,
And tear my hair off. Where's this changeable stuff?[9]

FLAMINIO

O'er head and ears in water,[10] I assure you.
She is not for your wearing.

BRACCIANO

In, you pander!

FLAMINIO

What me, my lord? Am I your dog?

1 *halter*: noose, echoing the use of 'hang', wishing that Francisco be hanged instead
2 *willow*: sign of a rejected lover
3 *bed-straw*: fruit was often ripened in straw
4 *lines . . . line*: the written line overpowers ('convinces') his lines of age, i.e., wrinkles
5 *atheists*: refers to the fact that Francisco has invoked the pagan gods
6 *atomies*: tiny particles
7 *irregular*: disorderly
8 *disease*: syphilis, its symptoms included hair loss
9 *changeable stuff*: fabric that appears to change colour depending on the angle, i.e., watered silk
10 *water*: tears

BRACCIANO
A bloodhound.[1] Do you brave?[2] Do you stand[3] me?
FLAMINIO
Stand you? Let those that have diseases run;[4]
I need no plasters.
BRACCIANO
Would you be kicked?
FLAMINIO
Would you have your neck broke?[5]
I tell you, Duke, I am not in Russia;[6]
My shins must be kept whole.
BRACCIANO
Do you know me?
FLAMINIO
Oh, my lord, methodically.
As in this world there are degrees of evils,
So in this world there are degrees of devils.
You're a great duke, I your poor secretary.
I do look now for a Spanish fig or an Italian sallet[7] daily.
BRACCIANO
Pander, ply your convoy,[8] and leave your prating.
FLAMINIO
All your kindness to me is like that miserable courtesy of Polyphemus to Ulysses:[9] you reserve me to be devoured last. You would dig turves[10] out of my grave to feed your larks – that would be music to you. Come, I'll lead you to her.
[*He walks out backwards.*]

1 *bloodhound*: as a pander, the 'blood' he pursues is also sexual desire
2 *brave*: defy
3 *stand*: withstand
4 *run*: move away, ooze
5 *neck broke*: an allusion to Camillo's fate
6 *Russia*: thought to punish bankrupts by beating them on the shins
7 *sallet*: salad; this and the fig were both forms of poisoning
8 *ply your convoy*: get on with your business
9 *courtesy . . . Ulysses*: in the *Odyssey* Polyphemus, a Cyclops, promised Ulysses the favour of being eaten last (9.369–70)
10 *turves*: turfs

BRACCIANO

Do you face me?

FLAMINIO

Oh sir, I would not go before a politic enemy with my back towards him, though there were behind me a whirlpool.

Enter VITTORIA *to* BRACCIANO *and* FLAMINIO.

BRACCIANO [*showing her the letter*]

Can you read, mistress? Look upon that letter.
There are no characters,[1] nor hieroglyphics.
You need no comment;[2] I am grown your receiver.[3]
God's precious,[4] you shall be a brave, great lady,
A stately and advanced whore!

VITTORIA

Say, sir?

BRACCIANO

Come, come, let's see your cabinet.[5] Discover
Your treasury of love-letters. Death and furies,
I'll see them all!

VITTORIA

Sir, upon my soul,
I have not any. Whence was this directed?

BRACCIANO

Confusion on[6] your politic ignorance!
You are reclaimed,[7] are you? I'll give you the bells[8]
And let you fly to the devil.

[BRACCIANO *gives her the letter.*]

FLAMINIO

'Ware hawks, my lord.

1 *characters*: cabbalistic signs
2 *comment*: commentary
3 *receiver*: an official who received petitions for Parliament, also a pimp
4 *God's precious*: by God's precious blood – an oath
5 *cabinet*: casket containing private letters and jewels
6 *Confusion on*: damn
7 *reclaimed*: a falconry term, meaning called back after being released
8 *bells*: attached to the hawk's legs to help them be reclaimed

VITTORIA
[*reads*] 'Florence'? This is some treacherous plot, my lord.
To me, he ne'er was lovely,[1] I protest,
So much as in my sleep.

BRACCIANO
Right: they are plots.
Your beauty – oh, ten thousand curses on't!
How long have I beheld the devil in crystal?[2]
Thou hast led me, like an heathen sacrifice,
With music and with fatal yokes of flowers,
To my eternal ruin. Woman to man
Is either a god or a wolf.[3]

VITTORIA [*weeping*]
My lord –

BRACCIANO
Away!
We'll be as differing as two adamants:[4]
The one shall shun the other. What? Dost weep?
Procure but ten of thy dissembling trade,
Ye'd furnish all the Irish funerals
With howling, past wild Irish.[5]

FLAMINIO
Fie, my lord.

BRACCIANO
That hand, that cursèd hand, which I have wearied
With doting kisses! O my sweetest Duchess,
How lovely art thou now! [*To* VITTORIA] Thy loose thoughts
Scatter like quicksilver. I was bewitched;
For all the world speaks ill of thee.

1 *lovely*: amorous, attractive
2 *beheld the devil in crystal*: proverbial for deceiving oneself
3 *Woman . . . wolf*: proverbial
4 *adamants*: magnets
5 *Irish*: supposedly hired women to mourn the dead, synonymous with false grief

VITTORIA

No matter.
I'll live so now I'll make that world recant
And change her speeches. You did name your Duchess.

BRACCIANO

Whose death God pardon.

VITTORIA

Whose death God revenge
On thee, most godless Duke.

FLAMINIO [*Aside*]

Now for two whirlwinds!

VITTORIA

What have I gained by thee but infamy?
Thou hast stained the spotless honour of my house,
And frighted thence noble society,
Like those which, sick o'th' palsy and retain
Ill-scenting foxes[1] 'bout them, are still shunned
By those of choicer nostrils. What do you call this house?
Is this your palace? Did not the judge style it
A house of penitent whores? Who sent me to it?
Who hath the honour to advance Vittoria
To this incontinent college? Is't not you?
Is't not your high preferment?[2] Go, go brag
How many ladies you have undone, like me.
Fare you well, sir; let me hear no more of you.
I had a limb corrupted to an ulcer,
But I have cut it off; and now I'll go
Weeping to heaven on crutches.[3] For your gifts,
I will return them all; and I do wish
That I could make you full executor
To all my sins. Oh, that I could toss myself
Into a grave as quickly. For all thou art worth
I'll not shed one tear more; I'll burst first.

She throws herself upon a bed.

1 *foxes*: known for their unpleasant smell, but used in the cure of palsy
2 *preferment*: promotion 3 *Weeping . . . crutches*: an echo of Mark 9:45

BRACCIANO
I have drunk Lethe.[1] Vittoria?
My dearest happiness! Vittoria?
What do you ail, my love? Why do you weep?

VITTORIA
Yes, I now weep poniards.[2] Do you see?

BRACCIANO
Are not those matchless eyes mine?

VITTORIA
I had rather
They were not matches.[3]

BRACCIANO
Is not this lip mine?

VITTORIA
Yes, thus to bite it off, rather than give it thee.

FLAMINIO
Turn to my lord, good sister.

VITTORIA
Hence, you pander!

FLAMINIO
Pander? Am I the author of your sin?

VITTORIA
Yes, he's a base thief that a thief lets in.

FLAMINIO
We're blown up,[4] my lord.

BRACCIANO
Wilt thou hear me?
Once to be jealous of thee is t'express
That I will love thee everlastingly,
And never more be jealous.

VITTORIA
O thou fool,
Whose greatness hath by much o'ergrown thy wit!

1 *Lethe*: a classical river, its waters prompted forgetfulness
2 *poniards*: daggers, i.e., angrily
3 *not matches*: not symmetrical, i.e., she regrets her beauty
4 *blown up*: shattered, destroyed by a mine

What dar'st thou do that I not dare to suffer,
Excepting to be still thy whore? For that,
In the sea's bottom sooner thou shalt make
A bonfire.

FLAMINIO

Oh, no oaths, for God's sake.

BRACCIANO

Will you hear me?

VITTORIA

Never.

FLAMINIO

What a damned impostume[1] is a woman's will!
Can nothing break it? [*Aside to* BRACCIANO] Fie, fie, my lord,
Women are caught as you take tortoises:
She must be turned on her back. [*To* VITTORIA] Sister, by this hand,
I am on your side. [*To* BRACCIANO] Come, come, you have wronged her.
[*Aside to* BRACCIANO] What a strange, credulous man were you, my lord,
To think the Duke of Florence could love her?
Will any mercer[2] take another's ware
When once 'tis toused[3] and sullied? [*To* VITTORIA] And yet, sister,
How scurvily this frowardness[4] becomes you!
[*Aside to* BRACCIANO] Young leverets stand not long;[5] and women's anger
Should, like their flight, procure a little sport:
A full cry[6] for a quarter of an hour,
And then be put to th'dead quat.[7]

1 *impostume*: abscess, festering sore
2 *mercer*: dealer in silks, velvets and other expensive fabrics
3 *toused*: rumpled 4 *frowardness*: perversity
5 *stand not long*: do not hold out long in the hunt
6 *full cry*: pursuit, weeping
7 *quat*: hare's squatting position when cornered

BRACCIANO

Shall these eyes,
Which have so long time dwelt upon your face,
Be now put out?

FLAMINIO

No cruel landlady i'th' world,
Which lends forth groats[1] to broom-men[2] and takes use[3] for them,
Would do't.
[*Aside to* BRACCIANO] Hand[4] her, my lord, and kiss her. Be not like
A ferret to let go your hold with blowing.[5]

BRACCIANO

Let us renew right hands.
[*He takes* VITTORIA*'s hand.*]

VITTORIA

Hence.

BRACCIANO

Never shall rage, or the forgetful[6] wine,
Make me commit like fault.

FLAMINIO [*Aside to* BRACCIANO]

Now you are i'th' way on't, follow't hard.

BRACCIANO

Be thou at peace with me; let all the world
Threaten the cannon.

FLAMINIO [*To* VITTORIA]

Mark his penitence.
Best natures do commit the grossest faults
When they're giv'n o'er to jealousy, as best wine
Dying makes strongest vinegar. I'll tell you,
The sea's more rough and raging than calm rivers,
But nor so sweet nor wholesome. A quiet woman

1 *groats*: pennies 2 *broom-men*: road-sweepers
3 *takes use*: collects interest 4 *Hand*: fondle
5 *ferret . . . blowing*: blowing on a ferret was supposed to loosen its grip
6 *forgetful*: causing forgetfulness

Is a still water under a great bridge:
A man may shoot her[1] safely.

VITTORIA
O ye dissembling men!

FLAMINIO
We sucked that, sister, from women's breasts
In our first infancy.

VITTORIA
To add misery to misery!

BRACCIANO
Sweetest –

VITTORIA
Am I not low enough?
Ay, ay, your good heart gathers like a snowball
Now your affection's cold.

FLAMINIO
Ud's foot, it shall melt
To a heart again, or all the wine in Rome
Shall run o'th' lees for't.

VITTORIA
Your dog or hawk should be rewarded better
Than I have been. I'll speak not one word more.

FLAMINIO
Stop her mouth with a sweet kiss, my lord.
[BRACCIANO *kisses* VITTORIA.]
So now the tide's turned, the vessel's come about.
He's a sweet armful. Oh, we curled-haired men
Are still[2] most kind to women. This is well.

BRACCIANO [*To* VITTORIA]
That you should chide thus!

FLAMINIO
Oh, sir, your little chimneys
Do ever cast most smoke; I sweat for you.
Couple together with as deep a silence

1 *shoot*: descend a river, sexually penetrate 2 *still*: always
3 *Grecians . . . horse*: the Greeks entered the besieged city of Troy by hiding in a wooden horse

As did the Grecians in their wooden horse.[3]
My lord, supply your promises with deeds;
You know that painted meat no hunger feeds.

BRACCIANO
Stay – Ingrateful Rome!

FLAMINIO
Rome? It deserves
To be called 'Barbary'[1] for our villainous usage.

BRACCIANO
Soft! The same project which the Duke of Florence –
Whether in love or gullery[2] I know not –
Laid down for her escape will I pursue.

FLAMINIO
And no time fitter than this night, my lord:
The Pope being dead, and all the cardinals entered
The conclave[3] for th'electing a new Pope;
The city in a great confusion.
We may attire her in a page's suit,
Lay her post-horse,[4] take shipping, and amain
For Padua.

BRACCIANO
I'll instantly steal forth the Prince Giovanni,
And make for Padua. You two, with your old mother
And young Marcello that attends on Florence,
If you can work him to it, follow me.
I will advance you all. For you, Vittoria,
Think of a duchess' title.

FLAMINIO
Lo you, sister!
Stay, my lord, I'll tell you a tale. The crocodile, which lives in the river Nilus, hath a worm breeds i'th' teeth of't which puts it to extreme anguish. A little bird, no bigger than a wren, is barber-surgeon[5] to this crocodile; flies into the jaws of't,

1 *Barbary*: a country in North Africa, associated with barbarousness
2 *gullery*: deception
3 *conclave*: place where cardinals meet to elect a new pope
4 *lay her post-horse*: supply her with horses (those kept for hire at inns)
5 *barber-surgeon*: barbers also served as dentists in this period

picks out the worm, and brings present remedy. The fish, glad of ease but ingrateful to her that did it, that the bird may not talk largely of her abroad for non-payment, closeth her chaps intending to swallow her, and so put her to perpetual silence. But nature, loathing such ingratitude, hath armed this bird with a quill or prick on the head, top o'th' which wounds the crocodile i'th' mouth, forceth her open her bloody prison, and away flies the pretty tooth-picker from her cruel patient.

BRACCIANO

Your application is I have not rewarded
The service you have done me.

FLAMINIO

No, my lord.

You, sister, are the crocodile: you are blemished in your fame; my lord cures it. And though the comparison hold not in every particle, yet observe, remember, what good the bird with the prick i'th' head hath done you, and scorn ingratitude.

[*Aside*] It may appear to some ridiculous
Thus to talk knave and madman; and sometimes
Come in with a dried sentence,[1] stuffed with sage.[2]
But this allows[3] my varying of shapes:
Knaves do grow great by being great men's apes. *Exeunt.*

ACT 4

Scene 3

Enter LODOVICO, GASPARO *and six* AMBASSADORS. *At another door* [FRANCISCO,] *the Duke of Florence.*

FRANCISCO [*To* LODOVICO]

So, my lord, I commend your diligence.
Guard well the conclave, and, as the order is,
Let none have conference with the cardinals.

1 *sentence*: maxim 2 *sage*: herb, also wisdom 3 *allows*: authorizes

LODOVICO
I shall, my lord. Room for the ambassadors!
GASPARO
They're wondrous brave[1] today. Why do they wear
These several[2] habits?
LODOVICO
Oh, sir, they're knights
Of several orders.
That lord i'th' black cloak with the silver cross
Is Knight of Rhodes;[3] the next, Knight of St Michael;[4]
That of the Golden Fleece;[5] the Frenchman there,
Knight of the Holy Ghost;[6] my lord of Savoy,
Knight of th'Annunciation;[7] the Englishman
Is Knight of th'honoured Garter,[8] dedicated
Unto their saint, St George. I could describe to you
Their several institutions, with the laws
Annexed to their orders, but that time
Permits not such discovery.
FRANCISCO
Where's Count Lodovic?
LODOVICO
Here, my lord.
FRANCISCO
'Tis o'th' point of dinner time.
Marshal the cardinals' service.
LODOVICO
Sir, I shall.
Enter SERVANTS *with several dishes covered.*
Stand, let me search your dish. Who's this for?

1 *brave*: finely dressed 2 *several*: various
3 *Rhodes*: the Maltese ambassador
4 *St Michael*: one of the French ambassadors, dressed in silver and white
5 *Golden Fleece*: the Spanish ambassador, dressed in crimson and gold
6 *Holy Ghost*: dressed in a cape of silver, orange and white
7 *Annunciation*: the Savoy ambassador, wearing white and purple, with a gold collar
8 *Garter*: dressed in crimson and purple with a jewelled chain around the neck and a gold garter on the left leg

[FIRST] SERVANT
For my Lord Cardinal Monticelso.

LODOVICO
Whose this?

[SECOND] SERVANT
For my Lord Cardinal of Bourbon.

FRENCH AMBASSADOR
Why doth he search the dishes? To observe
What meat is dressed?[1]

ENGLISH AMBASSADOR
No, sir, but to prevent
Lest any letters should be conveyed in
To bribe or to solicit the advancement
Of any cardinal. When first they enter
'Tis lawful for the ambassadors of princes
To enter with them, and to make their suit
For any man their prince affecteth best;
But after, till a general election,
No man may speak with them.

LODOVICO
You that attend on the lord cardinals,
Open the window and receive their viands.

A CARDINAL [*At the window*]
You must return the service. The lord cardinals
Are busied 'bout electing of the Pope.
They have given o'er scrutiny[2] and are fallen
To admiration.[3] [*Exit.*]

LODOVICO
Away, away! [*Exeunt* SERVANTS *with dishes.*]

FRANCISCO
I'll lay a thousand ducats you hear news
Of a Pope presently –
[*Sound of trumpets.*]
Hark! Sure, he's elected.

1 *meat is dressed*: food is prepared
2 *scrutiny*: the taking of individual votes
3 *admiration*: choice by divine instruction; each cardinal kneels before his preferred candidate

[*Enter*] *Cardinal* [*of* ARAGON] *on the terrace.*

Behold! My lord of Aragon appears
On the church battlements.

ARAGON [*Holding up a cross*]

De nuntio vobis gaudium magnum. Reverendissimus Cardinalis Lorenzo de Monticelso electus est in sedem apostolicam, et elegit sibi nomen Paulum quartum.[1]

ALL

Vivat Sanctus Pater Paulus Quartus![2]

[*Enter* SERVANT.]

SERVANT

Vittoria, my lord –

FRANCISCO

Well, what of her?

SERVANT

Is fled the city –

FRANCISCO

Ha?

SERVANT

With Duke Bracciano.

FRANCISCO

Fled? Where's the Prince Giovanni?

SERVANT

Gone with his father.

FRANCISCO

Let the matrona of the convertites
Be apprehended. Fled? Oh, damnable! [*Exit* SERVANT.]
[*Aside*] How fortunate are my wishes. Why, 'twas this
I only laboured. I did send the letter
T'instruct him what to do. Thy fame, fond[3] Duke,
I first have poisoned; directed thee the way
To marry a whore. What can be worse? This follows:

1 *De nuntio . . . quartum*: 'I bring you tidings of great joy. The Most Reverend Cardinal Lorenzo de Monticelso has been elected to the Apostolic See and has chosen for himself the title of Paul IV.'

2 *Vivat . . . Quartus*: 'Long live the Holy Father Paul IV'

3 *fond*: foolish, infatuated

The hand must act to drown the passionate tongue.
I scorn to wear a sword and prate of wrong.

Enter MONTICELSO *in state* [*as* POPE PAUL IV].

MONTICELSO

Concedimus vobis apostolicam benedictionem et remissionem peccatorum.[1]

[FRANCISCO *whispers to him.*]

My lord reports Vittoria Corombona
Is stol'n from forth the house of convertites
By Bracciano, and they're fled the city.
Now, though this be the first day of our state,
We cannot better please the divine power,
Than to sequester from the holy church
These cursèd persons. Make it therefore known,
We do denounce excommunication
Against them both. All that are theirs in Rome
We likewise banish. Set on.

Exeunt [*all except* FRANCISCO *and* LODOVICO].

FRANCISCO

Come, dear Lodovico,
You have ta'en the sacrament[2] to prosecute
Th'intended murder.

LODOVICO

With all constancy;
But, sir, I wonder you'll engage yourself
In person, being a great prince.

FRANCISCO

Divert me not.
Most of his court are of my faction,
And some are of my counsel. Noble friend,
Our danger shall be 'like in this design;

Enter MONTICELSO [*unseen*].

Give leave part of the glory may be mine. [*Exit* FRANCISCO.]

1 *Concedimus . . . peccatorum*: 'We grant you the Apostolic benediction and remission of sins'

2 *Ta'en the sacrament*: received Holy Communion to support his oath

MONTICELSO
Why did the Duke of Florence with such care
Labour your pardon? Say.
LODOVICO
Italian beggars will resolve you that,
Who, begging of an alms, bid those they beg of
Do good for their own sakes; or't may be
He spreads his bounty with a sowing[1] hand,
Like kings, who many times give out of measure,[2]
Not for desert so much as for their pleasure.
MONTICELSO
I know you're cunning. Come, what devil was that
That you were raising?
LODOVICO
Devil, my lord?
MONTICELSO
I ask you,
How doth the Duke employ you, that his bonnet
Fell with such compliment unto his knee
When he departed from you?
LODOVICO
Why, my lord,
He told me of a resty[3] Barbary horse
Which he would fain have brought to the career,[4]
The 'sault[5] and the ring-galliard.[6] Now, my lord,
I have a rare French rider –
MONTICELSO
Take you heed,
Lest the jade[7] break your neck. Do you put me off
With your wild horse-tricks? Sirrah, you do lie.
Oh, thou'rt a foul, black cloud, and thou dost threat
A violent storm.

1 *sowing*: scattering, with hopes to reap
2 *out of measure*: excessively 3 *resty*: stubborn, restive
4 *career*: a gallop brought up short 5 *'sault*: leaps and vaults
6 *ring-galliard*: circular manoeuvre 7 *jade*: an ill-tempered horse

LODOVICO

Storms are i'th' air, my lord.
I am too low to storm.

MONTICELSO

Wretched creature!
I know that thou art fashioned for all ill,
Like dogs, that once get blood, they'll ever kill.
About some murder, was't not?

LODOVICO

I'll not tell you;
And yet I care not greatly if I do.
Marry, with this preparation: holy father,
I come not to you as an intelligencer,[1]
But as a penitent sinner. What I utter
Is in confession merely, which you know
Must never be revealed.

MONTICELSO

You have o'erta'en[2] me.

LODOVICO

Sir, I did love Bracciano's Duchess dearly –
Or rather I pursued her with hot lust,
Though she ne'er knew on't. She was poisoned,
Upon my soul she was; for which I have sworn
T'avenge her murder.

MONTICELSO

To the Duke of Florence?

LODOVICO

To him I have.

MONTICELSO

Miserable creature!
If thou persist in this, 'tis damnable.
Dost thou imagine thou canst slide on blood
And not be tainted[3] with a shameful fall?
Or like the black and melancholic yew-tree,
Dost think to root thyself in dead men's graves,

1 *intelligencer*: spy, informer 2 *o'erta'en*: entrapped
3 *tainted*: injured, found guilty

And yet to prosper? Instruction to thee
Comes like sweet showers to over-hard'ned ground:
They wet, but pierce not deep. And so I leave thee
With all the furies hanging 'bout thy neck,
Till by thy penitence thou remove this evil,
In conjuring from thy breast that cruel devil.

Exit MONTICELSO.

LODOVICO

I'll give it o'er. He says 'tis damnable.
Besides, I did expect his suffrage[1]
By reason of Camillo's death.

Enter SERVANT *and* FRANCISCO [*apart*].

FRANCISCO

Do you know that count?

SERVANT

Yes, my lord.

FRANCISCO

Bear him these thousand ducats to his lodging.
Tell him the Pope hath sent them. Happily
That will confirm more than all the rest.

[*Exit* FRANCISCO.]

SERVANT

Sir – [*He hands* LODOVICO *the money.*]

LODOVICO

To me, sir?

SERVANT

His Holiness hath sent you a thousand crowns,
And wills you, if you travel, to make him
Your patron for intelligence.[2]

LODOVICO

His creature,
Ever to be commanded. [*Exit* SERVANT.]
Why, now 'tis come about. He railed upon me,
And yet these crowns were told out[3] and laid ready,
Before he knew my voyage. Oh, the art,

1 *suffrage*: support, prayers 2 *intelligence*: secret information
3 *told out*: counted out

The modest form[1] of greatness, that do sit
Like brides at wedding-dinners, with their looks turned
From the least wanton jests, their puling[2] stomach
Sick of the modesty, when their thoughts are loose,[3]
Even acting of those hot and lustful sports
Are to ensue about midnight – such his cunning!
He sounds my depth thus with a golden plummet.[4]
I am doubly armed now to th'act of blood.
There's but three Furies found in spacious hell,
But in a great man's breast three thousand dwell. [*Exit.*]

ACT 5

Scene 1

A passage over the stage of BRACCIANO, FLAMINIO, MARCELLO, HORTENSIO, [VITTORIA] COROMBONA [*dressed as a bride*], CORNELIA, ZANCHE *and others.*

[*Enter* FLAMINIO *and* HORTENSIO.]

FLAMINIO
In all the weary minutes of my life,
Day ne'er broke up till now. This marriage
Confirms me happy.

HORTENSIO
'Tis a good assurance.
Saw you not yet the Moor that's come to court?

FLAMINIO
Yes, and conferred with him i'th' Duke's closet.
I have not seen a goodlier personage,
Nor ever talked with man better experienced
In state affairs or rudiments of war.
He hath, by report, served the Venetian

1 *form*: outward appearance 2 *puling*: weak, sickly 3 *loose*: unchaste
4 *plummet*: ball of lead attached to a line, for measuring depth, i.e., money

In Candy[1] these twice seven years, and been chief
In many a bold design.

HORTENSIO

What are those two
That bear him company?

FLAMINIO

Two noblemen of Hungary that, living in the Emperor's service as commanders, eight years since, contrary to the expectation of all the court, entered into religion, into the strict order of Capuchins.[2] But being not well settled in their undertaking, they left their order and returned to court, for which, being after troubled in conscience, they vowed their service against the enemies of Christ; went to Malta; were there knighted; and in their return back, at this great solemnity, they are resolved forever to forsake the world, and settle themselves here in a house of Capuchins in Padua.

HORTENSIO

'Tis strange.

FLAMINIO

One thing makes it so: they have vowed forever to wear next their bare bodies those coats of mail they served in.

HORTENSIO

Hard penance. Is the Moor a Christian?

FLAMINIO

He is.

HORTENSIO

Why proffers he his service to our Duke?

FLAMINIO

Because he understands there's like to grow
Some wars between us and the Duke of Florence,
In which he hopes employment.
I never saw one in a stern, bold look
Wear more command, nor in a lofty phrase
Express more knowing, or more deep contempt

1 *Candy*: Crete

2 *Capuchins*: an order of monks, deriving from the Franciscans, who wore long, pointed hoods

Of our slight, airy courtiers. He talks
As if he had travelled all the princes' courts
Of Christendom; in all things strives t'express,
That all that should dispute with him may know,
Glories, like glow-worms, afar off shine bright,
But looked to near have neither heat nor light.[1]
The Duke!

Enter BRACCIANO, [FRANCISCO, *Duke of*] *Florence disguised like Mulinassar,* LODOVICO, ANTONELLI,[2] GASPARO [*all disguised*], FERNESE *bearing their swords and helmets* [CARLO, PEDRO].

BRACCIANO

You are nobly welcome. We have heard at full
Your honourable service 'gainst the Turk.
[*To* FRANCISCO] To you, brave Mulinassar, we assign
A competent pension, and are inly sorrow[3]
The vows of those two worthy gentlemen
[*indicating* LODOVICO *and* GASPARO]
Make them incapable of our proffered bounty.
Your wish is you may leave your warlike swords
For monuments in our chapel. I accept it
As a great honour done me, and must crave
Your leave to furnish out our Duchess's revels.
Only one thing, as the last vanity
You e'er shall view, deny me not to stay
To see a barriers prepared tonight;
You shall have private standings. It hath pleased
The great ambassadors of several princes,
In their return from Rome to their own countries,
To grace our marriage, and to honour me
With such a kind of sport.

1 *Glories . . . light*: a favourite couplet of Webster's, taken from Alexander's *Alexandrean Tragedy* and reused in *The Duchess of Malfi*, 4.2

2 ANTONELLI: despite beginning the play as one of Lodovico's two partners in crime, Antonelli plays no part in the murders and his inclusion here may be an error

3 *sorrow*: grieved, regretful

FRANCISCO

I shall persuade them
To stay, my lord.

BRACCIANO

Set on there to the presence.[1]

Exeunt BRACCIANO, FLAMINIO *and* [HORTENSIO].

CARLO [*To* FRANCISCO]

Noble my lord, most fortunately welcome.

The conspirators here embrace.

You have our vows, sealed with the sacrament,
To second your attempts.

PEDRO

And all things ready.
He could not have invented his own ruin,
Had he despaired, with more propriety.

LODOVICO

You would not take my way.

FRANCISCO

'Tis better ordered.

LODOVICO

T' have poisoned his prayer-book, or a pair of beads,
The pommel of his saddle,[2] his looking-glass,
Or th'handle of his racket – Oh that, that!
That while he had been bandying at tennis,
He might have sworn himself to hell, and struck
His soul into the hazard![3] O my lord,
I would have our plot be ingenious,
And have it hereafter recorded for example
Rather than borrow example.

FRANCISCO

There's no way
More speeding than this thought on.

1 *presence*: presence chamber, where a monarch or noble received visitors
2 *saddle*: a Catholic called Edward Squire was executed in 1598 for poisoning the Queen's saddle
3 *hazard*: peril, also the inner wall of a tennis court

LODOVICO

On then.

FRANCISCO

And yet methinks that this revenge is poor,
Because it steals upon him like a thief.
To have ta'en him by the casque[1] in a pitched field,
Led him to Florence –

LODOVICO

It had been rare. And there
Have crowned him with a wreath of stinking garlic,
T' have shown the sharpness of his government
And rankness of his lust.

Enter FLAMINIO, MARCELLO *and* ZANCHE.

Flaminio comes.

Exeunt LODOVICO, ANTONELLI [GASPARO, PEDRO *and* CARLO].

[FRANCISCO *stands apart.*]

MARCELLO

Why doth this devil haunt you? Say.

FLAMINIO

I know not;
For, by this light, I do not conjure for her.
'Tis not so great a cunning as men think
To raise the devil, for here's one up[2] already.
The greatest cunning were to lay him down.

MARCELLO

She is your shame.

FLAMINIO

I prithee, pardon her.
In faith, you see women are like to burs:
Where their affection throws them, there they'll stick.

ZANCHE [*indicating* FRANCISCO]

That is my countryman, a goodly person.
When he's at leisure, I'll discourse with him
In our own language.

1 *casque*: helmet
2 *one up*: perhaps an allusion to Flaminio's erect penis, as well as to Zanche

FLAMINIO

I beseech you, do. *Exit* ZANCHE.

How is't brave soldier? Oh, that I had seen
Some of your iron days! I pray, relate
Some of your service to us.

FRANCISCO

'Tis a ridiculous thing for a man to be his own chronicle. I did never wash my mouth with mine own praise for fear of getting a stinking breath.

MARCELLO

You're too stoical. The Duke will expect other discourse from you.

FRANCISCO

I shall never flatter him; I have studied man too much to do that. What difference is between the Duke and I?[1] No more than between two bricks, all made of one clay. Only't may be one is placed on the top of a turret; the other in the bottom of a well, by mere chance. If I were placed as high as the Duke, I should stick as fast, make as fair a show, and bear out weather equally.[2]

FLAMINIO

If this soldier had a patent to beg in churches,[3] then he would tell them stories.

MARCELLO

I have been a soldier too.

FRANCISCO

How have you thrived?

MARCELLO

'Faith, poorly.

1 *What difference . . . Duke and I*: particularly true, given that they are both Italian dukes with fair skin

2 *If . . . equally*: borrowed from Stefano Guazzo's *Civil Conversation* (English translation, 1581)

3 *soldier . . . churches*: unemployed soldiers were often forced into beggary, but needed a licence to avoid arrest

FRANCISCO

That's the misery of peace: only outsides are then respected. As ships seem very great upon the river which show very little upon the seas, so some men i'th' court seem Colossuses in a chamber who, if they came into the field, would appear pitiful pigmies.

FLAMINIO

Give me a fair room yet hung with arras,[1] and some great cardinal to lug me by th'ears as his endeared minion –

FRANCISCO

And thou may'st do the devil knows what villainy.

FLAMINIO

And safely.

FRANCISCO

Right; you shall see in the country in harvest time, pigeons, though they destroy never so much corn, the farmer dare not present the fowling-piece to them. Why? Because they belong to the lord of the manor, whilst your poor sparrows, that belong to the Lord of heaven, they go to the pot for't.

FLAMINIO

I will now give you some politic instruction. The Duke says he will give you pension – that's but bare promise; get it under his hand. For I have known men that have come from serving against the Turk; for three or four months they have had pension to buy them new wooden legs and fresh plasters, but after 'twas not to be had. And this miserable courtesy shows, as if a tormenter should give hot cordial drinks to one three-quarters dead o'th' rack, only to fetch the miserable soul again to endure more dog-days.

Enter HORTENSIO, *a* YOUNG LORD, ZANCHE *and two more.*

How now, gallants. What, are they ready for the barriers?

[*Exit* FRANCISCO.]

YOUNG LORD

Yes, the lords are putting on their armour.

1 *arras*: tapestry (for hiding behind)

HORTENSIO [*Aside to* FLAMINIO]
What's he?

FLAMINIO
A new upstart: one that swears like a falconer, and will lie in the Duke's ear day by day, like a maker of almanacs;[1] and yet, I knew him since he came to th'court smell worse of sweat than an under-tennis-court-keeper.

HORTENSIO
Look you, yonder's your sweet mistress.

FLAMINIO
Thou art my sworn brother; I'll tell thee, I do love that Moor, that witch, very constrainedly; she knows some of my villainy. I do love her just as a man holds a wolf by the ears.[2] But for fear of turning upon me and pulling out my throat, I would let her go to the devil.

HORTENSIO
I hear she claims marriage of thee.

FLAMINIO
'Faith, I made to her some such dark promise, and in seeking to fly from't I run on, like a frighted dog with a bottle at's tail, that fain would bite it off and yet dares not look behind him. [*To* ZANCHE] Now, my precious gipsy!

ZANCHE
Ay, your love to me rather cools[3] than heats.[4]

FLAMINIO
Marry, I am the sounder lover. We have many wenches about the town heat[5] too fast.

HORTENSIO
What do you think of these perfumed gallants then?

1 *maker of almanacs*: fortune-teller 2 *man . . . ears*: proverbial

3 *cools*: abates

4 *your love . . . heats*: this, and the reference to Zanche as 'gipsy', recalls Shakespeare's *Antony and Cleopatra*

5 *heat*: become lustful, infected with venereal disease

FLAMINIO

Their satin[1] cannot save them. I am confident
They have a certain spice of the disease,
For they that sleep with dogs shall rise with fleas.

ZANCHE

Believe it! A little painting and gay clothes[2]
Make you loathe me.

FLAMINIO

How? Love a lady for painting or gay apparel? I'll unkennel one example more for thee. Aesop had a foolish dog that let go the flesh to catch the shadow; I would have courtiers be better diners.

ZANCHE

You remember your oaths?

FLAMINIO

Lovers' oaths are like mariners' prayers – uttered in extremity, but when the tempest is o'er, and that the vessel leaves tumbling, they fall from protesting to drinking. And yet, amongst gentlemen, protesting and drinking go together, and agree as well as shoemakers and Westphalia bacon. They are both drawers-on;[3] for drink draws on protestation, and protestation draws on more drink. Is not this discourse better now than the morality of your sunburnt gentleman?

Enter CORNELIA.

CORNELIA

Is this your perch, you haggard?[4] Fly to th'stews.[5]
[*Strikes* ZANCHE.]

FLAMINIO

You should be clapped by th'heels[6] now. Strike i'th' court?[7]
[*Exit* CORNELIA.]

1 *satin*: perhaps with a pun on 'Satan'

2 *painting . . . clothes*: i.e., the attractions of other women

3 *shoemakers . . . drawers-on*: the shoemaker puts shoes on feet; bacon draws on thirst

4 *haggard*: a wild female hawk, also a promiscuous woman

5 *stews*: brothel

6 *clapped by th'heels*: imprisoned in iron chains or the stocks

7 *Strike i'th' court*: punishments for this included having one's right hand cut off

ZANCHE
She's good for nothing but to make her maids
Catch cold o'nights. They dare not use a bed-staff[1]
For fear of her light[2] fingers.

MARCELLO
You're a strumpet –
An impudent one!
[*He kicks* ZANCHE.]

FLAMINIO
Why do you kick her? Say.
Do you think that she's like a walnut-tree?
Must she be cudgelled ere she bear good fruit?[3]

MARCELLO
She brags that you shall marry her.

FLAMINIO
What then?

MARCELLO
I had rather she were pitched upon a stake
In some new-seeded garden, to affright
Her fellow crows thence.

FLAMINIO
You're a boy, a fool.
Be guardian to your hound; I am of age.

MARCELLO
If I take her near you, I'll cut her throat.

FLAMINIO
With a fan of feathers?[4]

MARCELLO
And for you, I'll whip
This folly from you.

FLAMINIO
Are you choleric?[5]
I'll purge't with rhubarb.

1 *bed-staff*: a stick for making the bed, but also possibly a male companion
2 *light*: thieving, unchaste 3 *Must . . . fruit*: proverbial
4 *feathers*: indicating his transformation into a courtier
5 *choleric*: angry, produced by an excess of choler

HORTENSIO

O your brother!

FLAMINIO

Hang him!
He wrongs me most that ought t'offend me least.
[*To* MARCELLO] I do suspect my mother played foul-play
When she conceived thee.

MARCELLO

Now, by all my hopes,
Like the two slaughtered sons of Oedipus,
The very flames of our affection
Shall turn two ways.[1] Those words I'll make thee answer
With thy heart-blood.

FLAMINIO

Do. Like the geese[2] in the progress,
You know where you shall find me.

MARCELLO

Very good.

[*Exit* FLAMINIO.]

[*To* YOUNG LORD] And thou be'st a noble friend, bear him my sword,
And bid him fit the length on't.

YOUNG LORD

Sir, I shall.

[*Exeunt all but* ZANCHE.]

Enter FRANCISCO *the Duke of Florence* [*disguised as Mulinassar*].

ZANCHE [*Aside*]

He comes. Hence, petty thought of my disgrace!
[*To* FRANCISCO] I ne'er loved my complexion till now,
'Cause I may boldly say, without a blush,
I love you.

1 *Like . . . two ways*: Oedipus' sons Eteocles and Polinices were killed in their struggle to claim his throne; at their joint funeral the flames parted to show their ongoing hatred

2 *geese*: prostitutes who followed the progress, with a pun on 'gesses' or stopping-places

FRANCISCO

Your love is untimely sown.
There's a spring at Michaelmas, but 'tis but a faint one.
I am sunk in years, and I have vowed never to marry.

ZANCHE

Alas, poor maids get more lovers than husbands.
Yet you may mistake my wealth; for, as when ambassadors are sent to congratulate princes, there's commonly sent along with them a rich present, so that, though the prince like not the ambassador's person nor words, yet he likes well of the presentment, so I may come to you in the same manner, and be better loved for my dowry than my virtue.

FRANCISCO

I'll think on the motion.

ZANCHE

Do. I'll now detain you no longer. At your better leisure, I'll tell you things shall startle your blood.
Nor blame me that this passion I reveal:
Lovers die inward that their flames conceal.

FRANCISCO [*Aside*]

Of all intelligence this may prove the best.
Sure, I shall draw strange fowl from this foul nest. *Exeunt.*

ACT 5

Scene 2

Enter MARCELLO *and* CORNELIA [*with the* PAGE].

CORNELIA

I hear a whispering all about the court
You are to fight. Who is your opposite?
What is the quarrel?

MARCELLO

'Tis an idle rumour.

CORNELIA

Will you dissemble? Sure, you do not well
To fright me thus. You never look thus pale

But when you are most angry. I do charge you,
Upon my blessing – Nay, I'll call the Duke
And he shall school you.

MARCELLO

Publish not a fear
Which would convert to laughter; 'tis not so.
Was not this crucifix my father's?

CORNELIA

Yes.

MARCELLO

I have heard you say, giving my brother suck,
He took the crucifix between his hands
And broke a limb off.

CORNELIA

Yes, but 'tis mended.

Enter FLAMINIO.

FLAMINIO

I have brought your weapon back.

FLAMINIO *runs* MARCELLO *through*.

CORNELIA

Ha? Oh, my horror!

MARCELLO

You have brought it home indeed.

CORNELIA

Help! Oh, he's murdered!

FLAMINIO

Do you turn your gall up?[1] I'll to sanctuary,
And send a surgeon to you. [*Exit*.]

Enter CARLO, HORTENSIO, PEDRO.

HORTENSIO

How? O'th' ground?

MARCELLO

O mother, now remember what I told
Of breaking off the crucifix. Farewell.
There are some sins which heaven doth duly punish

1 *turn your gall up*: become more angry; Flaminio expresses surprise because bloodletting was supposed to cure anger

In a whole family. This it is to rise
By all dishonest means. Let all men know
That tree shall long time keep a steady foot
Whose branches spread no wider than the root. [*He dies.*]

CORNELIA

O my perpetual sorrow!

HORTENSIO

Virtuous Marcello!
He's dead. Pray, leave him, lady. Come, you shall.
[*He restrains* CORNELIA.]

CORNELIA

Alas, he is not dead: he's in a trance.
Why, here's nobody shall get anything by his death. Let me call him again, for God's sake.

CARLO

I would you were deceived.

CORNELIA

Oh, you abuse me, you abuse me, you abuse me! How many have gone away thus for lack of tendance. Rear up's head, rear up's head! His bleeding inward will kill him.

HORTENSIO

You see he is departed.

CORNELIA

Let me come to him. Give me him as he is. If he be turned to earth, let me but give him one hearty kiss, and you shall put us both into one coffin. Fetch a looking-glass – see if his breath will not stain it; or pull out some feathers from my pillow and lay them to his lips.[1] Will you lose him for a little pains-taking?

HORTENSIO

Your kindest office is to pray for him.

CORNELIA

Alas! I would not pray for him yet. He may live to lay me i'th' ground and pray for me, if you'll let me come to him.

1 *Fetch . . . lips*: borrows from the death of Cordelia in Shakespeare's *King Lear*

Enter BRACCIANO *all armed, save the beaver, with* FLAMINIO
[*and* FRANCISCO *and* LODOVICO *both disguised*].

BRACCIANO
Was this your handiwork?

FLAMINIO
It was my misfortune.

CORNELIA
He lies, he lies! He did not kill him. These have killed him that would not let him be better looked to.

BRACCIANO
Have comfort, my grieved mother.

CORNELIA
O you screech-owl![1]
[*She tries to strike* BRACCIANO.]

HORTENSIO
Forbear, good madam!
[*He holds* CORNELIA *back.*]

CORNELIA
Let me go, let me go.
She runs to FLAMINIO *with her knife drawn and, coming to him, lets it fall.*
The God of heaven forgive thee. Dost not wonder
I pray for thee? I'll tell thee what's the reason:
I have scarce breath to number twenty minutes;
I'd not spend that in cursing. Fare thee well.
Half of thyself lies there, and may'st thou live
To fill an hour-glass with his mouldered ashes,
To tell how thou shouldst spend the time to come
In blessed repentance.

BRACCIANO
Mother, pray tell me,
How came he by his death? What was the quarrel?

1 *screech-owl*: bird of ill-omen

CORNELIA

Indeed, my younger boy[1] presumed too much
Upon his manhood; gave him bitter words;
Drew his sword first; and so, I know not how –
For I was out of my wits – he fell with's head
Just in my bosom.

PAGE

This is not true, madam.

CORNELIA

I pray thee, peace.
One arrow's grazed[2] already; it were vain
T' lose this, for that will ne'er be found again.

BRACCIANO

Go, bear the body to Cornelia's lodging;

[*Exeunt* CARLO, PEDRO *and* HORTENSIO *with* MARCELLO*'s body.*]

And we command that none acquaint our Duchess
With this sad accident. For you, Flaminio,
Hark you, I will not grant your pardon.

FLAMINIO

No?

BRACCIANO

Only a lease of your life. And that shall last
But for one day. Thou shalt be forced each evening
To renew it, or be hanged.

FLAMINIO

At your pleasure.

LODOVICO *sprinkles* BRACCIANO*'s beaver*[3] *with a poison.*

Your will is law now; I'll not meddle with it.

BRACCIANO

You once did brave me in your sister's lodging;
I'll now keep you in awe for't. Where's our beaver?

1 *my younger boy*: younger sons were famously disgruntled, given that they would not inherit the estate

2 *graz'd*: lost in the grass ('grassed'), also wounded

3 *beaver*: the lower part of a helmet's face-guard

FRANCISCO [*Aside*]
He calls for his destruction. Noble youth,
I pity thy sad fate. Now to the barriers!
This shall his passage to the black lake[1] further:
The last good deed he did, he pardoned murder. *Exeunt.*

ACT 5

Scene 3

Charges and shouts. They fight at barriers; first single pairs, then three to three.
Enter BRACCIANO [*in armour*] *and* FLAMINIO *with others* [VITTORIA, GIOVANNI *and* FRANCISCO, *disguised as Mulinassar,* GUARDS *and* ATTENDANTS].

BRACCIANO
An armourer! Ud's death, an armourer!

FLAMINIO
Armourer! Where's the armourer?

BRACCIANO
Tear off my beaver!

FLAMINIO
Are you hurt, my lord?

BRACCIANO
Oh, my brain's on fire!
Enter ARMOURER.
The helmet is poisoned!

ARMOURER
My lord, upon my soul –

BRACCIANO
Away with him to torture!
[*Exeunt* GUARDS *with* ARMOURER.]
There are some great ones that have hand in this,
And near about me.

1 *black lake*: Acheron, a black river in the classical hell

VITTORIA

O my loved lord, poisoned?

FLAMINIO

Remove the bar.[1] Here's unfortunate revels!
Call the physicians.

Enter two PHYSICIANS.

A plague upon you!
We have too much of your cunning here already.
I fear the ambassadors are likewise poisoned.

BRACCIANO

Oh, I am gone already. The infection
Flies to the brain and heart. O thou strong heart!
There's such a covenant 'tween the world and it,
They're loath to break.

GIOVANNI

O my most loved father!

BRACCIANO

Remove the boy away.

[*Exeunt* ATTENDANTS *with* GIOVANNI.]

Where's this good woman? Had I infinite worlds
They were too little for thee. Must I leave thee?
What say yon screech-owls?[2] Is the venom mortal?

PHYSICIAN

Most deadly.

BRACCIANO

Most corrupted, politic hangman!
You kill without book, but your art to save
Fails you as oft as great men's needy friends.
I, that have given life to offending slaves
And wretched murderers, have I not power
To lengthen mine own a twelvemonth?
[*To* VITTORIA] Do not kiss me, for I shall poison thee.
This unction is sent from the great Duke of Florence.

1 *bar*: barrier, at which they have been fighting onstage
2 *screech-owls*: referring to the doctors who predict his death

FRANCISCO
Sir, be of comfort.

BRACCIANO
O thou soft, natural death, that art joint-twin
To sweetest slumber, no rough-bearded comet
Stares on thy mild departure. The dull owl
Beats not against thy casement. The hoarse wolf
Scents not thy carrion.[1] Pity winds thy corpse,
Whilst horror waits on princes.

VITTORIA
I am lost forever!

BRACCIANO
How miserable a thing it is to die
'Mongst women howling!
[*Enter* LODOVICO *and* GASPARO, *disguised as Capuchins.*]
What are those?

FLAMINIO
Franciscans.[2]
They have brought the extreme unction.[3]

BRACCIANO
On pain of death, let no man name death to me;
It is a word infinitely terrible.
Withdraw into our cabinet.[4]
Exeunt [*all*] *but* FRANCISCO *and* FLAMINIO.

FLAMINIO
To see what solitariness is about dying princes. As heretofore they have unpeopled towns, divorced friends, and made great houses unhospitable, so now, O justice, where are their flatterers now? Flatterers are but the shadows of princes' bodies – the least thick cloud makes them invisible.

FRANCISCO
There's great moan made for him.

1 *comet . . . carrion*: all portents of doom
2 *Franciscans*: both Franciscan monks and followers of Francisco
3 *extreme unction*: sacrament involving the anointing of the dying, but here also poison
4 *cabinet*: private room, perhaps the curtained discovery space

FLAMINIO

'Faith, for some few hours salt water will run most plentifully in every office o'th' court; but, believe it, most of them do but weep over their stepmothers' graves.[1]

FRANCISCO

How mean you?

FLAMINIO

Why, they dissemble, as some men do that live within compass o'th' verge.[2]

FRANCISCO

Come, you have thrived well under him.

FLAMINIO

'Faith, like a wolf in a woman's breast, I have been fed with poultry.[3] But for money? Understand me, I had as good a will to cozen him as e'er an officer of them all, but I had not cunning enough to do it.

FRANCISCO

What didst thou think of him? 'Faith, speak freely.

FLAMINIO

He was a kind of statesman that would sooner have reckoned how many cannon-bullets he had discharged against a town, to count his expense that way, than how many of his valiant and deserving subjects he lost before it.

FRANCISCO

Oh, speak well of the Duke.

FLAMINIO

I have done.

Wilt hear some of my court wisdom?

Enter LODOVICO [*disguised*].

To reprehend princes is dangerous, and to over-commend some of them is palpable lying.

1 *stepmothers' graves*: another example of false grief, stepmothers standing in the way of the children's inheritance

2 *within ... th' verge*: within twelve miles of court, ruled over by the Lord High Steward

3 *like a wolf ... poultry*: the 'wolf' is an ulcer, usually treated by applying raw meat; there may be a pun on poultry/paltry

FRANCISCO
How is it with the Duke?
LODOVICO
Most deadly ill.
He's fall'n into a strange distraction.
He talks of battles and monopolies,
Levying of taxes, and from that descends
To the most brain-sick language. His mind fastens
On twenty several objects, which confound
Deep sense with folly. Such a fearful end
May teach some men that bear too lofty crest,
Though they live happiest, yet they die not best.
He hath conferred the whole state of the dukedom
Upon your sister, till the Prince arrive
At mature age.
FLAMINIO
There's some good luck in that yet.
FRANCISCO
See, here he comes.

Enter BRACCIANO, *presented in a bed,* VITTORIA *and others* [*including* GASPARO, *disguised*].

There's death in's face already.
VITTORIA
O my good lord!

These speeches are several kinds of distractions and in the action should appear so.

BRACCIANO
Away! You have abused me!
You have conveyed coin forth our territories,[1]
Bought and sold offices, oppressed the poor,
And I ne'er dreamt on't! Make up your accounts;
I'll now be mine own steward.
FLAMINIO
Sir, have patience.

1 *conveyed . . . territories*: exporting money was a serious offence; Henry VIII issued a statute forbidding it

BRACCIANO

Indeed, I am too blame,[1]
For did you ever hear the dusky raven[2]
Chide blackness? Or was't ever known the devil
Railed against cloven creatures?

VITTORIA

O my lord!

BRACCIANO

Let me have some quails to supper.

FLAMINIO

Sir, you shall.

BRACCIANO

No, some fried dog-fish;[3] your quails feed on poison.
That old dog-fox,[4] that politician, Florence –
I'll forswear hunting and turn dog-killer.
Rare! I'll be friends with him, for, mark you, sir, one dog
Still sets another a-barking. Peace, peace!
Yonder's a fine slave come in now.

FLAMINIO

Where?

BRACCIANO

Why, there:
In a blue bonnet, and a pair of breeches
With a great cod-piece. Ha, ha, ha!
Look you, his cod-piece is stuck full of pins
With pearls o'th head of them. Do not you know him?

FLAMINIO

No, my lord.

BRACCIANO

Why, 'tis the devil!
I know him by a great rose he wears on's shoe
To hide his cloven foot. I'll dispute with him;
He's a rare linguist.[5]

1 *blame*: blameworthy 2 *raven*: another bird predicting death
3 *dog-fish*: a small shark 4 *dog-fox*: a male fox
5 *linguist*: one who knows many languages, a rhetorician

VITTORIA

My lord, here's nothing.

BRACCIANO

Nothing? Rare! Nothing? When I want money
Our treasury is empty; there is nothing.
I'll not be used thus.
[*He tries to get up.*]

VITTORIA

Oh, lie still, my lord!

BRACCIANO

See, see – Flaminio, that killed his brother,
Is dancing on the ropes[1] there; and he carries
A money-bag in each hand to keep him even,
For fear of breaking's neck. And there's a lawyer,
In a gown whipped[2] with velvet, stares and gapes
When the money will fall. How the rogue cuts capers!
It should have been in a halter.[3]
'Tis there. [*Pointing to* VITTORIA] What's she?

FLAMINIO

Vittoria, my lord.

BRACCIANO

Ha, ha, ha! Her hair is sprinkled with orris[4] powder
That makes her look as if she had sinned in the pastry.[5]
[*Points to* LODOVICO] What's he?

FLAMINIO

A divine, my lord.

BRACCIANO

He will be drunk; avoid him. Th'argument
Is fearful when churchmen stagger in't.
Look you: six grey rats that have lost their tails
Crawl up the pillow. Send for a rat-catcher.
I'll do a miracle: I'll free the court
From all foul vermin. Where's Flaminio?

1 *the ropes*: a tightrope 2 *whipped*: trimmed
3 *halter*: the rope, indicating that Flaminio deserves hanging
4 *orris*: iris root, used for whitening and perfuming hair, reflecting Vittoria's status as a bride
5 *pastry*: a place where pastry is made

FLAMINIO [*Aside*]

I do not like that he names me so often,
Especially on's death-bed. 'Tis a sign
I shall not live long. [*Aloud*] See, he's near his end.

LODOVICO

Pray, give us leave.

BRACCIANO *seems here near his end.* LODOVICO *and* GASPARO, *in the habit of Capuchins, present him, in his bed, with a crucifix and hallowed candle.*[1]

Attende, Domine Bracciane – [2]

FLAMINIO

See, see, how firmly he doth fix his eye
Upon the crucifix.

VITTORIA

Oh, hold it constant.
It settles his wild spirits; and so his eyes
Melt into tears.

LODOVICO (*By the crucifix*)

Domine Bracciane, solebas in bello tutus esse tuo clypeo, nunc hunc clypeum hosti tuo opponas infernali.[3]

GASPARO (*By the hallowed taper*)

Olim hasta valuisti in bello; nunc hanc sacram hastam vibrabis contra hostem animarum.[4]

LODOVICO

Attende, Domine Bracciane, si nunc quoque probas ea quae acta sunt inter nos, flecte caput in dextrum.[5]

[BRACCIANO *turns his head to the right.*]

1 *crucifix . . . candle*: symbols of hope and comfort to the dying; the murderers perform the *Commendatio Animae* or ritual commending of the soul to God

2 *Attende . . . Bracciane*: 'Listen, Lord Bracciano'

3 *Domine . . . infernali*: 'Lord Bracciano, you were accustomed to be guarded in battle by your shield; now this shield [the crucifix] you shall oppose against your infernal enemy'

4 *Olim . . . animarum*: 'Once with your spear you prevailed in battle; now this holy spear [the hallowed taper] you shall wield against the enemy of souls'

5 *Attende . . . dextrum*: 'Listen, Lord Bracciano, if you now also approve what has been done between us, turn your head to the right'

GASPARO

Esto securus, Domine Bracciane: cogita quantum habeas meritorum – denique memineris meam animam pro tua oppignoratam si quid esset periculi.[1]

LODOVICO

Si nunc quoque probas ea quae acta sunt inter nos, flecte caput in laevum.[2]

[BRACCIANO *turns his head to the left.*]

He is departing. Pray, stand all apart,
And let us only whisper in his ears
Some private meditations which our order
Permits you not to hear.

Here, the rest being departed, LODOVICO *and* GASPARO *discover themselves.*

GASPARO

Bracciano.

LODOVICO

Devil Bracciano! Thou art damned.

GASPARO

Perpetually.

LODOVICO

A slave condemned and given up to the gallows
Is thy great lord and master.[3]

GASPARO

True, for thou
Art given up to the devil.

LODOVICO

O you slave!
You that were held the famous politician,
Whose art was poison –

1 *Esto . . . periculi*: 'Rest assured, Lord Bracciano: think how many good deeds you have done – lastly remember that my soul is pledged for yours if there should be any peril'

2 *Si . . . laevum*: 'If you now also approve what has been between us, turn your head to the left'

3 *A slave . . . master*: the *Commendatio animae* ought to commend Bracciano's soul to God

GASPARO

And whose conscience[1] murder.

LODOVICO

– That would have broke your wife's neck down the stairs
Ere she was poisoned.[2]

GASPARO

That had your villainous sallets –

LODOVICO

And fine, embroidered bottles and perfumes,
Equally mortal with a winter plague.[3]

GASPARO

Now there's mercury –

LODOVICO

And copperas[4] –

GASPARO

And quicksilver[5] –

LODOVICO

With other devilish, 'pothecary stuff
A-melting in your politic brains. Dost hear?

GASPARO

This is Count Lodovico.

LODOVICO

This Gasparo;
And thou shalt die like a poor rogue.

GASPARO

And stink
Like a dead, fly-blown dog.

LODOVICO

And be forgotten before thy funeral sermon.

1 *conscience*: inmost thought

2 *broke . . . poisoned*: probably a reference to the Earl of Leicester, who was suspected of attempting to poison his wife, Amy Robsart, and of having her thrown down the stairs in order to clear a path for his marriage to Elizabeth I; according to the pamphlet *Leicester's Commonwealth* (1584) he employed a poisoner named Doctor Julio

3 *winter plague*: a plague that could survive winter was regarded as particularly deadly

4 *copperas*: a sulphate of copper, iron or zinc

5 *quicksilver*: mercury

BRACCIANO
Vittoria! Vittoria!
LODOVICO
O the cursèd devil,
Come to himself again! We are undone.
[*They quickly resume their disguises.*]
Enter VITTORIA *and the* ATTENDANTS.
GASPARO [*Aside to* LODOVICO]
Strangle him in private.
[*To* VITTORIA] What? Will you call him again
To live in treble torments? For charity,
For Christian charity, avoid the chamber.
[*Exeunt* VITTORIA *and* ATTENDANTS.]
LODOVICO
You would prate, sir. This is a true-love knot,[1]
Sent from the Duke of Florence.
BRACCIANO *is strangled.*
GASPARO
What, is it done?
LODOVICO
The snuff[2] is out. No woman-keeper[3] i'th' world,
Though she had practised seven year at the pest-house,[4]
Could have done't quaintlier.[5]
[*Enter* VITTORIA, FRANCISCO, FLAMINIO
and ATTENDANTS.]
My lords, he's dead.
ALL
Rest to his soul.
VITTORIA
O me! This place is hell.

1 *true-love knot*: a noose, also recalls Francisco's fake courtship of Vittoria
2 *snuff*: proverbial description of death as a candle going out in a snuff
3 *woman-keeper*: nurse, often suspected of killing their patients
4 *pest-house*: plague hospital 5 *quaintlier*: more skilfully

Exeunt VITTORIA [*weeping*, GASPARO *and* ATTENDANTS.]
[LODOVICO *stands aside.*]

FRANCISCO
How heavily she takes it!

FLAMINIO
Oh, yes, yes.
Had women navigable rivers in their eyes
They would dispend[1] them all. Surely, I wonder
Why we should wish more rivers to the city,[2]
When they sell water so good cheap. I'll tell thee,
These are but moonish[3] shades of griefs or fears;
There's nothing sooner dry than women's tears.
Why, here's an end of all my harvest: he has given me nothing.
Court promises! Let wise men count them cursed,
For while you live he that scores best pays worst.[4]

FRANCISCO
Sure, this was Florence' doing.

FLAMINIO
Very likely.
Those are found weighty strokes which come from th'hand,
But those are killing strokes which come from th'head.
Oh, the rare tricks of a Machiavellian!
He doth not come like a gross, plodding slave
And buffet you to death. No, my quaint[5] knave
He tickles you to death, makes you die laughing,
As if you had swallowed down a pound of saffron.[6]
You see the feat; 'tis practised in a trice –
To teach court-honesty it jumps on ice.[7]

1 *dispend*: spend, exhaust
2 *I . . . city*: a scheme to create a new river that would provide Londoners with water had begun in 1608
3 *moonish*: changeable
4 *he that . . . worst*: he that runs up the most credit pays most for it
5 *quaint*: ingenious
6 *saffron*: supposed to cause merriment, but fatal in large doses
7 *jumps on ice*: is precarious

FRANCISCO

Now have the people liberty to talk
And descant[1] on his vices.

FLAMINIO

Misery of princes,
That must of force be censured by their slaves!
Not only blamed for doing things are ill,
But for not doing all that all men will.
One were better be a thresher.
Ud's death, I would fain speak with this Duke yet.

FRANCISCO

Now he's dead?

FLAMINIO

I cannot conjure, but if prayers or oaths
Will get to th'speech of him, though forty devils
Wait on him in his livery of flames,
I'll speak to him and shake him by the hand,
Though I be blasted.[2] *Exit* FLAMINIO.

[LODOVICO *comes forward.*]

FRANCISCO

Excellent Lodovico!
What? Did you terrify him at the last gasp?

LODOVICO

Yes; and so idly, that the Duke had like
T'have terrified us.

FRANCISCO

How?

Enter [ZANCHE] *the Moor.*

LODOVICO

You shall hear that hereafter.
See, yon's the infernal[3] that would make up sport.[4]
Now to the revelation of that secret
She promised when she fell in love with you.

1 *descant*: expound 2 *blasted*: struck down by supernatural force
3 *infernal*: devil 4 *make up sport*: complete our entertainment

FRANCISCO [*To* ZANCHE]
You're passionately met in this sad world.

ZANCHE
I would have you look up, sir. These court tears
Claim not your tribute to them. Let those weep
That guiltily partake in the sad cause.
I knew last night, by a sad dream I had,
Some mischief would ensue. Yet, to say truth,
My dream most concerned you.

LODOVICO [*Aside to* FRANCISCO]
Shall's fall a-dreaming?

FRANCISCO [*Aside to* LODOVICO]
Yes, and for fashion sake I'll dream with her.

ZANCHE
Methought, sir, you came stealing to my bed.

FRANCISCO
Wilt thou believe me, sweeting? By this light,
I was a-dreamt on thee too, for methought
I saw thee naked.

ZANCHE
Fie, sir! As I told you,
Methought you lay down by me.

FRANCISCO
So dreamt I;
And lest thou shouldst take cold, I covered thee
With this Irish mantle.

ZANCHE
Verily, I did dream
You were somewhat bold with me; but to come to't –

LODOVICO [*Aside*]
How, how? I hope you will not go to't here.

FRANCISCO
Nay, you must hear my dream out.

ZANCHE
Well, sir, forth.

FRANCISCO
When I threw the mantle o'er thee, thou didst laugh
Exceedingly methought.

ZANCHE

Laugh?

FRANCISCO

And cried'st out
The hair did tickle thee.

ZANCHE

There was a dream indeed.

LODOVICO [*Aside to* FRANCISCO]

Mark her, I prithee. She simpers like the suds
A collier[1] hath been washed in.

ZANCHE

Come, sir, good fortune 'tends you. I did tell you
I would reveal a secret: Isabella,
The Duke of Florence' sister, was empoisoned
By a fumed[2] picture; and Camillo's neck
Was broke by damned Flaminio, the mischance
Laid on a vaulting-horse.

FRANCISCO

Most strange!

ZANCHE

Most true.

LODOVICO [*Aside*]

The bed of snakes is broke.

ZANCHE

I sadly do confess I had a hand
In the black deed.

FRANCISCO

Thou kept'st their counsel?

ZANCHE

Right;
For which, urged with contrition, I intend
This night to rob Vittoria.

LODOVICO [*Aside*]

Excellent penitence!
Usurers dream on't while they sleep out sermons.

1 *collier*: coal-miner, i.e., producing black suds when washed
2 *fumed*: perfumed

ZANCHE

To further our escape, I have entreated
Leave to retire me, till the funeral,
Unto a friend i'th' country. That excuse
Will further our escape. In coin and jewels
I shall, at least, make good unto your use
An hundred thousand crowns.

FRANCISCO

O noble wench!

LODOVICO [*Aside*]

Those crowns we'll share.

ZANCHE

It is a dowry,
Methinks, should make that sunburnt proverb false,
And 'wash the Ethiop white'.[1]

FRANCISCO

It shall. Away!

ZANCHE

Be ready for our flight.

FRANCISCO

An hour 'fore day.

Exit [ZANCHE] *the Moor.*

O strange discovery! Why, till now we knew not
The circumstance of either of their deaths.

Enter [ZANCHE *the*] *Moor.*

ZANCHE

You'll wait about midnight in the chapel?

FRANCISCO

There.

[*Exit* ZANCHE.]

LODOVICO

Why, now our action's justified.

FRANCISCO

Tush for justice!
What harms it justice? We now, like the partridge,

1 *wash . . . white*: proverbial, based on Jeremiah 13:23

Purge the disease with laurel,[1] for the fame
Shall crown the enterprise and quit the shame. *Exeunt.*

ACT 5

Scene 4

Enter FLAMINIO *and* GASPARO *at one door; another way* GIOVANNI, *attended.*

GASPARO [*To* FLAMINIO]

The young Duke – Did you e'er see a sweeter prince?

FLAMINIO

I have known a poor woman's bastard better favoured[2] – this is behind him. Now, to his face: all comparisons were hateful. Wise was the courtly peacock that, being a great minion, and being compared for beauty by some dottrels[3] that stood by to the kingly eagle, said the eagle was a far fairer bird than herself, not in respect of her feathers but in respect of her long tallants.[4] His will grow out in time. [*To* GIOVANNI] My gracious lord –

GIOVANNI

I pray, leave me, sir.

FLAMINIO

Your grace must be merry. 'Tis I have cause to mourn, for wot[5] you what said the little boy that rode behind his father on horseback?

GIOVANNI

Why, what said he?

FLAMINIO

'When you are dead, father,' said he, 'I hope then I shall ride in the saddle.' Oh, 'tis a brave thing for a man to sit by himself: he may stretch himself in the stirrups, look about, and

1 *laurel*: the plant from which victory wreaths were woven
2 *better favoured*: more good-looking
3 *dottrels*: proverbially stupid birds
4 *tallants*: talons, talents 5 *wot*: know

see the whole compass of the hemisphere. You're now, my lord, i'th' saddle.

GIOVANNI

Study your prayers, sir, and be penitent.
'Twere fit you'd think on what hath former been;
I have heard Grief named the eldest child of Sin.

Exeunt GIOVANNI [*with* ATTENDANTS *and* GASPARO].

FLAMINIO

Study my prayers? He threatens me divinely. I am falling to pieces already. I care not, though like Anacharsis[1] I were pounded to death in a mortar. And yet that death were fitter for usurers: gold and themselves to be beaten together to make a most cordial cullis[2] for the devil.
He hath his uncle's villainous look already,
In *decimo-sexto*.[3]

Enter COURTIER.

Now sir, what are you?

COURTIER

It is the pleasure, sir, of the young Duke
That you forbear the presence,[4] and all rooms
That owe him reverence.

FLAMINIO

So, the wolf and the raven
Are very pretty fools when they are young.
Is it your office, sir, to keep me out?

COURTIER

So the Duke wills.

FLAMINIO

Verily, Master Courtier, extremity is not to be used in all offices. Say that a gentlewoman were taken out of her bed

1 *Anacharsis*: a Scythian philosopher, killed by his brother with an arrow; Webster has him confused with Anaxarchus, who was pounded to death in a pestle and mortar because he challenged the authority of a tyrant

2 *cullis*: health-giving broth

3 *In decimo-sexto*: i.e., in a smaller version; a decimo-sexto page was one sixteenth of a full sheet of paper

4 *presence*: presence chamber

about midnight, and committed to Castle Angelo,[1] to the tower yonder,[2] with nothing about her but her smock. Would it not show a cruel part in the gentleman-porter to lay claim to her upper garment, pull it o'er her head and ears, and put her in naked?

COURTIER

Very good, you are merry. [*Exit*.]

FLAMINIO

Doth he make a court ejectment of me? A flaming[3] firebrand casts more smoke without[4] a chimney than within't. I'll smoor[5] some of them.

Enter [FRANCISCO, *Duke of*] *Florence* [*disguised as Mulinassar*].

How now? Thou art sad.

FRANCISCO

I met, even now, with the most piteous sight.

FLAMINIO

Thou met'st another here: a pitiful,
Degraded courtier.

FRANCISCO

Your reverend mother
Is grown a very old woman in two hours.
I found them winding of Marcello's corpse,[6]
And there is such a solemn melody
'Tween doleful songs, tears and sad elegies –
Such as old grandams, watching by the dead,[7]
Were wont t'outwear the nights with – that, believe me,

1 *Castle Angelo*: the Castel Sant'Angelo in Rome was the site of the real Vittoria's imprisonment
2 *tower yonder*: the audience might think of the Tower of London in which Arbella Stuart had lately been imprisoned for marrying without James I's permission
3 *flaming*: Flaminio puns on his own name
4 *without*: outside
5 *smoor*: suffocate
6 *winding . . . corpse*: wrapping it in the winding sheet, leaving the face uncovered
7 *watching . . . dead*: the practice of staying with the dead through the night, with candles burning, was dying out in England

I had no eyes to guide me forth the room,
They were so o'er-charged with water.

FLAMINIO
I will see them.

FRANCISCO
'Twere much uncharity in you, for your sight
Will add unto their tears.

FLAMINIO
I will see them.

FRANCISCO
They are behind the traverse.[1] I'll discover
Their superstitious[2] howling.
[*He draws the traverse.*]

CORNELIA, [ZANCHE] *the Moor and three other* LADIES *discovered, winding* MARCELLO*'s corpse. A song.*

CORNELIA
This rosemary[3] is withered; pray, get fresh.
I would have these herbs grow up in his grave
When I am dead and rotten. Reach the bays.[4]
I'll tie a garland here about his head:
'Twill keep my boy from lightning. This sheet
I have kept this twenty year, and every day
Hallowed it with my prayers. I did not think
He should have wore it.

ZANCHE
Look you who are yonder.

CORNELIA
Oh, reach me the flowers.

ZANCHE [*To* LADIES]
Her ladyship's foolish.[5]

1 *traverse*: a curtain at the back of the stage, covering the discovery space
2 *superstitious*: excessive
3 *rosemary*: an evergreen herb, symbolizing immortality and remembrance
4 *bays*: laurel leaves, associated with fame and supposed to protect from lightning
5 *foolish*: not making sense

LADY

Alas! Her grief
Hath turned her child again.

CORNELIA (*To* FLAMINIO)

You're very welcome.
There's rosemary for you, and rue[1] for you.
[*To* FRANCISCO] Heart's-ease[2] for you – I pray make much of it;
I have left more for myself.[3]

FRANCISCO

Lady, who's this?

CORNELIA

You are, I take it, the grave-maker.

FLAMINIO

So.

ZANCHE

'Tis Flaminio.

[CORNELIA *takes* FLAMINIO'*s hand.*]

CORNELIA

Will you make me such a fool? Here's a white hand –
Can blood so soon be washed out?[4] Let me see:
'When screech-owls croak upon the chimney-tops,
And the strange cricket i'th' oven sings and hops,
When yellow spots do on your hands appear,
Be certain then you of a corpse shall hear.'
Out upon't! How 'tis speckled! H'as handled a toad, sure.
Cowslip-water is good for the memory;
Pray, buy me three ounces of't.

FLAMINIO

I would I were from hence.

CORNELIA

Do you hear, sir?
I'll give you a saying which my grandmother

1 *rue*: evergreen shrub, symbolizing sorrow and repentance
2 *Heart's-ease*: pansy, representing thoughts and tranquillity
3 *I pray . . . myself*: Webster is clearly recalling Ophelia in *Hamlet*, 4.5
4 *Can . . . out*: echoes *Macbeth*, 5.1

Was wont, when she heard the bell toll, to sing o'er
Unto her lute.[1]

FLAMINIO

Do, an you will, do.

CORNELIA *doth this in several forms of distraction.*

CORNELIA [*Sings*]

Call for the robin redbreast and the wren,[2]
Since o'er shady groves they hover,
And with leaves and flow'rs do cover
The friendless bodies of unburied men.
Call unto his funeral dole[3]
The ant, the field-mouse and the mole,
To rear him hillocks that shall keep him warm,
And, when gay tombs are robbed, sustain no harm.
But keep the wolf far thence that's foe to men,
For with his nails he'll dig them up again.[4]

They would not bury him 'cause he died in a quarrel,
But I have an answer for them.
[*Sings*] *Let holy church receive him duly*
Since he paid the church tithes truly.
His wealth is summed,[5] and this is all his store;[6]
This poor men get, and great men get no more.
Now the wares are gone, we may shut up shop.[7]
Bless you all, good people.

Exeunt CORNELIA [ZANCHE] *and* LADIES.

FLAMINIO

I have a strange thing in me, to th'which
I cannot give a name, without it be
Compassion. I pray, leave me. *Exit* FRANCISCO.

1 *lute*: mad Ophelia carries a lute in Q1 *Hamlet* and perhaps Cornelia does so here

2 *robin . . . wren*: both birds were thought to cover up dead bodies

3 *dole*: rites

4 *wolf . . . again*: the wolf was believed to dig up the corpses of those who had been murdered and thence to act as an agent of revenge

5 *summed*: reckoned

6 *store*: perhaps indicating his corpse

7 *shut up shop*: Cornelia might have retreated to the discovery space where she now draws the curtain

This night I'll know the utmost of my fate;
I'll be resolved what my rich sister means
T'assign me for my service. I have lived
Riotously ill, like some that live in court;
And sometimes, when my face was full of smiles,
Have felt the maze[1] of conscience in my breast.
Oft gay and honoured robes those tortures try;[2]
We think caged birds sing, when indeed they cry.

Enter BRACCIANO*'s* GHOST, *in his leather cassock*[3] *and breeches, boots* [*and*] *a cowl,*[4] [*carrying*] *a pot of lily-flowers with a skull in't.*

Ha! I can stand thee. [*The* GHOST *approaches*] Nearer, nearer yet.
What a mockery[5] hath death made of thee! Thou look'st sad.
In what place art thou? In yon starry gallery
Or in the cursèd dungeon?[6] No? Not speak?
Pray, sir, resolve me: what religion's best
For a man to die in? Or is it in your knowledge
To answer me how long I have to live?
That's the most necessary question.
Not answer? Are you still like some great men
That only walk like shadows[7] up and down,
And to no purpose? Say.

The GHOST *throws earth upon him and shows him the skull.*

What's that? Oh, fatal! He throws earth upon me.
A dead man's skull beneath the roots of flowers.
I pray, speak, sir. Our Italian churchmen
Make us believe dead men hold conference
With their familiars, and many times
Will come to bed to them, and eat with them. *Exit* GHOST.

1 *maze*: labyrinth, confusion 2 *try*: experience
3 *cassock*: long coat or cloak worn by soldiers; a leather version was often worn by stage ghosts
4 *cowl*: monastic hood 5 *mockery*: counterfeit, absurdity
6 *starry gallery . . . dungeon*: probably gesturing to the gallery of the theatre and the 'hell' space below the stage
7 *shadows*: insubstantial persons, actors

He's gone, and see: the skull and earth are vanished.
This is beyond melancholy.[1] I do dare my fate
To do its worst. Now to my sister's lodging
And sum up all these horrors: the disgrace
The Prince threw on me; next the piteous sight
Of my dead brother and my mother's dotage;
And last this terrible vision. All these
Shall with Vittoria's bounty turn to good,
Or I will drown this weapon in her blood.
[*Draws his sword and*] *Exit.*

ACT 5

Scene 5

Enter FRANCISCO, LODOVICO, *and* HORTENSIO [*watching them*].

LODOVICO
My lord, upon my soul, you shall no further.
You have most ridiculously engaged yourself
Too far already. For my part, I have paid
All my debts, so if I should chance to fall
My creditors fall not with me; and I vow
To 'quite[2] all in this bold assembly
To the meanest follower. My lord, leave the city,
Or I'll forswear the murder.

FRANCISCO
Farewell, Lodovico.
If thou dost perish in this glorious act,
I'll rear unto thy memory that fame
Shall in the ashes keep alive thy name.
[*Exeunt* FRANCISCO *and* LODOVICO.]

1 *beyond melancholy*: i.e., something more than the projection of Flaminio's mood
2 *'quite*: revenge

HORTENSIO
There's some black deed on foot. I'll presently[1]
Down to the citadel and raise some force.
These strong court factions that do brook no checks
In the career[2] oft break the riders' necks. [*Exit.*]

ACT 5

Scene 6

Enter VITTORIA *with a book in her hand* [*and*] ZANCHE; FLAMINIO *following them.*

FLAMINIO
What, are you at your prayers? Give o'er.

VITTORIA
How, Ruffin?[3]

FLAMINIO
I come to you 'bout worldly business.
Sit down, sit down. [ZANCHE *makes to leave.*] Nay, stay, blowze,[4] you may hear it.
The doors are fast enough.

VITTORIA
Ha, are you drunk?

FLAMINIO
Yes, yes, with wormwood[5] water. You shall taste
Some of it presently.

VITTORIA
What intends the fury?

FLAMINIO
You are my lord's executrix, and I claim
Reward for my long service.

1 *presently*: immediately 2 *career*: gallop at full speed
3 *Ruffin*: a name for a devil
4 *blowze*: a fat, red-faced woman, which Zanche is not
5 *wormwood*: a bitter-tasting plant

VITTORIA

For your service?

FLAMINIO

Come, therefore, here is pen and ink. Set down
What you will give me.

She writes.

VITTORIA

There.

FLAMINIO

Ha? Have you done already?
'Tis a most short conveyance.

VITTORIA

I will read it.
[*Reads*] 'I give that portion to thee, and no other,
Which Cain groaned under, having slain his brother'.[1]

FLAMINIO

A most courtly patent to beg by.

VITTORIA

You are a villain.

FLAMINIO

Is't come to this? They say affrights cure agues.
Thou hast a devil in thee; I will try
If I can scare him from thee. Nay, sit still.
My lord hath left me yet two case[2] of jewels
Shall make me scorn your bounty. You shall see them.

[*Exit.*]

VITTORIA

Sure, he's distracted.

ZANCHE

Oh, he's desperate!
For your own safety give him gentle language.

[FLAMINIO] *enters with two case of pistols.*

1 *I . . . brother*: according to Genesis, Cain was accursed after slaying his brother Abel and became the first exile

2 *case*: a pair

FLAMINIO

Look, these are better far at a dead lift[1]
Than all your jewel-house.

VITTORIA

And yet, methinks,
These stones have no fair lustre; they are ill-set.

FLAMINIO

I'll turn the right side towards you. You shall see
How they will sparkle.

VITTORIA

Turn this horror from me.
What do you want? What would you have me do?
Is not all mine, yours? Have I any children?

FLAMINIO

Pray thee, good woman, do not trouble me
With this vain, worldly business. Say your prayers.
I made a vow to my deceasèd lord
Neither yourself nor I should outlive him
The numb'ring of four hours.

VITTORIA

Did he enjoin it?

FLAMINIO

He did, and 'twas a deadly jealousy,
Lest any should enjoy thee after him,
That urged him vow me to it.[2] For my death,
I did propound it voluntarily, knowing
If he could not be safe in his own court,
Being a great duke, what hope then for us?

VITTORIA

This is your melancholy and despair.

FLAMINIO

Away!
Fool thou art to think that politicians

1 *at a dead lift*: in a sudden emergency
2 *He did . . . to it*: perhaps alluding to King Herod, who ordered his wife Mariam to be killed; Webster may have known Elizabeth Cary's *The Tragedy of Mariam* (1613)

Do use to kill the effects of injuries
And let the cause live. Shall we groan in irons,
Or be a shameful and a weighty burden
To a public scaffold? This is my resolve:
I would not live at any man's entreaty,
Nor die at any's bidding.

VITTORIA

Will you hear me?

FLAMINIO

My life hath done service to other men;
My death shall serve mine own turn. Make you ready.

VITTORIA

Do you mean to die indeed?

FLAMINIO

With as much pleasure
As e'er my father 'gat me.

VITTORIA [*Aside to* ZANCHE]

Are the doors locked?

ZANCHE [*Aside*]

Yes, madam.

VITTORIA

Are you grown an atheist? Will you turn your body,
Which is the goodly palace of the soul,
To the soul's slaughter-house? O the cursed devil,
Which doth present us with all other sins
Thrice candied[1] o'er; despair with gall and stibium,[2]
Yet we carouse it off[3] – [*Aside to* ZANCHE] Cry out for help!
– Makes us forsake that which was made for man,
The world, to sink to that was made for devils,
Eternal darkness.

ZANCHE

Help! Help!

1 *candied*: sugared 2 *stibium*: antimony, a poison
3 *despair... off*: unlike other sins, despair tastes bitter yet we drink it, prompting suicide

FLAMINIO

I'll stop your throat
With winter plums.[1]
[*He threatens* ZANCHE *with the pistols.*]

VITTORIA

I prithee, yet remember
Millions are now in graves which at last day
Like mandrakes shall rise shrieking.

FLAMINIO

Leave your prating,
For these are but grammatical[2] laments,
Feminine[3] arguments, and they move me
As some in pulpits move their auditory –
More with their exclamation[4] than sense
Of reason or sound doctrine.

ZANCHE [*Aside to* VITTORIA]

Gentle madam,
Seem to consent. Only persuade him teach
The way to death: let him die first.

VITTORIA [*Aside to* ZANCHE]
'Tis good; I apprehend it.
[*To* FLAMINIO] To kill oneself is meat that we must take
Like pills: not chew't but quickly swallow it.
The smart o'th' wound or weakness of the hand
May else bring treble torments.

FLAMINIO

I have held it
A wretched and most miserable life
Which is not able to die.

VITTORIA

Oh, but frailty –
Yet I am now resolved. Farewell, affliction!
Behold, Bracciano, I, that while you lived
Did make a flaming altar of my heart

1 *winter plums*: hard fruit, i.e., bullets
2 *grammatical* : conventional, merely following the rules
3 *Feminine*: i.e., weak 4 *exclamation*: emphatic speech

To sacrifice unto you, now am ready
To sacrifice heart and all. Farewell, Zanche.

ZANCHE
How, madam? Do you think that I'll outlive you,
Especially when my best self, Flaminio,
Goes the same voyage?

FLAMINIO
O most lovèd Moor!

ZANCHE [*To* FLAMINIO]
Only, by all my love, let me entreat you,
Since it is most necessary none of us
Do violence on ourselves, let you or I
Be her sad taster[1] – teach her how to die.

FLAMINIO
Thou dost instruct me nobly. Take these pistols.
[*He gives* VITTORIA *and* ZANCHE *two pistols each.*]
Because my hand is stained with blood already,
Two of these you shall level at my breast,
Th'other 'gainst your own, and so we'll die,
Most equally contented. But first, swear
Not to outlive me.

VITTORIA *and* [ZANCHE *the*] MOOR
Most religiously.

FLAMINIO
Then here's an end of me. Farewell, daylight!
And O contemptible physic,[2] that dost take
So long a study only to preserve
So short a life, I take my leave of thee.
(*Showing the pistols*) These are two cupping-glasses[3] that shall draw
All my infected blood out. Are you ready?

BOTH
Ready.

1 *taster*: a servant who tastes his master's food and drink to detect poison
2 *physic*: medical science
3 *cupping-glasses*: surgical vessels, heated and then placed on the body to draw off blood

FLAMINIO

Whither shall I go now? O Lucian, thy ridiculous purgatory![1] To find Alexander the Great cobbling shoes, Pompey tagging points,[2] and Julius Caesar making hair buttons,[3] Hannibal selling blacking,[4] and Augustus crying garlic, Charlemagne selling lists[5] by the dozen, and King Pippin[6] crying apples in a cart drawn with one horse.

Whether I resolve to fire, earth, water, air,
Or all the elements by scruples,[7] I know not,
Nor greatly care. Shoot, shoot!
Of all deaths the violent death is best,
For from ourselves it steals ourselves so fast,
The pain once apprehended is quite past.

They shoot and run to him and tread upon him.

VITTORIA

What, are you dropped?

FLAMINIO

I am mixed with earth already. As you are noble,
Perform your vows and bravely follow me.

VITTORIA

Whither? To hell?

ZANCHE

To most assured damnation.

VITTORIA

O thou most cursèd devil!

ZANCHE

Thou art caught –

1 *O Lucian . . . purgatory*: Lucian's *Menippos* includes such examples of great men's absurd fates

2 *tagging points*: fixing metal tips on the laces that held together Jacobean clothing

3 *hair buttons*: Caesar was famously bald

4 *blacking*: boot polish, here sold by Hannibal, who was black-skinned

5 *lists*: strips of cloth

6 *Pippin*: a variety of apple; the correct French spelling of the king's name is Pepin

7 *scruples*: small degrees

VITTORIA
In thine own engine. I tread the fire out
That would have been my ruin.

FLAMINIO
Will you be perjured? What a religious oath was Styx[1] that the gods never durst swear by and violate! Oh, that we had such an oath to minister, and to be so well kept in our courts of justice.

VITTORIA
Think whither thou art going.

ZANCHE
And remember
What villainies thou hast acted.

VITTORIA
This thy death
Shall make me, like a blazing, ominous star,[2]
Look up and tremble.

FLAMINIO
Oh, I am caught with a springe![3]

VITTORIA
You see the fox comes many times short[4] home;
'Tis here proved true.

FLAMINIO
Killed with a couple of braches.[5]

VITTORIA
No fitter off'ring for the infernal furies
Than one in whom they reigned while he was living.

FLAMINIO
Oh, the way's dark and horrid! I cannot see.
Shall I have no company?

1 *Styx*: river in the classical underworld, used by the ancients to swear by
2 *ominous star*: a comet, thought to foretell the fall of princes
3 *springe*: snare for trapping birds and small mammals
4 *short*: without his tail 5 *braches*: bitches (female dogs)

VITTORIA

Oh, yes, thy sins
Do run before thee to fetch fire from hell
To light thee thither.

FLAMINIO

Oh, I smell soot,
Most stinking soot; the chimney is a-fire.
My liver's parboiled like Scotch holy-bread.[1]
There's a plumber laying pipes in my guts; it scalds.
Wilt thou outlive me?

ZANCHE

Yes, and drive a stake
Through thy body;[2] for we'll give it out
Thou didst this violence upon thyself.

FLAMINIO

O cunning devils! Now I have tried your love
And doubled all your reaches.[3] I am not wounded!

FLAMINIO *riseth.*

The pistols held no bullets. 'Twas a plot
To prove your kindness to me, and I live
To punish your ingratitude. I knew,
One time or other, you would find a way
To give me a strong potion. O men
That lie upon your death-beds, and are haunted
With howling wives, ne'er trust them! They'll remarry
Ere the worm pierce your winding-sheet, ere the spider
Make a thin curtain for your epitaphs.
How cunning you were to discharge! Do you practise at the artillery yard?[4] Trust a woman? Never, never! Bracciano be my precedent. We lay our souls to pawn to the devil for a little pleasure, and a woman makes the bill of sale. That ever man should marry! For one Hypermnestra that saved her lord and husband, forty-nine of her sisters cut their husbands'

1 *Scotch holy-bread*: sodden sheep's liver
2 *drive . . . body*: treatment of suicides who were then buried at crossroads
3 *reaches*: plots, contrivances
4 *artillery yard*: in 1610 the Artillery Gardens at Billingsgate became a popular resort for gentlemen and merchants to practise shooting

throats all in one night.[1] There was a shoal of virtuous horse-leeches.[2]
Here are two other instruments.[3]

Enter LODOVICO, GASPARO [*still disguised as Capuchins, with swords aloft*], PEDRO [*and*] CARLO.

VITTORIA
Help, help!

FLAMINIO
What noise is that? Ha? False keys i'th' court!

LODOVICO
We have brought you a masque.[4]

FLAMINIO
A matachin[5] it seems,
By your drawn swords. Churchmen turned revellers?

CONSPIRATORS
Isabella, Isabella!

[*They throw off their disguises.*]

LODOVICO
Do you know us now?

FLAMINIO
Lodovico and Gasparo!

LODOVICO
Yes, and that Moor the Duke gave pension to
Was the great Duke of Florence.

VITTORIA
Oh, we are lost.

[GASPARO *seizes* VITTORIA. PEDRO *takes* FLAMINIO. CARLO *seizes* ZANCHE.]

1 *For one . . . night*: Danaus learned in an oracle that he would be killed by one of his brother's fifty sons; he married his fifty daughters to those sons and ordered them to kill their husbands on the wedding night; only Hypermnestra refused

2 *horse-leeches*: bloodsuckers, rhetoricians

3 *instruments*: i.e., Vittoria and Zanche

4 *masque*: Jacobean courtly entertainment, usually featuring masked dancers; often used to bring revenge tragedy to a close, e.g., Middleton's *The Revenger's Tragedy*

5 *matachin*: sword dance, with masks and elaborate costumes

FLAMINIO
You shall not take justice from forth my hands.
Oh, let me kill her! I'll cut my safety
Through your coats of steel. Fate's a spaniel:
We cannot beat it from us. What remains now?
Let all that do ill take this precedent:
Man may his fate foresee, but not prevent.
And of all axioms this shall win the prize:
'Tis better to be fortunate than wise.

GASPARO
Bind him to the pillar.
[PEDRO *ties up* FLAMINIO.]

VITTORIA
Oh, your gentle pity!
I have seen a blackbird that would sooner fly
To a man's bosom, than to stay[1] the gripe
Of the fierce sparrow-hawk.

GASPARO
Your hope deceives you.

VITTORIA
If Florence be i'th' court, would he would kill me.

GASPARO
Fool! Princes give rewards with their own hands,
But death or punishment by the hands of others.

LODOVICO [*To* FLAMINIO]
Sirrah, you once did strike me – I'll strike you
Into the centre.[2]

FLAMINIO
Thou'lt do it like a hangman, a base hangman,
Not like a noble fellow, for thou seest
I cannot strike again.

LODOVICO
Dost laugh?

1 *stay*: wait for
2 *centre*: heart, soul

FLAMINIO
Wouldst have me die, as I was born, in whining?
GASPARO
Recommend yourself to heaven.
FLAMINIO
No, I will carry mine own commendations thither.
LODOVICO
Oh, could I kill you forty times a day
And use't four year together, 'twere too little!
Nought grieves's but that you are too few to feed
The famine of our vengeance. What dost think on?
FLAMINIO
Nothing, of nothing. Leave thy idle[1] questions.
I am i'th' way to study a long silence;
To prate were idle. I remember nothing.
There's nothing of so infinite vexation
As man's own thoughts.
LODOVICO [*To* VITTORIA]
O thou glorious strumpet,
Could I divide thy breath from this pure air
When't leaves thy body, I would suck it up
And breathe't upon some dunghill.
VITTORIA
You my death's-man?
Methinks thou dost not look horrid enough;
Thou hast too good a face to be a hangman.
If thou be, do thy office in right form:[2]
Fall down upon thy knees, and ask forgiveness.
LODOVICO
Oh, thou hast been a most prodigious comet,
But I'll cut off your train.[3] [*To* CARLO] Kill the Moor first.

1 *idle*: foolish, irrelevant
2 *Do . . . form*: executioners conventionally sought their victim's forgiveness beforehand
3 *train*: tail of the comet, but also attendants

VITTORIA

You shall not kill her first. Behold my breast!
I will be waited on in death; my servant
Shall never go before me.

GASPARO

Are you so brave?

VITTORIA

Yes, I shall welcome death
As princes do some great ambassadors:
I'll meet thy weapon halfway.

LODOVICO

Thou dost tremble;
Methinks fear should dissolve thee into air.

VITTORIA

Oh, thou art deceived. I am too true a woman:
Conceit[1] can never kill me. I'll tell thee what,
I will not in my death shed one base tear,
Or if look pale, for want of blood not fear.

CARLO

Thou art my task, black fury.

ZANCHE

I have blood
As red as either of theirs. Wilt drink some?
'Tis good for the falling sickness.[2] I am proud
Death cannot alter my complexion,
For I shall ne'er look pale.

LODOVICO

Strike, strike,
With a joint motion!

[*They stab* VITTORIA, FLAMINIO *and* ZANCHE.]

VITTORIA

'Twas a manly blow.
The next thou giv'st, murder some sucking infant,
And then thou wilt be famous.

1 *Conceit*: the imagining of death, female vanity, the conception of a child
2 *falling sickness*: epilepsy

FLAMINIO

Oh, what blade is't?
A Toledo or an English fox?[1]
I ever thought a cutler[2] should distinguish
The cause of my death, rather than a doctor.
Search my wound deeper; tent[3] it with the steel
That made it.

VITTORIA

Oh, my greatest sin lay in my blood.[4]
Now my blood pays for't.

FLAMINIO

Th'art a noble sister.
I love thee now. If woman do breed man
She ought to teach him manhood. Fare thee well.
Know many glorious women, that are famed
For masculine virtue, have been vicious;
Only a happier silence did betide them:
She hath no faults who hath the art to hide them.

VITTORIA

My soul, like to a ship in a black storm,
Is driven I know not whither.

FLAMINIO

Then cast anchor.
Prosperity doth bewitch men, seeming clear,
But seas do laugh, show white, when rocks are near.
We cease to grieve, cease to be Fortune's slaves,
Nay, cease to die by dying.
[ZANCHE *dies.*]
Art thou gone?
[*To* VITTORIA] And thou so near the bottom? False report
Which says that women vie with the nine Muses
For nine tough, durable lives. I do not look
Who went before, nor who shall follow me.

1 *Toledo . . . fox*: different kinds of short sword
2 *cutler*: a trader in knives and cutting implements
3 *tent*: clean out the wound to heal it, but also 'heal' Flaminio by stabbing him again
4 *blood*: sexual passion, kinship

No, at myself I will begin and end:
While we look up to heaven we confound
Knowledge with knowledge. Oh, I am in a mist!

VITTORIA

Oh, happy they that never saw the court,
Nor ever knew great man but by report. VITTORIA *dies.*

FLAMINIO

I recover, like a spent taper, for a flash –
And instantly go out.
Let all that belong to great men remember th'old wives' tradition, to be like the lions i'th' Tower on Candlemas day, to mourn if the sun shine, for fear of the pitiful remainder of winter to come.[1]
'Tis well; yet there's some goodness in my death:
My life was a black charnel. I have caught
An everlasting cold; I have lost my voice[2]
Most irrecoverably. Farewell, glorious villains!
This busy trade[3] of life appears most vain,
Since rest breeds rest, where all seek pain by pain.
Let no harsh, flattering bells resound my knell.
Strike, thunder, and strike loud to my farewell!

[FLAMINIO] *dies.*

ENGLISH AMBASSADOR [*Within*]

This way, this way. Break ope the doors! This way.

LODOVICO

Ha, are we betrayed?
Why then, let's constantly[4] die all together,
And having finished this most noble deed,
Defy the worst of fate, not fear to bleed.

Enter AMBASSADORS *and* GIOVANNI [*with* GUARDS].

ENGLISH AMBASSADOR

Keep back the Prince! Shoot, shoot!

[GUARDS *shoot at the conspirators.*]

1 *Let all . . . to come*: it was proverbial that if Candlemas day (2nd February) was fair, winter would last longer

2 *I . . . voice*: perhaps another metatheatrical joke, given the length of Flaminio's part

3 *trade*: habitual course 4 *constantly*: resolutely

LODOVICO

Oh, I am wounded!
I fear I shall be ta'en.

GIOVANNI

You bloody villains,
By what authority have you committed
This massacre?

LODOVICO

By thine.

GIOVANNI

Mine?

LODOVICO

Yes; thy uncle,
Which is a part of thee, enjoined us to't.
Thou know'st me, I am sure. I am Count Lodovic;
And thy most noble uncle, in disguise,
Was last night in thy court.

GIOVANNI

Ha?

CARLO

Yes, that Moor
Thy father chose his pensioner.

GIOVANNI

He turned murderer?
Away with them to prison and to torture! [GUARDS *seize hold of them*]
All that have hands in this shall taste our justice,
As I hope heaven.

LODOVICO

I do glory yet
That I can call this act mine own. For my part,
The rack, the gallows and the torturing wheel
Shall be but sound sleeps to me. Here's my rest:
I limned[1] this night-piece,[2] and it was my best.

1 *limned*: painted, fashioned
2 *night-piece*: painting of a night scene or other tragic composition

GIOVANNI

Remove the bodies.
[*To the* ENGLISH AMBASSADOR] See, my honoured lord,
What use you ought make of their punishment.
Let guilty men remember their black deeds
Do lean on crutches made of slender reeds. [*Exeunt.*]

Instead of an Epilogue only this of Martial supplies me:

Haec fuerint nobis praemia si placui.[1]

For the action of the play, 'twas generally well, and I dare affirm, with the joint testimony of some of their own quality[2] *– for the true imitation of life, without striving to make nature a monster – the best that ever became them; whereof, as I make a general acknowledgement, so in particular I must remember the well-approved industry of my friend, Master Perkins,*[3] *and confess the worth of his action did crown both the beginning and end.*

FINIS.

1 *Haec ... placui*: 'These things will be our reward, if I have pleased' (Martial, 2.91.8)
2 *quality*: profession
3 *Master Perkins*: Richard Perkins, leading player of the Queen Anne's Men, probably took the role of Flaminio

JOHN WEBSTER

THE DUCHESS OF MALFI

LIST OF CHARACTERS

The DUCHESS *of Malfi, a young widow, later secretly married to Antonio*
FERDINAND, *Duke of Calabria, the Duchess's twin*
The CARDINAL *of Aragon, elder brother of the Duchess and Ferdinand*

Daniel de BOSOLA *the Duchess's Master of the Horse, spying for the Cardinal and Ferdinand*
ANTONIO *Bologna the Duchess's steward, later her husband*
CARIOLA *the Duchess's waiting-maid*
DELIO *a courtier, Antonio's friend*
THREE CHILDREN[1] *of the Duchess and Antonio*

JULIA *wife of Castruchio, mistress of the Cardinal*
CASTRUCHIO[2] *an old courtier, Julia's husband*
OLD LADY *a courtier*
DOCTOR

Count MALATESTE *a Roman courtier*
Marquis of PESCARA *a soldier and courtier*
RODERIGO, GRISOLAN, SILVIO *courtiers at Amalfi*
FOROBOSCO* *an official at the Duchess's court*

*Court Officers, Two Pilgrims, Eight Madmen, Executioners, Servants, Attendants, Ladies-in-Waiting, Guards, Churchmen**

*non-speaking parts

1 *THREE CHILDREN*: a small boy and girl and a male infant, perhaps represented by a doll

2 *CASTRUCHIO*: his name suggests 'castrated', providing a motive for Julia's sexual betrayal

To the Right Honourable GEORGE HARDING,[1] BARON BERKELEY *of Berkeley Castle and Knight of the Order of the Bath to the Illustrious Prince* CHARLES.

My Noble Lord,

That I may present my excuse why, being a stranger to your Lordship, I offer this poem[2] to your patronage, I plead this warrant: men who never saw the sea yet desire to behold that regiment of waters, choose some eminent river to guide them thither, and make that, as it were, their conduct[3] or postilion.[4] By the like ingenious means has your fame arrived at my knowledge, receiving it from some of worth who, both in contemplation and practice, owe to your Honour their clearest service. I do not altogether look up at your title; the ancient'st nobility being but a relic of time past, and the truest honour, indeed, being for a man to confer honour on himself – which your learning strives to propagate, and shall make you arrive at the dignity of a great example. I am confident this work is not unworthy your Honour's perusal; for by such poems as this, poets have kissed the hands of great princes, and drawn their gentle eyes to look down upon their sheets of paper, when the poets themselves were bound up in their winding-sheets. The like courtesy from your Lordship shall make you live in your grave, and laurel spring out of it, when the ignorant scorners of the Muses, that, like worms in libraries, seem to live only to destroy learning, shall wither, neglected and forgotten. This

1 *GEORGE HARDING*: eighth Baron of Berkeley (1601–58), son and grandson to the Lords Hunsdon, who patronized the Lord Chamberlain's Men, and a prominent literary patron, the dedicatee of Robert Burton's *The Anatomy of Melancholy* (1621)

2 *poem*: fictional work 3 *conduct*: conductor 4 *postilion*: escort

work, and myself, I humbly present to your approved censure;[1] it being the utmost of my wishes to have your honourable self my weighty and perspicuous comment; which grace so done me, shall ever be acknowledged

By your Lordship's in all duty and observance,
John Webster

1 *approved censure*: tested judgement

In the just worth of that well-deserver,
Mr JOHN WEBSTER, *and upon this*
masterpiece of tragedy.

In this thou imitat'st one rich and wise,
That sees his good deeds done before he dies.
As he by works, thou by this work of fame
Hast well provided for thy living name.
To trust to others' honourings is worth's crime;
Thy monument is raised in thy lifetime,
And 'tis most just; for every worthy man
Is his own marble, and his merit can
Cut him to any figure, and express
More art than Death's cathedral palaces,
Where royal ashes keep their court. Thy note
Be ever plainness; 'tis the richest coat.
Thy epitaph only the title be,
Write 'Duchess' – that will fetch a tear for thee.
For who e'er saw this Duchess live and die
That could get off under a bleeding eye?

In Tragaediam.
Ut lux ex tenebris ictu percussa Tonantis,
Illa, ruina malis, claris fit vita poetis.[1]

Thomas Middletonus,[2] *Poeta & Chron*
Londinensis

1 *In . . . poetis*: 'To Tragedy', 'As light springs from darkness at the stroke of the Thunderer, /May it – ruin to evil! – be life for famous poets'
2 *Thomas Middleton*: poet and dramatist (1580–1628), who collaborated with Webster, appointed to the post of London Chronologer in 1620

To his friend, Master John Webster, upon his *Duchess of Malfi*

I never saw thy Duchess till the day
That she was lively bodied in thy play.
Howe'er she answered[1] her low-rated love,
Her brothers' anger did so fatal prove;
Yet, my opinion is, she might speak[2] more,
But never in her life so well before.[3]

William Rowley[4]

To the reader of the author, and his DUCHESS OF MALFI

Crown him a poet, whom nor Rome nor Greece
Transcend in all theirs, for a masterpiece
In which, whiles words and matter change, and men
Act one another, he, from whose clear pen
They all took life, to Memory hath lent
A lasting fame, to raise his monument.

John Ford

1 *answered*: defended 2 *speak*: have spoken
3 *so well before*: i.e., as in the play
4 *William Rowley*: (*c.* 1585–1626) dramatist, actor and playwright, who collaborated with Webster

ACT 1

Scene 1

[*Enter*] ANTONIO *and* DELIO.

DELIO

You are welcome to your country, dear Antonio.
You have been long in France, and you return
A very formal Frenchman in your habit.[1]
How do you like the French court?

ANTONIO

I admire it;
In seeking to reduce both state and people
To a fixed order, their judicious king
Begins at home: quits first his royal palace
Of flatt'ring sycophants, of dissolute
And infamous persons – which[2] he sweetly terms
His Master's masterpiece, the work of heaven –
Consid'ring duly that a prince's court
Is like a common fountain, whence should flow
Pure silver drops in general; but if't chance
Some cursed example poison't near the head,
Death and diseases through the whole land spread.
And what is't makes this blessèd government
But a most provident council, who dare freely
Inform him the corruption of the times?
Though some o'th' court hold it presumption
To instruct princes what they ought to do,
It is a noble duty to inform them
What they ought to foresee.
[*Enter* BOSOLA.]

1 *habit*: dress 2 *which*: i.e., the act of clearing out sycophants

Here comes Bosola,
The only court-gall;[1] yet I observe his railing[2]
Is not for simple love of piety;
Indeed, he rails at those things which he wants;
Would be as lecherous, covetous or proud,
Bloody or envious, as any man,
If he had means to be so.
[*Enter* CARDINAL.]
Here's the Cardinal.
[ANTONIO *and* DELIO *stand aside.*]

BOSOLA
I do haunt you still.

CARDINAL
So.

BOSOLA
I have done you
Better service than to be slighted thus.
Miserable age, where only the[3] reward
Of doing well is the doing of it!

CARDINAL
You enforce your merit too much.

BOSOLA
I fell into the galleys in your service, where, for two years together, I wore two towels instead of a shirt, with a knot on the shoulder, after the fashion of a Roman mantle. Slighted thus? I will thrive some way: blackbirds fatten best in hard weather; why not in these dog-days?[4]

CARDINAL
Would you could become honest.

BOSOLA
With all your divinity, do but direct me the way to it. I have known many travel far for it, and yet return as arrant knaves

1 *court-gall*: a court satirist or malcontent 2 *railing*: abusive language
3 *only the*: the only
4 *dog-days*: a period of oppressively hot weather in which malignant influences were thought to prevail

as they went forth, because they carried themselves always along with them. [*Exit* CARDINAL.]
Are you gone? [*To* ANTONIO *and* DELIO] Some fellows, they say, are possessed with the devil, but this great fellow were able to possess the greatest devil and make him worse.

ANTONIO

He hath denied thee some suit?

BOSOLA

He and his brother are like plum trees that grow crooked over standing[1] pools: they are rich, and o'erladen with fruit, but none but crows, pies[2] and caterpillars feed on them. Could I be one of their flattering panders, I would hang on their ears like a horse-leech till I were full, and then drop off. I pray, leave me. Who would rely upon these miserable dependences in expectation to be advanced tomorrow? What creature ever fed worse than hoping Tantalus?[3] Nor ever died any man more fearfully than he that hoped for a pardon. There are rewards for hawks and dogs when they have done us service, but for a soldier that hazards his limbs in a battle – nothing but a kind of geometry is his last supportation.

DELIO

Geometry?

BOSOLA

Ay, to hang in a fair pair of slings, take his latter swing in the world upon an honourable pair of crutches, from hospital to hospital. Fare ye well, sir; and yet do not you scorn us, for places in the court are but like beds in the hospital, where this man's head lies at that man's foot, and so lower and lower. [*Exit* BOSOLA.]

DELIO

I knew this fellow seven years in the galleys
For a notorious murder, and 'twas thought
The Cardinal suborned it. He was released

1 *standing*: stagnant 2 *pies*: magpies
3 *Tantalus*: a mythological figure, punished in Hades with hunger and thirst, while food and drink remained tantalisingly beyond his reach

By the French general, Gaston de Foix,[1]
When he recovered Naples.

ANTONIO

'Tis great pity
He should be thus neglected; I have heard
He's very valiant. This foul melancholy
Will poison all his goodness, for, I'll tell you,
If too immoderate sleep be truly said
To be an inward rust unto the soul,
It then doth follow want of action
Breeds all black malcontents, and their close rearing,
Like moths in cloth, do hurt for want of wearing.

ACT 1

Scene 2

[*Enter*] CASTRUCCIO, SILVIO, RODERIGO *and* GRISOLAN.

DELIO

The presence[2] 'gins to fill. You promised me
To make me the partaker of the natures
Of some of your great courtiers.

ANTONIO

The Lord Cardinal's,
And other strangers that are now in court?
I shall.

[*Enter* FERDINAND.]

Here comes the great Calabrian Duke.

[ANTONIO *and* DELIO *stand aside.*]

FERDINAND

Who took the ring[3] oft'nest?

1 *Gaston de Foix*: historically, he was a child when Naples was recovered in 1501

2 *presence*: presence chamber, where a monarch or noble would receive visitors

3 *took the ring*: a game in which jousters vied to carry a ring on the end of their lance, introduced to the English court by James I

SILVIO
Antonio Bologna, my lord.

FERDINAND
Our sister Duchess's great master of her household? Give him the jewel.[1] When shall we leave this sportive action and fall to action indeed?

CASTRUCCIO
Methinks, my lord, you should not desire to go to war in person.

FERDINAND [*Aside*]
Now for some gravity – why, my lord?

CASTRUCCIO
It is fitting a soldier arise to be a prince, but not necessary a prince descend to be a captain.

FERDINAND
No?

CASTRUCCIO
No, my lord, he were far better do it by a deputy.

FERDINAND
Why should he not as well sleep or eat by a deputy? This might take idle, offensive and base office from him, whereas the other deprives him of honour.

CASTRUCCIO
Believe my experience: that realm is never long in quiet where the ruler is a soldier.

FERDINAND
Thou told'st me thy wife could not endure fighting.

CASTRUCCIO
True, my lord.

FERDINAND
And of a jest she broke, of a captain she met, full of wounds – I have forgot it.

CASTRUCCIO
She told him, my lord, he was a pitiful fellow to lie, like the children of Ismael, all in tents.[2]

1 *jewel*: a tournament prize, also anticipates Antonio's winning of the Duchess and her chastity

2 *tents*: outdoor shelters, dressings for a wound

FERDINAND

Why, there's a wit were able to undo all the chirurgeons[1] o'the city; for although gallants should quarrel, and had drawn their weapons and were ready to go to it, yet her persuasions would make them put up.[2]

CASTRUCCIO

That she would, my lord,

FERDINAND

How do you like my Spanish jennet?[3]

RODERIGO

He is all fire.

FERDINAND

I am of Pliny's opinion:[4] I think he was begot by the wind. He runs as if he were ballasted[5] with quicksilver.

SILVIO

True, my lord, he reels[6] from the tilt[7] often.

RODERIGO [*and*] GRISOLAN

Ha, ha, ha!

FERDINAND

Why do you laugh? Methinks you that are courtiers should be my touchwood – take fire when I give fire; that is, laugh when I laugh, were the subject never so witty.

CASTRUCCIO

True, my lord. I myself have heard a very good jest, and have scorned to seem to have so silly a wit as to understand it.

FERDINAND

But I can laugh at your fool, my lord.

CASTRUCCIO

He cannot speak, you know, but he makes faces. My lady cannot abide him.

FERDINAND

No?

1 *chirurgeons*: surgeons 2 *put up*: sheathe their weapons
3 *Spanish jennet*: a light, sporting horse
4 *Pliny's opinion*: Pliny claimed that Portuguese mares conceived by means of the West Wind, which made their colts swift
5 *ballasted*: weighted with 6 *reels*: swings about, staggers away from
7 *tilt*: listing of a ship, jousting tournament and also copulation

CASTRUCCIO

Nor endure to be in merry company, for she says too much laughing and too much company fills her too full of the wrinkle.

FERDINAND

I would then have a mathematical instrument made for her face, that she might not laugh out of compass.[1] I shall shortly visit you at Milan, Lord Silvio.

SILVIO

Your grace shall arrive most welcome.

FERDINAND

You are a good horseman, Antonio. You have excellent riders in France. What do you think of good horsemanship?

ANTONIO [*coming forward*]

Nobly, my lord. As out of the Grecian horse[2] issued many famous princes, so out of brave horsemanship arise the first sparks of growing resolution that raise the mind to noble action.

FERDINAND

You have bespoke it worthily.

[*Enter* CARDINAL, DUCHESS, CARIOLA, JULIA *and* ATTENDANTS.]

SILVIO

Your brother, the Lord Cardinal, and sister Duchess.

CARDINAL

Are the galleys come about?

GRISOLAN

They are, my lord.

FERDINAND

Here's the Lord Silvio is come to take his leave.

[*All except* ANTONIO *and* DELIO *stand apart.*]

DELIO [*To* ANTONIO]

Now, sir, your promise: what's that Cardinal –
I mean his temper? They say he's a brave fellow,

1 *out of compass*: immoderately

2 *Grecian horse*: a wooden horse, filled with Greek soldiers, which was taken inside the besieged city of Troy and led to its destruction

Will play his five thousand crowns at tennis, dance,
Court ladies, and one that hath fought single combats.

ANTONIO

Some such flashes superficially hang on him, for form;[1] but observe his inward character: he is a melancholy churchman. The spring in his face is nothing but the engendering of toads.[2] Where he is jealous of any man he lays worse plots for them than ever was imposed on Hercules, for he strews in his way flatterers, panders, intelligencers,[3] atheists, and a thousand such political monsters. He should have been Pope, but instead of coming to it by the primitive decency of the Church, he did bestow bribes so largely, and so impudently, as if he would have carried it away without heaven's knowledge. Some good he hath done –

DELIO

You have given too much of him. What's his brother?

ANTONIO

The Duke there? A most perverse and turbulent nature;
What appears in him mirth is merely outside.
If he laugh heartily, it is to laugh
All honesty out of fashion.

DELIO

Twins?

ANTONIO

In quality.
He speaks with others' tongues, and hears men's suits
With others' ears; will seem to sleep o'th' bench
Only to entrap offenders in their answers;
Dooms men to death by information,[4]
Rewards by hearsay.

DELIO

Then the law to him
Is like a foul, black cobweb to a spider:

1 *form*: external appearance
2 *The spring . . . toads*: his capacity for tears, usually a sign of humanity, is the slime which breeds toads
3 *intelligencers*: spies 4 *information*: private intelligence

He makes it his dwelling, and a prison
To entangle those shall feed him.

ANTONIO

Most true.
He never pays debts, unless they be shrewd turns,[1]
And those he will confess that he doth owe.
Last, for his brother there, the Cardinal:
They that do flatter him most say oracles
Hang at his lips; and verily I believe them,
For the devil speaks in them.
But for their sister, the right noble Duchess,
You never fixed your eye on three fair medals,
Cast in one figure, of so different temper.
For her discourse, it is so full of rapture
You only will begin then to be sorry
When she doth end her speech; and wish, in wonder,
She held it less vainglory to talk much,
Than your penance to hear her.[2] Whilst she speaks,
She throws upon a man so sweet a look
That it were able raise one to a galliard[3]
That lay in a dead palsy, and to dote
On that sweet countenance; but in that look
There speaketh so divine a continence
As cuts off all lascivious and vain hope.
Her days are practised in such noble virtue
That sure her nights – nay more, her very sleeps –
Are more in heaven than other ladies' shrifts.[4]
Let all sweet ladies break their flatt'ring glasses,
And dress themselves in her.[5]

DELIO

Fie, Antonio,
You play the wire-drawer[6] with her commendations.

1 *shrewd turns*: injuries
2 *Than . . . her*: than you hold it spiritually redemptive
3 *galliard*: an energetic dance 4 *shrifts*: confessions
5 *dress themselves in her*: use her as their mirror, model themselves on her
6 *play the wire-drawer*: spin out

ANTONIO
I'll case the picture up.[1] Only thus much –
All her particular worth grows to this sum:
She stains[2] the time past, lights the time to come.

CARIOLA
You must attend my lady in the gallery,
Some half an hour hence.

ANTONIO
I shall.
[*Exeunt* ANTONIO AND DELIO.]

FERDINAND
Sister, I have a suit to you.

DUCHESS
To me, sir?

FERDINAND
A gentleman here, Daniel de Bosola,
One that was in the galleys –

DUCHESS
Yes, I know him.

FERDINAND
A worthy fellow h'is. Pray, let me entreat for
The provisorship of your horse.[3]

DUCHESS
Your knowledge of him
Commends him and prefers him.

FERDINAND
Call him hither.
[*Exit* ATTENDANT.]
We are now upon parting. Good Lord Silvio,
Do us commend to all our noble friends
At the leaguer.[4]

1 *case . . . up*: put the picture away in its case
2 *stains*: eclipses, but also makes appear tainted
3 *provisorship . . . horse*: an important court appointment, given by Elizabeth I to her favourite (and sometime potential husband) the Earl of Leicester
4 *leaguer*: military camp

SILVIO
Sir, I shall.
DUCHESS
You are for Milan?
SILVIO
I am.
DUCHESS
Bring the caroches.[1] We'll bring you down to the haven.
[*Exeunt all but* CARDINAL *and* FERDINAND.]
CARDINAL
Be sure you entertain that Bosola
For your intelligence.[2] I would not be seen in't;
And therefore many times I have slighted him
When he did court our furtherance,[3] as this morning.
FERDINAND
Antonio, the great master of her household,
Had been far fitter.
CARDINAL
You are deceived in him;
His nature is too honest for such business.
[*Enter* BOSOLA.]
He comes. I'll leave you. [*Exit* CARDINAL.]
BOSOLA
I was lured to you.
FERDINAND
My brother here, the Cardinal, could never
Abide you.
BOSOLA
Never since he was in my debt.
FERDINAND
Maybe some oblique character in your face
Made him suspect you?

1 *caroches*: luxurious coaches for town use
2 *entertain . . . intelligence*: keep Bosola on the payroll as your spy
3 *court our furtherance*: ask us for reward or promotion

BOSOLA

Doth he study physiognomy?
There's no more credit to be given to th'face
Than to a sick man's urine, which some call
The physician's whore because she cozens[1] him.
He did suspect me wrongfully.

FERDINAND

For that
You must give great men leave to take their times.
Distrust doth cause us seldom be deceived;
You see the oft shaking of the cedar tree
Fastens it more at root.

BOSOLA

Yet take heed,
For to suspect a friend unworthily
Instructs him the next[2] way to suspect you,
And prompts him to deceive you.

FERDINAND

There's gold.

[*He gives* BOSOLA *money.*]

BOSOLA

So:
What follows? Never rained such showers as these
Without thunderbolts i'th' tail of them.[3]
Whose throat must I cut?

FERDINAND

Your inclination to shed blood rides post[4]
Before my occasion to use you. I give you that
To live i'th' court here, and observe the Duchess,
To note all the particulars of her 'haviour:
What suitors do solicit her for marriage,
And whom she best affects. She's a young widow;
I would not have her marry again.

1 *cozens*: deceives 2 *next*: nearest

3 *showers . . . them*: an allusion to Jupiter, who famously wielded thunderbolts, but visited Danae in a shower of gold

4 *rides post*: runs ahead

BOSOLA

No, sir?

FERDINAND

Do not you ask the reason, but be satisfied
I say I would not.

BOSOLA

It seems you would create me
One of your familiars.[1]

FERDINAND

Familiar? What's that?

BOSOLA

Why, a very quaint,[2] invisible devil in flesh:
An intelligencer.

FERDINAND

Such a kind of thriving thing
I would wish thee, and ere long thou may'st arrive
At a higher place by't.

BOSOLA [*scorning the money*]

Take your devils,
Which hell calls angels.[3] These cursed gifts would make
You a corrupter, me an impudent traitor;
And should I take these they'd take me to hell.

FERDINAND

Sir, I'll take nothing from you that I have given.
There is a place that I procured for you
This morning: the provisorship o'th' horse.
Have you heard on't?

BOSOLA

No.

FERDINAND

'Tis yours. Is't not worth thanks?

1 *familiars*: servants, intimate friends, also spirits through whom magic is worked

2 *quaint*: cunning

3 *angels*: gold coins, bearing an image of St Michael killing a dragon

BOSOLA
I would have you curse yourself now, that your bounty,
Which makes men truly noble, e'er should make
Me a villain. Oh, that to avoid ingratitude
For the good deed you have done me, I must do
All the ill man can invent! Thus the devil
Candies all sins o'er, and what heaven terms vile,
That names he complemental.[1]

FERDINAND
Be yourself:
Keep your old garb of melancholy. 'Twill express
You envy those that stand above your reach,
Yet strive not to come near 'em. This will gain
Access to private lodgings, where yourself
May, like a politic[2] dormouse[3] –

BOSOLA
As I have seen some
Feed in a lord's dish,[4] half asleep, not seeming
To listen to any talk, and yet these rogues
Have cut his throat in a dream. What's my place?
The provisorship o'th' horse? Say, then, my corruption
Grew out of horse-dung. I am your creature.

FERDINAND
Away!

BOSOLA
Let good men for good deeds covet good fame,
Since place and riches oft are bribes of shame.
Sometimes the devil doth preach. *Exit* BOSOLA.

[*Enter* CARDINAL *and* DUCHESS.]

CARDINAL [*To* DUCHESS]
We are to part from you, and your own discretion
Must now be your director.

1 *complemental*: a mark of courtly accomplishment 2 *politic*: cunning
3 *dormouse*: according to Pliny, the dormouse sleeps all winter and thereby renews its vigour
4 *Feed . . . dish*: dine at a lord's table

FERDINAND

You are a widow:
You know already what man is; and, therefore,
Let not youth, high promotion, eloquence –

CARDINAL

No, nor anything without the addition, honour,
Sway your high blood.

FERDINAND

Marry? They are most luxurious[1]
Will wed twice.

CARDINAL

Oh, fie!

FERDINAND

Their livers[2] are more spotted
Than Laban's sheep.[3]

DUCHESS

Diamonds are of most value,
They say, that have passed through most jewellers' hands.

FERDINAND

Whores, by that rule, are precious.

DUCHESS

Will you hear me?
I'll never marry.

CARDINAL

So most widows say,
But commonly that motion[4] lasts no longer
Than the turning of an hour-glass; the funeral sermon
And it end both together.

FERDINAND

Now hear me:
You live in a rank pasture here, i'th' court.
There is a kind of honey-dew[5] that's deadly:
'Twill poison your fame. Look to't. Be not cunning,
For they whose faces do belie their hearts

1 *luxurious*: lecherous 2 *livers*: regarded as the seat of passion, including lust
3 *Laban's sheep*: parti-coloured, see Genesis 30:31–3
4 *motion*: impulse 5 *honey-dew*: a sweet, sticky substance found on plants

Are witches ere they arrive at twenty years,
Ay, and give the devil suck.

DUCHESS

This is terrible good counsel.

FERDINAND

Hypocrisy is woven of a fine, small thread,
Subtler than Vulcan's engine.[1] Yet, believe't,
Your darkest actions – nay, your privat'st thoughts –
Will come to light.

CARDINAL

You may flatter yourself,
And take your own choice: privately be married
Under the eves of night –

FERDINAND

Think't the best voyage
That e'er you made, like the irregular crab
Which, though't goes backward, thinks that it goes right
Because it goes its own way. But observe:
Such weddings may more properly be said
To be executed than celebrated.

CARDINAL

The marriage night
Is the entrance into some prison.

FERDINAND

And those joys,
Those lustful pleasures, are like heavy sleeps
Which do forerun man's mischief.

CARDINAL

Fare you well.
Wisdom begins at the end:[2] remember it.

[*Exit* CARDINAL.]

DUCHESS

I think this speech between you both was studied,[3]
It came so roundly off.

1 *Vulcan's engine*: Vulcan used a net to catch the adulterous Venus and Mars
2 *Wisdom . . . end*: proverbial, e.g., 'Think on the end before you begin'
3 *studied*: rehearsed

FERDINAND

You are my sister;
This was my father's poniard [*drawing a dagger*].
Do you see?
I'd be loath to see't look rusty,[1] 'cause 'twas his.
I would have you to give o'er these chargeable[2] revels;
A visor and a masque are whispering-rooms
That were ne'er built for goodness. Fare ye well –
And women like that part which, like the lamprey,[3]
Hath ne'er a bone in't.

DUCHESS

Fie, sir![4]

FERDINAND

Nay,
I mean the tongue: variety of courtship.
What cannot a neat knave with a smooth tale[5]
Make a woman believe? Farewell, lusty widow.
[*Exit* FERDINAND.]

DUCHESS

Shall this move me? If all my royal kindred
Lay in my way unto this marriage
I'd make them my low foot-steps.[6] And, even now,
Even in this hate, as men in some great battles,
By apprehending danger, have achieved
Almost impossible actions – I have heard soldiers say so –
So I, through frights and threat'nings, will assay
This dangerous venture. Let old wives report
I winked[7] and chose a husband.

1 *rusty*: because it has first been covered in blood
2 *chargeable*: expensive 3 *lamprey*: eel-like fish
4 *Fie, sir!*: the Duchess's shock suggests that she is thinking of the penis, an assumption that Ferdinand can take as evidence of her lustfulness
5 *tale*: also implies 'tail', penis
6 *low foot-steps*: steps up to the altar; there may also be a reference to Marlowe's *Tamburlaine*, in which the conqueror uses his enemy king as a footstool
7 *winked*: closed my eyes, in the sense of ignoring the consequences or the immorality of her actions

[*Enter* CARIOLA.]

Cariola,
To thy known secrecy I have given up
More than my life: my fame.[1]

CARIOLA

Both shall be safe;
For I'll conceal this secret from the world
As warily as those that trade in poison
Keep poison from their children.

DUCHESS

Thy protestation
Is ingenious and hearty;[2] I believe it.
Is Antonio come?

CARIOLA

He attends you.

DUCHESS

Good. Dear soul,
Leave me, but place thyself behind the arras,[3]
Where thou may'st overhear us. Wish me good speed,
For I am going into a wilderness
Where I shall find nor path nor friendly clew[4]
To be my guide.

[CARIOLA *goes behind the arras. Enter* ANTONIO.]

I sent for you. Sit down.
Take pen and ink, and write. Are you ready?

ANTONIO [*sitting at a desk*]

Yes.

DUCHESS

What did I say?

ANTONIO

That I should write somewhat.

1 *fame*: reputation 2 *hearty*: heartfelt
3 *arras*: curtain, perhaps the one at the back of the stage over the discovery space
4 *clew*: ball of thread, as used by Theseus to find his way through the labyrinth

DUCHESS

Oh, I remember:
After these triumphs,[1] and this large expense,
It's fit, like thrifty husbands,[2] we enquire
What's laid up for tomorrow.

ANTONIO

So please your beauteous excellence.

DUCHESS

Beauteous?
Indeed, I thank you. I look young for your sake:[3]
You have ta'en my cares upon you.

ANTONIO [*rising*]

I'll fetch your Grace the particulars
Of your revenue and expense.

DUCHESS

Oh, you are an upright[4] treasurer, but you mistook;
For when I said I meant to make enquiry
What's laid up for tomorrow, I did mean
What's laid up yonder for me.

ANTONIO

Where?

DUCHESS

In heaven.
I am making my will, as 'tis fit princes should
In perfect memory; and I pray, sir, tell me:
Were not one better make it smiling thus,
Than in deep groans and terrible, ghastly looks,
As if the gifts we parted with procured[5]
That violent destruction?

ANTONIO

Oh, much better.

1 *triumphs*: court festivities
2 *husbands*: managers of a household, as well as in the marital sense
3 *for your sake*: thanks to you
4 *upright*: with a pun on the fact that Antonio is now standing
5 *procured*: brought about

DUCHESS
If I had a husband now, this care were quit;
But I intend to make you overseer.[1]
What good deed shall we first remember? Say.

ANTONIO
Begin with that first good deed began i'th' world,
After man's creation: the sacrament of marriage.
I'd have you first provide for a good husband;
Give him all.

DUCHESS
All?

ANTONIO
Yes, your excellent self.

DUCHESS
In a winding-sheet?

ANTONIO
In a couple.[2]

DUCHESS
St Winifred,[3] that were a strange will!

ANTONIO:
'Twere strange if there were no will in you
To marry again.

DUCHESS
What do you think of marriage?

ANTONIO
I take't as those that deny purgatory:
It locally contains or heaven or hell;
There's no third place in't.

DUCHESS
How do you affect[4] it?

1 *overseer*: specifically, a person appointed to assist or oversee the work of the executors of a will

2 *couple*: bond of wedlock

3 *St Winifred*: a seventh-century Welsh saint, whose head was struck off by a rejected suitor, but restored by St Bruno

4 *affect*: feel about

ANTONIO
My banishment,[1] feeding my melancholy,
Would often reason thus –

DUCHESS
Pray, let's hear it.

ANTONIO
Say a man never marry, nor have children,
What takes that from him? Only the bare name
Of being a father, or the weak delight
To see the little wanton[2] ride a-cock-horse
Upon a painted stick, or hear him chatter
Like a taught starling.

DUCHESS
Fie, fie, what's all this?
One of your eyes is bloodshot. Use my ring to't;
[*She gives him a ring.*]
They say 'tis very sovereign.[3] 'Twas my wedding-ring,
And I did vow never to part with it
But to my second husband.

ANTONIO
You have parted with it now.

DUCHESS
Yes, to help your eyesight.

ANTONIO
You have made me stark blind.

DUCHESS
How?

ANTONIO
There is a saucy and ambitious devil
Is dancing in this circle.

DUCHESS
Remove him.

1 *my banishment*: historically, Antonio followed the deposed King of Naples, Federico, to exile in France
2 *wanton*: rogue, term of endearment for a child
3 *sovereign*: effective; gold was believed to cure a stye on the eyelid

ANTONIO

How?

DUCHESS

There needs small conjuration when your finger
May do it thus –
[*She puts the ring on his finger.*]
Is it fit?

ANTONIO

What said you?
He kneels.

DUCHESS

Sir,
This goodly roof of yours is too low-built.
I cannot stand upright in't, nor discourse
Without I raise it higher. Raise yourself,
Or, if you please, my hand to help you: so.
[*The* DUCHESS *raises him up.*]

ANTONIO

Ambition, madam, is a great man's madness,
That is not kept in chains and close-pent rooms
But in fair, lightsome lodgings, and is girt
With the wild noise of prattling visitants,
Which makes it lunatic beyond all cure.
Conceive not I am so stupid but I aim[1]
Whereto your favours tend, but he's a fool
That, being a-cold, would thrust his hands i'th' fire
To warm them.

DUCHESS

So, now the ground's broke,
You may discover what a wealthy mine
I make you lord of.

ANTONIO

Oh, my unworthiness!

DUCHESS

You were ill to sell yourself.
This dark'ning of your worth is not like that

1 *aim*: guess

Which tradesmen use i'th' city: their false lights
Are to rid bad wares off;[1] and I must tell you,
If you will know where breathes a complete man –
I speak it without flattery – turn your eyes
And progress through yourself.

ANTONIO

Were there nor heaven nor hell,
I should be honest. I have long served Virtue
And ne'er ta'en wages of her.

DUCHESS

Now she pays it.
The misery of us that are born great!
We are forced to woo because none dare woo us;
And, as a tyrant doubles with his words,
And fearfully equivocates, so we
Are forced to express our violent passions
In riddles and in dreams, and leave the path
Of simple virtue, which was never made
To seem the thing it is not. Go, go brag
You have left me heartless. Mine is in your bosom;
I hope 'twill multiply love there. You do tremble.
Make not your heart so dead a piece of flesh
To fear more than to love me. Sir, be confident.
What is't distracts you? This is flesh and blood, sir;
'Tis not the figure, cut in alabaster,
Kneels at my husband's tomb. Awake, awake, man!
I do here put off all vain ceremony,
And only do appear to you a young widow
That claims you for her husband, and, like a widow,
I use but half a blush in't.

ANTONIO

Truth speak for me:
I will remain the constant sanctuary
Of your good name.

1 *rid bad wares off*: get rid of spoiled merchandise

DUCHESS

I thank you, gentle love,
And 'cause you shall not come to me in debt,
Being now my steward, here upon your lips
I sign your *Quietus est*.[1]
[*She kisses him.*]
This you should have begged now.
I have seen children oft eat sweetmeats thus,
As fearful to devour them too soon.

ANTONIO

But for your brothers?

DUCHESS

Do not think of them.
[*She embraces him.*]
All discord, without this circumference,[2]
Is only to be pitied, and not feared.
Yet, should they know it, time will easily
Scatter the tempest.

ANTONIO

These words should be mine,
And all the parts[3] you have spoke, if some part of it
Would not have savoured flattery.

DUCHESS

Kneel.
[*They kneel.* CARIOLA *comes from behind the arras.*]

ANTONIO

Ha?

DUCHESS

Be not amazed. This woman's of my counsel.
I have heard lawyers say a contract in a chamber,
Per verba de presenti,[4] is absolute marriage.

1 *Quietus est*: written at the end of an account, meaning that all debts are settled, synonymous with paying one's debt to Death

2 *without . . . circumference*: i.e., outside of her arms

3 *parts*: particulars, with a theatrical sense, i.e., the Duchess is playing the male role

4 *Per . . . presenti*: a kind of marriage that involved no more than the couple's verbal agreement made before a witness

Bless, heaven, this sacred Gordian,[1] which let violence
Never untwine.

ANTONIO

And may our sweet affections, like the spheres,
Be still[2] in motion –

DUCHESS

Quick'ning, and make
The like soft music –

ANTONIO

That we may imitate the loving palms,[3]
Best emblem of a peaceful marriage,
That ne'er bore fruit divided.

DUCHESS

What can the Church force[4] more?

ANTONIO

That Fortune may not know an accident,
Either of joy or sorrow, to divide
Our fixèd wishes.

DUCHESS

How can the Church build faster?[5]
[*They stand up.*]
We now are man and wife, and 'tis the Church
That must but echo this. [*To* CARIOLA] Maid, stand apart.
[*Covering her eyes*] I now am blind.

ANTONIO

What's your conceit in this?

DUCHESS

I would have you lead your Fortune[6] by the hand
Unto your marriage bed.

1 *this sacred Gordian*: i.e., the Duchess's hand holding Antonio's; in ancient history an oracle predicted that whoever cut the knot tied by King Gordius would rule Asia; Alexander the Great was successful

2 *still*: perpetually

3 *loving palms*: according to Pliny, single palm trees do not bear fruit

4 *force*: enforce 5 *faster*: stronger, more lastingly

6 *Fortune*: the personification of Fortune was often depicted as blind in order to suggest impartiality

You speak in me this, for we now are one.
We'll only lie and talk together, and plot
T'appease my humorous[1] kindred; and, if you please,
Like the old tale in *Alexander and Lodowick*,[2]
Lay a naked sword between us; keep us chaste.
Oh, let me shroud[3] my blushes in your bosom,
Since 'tis the treasury of all my secrets.

CARIOLA [*Aside*]

Whether the spirit of greatness or of woman
Reign most in her, I know not, but it shows
A fearful madness. I owe her much of pity. *Exeunt.*

ACT 2

Scene 1

[*Enter*] BOSOLA [*and*] CASTRUCCIO.

BOSOLA

You say you would fain be taken for an eminent courtier?[4]

CASTRUCCIO

'Tis the very main of my ambition.

BOSOLA

Let me see: you have a reasonable good face for't already, and your night-cap[5] expresses your ears sufficient largely. I would have you learn to twirl the strings of your band with a good grace, and in a set speech at th'end of every sentence to hum three or four times, or blow your nose, till it smart again, to recover your memory. When you come to be a

1 *humorous*: ill-humoured, capricious
2 *Alexander and Lodowick*: in legend, two friends so alike they were mistaken for each other; when Lodowick married a princess in Alexander's name, he placed a sword between them in bed so as not to betray his friend
3 *shroud*: hide from view, but also to cover with a death shroud
4 *courtier*: both in the usual sense and meaning a lawyer or judge
5 *night-cap*: the sergeant-at-law wore a white skullcap; here it emphasizes Castruccio's large ears, implying he is an ass

president[1] in criminal causes, if you smile upon a prisoner, hang him, but if you frown upon him and threaten him, let him be sure to 'scape the gallows.

CASTRUCCIO

I would be a very merry president.

BOSOLA

Do not sup a' nights; 'twill beget you an admirable wit.

CASTRUCCIO

Rather it would make me have a good stomach to quarrel, for they say your roaring-boys[2] eat meat seldom, and that makes them so valiant. But how shall I know whether the people take me for an eminent fellow?

BOSOLA

I will teach a trick to know it: give out you lie a-dying, and if you hear the common people curse you, be sure you are taken for one of the prime night-caps.

[*Enter* OLD LADY.]

You come from painting[3] now?

OLD LADY

From what?

BOSOLA

Why, from your scurvy face-physic. To behold thee not painted inclines somewhat near a miracle. These in thy face, here, were deep ruts and foul sloughs[4] the last progress.[5] There was a lady in France that, having had the smallpox, flayed the skin off her face to make it more level; and whereas before she looked like a nutmeg-grater, after she resembled an abortive hedgehog.

OLD LADY

Do you call this painting?

1 *president*: judge 2 *roaring-boys*: rowdy youths
3 *painting*: applying cosmetics 4 *sloughs*: potholes
5 *progress*: a spectacular ceremonial tour taken by royalty or nobility

BOSOLA

No, no, but careening[1] of an old, morphewed[2] lady, to make her disembogue[3] again. There's rough-cast[4] phrase to your plastic.[5]

OLD LADY

It seems you are well acquainted with my closet.[6]

BOSOLA

One would suspect it for a shop of witchcraft, to find in it the fat of serpents, spawn of snakes, Jews' spittle, and their young children's ordure, and all these for the face. I would sooner eat a dead pigeon, taken from the soles of the feet of one sick of the plague,[7] than kiss one of you fastings.[8] Here are two of you whose sin of your youth is the very patrimony of the physician – makes him renew his footcloth[9] with the spring, and change his high-priced courtesan with the fall of the leaf. I do wonder you do not loathe yourselves.

Observe my meditation now:
What thing is in this outward form of man
To be beloved? We account it ominous
If nature do produce a colt or lamb,
A fawn or goat, in any limb resembling
A man, and fly from't as a prodigy.
Man stands amazed to see his deformity
In any other creature but himself;
But in our own flesh, though we bear diseases
Which have their true names only ta'en from beasts,

1 *careening*: cleaning or scraping, usually of the hull of a ship
2 *morphewed*: having diseased and (specifically) discoloured skin
3 *disembogue*: put out to sea
4 *rough-cast*: made of lime and gravel, i.e., putting it in crude terms
5 *plastic*: a smooth complexion, a more delicate turn of phrase
6 *closet*: a private room, also a chest for valuables
7 *a dead pigeon ... the plague*: a recognized treatment for plague; Prince Henry had freshly killed pigeons applied to the soles of his feet in 1612
8 *fasting*: self-starvation, causing bad breath
9 *footcloth*: a decorative cloth placed over the back of a horse, symbolic of high status

As the most ulcerous wolf[1] and swinish measle;[2]
Though we are eaten up of lice and worms,
And though continually we bear about us
A rotten and dead body, we delight
To hide it in rich tissue.[3] All our fear –
Nay, all our terror – is lest our physician
Should put us in the ground to be made sweet.
[*To* CASTRUCCIO] Your wife's gone to Rome. You two couple, and get you
To the wells at Lucca,[4] to recover your aches.
[*Exeunt* CASTRUCCIO *and* OLD LADY.]
I have other work on foot. I observe our Duchess
Is sick a'days. She pukes, her stomach seethes,
The fins[5] of her eyelids look most teeming blue,
She wanes i'th' cheek and waxes fat i'th' flank;
And, contrary to our Italian fashion,
Wears a loose-bodied[6] gown. There's somewhat in't.
I have a trick may chance discover it,
A pretty one. I have bought some apricots,
The first our spring yields.
[*Enter* DELIO *and* ANTONIO *who talk apart.*]

DELIO
And so long since married?
You amaze me.

ANTONIO
Let me seal your lips forever;
For did I think that anything but th'air
Could carry these words from you, I should wish
You had no breath at all.
[*To* BOSOLA] Now, sir, in your contemplation?
You are studying to become a great, wise fellow.

1 *wolf*: a type of ulcer; in Latin *lupus* means ulcer
2 *measle*: a disease in swine as well as humans 3 *tissue*: delicate fabric
4 *Lucca*: Italian city, famous as a spa 5 *fins*: edges
6 *loose-bodied*: with a pun on morally 'loose'

BOSOLA

Oh sir, the opinion of wisdom is a foul tetter[1] that runs all over a man's body. If simplicity direct us to have no evil, it directs us to a happy being; for the subtlest folly proceeds from the subtlest wisdom. Let me be simply honest.

ANTONIO

I do understand your inside.

BOSOLA

Do you so?

ANTONIO

Because you would not seem to appear to th'world
Puffed up with your preferment, you continue
This out-of-fashion melancholy. Leave it, leave it.

BOSOLA

Give me leave to be honest in any phrase, in any compliment whatsoever. Shall I confess myself to you? I look no higher than I can reach. They are the gods that must ride on winged horses. A lawyer's mule of a slow pace will both suit my disposition and business; for, mark me, when a man's mind rides faster than his horse can gallop, they quickly both tire.

ANTONIO

You would look up to heaven, but I think
The devil, that rules i'th' air, stands in your light.

BOSOLA

Oh, sir, you are lord of the ascendant,[2] chief man with the Duchess. A duke was your cousin-german, removed.[3] Say you were lineally descended from King Pippin,[4] or he himself, what of this? Search the heads of the greatest rivers in the world, you shall find them but bubbles of water. Some would think the souls of princes were brought forth by some more weighty cause than those of meaner persons. They are deceived. There's the same hand to them; the like passions sway them; the same reason that makes a vicar go to law for

1 *tetter*: a skin disease
2 *lord of the ascendant*: dominant influence, rising star
3 *cousin-german, removed*: first cousin, once removed
4 *Pippin*: Pepin, king of the Franks and father of Charlemagne

a tithe-pig and undo his neighbours makes them spoil a whole province, and batter down goodly cities with the cannon.

[*Enter* DUCHESS *and* ATTENDANTS.]

DUCHESS

Your arm, Antonio.

[*She leans upon him.*]

Do I not grow fat?
I am exceeding short-winded. Bosola,
I would have you, sir, provide for me a litter –
Such a one as the Duchess of Florence rode in.

BOSOLA

The Duchess used one when she was great with child.

DUCHESS

I think she did. [*To* ATTENDANT] Come hither; mend my ruff.
Here. When? Thou art such a tedious lady, and
Thy breath smells of lemon pills.[1] Would thou hadst done!
Shall I swoon under thy fingers? I am
So troubled with the mother.[2]

BOSOLA [*Aside*]

I fear too much.

DUCHESS [*To* ANTONIO]

I have heard you say that the French courtiers
Wear their hats on 'fore the King.

ANTONIO

I have seen it.

DUCHESS

In the presence?

ANTONIO

Yes.

DUCHESS

Why should not we bring up that fashion?
'Tis ceremony more than duty that consists
In the removing of a piece of felt.

1 *smells of lemon pills*: an extra sensitivity to smells is another symptom of pregnancy
2 *the mother*: hysteria, with an obvious pun

Be you the example to the rest o'th' court:
Put on your hat first.

ANTONIO

You must pardon me.
I have seen, in colder countries than in France,
Nobles stand bare to th'prince; and the distinction
Methought showed reverently.

BOSOLA

I have a present for your Grace.

DUCHESS

For me, sir?

BOSOLA

Apricots, madam.

DUCHESS

Oh, sir, where are they?
I have heard of none to-year.
[BOSOLA *gives her the fruit.*]

BOSOLA [*Aside*]

Good, her colour rises.

DUCHESS [*eating greedily*]

Indeed, I thank you. They are wondrous fair ones.
What an unskilful fellow is our gardener!
We shall have none this month.

BOSOLA

Will not your Grace pare them?

DUCHESS

No – they taste of musk, methinks; indeed, they do.

BOSOLA

I know not; yet I wish your Grace had pared 'em.

DUCHESS

Why?

BOSOLA

I forgot to tell you: the knave gardener,
Only to raise his profit by them the sooner,
Did ripen them in horse-dung.

DUCHESS

Oh, you jest!
[*To* ANTONIO] You shall judge. Pray, taste one.

ANTONIO [*refusing*]
Indeed, madam,
I do not love the fruit.

DUCHESS
Sir, you are loath
To rob us of our dainties.[1] 'Tis a delicate fruit.
They say they are restorative.

BOSOLA
'Tis a pretty art,
This grafting.[2]

DUCHESS
'Tis so: a bett'ring of nature.

BOSOLA
To make a pippin grow upon a crab,
A damson on a blackthorn. [*Aside*] How greedily she eats them!
A whirlwind strike off these bawd-farthingales,[3]
For, but for that and the loose-bodied gown,
I should have discovered apparently[4]
The young springal[5] cutting a caper[6] in her belly.

DUCHESS
I thank you, Bosola. They were right good ones –
If they do not make me sick.
[*The* DUCHESS *appears unwell.*]

ANTONIO
How now, madam?

DUCHESS
This green fruit and my stomach are not friends.
How they swell me!

BOSOLA [*Aside*]
Nay, you are too much swelled already.

1 *dainties*: choice foods, luxuries
2 *grafting*: gardening method, with an ironic allusion to the Duchess's breeding with the lower-class Antonio
3 *farthingales*: hooped petticoats; 'bawd' because they hide the evidence of sexual sin
4 *apparently*: clearly 5 *springal*: stripling
6 *cutting a caper*: dancing

DUCHESS
Oh, I am in an extreme cold sweat!
BOSOLA
I am very sorry. [*Exit.*]
DUCHESS [*To* SERVANTS]
Lights to my chamber! [*Aside*] O good Antonio,
I fear I am undone. *Exeunt* DUCHESS [*and* ATTENDANTS].
DELIO
Lights there, lights!
ANTONIO
O my most trusty Delio, we are lost!
I fear she's fall'n in labour, and there's left
No time for her remove.
DELIO
Have you prepared
Those ladies to attend her, and procured
That politic, safe conveyance for the midwife
Your Duchess plotted?
ANTONIO
I have.
DELIO
Make use, then, of this forced occasion.
Give out that Bosola hath poisoned her
With these apricots – that will give some colour
For her keeping close.
ANTONIO
Fie, fie! The physicians
Will then flock to her.
DELIO
For that you may pretend
She'll use some prepared antidote of her own,
Lest the physicians should re-poison her.
ANTONIO
I am lost in amazement. I know not what to think on't.
Exeunt.

ACT 2

Scene 2

[*Enter*] BOSOLA [*and*] OLD LADY.

BOSOLA [*Aside*]

So, so, there's no question but her tetchiness and most vulturous eating of the apricots are apparent signs of breeding. [*To* OLD LADY] Now –

OLD LADY

I am in haste, sir.[1]

BOSOLA

There was a young waiting-woman had a monstrous desire to see the glass-house – [2]

OLD LADY

Nay, pray let me go.

BOSOLA

– And it was only to know what strange instrument it was should swell up a glass to the fashion of a woman's belly.

OLD LADY

I will hear no more of the glass-house. You are still abusing women.

BOSOLA

Who, I? No, only by the way, now and then, mention your frailties. The orange tree bears ripe and green fruit, and blossoms all together; and some of you give entertainment[3] for pure love, but more, for more precious reward. The lusty spring smells well, but drooping autumn tastes well. If we have the same golden showers that rained in the time of Jupiter the Thunderer, you have the same Danäes still, to hold up their laps to receive them.[4] Didst thou never study the mathematics?

1 *in haste, sir*: the Old Lady may be hurrying to attend the Duchess's lying-in
2 *glass-house*: there was a glass factory near the Blackfriars Theatre
3 *entertainment*: sexual favours
4 *If we . . . receive them*: because she had received Jupiter in a shower of gold, Danae became an emblem of the mercenary woman

OLD LADY

What's that, sir?

BOSOLA

Why, to know the trick how to make a many lines meet in one centre. Go, go give your foster-daughters good counsel. Tell them that the devil takes delight to hang at a woman's girdle, like a false, rusty watch, that she cannot discern how the time passes. [*Exit* OLD LADY.]

[*Enter* ANTONIO, DELIO, RODERIGO *and* GRISOLAN.]

ANTONIO

Shut up the court gates!

RODERIGO

Why, sir? What's the danger?

ANTONIO

Shut up the posterns presently,[1] and call
All the officers o'th' court.

GRISOLAN

I shall, instantly. [*Exit.*]

ANTONIO

Who keeps the key o'th' park-gate?

RODERIGO

Forobosco.

ANTONIO

Let him bring't presently.

[*Exeunt* ANTONIO *and* RODERIGO.]

[*Enter* OFFICERS.]

[FIRST] OFFICER

Oh, gentlemen o'th' court, the foulest treason!

BOSOLA [*Aside*]

If that these apricots should be poisoned now,
Without my knowledge!

[FIRST] OFFICER

There was taken even now a Switzer[2] in the Duchess's bedchamber.

SECOND OFFICER

A Switzer?

1 *presently*: immediately 2 *Switzer*: Swiss mercenary

[FIRST] OFFICER
With a pistol[1] in his great codpiece.

BOSOLA
Ha, ha, ha!

[FIRST] OFFICER
The codpiece was the case for't.

SECOND OFFICER
There was a cunning traitor! Who would have searched his codpiece?

[FIRST] OFFICER
True, if he had kept out of the ladies' chambers – and all the moulds of his buttons were leaden bullets.

SECOND OFFICER
Oh wicked cannibal![2] A fire-lock[3] in's codpiece?

[FIRST] OFFICER
'Twas a French plot,[4] upon my life!

SECOND OFFICER
To see what the devil can do!

[*Enter* ANTONIO, RODERIGO *and* GRISOLAN.]

ANTONIO
All the officers here?

OFFICERS
We are.

ANTONIO
Gentlemen,
We have lost much plate, you know; and but this evening
Jewels to the value of four thousand ducats
Are missing in the Duchess's cabinet.[5]
Are the gates shut?

OFFICERS
Yes.

1 *pistol*: pronounced without the 't', rendering it more like pizzle, i.e., penis
2 *cannibal*: a more general term of abuse for a villain
3 *fire-lock*: a gun or musket
4 *French plot*: syphilis, its symptoms including a burning sensation, was often called the 'French disease'
5 *cabinet*: a private room or box for treasured belongings

ANTONIO

'Tis the Duchess's pleasure
Each officer be locked into his chamber
Till the sun-rising, and to send the keys
Of all their chests, and of their outward doors,
Into her bedchamber. She is very sick.

RODERIGO

At her pleasure.

ANTONIO

She entreats you take't not ill. The innocent
Shall be the more approved by it.

BOSOLA

Gentleman o'th' wood-yard,[1] where's your Switzer now?

[FIRST] OFFICER

By this hand, 'twas credibly reported by one o'th' black-guard.[2]

[*Exeunt all but* ANTONIO *and* DELIO.]

DELIO

How fares it with the Duchess?

ANTONIO

She's exposed
Unto the worst of torture, pain and fear.

DELIO

Speak to her all happy comfort.

ANTONIO

How I do play the fool with mine own danger!
You are this night, dear friend, to post to Rome;
My life lies in your service.

DELIO

Do not doubt me.

ANTONIO

Oh, 'tis far from me, and yet fear presents me
Somewhat that looks like danger.

1 *Gentleman o'th' wood-yard*: Bosola is mocking his low status
2 *black-guard*: scullions or low kitchen servants

DELIO

Believe it,
'Tis but the shadow of your fear, no more.
How superstitiously we mind[1] our evils!
The throwing-down salt, or crossing of a hare,
Bleeding at nose, the stumbling of a horse,
Or singing of a cricket,[2] are of power
To daunt whole man[3] in us. Sir, fare you well.
I wish you all the joys of a blessed father,
And, for my faith, lay this unto your breast:
Old friends, like old swords, still are trusted best.

[*Exit* DELIO.]

[*Enter* CARIOLA, *holding an infant.*]

CARIOLA

Sir, you are the happy father of a son.
Your wife commends him to you.

ANTONIO

Blessed comfort!
For heaven's sake, tend her well. I'll presently
Go set a figure for's nativity.[4] *Exeunt.*

ACT 2

Scene 3

[*Enter*] BOSOLA [*with a dark lantern*].[5]

BOSOLA

Sure, I did hear a woman shriek. List! Ha?
And the sound came, if I received it right,
From the Duchess's lodgings. There's some stratagem
In the confining all our courtiers
To their several wards. I must have part of it;

1 *mind*: remember, think upon 2 *throwing . . . cricket*: all bad omens
3 *whole man*: resolution 4 *set . . . nativity*: cast his horoscope
5 *dark lantern*: designed to conceal its light, indicates to the audience that the scene is night, but also associated with villainy

My intelligence will freeze else. List again!
It may be 'twas the melancholy bird,
Best friend of silence and of solitariness,
The owl, that screamed so –
[*Enter* ANTONIO, *with a light and his sword drawn.*]
Ha? Antonio?

ANTONIO
I heard some noise. Who's there? What art thou? Speak.

BOSOLA
Antonio! Put not your face nor body
To such a forced expression of fear.
I am Bosola, your friend.

ANTONIO
Bosola?
[*Aside*] This mole does undermine me. [*Aloud*] Heard you not
A noise even now?

BOSOLA
From whence?

ANTONIO
From the Duchess's lodging?

BOSOLA
Not I. Did you?

ANTONIO
I did, or else I dreamed.

BOSOLA
Let's walk towards it.

ANTONIO
No. It may be 'twas
But the rising of the wind.
[*He sheathes his sword.*]

BOSOLA
Very likely.
Methinks 'tis very cold, and yet you sweat.
You look wildly.

ANTONIO

I have been setting a figure[1]
For the Duchess's jewels.[2]

BOSOLA

Ah, and how falls your question?
Do you find it radical?[3]

ANTONIO

What's that to you?
'Tis rather to be questioned what design,
When all men were commanded to their lodgings,
Makes you a night-walker.[4]

BOSOLA

In sooth, I'll tell you:
Now all the court's asleep, I thought the devil
Had least to do here. I came to say my prayers;
And if it do offend you I do so,
You are a fine courtier.

ANTONIO [*Aside*]

This fellow will undo me.
[*Aloud*] You gave the Duchess apricots today.
Pray heaven they were not poisoned!

BOSOLA

Poisoned? A Spanish fig[5]
For the imputation!

ANTONIO

Traitors are ever confident
Till they are discovered. There were jewels stol'n too.
In my conceit, none are to be suspected
More than yourself.

1 *setting a figure*: casting a horoscope
2 *jewels*: astrology was often used in an attempt to find stolen goods
3 *how . . . radical*: both 'question' and 'radical' are astrological terms: is the governing planet also the planet in the ascendant?
4 *night-walker*: nocturnal criminal
5 *Spanish fig*: a rude gesture made by thrusting the thumb between two fingers, also poison

BOSOLA

You are a false steward.

ANTONIO

Saucy slave, I'll pull thee up by the roots!

BOSOLA

Maybe the ruin will crush you to pieces.

ANTONIO

You are an impudent snake, indeed, sir.
Are you scarce warm, and do you show your sting?

BOSOLA

. . .[1]

ANTONIO

You libel well, sir.

BOSOLA

No, sir. Copy it out,
And I will set my hand to't.

ANTONIO

My nose bleeds.

[*He takes out a handkerchief, and drops a paper.*]

One that were superstitious would count
This ominous, when it merely comes by chance.
Two letters[2] that are wrought here for my name
Are drowned in blood. Mere accident.
[*To* BOSOLA] For you, sir, I'll take order.
I'th' morn you shall be safe. [*Aside*] 'Tis that must colour
Her lying-in. [*Aloud*] Sir, this door you pass not:
I do not hold it fit that you come near
The Duchess's lodgings till you have quit yourself.
[*Aside*] The great are like the base – nay, they are the same –
When they seek shameful ways to avoid shame. *Exit.*

BOSOLA

Antonio hereabout did drop a paper.
Some of your help, false friend. [*Holding up the lantern*]
Oh, here it is.

[*He takes up the paper.*]

1 *BOSOLA*: . . .: there is a line missing here
2 *letters*: embroidered onto the handkerchief

What's here? A child's nativity calculated!
[*Reads*] 'The Duchess was delivered of a son, 'tween the hours twelve and one, in the night, Anno Domini 1504' – that's this year – 'decimo nono Decembris' – that's this night – 'taken according to the meridian of Malfi' – that's our Duchess. Happy discovery! – 'The lord of the first house, being combust[1] in the ascendant, signifies short life; and Mars being in a human sign,[2] joined to the tail of the Dragon,[3] in the eighth house,[4] doth threaten a violent death. *Caetera non scrutantur.*'[5]
Why, now 'tis most apparent. This precise[6] fellow
Is the Duchess's bawd! I have it to my wish.
This is a parcel of intelligency
Our courtiers were cased-up for. It needs must follow
That I must be committed on pretence
Of poisoning her, which I'll endure and laugh at.
If one could find the father now – but that
Time will discover. Old Castruccio
I'th' morning posts to Rome. By him I'll send
A letter that shall make her brothers' galls
O'erflow their livers. This was a thrifty[7] way.
Though Lust do masque in ne'er so strange disguise,
She's oft found witty, but is never wise. [*Exit.*]

1 *combust*: burnt up, losing influence
2 *human sign*: i.e., Aquarius, Gemini, Virgo or Sagittarius
3 *tail of the Dragon*: where the moon crosses the sun's orbit as it descends
4 *eighth house*: associated with death
5 *Caetera . . . scrutantur*: 'The rest is not examined'
6 *precise*: strict, puritanical 7 *thrifty*: successful, prosperous

ACT 2

Scene 4

[*Enter*] CARDINAL *and* JULIA.

CARDINAL
Sit; thou art my best of wishes. Prithee tell me,
What trick didst thou invent to come to Rome
Without thy husband?

JULIA
Why, my lord, I told him
I came to visit an old anchorite[1]
Here, for devotion.

CARDINAL
Thou art a witty, false one –
I mean, to him.

JULIA
You have prevailed with me
Beyond my strongest thoughts. I would not now
Find you inconstant.

CARDINAL
Do not put thyself
To such a voluntary torture, which proceeds
Out of your own guilt.

JULIA
How, my lord?

CARDINAL
You fear
My constancy, because you have approved
Those giddy and wild turnings in yourself.

JULIA
Did you e'er find them?

1 *anchorite*: religious recluse or hermit

CARDINAL

Sooth, generally, for women.
A man might strive to make glass malleable
Ere he should make them fixed.

JULIA

So, my lord.

CARDINAL

We had need go borrow that fantastic glass[1]
Invented by Galileo the Florentine,
To view another spacious world i'th' moon,
And look to find a constant woman there.

JULIA [*weeping*]

This is very well, my lord.

CARDINAL

Why do you weep?
Are tears your justification? The self-same tears
Will fall into your husband's bosom, lady,
With a loud protestation that you love him
Above the world. Come, I'll love you wisely –
That's jealously – since I am very certain
You cannot me make cuckold.

JULIA

I'll go home
To my husband.

CARDINAL

You may thank me, lady.
I have taken you off your melancholy perch,
Bore you upon my fist, and showed you game,
And let you fly at it.[2] I pray thee, kiss me.
When thou wast with thy husband, thou wast watched
Like a tame elephant[3] – still you are to thank me.
Thou hadst only kisses from him, and high feeding,
But what delight was that? 'Twas just like one

1 *glass*: Galileo's telescope, built in 1609
2 *I have . . . fly at it*: imagining Julia as a falcon
3 *tame elephant*: a real elephant had been put on display in London in 1594; tame could also mean sexually frustrated

That hath a little fing'ring on the lute,
Yet cannot tune it – still you are to thank me.

JULIA
You told me of a piteous wound i'th' heart
And a sick liver, when you wooed me first,
And spake like one in physic.[1]
[*Knocking*]

CARDINAL
Who's that?
Rest firm. For my affection to thee,
Lightning moves slow to't.
[*Enter* SERVANT.]

SERVANT
Madam, a gentleman
That's come post from Malfi desires to see you.

CARDINAL
Let him enter. I'll withdraw. *Exit.*

SERVANT
He says
Your husband, old Castruccio, is come to Rome,
Most pitifully tired with riding post. [*Exit.*]
[*Enter* DELIO.]

JULIA
Signor Delio! [*Aside*] 'Tis one of my old suitors.

DELIO
I was bold to come and see you.

JULIA
Sir, you are welcome.

DELIO
Do you lie here?

JULIA
Sure, your own experience
Will satisfy you, no. Our Roman prelates
Do not keep lodging for ladies.

1 *in physic*: undergoing medical treatment

DELIO

Very well.
I have brought you no commendations from your husband,
For I know none by him.

JULIA

I hear he's come to Rome?

DELIO

I never knew man and beast, of a horse and a knight,
So weary of each other. If he had had a good back,
He would have undertook to have borne his horse,
His breech was so pitifully sore.

JULIA

Your laughter
Is my pity.

DELIO

Lady, I know not whether
You want money, but I have brought you some.

JULIA

From my husband?

DELIO

No, from mine own allowance.

JULIA

I must hear the condition, ere I be bound to take it.

DELIO

Look on't; 'tis gold. Hath it not a fine colour?

JULIA

I have a bird more beautiful.

DELIO

Try the sound on't.

JULIA

A lute-string far exceeds it.
It hath no smell, like cassia or civet;[1]
Nor is it physical,[2] though some fond doctors

1 *cassia or civet*: both are perfumes 2 *physical*: medicinal

Persuade us seeth't in cullisses.[1] I'll tell you,
This is a creature bred by –
[*Enter* SERVANT.]

SERVANT

Your husband's come,
Hath delivered a letter to the Duke of Calabria
That, to my thinking, hath put him out of his wits. [*Exit.*]

JULIA

Sir, you hear?
Pray, let me know your business and your suit
As briefly as can be.

DELIO

With good speed. I would wish you –
At such time as you are non-resident
With your husband – my mistress.

JULIA

Sir, I'll go ask my husband if I shall,
And straight return your answer. *Exit.*

DELIO

Very fine.
Is this her wit or honesty that speaks thus?
I heard one say the Duke was highly moved
With a letter sent from Malfi. I do fear
Antonio is betrayed. How fearfully
Shows his ambition now: unfortunate Fortune!
They pass through whirlpools, and deep woes do shun,
Who the event weigh, ere the action's done. *Exit.*

1 *cullisses*: healthful broths

ACT 2

Scene 5

[*Enter*] CARDINAL *and* FERDINAND *with a letter.*

FERDINAND

I have this night digged up a mandrake.[1]

CARDINAL

Say you?

FERDINAND

And I am grown mad with't.

CARDINAL

What's the prodigy?[2]

FERDINAND

Read there [*handing him the letter*]. A sister damned! She's loose i'th' hilts;[3]
Grown a notorious strumpet!

CARDINAL

Speak lower.

FERDINAND

Lower?
Rogues do not whisper't now but seek to publish't,
As servants do the bounty of their lords:
Aloud, and with a covetous, searching eye
To mark who note them. Oh, confusion seize her!
She hath had most cunning bawds to serve her turn,
And more secure conveyances for lust,
Than towns of garrison for service.

CARDINAL

Is't possible?
Can this be certain?

1 *mandrake*: a medicinal plant that supposedly shrieked when it was pulled from the earth, the sound inducing madness in the hearer

2 *prodigy*: surprising news 3 *loose i'th' hilts*: unchaste

FERDINAND

Rhubarb![1] Oh, for rhubarb
To purge this choler! Here's the cursèd day[2]
To prompt my memory, and here it shall stick,
Till of her bleeding heart I make a sponge
To wipe it out.

CARDINAL

Why do you make yourself
So wild a tempest?

FERDINAND

Would I could be one,
That I might toss her palace 'bout her ears,
Root up her goodly forests, blast her meads,
And lay her general territory as waste
As she hath done her honours.

CARDINAL

Shall our blood,
The royal blood of Aragon and Castile,
Be thus attainted?[3]

FERDINAND

Apply desperate physic!
We must not now use balsamum[4] but fire,
The smarting cupping-glass, for that's the mean
To purge infected blood, such blood as hers.
[*Weeping*] There is a kind of pity in mine eye.
I'll give it to my handkercher – [*wiping his eyes*] and now 'tis here.
I'll bequeath this to her bastard!

CARDINAL

What to do?

FERDINAND

Why, to make soft lint for his mother's wounds
When I have hewed her to pieces!

1 *Rhubarb*: customarily used to treat anger
2 *cursèd day*: the horoscope that Bosola has included in his letter
3 *attainted*: a legal term for a familial line being tainted, also diseased
4 *balsamum*: balm

CARDINAL

Curs'd creature!
Unequal Nature, to place women's hearts
So far upon the left[1] side!

FERDINAND

Foolish men,
That e'er will trust their honour in a bark[2]
Made of so slight, weak bulrush as is woman,
Apt every minute to sink it.

CARDINAL

Thus
Ignorance, when it hath purchased honour,
It cannot wield it.

FERDINAND

Methinks I see her laughing –
Excellent hyena! Talk to me somewhat, quickly,
Or my imagination will carry me
To see her in the shameful act of sin.

CARDINAL

With whom?

FERDINAND

Happily with some strong-thighed bargeman,
Or one o'th' wood-yard that can quoit the sledge[3]
Or toss the bar; or else some lovely squire
That carries coals[4] up to her privy lodgings.[5]

CARDINAL

You fly beyond your reason.

FERDINAND

Go to, mistress!
'Tis not your whore's milk that shall quench my wild-fire,
But your whore's blood!

1 *left*: the Latin 'sinistra' means left, but also unlucky 2 *bark*: ship
3 *quoit the sledge*: throw the hammer
4 *carries coals*: proverbial for any menial work
5 *privy lodgings*: a private apartment, with a bawdy meaning

CARDINAL

How idly shows this rage, which carries you,
As men conveyed by witches, through the air
On violent whirlwinds. This intemperate noise
Fitly resembles deaf men's shrill discourse,
Who talk aloud, thinking all other men
To have their imperfection.

FERDINAND

Have not you
My palsy?[1]

CARDINAL

Yes, I can be angry
Without this rupture. There is not in nature
A thing that makes man so deformed, so beastly,
As doth intemperate anger. Chide yourself.
You have divers men who never yet expressed
Their strong desire of rest, but by unrest,
By vexing of themselves. Come, put yourself
In tune.

FERDINAND

So I will only study to seem
The thing I am not. I could kill her now,
In you or in myself, for I do think
It is some sin in us heaven doth revenge
By her.

CARDINAL

Are you stark mad?

FERDINAND

I would have their bodies
Burnt in a coal-pit, with the ventage stopped,
That their curs'd smoke might not ascend to heaven;
Or dip the sheets they lie in in pitch or sulphur,
Wrap them in't, and then light them like a match;
Or else to boil their bastard to a cullis,[2]

1 *palsy*: shaking disease 2 *cullis*: a curative broth

And give't his lecherous father to renew
The sin of his back.[1]

CARDINAL

I'll leave you.

FERDINAND

Nay, I have done.
I am confident, had I been damned in hell
And should have heard of this, it would have put me
Into a cold sweat. In, in, I'll go sleep.
Till I know who leaps[2] my sister, I'll not stir.
That known, I'll find scorpions to string my whips,[3]
And fix her in a general eclipse.[4] *Exeunt.*

ACT 3

Scene 1

[*Enter*] ANTONIO *and* DELIO.

ANTONIO

Our noble friend, my most beloved Delio,
Oh, you have been a stranger long at court.
Came you along with the Lord Ferdinand?

DELIO

I did, sir; and how fares your noble Duchess?

ANTONIO

Right fortunately well. She's an excellent
Feeder of pedigrees. Since you last saw her,
She hath had two children more – a son and daughter.

DELIO

Methinks 'twas yesterday! Let me but wink,
And not behold your face – which to mine eye

1 *sin of his back*: sexual intercourse
2 *leaps*: has sex with, usually used of animals
3 *scorpions*: knotted or barbed scourges, see 1 Kings 12:11
4 *general*: total

Is somewhat leaner – verily, I should dream
It were within this half-hour.

ANTONIO

You have not been in law, friend Delio,
Nor in prison, nor a suitor at the court,
Nor begged the reversion of some great man's place,
Nor troubled with an old wife, which doth make
Your time so insensibly hasten.

DELIO

Pray, sir, tell me:
Hath not this news arrived yet to the ear
Of the Lord Cardinal?

ANTONIO

I fear it hath.
The Lord Ferdinand, that's newly come to court,
Doth bear himself right dangerously.

DELIO

Pray, why?

ANTONIO

He is so quiet that he seems to sleep
The tempest out, as dormice do in winter.
Those houses that are haunted are most still
Till the devil be up.

DELIO

What say the common people?

ANTONIO

The common rabble do directly say
She is a strumpet.

DELIO

And your graver heads,
Which would be politic, what censure they?

ANTONIO

They do observe I grow to infinite purchase[1]
The left-hand[2] way, and all suppose the Duchess
Would amend it if she could. For, say they,
Great princes, though they grudge their officers

1 *purchase*: wealth 2 *left-hand*: corrupt

Should have such large and unconfinèd means
To get wealth under them, will not complain,
Lest thereby they should make them odious
Unto the people; for other obligation
Of love or marriage between her and me,
They never dream of.

[*Enter* FERDINAND, DUCHESS *and* BOSOLA.]

DELIO

The Lord Ferdinand
Is going to bed.

[DELIO *and* ANTONIO *withdraw.*]

FERDINAND

I'll instantly to bed,
For I am weary. I am to bespeak
A husband for you.

DUCHESS

For me, sir? Pray, who is't?

FERDINAND

The great Count Malateste.

DUCHESS

Fie upon him!
A count? He's a mere stick of sugar-candy;
You may look quite through him. When I choose
A husband, I will marry for your honour.

FERDINAND

You shall do well in't. [*Seeing* ANTONIO] How is't, worthy Antonio?

DUCHESS [*interrupts*]

But sir, I am to have private conference with you
About a scandalous report is spread
Touching mine honour.

FERDINAND

Let me be ever deaf to't:
One of Pasquil's paper bullets.[1] Court-calumny –

1 *Pasquil's paper bullets*: satires or lampoons; Pasquillo was the name of a statue to which lampoons were traditionally attached in sixteenth-century France

A pestilent air which princes' palaces
Are seldom purged of. Yet, say that it were true:
I pour it in your bosom, my fixed love
Would strongly excuse, extenuate, nay deny
Faults, were they apparent in you. Go, be safe
In your own innocency.

DUCHESS

Oh bless'd comfort!
This deadly air is purged.

Exeunt [DUCHESS, ANTONIO *and* DELIO.]

FERDINAND

Her guilt treads on
Hot, burning coulters.[1] Now, Bosola,
How thrives our intelligence?

BOSOLA

Sir, uncertainly.
'Tis rumoured she hath had three bastards, but
By whom we may go read i'th' stars.

FERDINAND

Why, some
Hold opinion all things are written there.

BOSOLA

Yes, if we could find spectacles to read them.
I do suspect there hath been some sorcery
Used on the Duchess.

FERDINAND

Sorcery? To what purpose?

BOSOLA

To make her dote on some desertless fellow
She shames to acknowledge.

FERDINAND

Can your faith give way
To think there's power in potions or in charms
To make us love, whether we will or no?

1 *coulters*: the blades in front of a ploughshare; to walk on hot coulters was a trial of chastity in Old English law

BOSOLA

Most certainly.

FERDINAND

Away! These are mere gulleries,[1] horrid things
Invented by some cheating mountebanks
To abuse us. Do you think that herbs or charms
Can force the will? Some trials have been made
In this foolish practice, but the ingredients
Were lenitive[2] poisons, such as are of force
To make the patient mad; and straight the witch
Swears, by equivocation, they are in love.
The witchcraft lies in her rank blood. This night
I will force confession from her. You told me
You had got, within these two days, a false key
Into her bedchamber?

BOSOLA

I have.

FERDINAND

As I would wish.

BOSOLA

What do you intend to do?

FERDINAND

Can you guess?

BOSOLA

No.

FERDINAND

Do not ask then.
He that can compass me, and know my drifts,
May say he hath put a girdle 'bout the world,
And sounded all her quick-sands.

BOSOLA

I do not
Think so.

FERDINAND

What do you think then, pray?

1 *gulleries*: tricks
2 *lenitive*: gentle so as to go unnoticed, also aphrodisiac

BOSOLA

That you are
Your own chronicle too much, and grossly
Flatter yourself.

FERDINAND

Give me thy hand; I thank thee.
I never gave pension but to flatterers
Till I entertained thee. Farewell;
That friend a great man's ruin strongly checks,
Who rails into his belief all his defects. *Exeunt.*

ACT 3

Scene 2

[*Enter*] DUCHESS, ANTONIO [*and*] CARIOLA.

DUCHESS [*To* CARIOLA]

Bring me the casket hither, and the glass.
[*To* ANTONIO] You get no lodging here tonight, my lord.

ANTONIO

Indeed, I must persuade one.

DUCHESS

Very good;
I hope in time 'twill grow into a custom
That noblemen shall come with cap and knee
To purchase a night's lodging of their wives.

ANTONIO

I must lie here.

DUCHESS

Must? You are a lord of misrule.[1]

ANTONIO

Indeed, my rule is only in the night.

DUCHESS

To what use will you put me?

1 *lord of misrule*: a person of low social status chosen to preside over feasts and revels, representing a temporary reversal of hierarchy

ANTONIO

We'll sleep together.

DUCHESS

Alas, what pleasure can two lovers find in sleep?

CARIOLA

My lord, I lie with her often, and I know
She'll much disquiet you –

ANTONIO

See, you are complained of.

CARIOLA

– for she's the sprawling'st bedfellow.

ANTONIO

I shall like her the better for that.

CARIOLA

Sir, shall I ask you a question?

ANTONIO

I pray thee, Cariola.

CARIOLA

Wherefore still when you lie with my lady
Do you rise so early?

ANTONIO

Labouring men
Count the clock oft'nest, Cariola;
Are glad when their task's ended.

DUCHESS

I'll stop your mouth.

[*She k.isses him.*]

ANTONIO

Nay, that's but one. Venus had two soft doves
To draw her chariot – I must have another.
[*He kisses her.*]
When wilt thou marry, Cariola?

CARIOLA

Never, my lord.

ANTONIO

Oh, fie upon this single life! Forgo it.
We read how Daphne, for her peevish flight,
Became a fruitless bay-tree; Syrinx turned

To the pale, empty reed; Anaxarete[1]
Was frozen into marble; whereas those
Which married, or proved kind unto their friends,[2]
Were, by a gracious influence, trans-shaped
Into the olive, pomegranate, mulberry;
Became flowers, precious stones or eminent stars.

CARIOLA

This is a vain poetry; but, I pray you, tell me:
If there were proposed me wisdom, riches and beauty,
In three several young men, which should I choose?

ANTONIO

'Tis a hard question. This was Paris's case
And he was blind in't, and there was great cause:
For how was't possible he could judge right,
Having three amorous goddesses in view,
And they stark naked? 'Twas a motion[3]
Were able to benight the apprehension
Of the severest counsellor of Europe.
Now I look on both your faces, so well formed,
It puts me in mind of a question I would ask.

CARIOLA

What is't?

ANTONIO

I do wonder why hard-favoured ladies,
For the most part, keep worse-favoured waiting-women
To attend them, and cannot endure fair ones?

DUCHESS

Oh, that's soon answered.
Did you ever in your life know an ill painter
Desire to have his dwelling next door to the shop
Of an excellent picture-maker? 'Twould disgrace
His face-making,[4] and undo him. I prithee,
When were we so merry? My hair tangles.

1 *Daphne . . . Syrinx . . . Anaxarete*: figures from Ovid's *Metamorphoses*; unlike Daphne and Syrinx, whose metamorphoses preserved their chastity, Anaxarete's refusal of love was punished by her transformation into a stone statue

2 *friends*: lovers 3 *motion*: show 4 *face-making*: portrait-painting

ANTONIO [*Aside*]
Pray thee, Cariola, let's steal forth the room
And let her talk to herself. I have divers times
Served her the like, when she hath chafed extremely.
I love to see her angry. Softly, Cariola.
Exeunt [ANTONIO *and* CARIOLA].

DUCHESS
Doth not the colour of my hair 'gin to change?
When I wax grey, I shall have all the court
Powder their hair with orris[1] to be like me.
[*Enter* FERDINAND *behind.*]
You have cause to love me: I entered you into my heart
Before you would vouchsafe to call for the keys.
We shall one day have my brothers take you napping.
Methinks his presence, being now in court,
Should make you keep your own bed; but you'll say
Love mixed with fear is sweetest. I'll assure you,
You shall get no more children till my brothers
Consent to be your gossips.[2] Have you lost your tongue?
[*Sees* FERDINAND *holding a poniard.*]
'Tis welcome;
For know, whether I am doomed to live or die,
I can do both like a prince.
FERDINAND *gives her a poniard.*

FERDINAND
Die then, quickly.
Virtue, where art thou hid? What hideous thing
Is it that doth eclipse thee?

DUCHESS
Pray sir, hear me –

FERDINAND
Or is it true, thou art but a bare name,
And no essential thing?

DUCHESS
Sir –

1 *orris*: iris root, used to whiten and perfume the hair
2 *gossips*: godparents for their children

FERDINAND

Do not speak.

DUCHESS

No, sir:
I will plant my soul in mine ears to hear you.

FERDINAND

O most imperfect light of human reason,
That mak'st us so unhappy to foresee
What we can least prevent! Pursue thy wishes
And glory in them. There's in shame no comfort,
But to be past all bounds and sense of shame.

DUCHESS

I pray, sir, hear me! I am married.

FERDINAND

So.

DUCHESS

Happily,[1] not to your liking; but for that,
Alas, your shears do come untimely now
To clip the bird's wings that's already flown.
Will you see my husband?

FERDINAND

Yes, if I could change
Eyes with a basilisk.[2]

DUCHESS

Sure, you came hither
By his confederacy?

FERDINAND

The howling of a wolf
Is music to[3] thee, screech-owl. Prithee, peace!
[*More loudly*] Whate'er thou art that hast enjoyed my sister –
For I am sure thou hear'st me – for thine own sake
Let me not know thee. I came hither prepared
To work thy discovery, yet am now persuaded
It would beget such violent effects

1 *Happily*: perhaps
2 *basilisk*: mythical serpent whose gaze was supposed to be fatal
3 *to*: compared to

As would damn us both. I would not for ten millions
I had beheld thee; therefore, use all means
I never may have knowledge of thy name.
Enjoy thy lust still, and a wretched life,
On that condition. [*To* DUCHESS] And for thee, vile woman,
If thou do wish thy lecher may grow old
In thy embracements, I would have thee build
Such a room for him as our anchorites
To holier use inhabit. Let not the sun
Shine on him till he's dead. Let dogs and monkeys
Only converse with him, and such dumb things
To whom nature denies use to sound his name.
Do not keep a paraquito,[1] lest she learn it.
If thou do love him, cut out thine own tongue
Lest it bewray him.

DUCHESS

Why might not I marry?
I have not gone about in this to create
Any new world or custom.

FERDINAND

Thou art undone;
And thou hast ta'en that massy sheet of lead
That hid thy husband's bones and folded it
About my heart.

DUCHESS

Mine bleeds for't.

FERDINAND

Thine? Thy heart?
What should I name't, unless a hollow bullet[2]
Filled with unquenchable wild-fire?

DUCHESS

You are in this
Too strict; and were you not my princely brother,
I would say too wilful. My reputation
Is safe.

1 *paraquito*: a small parrot 2 *bullet*: cannon ball

FERDINAND

Dost thou know what reputation is?
I'll tell thee – to small purpose, since th'instruction
Comes now too late.
Upon a time, Reputation, Love and Death
Would travel o'er the world; and it was concluded
That they should part and take three several ways.
Death told them they should find him in great battles,
Or cities plagued with plagues. Love gives them counsel
To enquire for him 'mongst unambitious shepherds,
Where dowries were not talked of, and sometimes
'Mongst quiet kindred that had nothing left
By their dead parents. 'Stay,' quoth Reputation,
'Do not forsake me, for it is my nature
If once I part from any man I meet
I am never found again.' And so, for you:
You have shook hands with Reputation,
And made him invisible. So, fare you well.
I will never see you more.

DUCHESS

Why should only I,
Of all the other princes of the world,
Be cased-up like a holy relic? I have youth
And a little beauty.

FERDINAND

So you have some virgins
That are witches. I will never see thee more. *Exit.*

Enter ANTONIO *with a pistol* [*and* CARIOLA].

DUCHESS

You saw this apparition?

ANTONIO

Yes, we are
Betrayed. How came he hither? I should turn
This to thee for that.

[*He points the pistol at* CARIOLA.]

CARIOLA

Pray, sir, do; and when
That you have cleft my heart, you shall read there
Mine innocence.

DUCHESS

That gallery gave him entrance.

ANTONIO

I would this terrible thing would come again
That, standing on my guard, I might relate
My warrantable love.

She shows the poniard.

Ha, what means this?

DUCHESS

He left this with me.

ANTONIO

And, it seems, did wish
You would use it on yourself.

DUCHESS

His action seemed
To intend so much.

ANTONIO

This hath a handle to't
As well as a point. Turn it towards him,
And so fasten the keen edge in his rank gall.
[*Knocking*]
How now! Who knocks? More earthquakes?

DUCHESS

I stand
As if a mine, beneath my feet, were ready
To be blown up.

CARIOLA

'Tis Bosola.

DUCHESS

Away!
O misery, methinks unjust actions
Should wear these masks and curtains, and not we.
You must instantly part hence. I have fashioned it already.

Exit ANTONIO.

[*Enter* BOSOLA.]

BOSOLA

The Duke your brother is ta'en up in a whirlwind;
Hath took horse and's rid post to Rome.

DUCHESS

So late?

BOSOLA

He told me, as he mounted into th'saddle,
You were undone.

DUCHESS

Indeed, I am very near it.

BOSOLA

What's the matter?

DUCHESS

Antonio, the master of our household,
Hath dealt so falsely with me in's accounts.
My brother stood engaged[1] with me for money,
Ta'en up of certain Neapolitan Jews,
And Antonio lets the bonds be forfeit.[2]

BOSOLA

Strange! [*Aside*] This is cunning.

DUCHESS

And hereupon
My brother's bills at Naples are protested
Against.[3] Call up our officers.

BOSOLA

I shall. *Exit.*

[*Enter* ANTONIO.]

DUCHESS

The place that you must fly to is Ancona.
Hire a house there. I'll send after you
My treasure and my jewels. Our weak safety
Runs upon enginous wheels;[4] short syllables

1 *stood engaged*: acted as security
2 *lets the bonds be forfeit*: i.e., by falling behind in the payments
3 *bills . . . Against*: promissory notes are not accepted
4 *enginous wheels*: as in a clock, where small movements produce the larger motion of the hands

Must stand for periods.[1] I must now accuse you
Of such a feignèd crime, as Tasso[2] calls
Magnanima mensogna – a noble lie,
'Cause it must shield our honours. Hark, they are coming!
[*Enter* BOSOLA *and* OFFICERS.]

ANTONIO

Will your Grace hear me?

DUCHESS

I have got well by you;[3] you have yielded me
A million of loss. I am like to inherit
The people's curses for your stewardship.
You had the trick in audit-time to be sick,
Till I had signed your *Quietus*,[4] and that cured you
Without help of a doctor. Gentlemen,
I would have this man be an example to you all;
So shall you hold my favour. I pray, let him;[5]
For h'as done that, alas, you would not think of,
And, because I intend to be rid of him,
I mean not to publish. [*To* ANTONIO] Use your fortune
elsewhere.

ANTONIO

I am strongly armed to brook my overthrow,
As commonly men bear with a hard year.
I will not blame the cause on't, but do think
The necessity of my malevolent star
Procures this, not her humour. Oh, the inconstant
And rotten ground of service you may see:
'Tis ev'n like him that in a winter night
Takes a long slumber o'er a dying fire,
As loath to part from't, yet parts thence as cold
As when he first sat down.

1 *periods*: in oratory, the peroration or summing-up

2 *Tasso*: (1544–95) Italian poet, author of *Gerusalemme Liberata*, in which a character called Soprina falsely accuses herself of a crime to save the lives of many Christians

3 *got well*: with a pun on begot well, referring to their children

4 *Quietus*: agreement that the account was settled, a receipt

5 *let him*: let him go free

DUCHESS

We do confiscate,
Towards the satisfying of your accounts,
All that you have.

ANTONIO

I am all yours, and 'tis very fit
All mine should be so.

DUCHESS

So, sir, you have your pass.

ANTONIO

You may see, gentlemen, what 'tis to serve
A prince with body and soul. *Exit.*

BOSOLA

Here's an example for extortion! What moisture is drawn out of the sea, when foul weather comes, pours down and runs into the sea again.

DUCHESS

I would know what are your opinions
Of this Antonio.

SECOND OFFICER

He could not abide to see a pig's head gaping; I thought your Grace would find him a Jew.[1]

THIRD OFFICER

I would you had been his officer, for your own sake.

FOURTH OFFICER

You would have had more money.

FIRST OFFICER

He stopped his ears with black wool; and to those came to him for money said he was thick of hearing.

SECOND OFFICER

Some said he was an hermaphrodite, for he could not abide a woman.

FOURTH OFFICER

How scurvy proud he would look when the treasury was full! Well, let him go.

1 *Jew*: conventionally greedy and financially untrustworthy

FIRST OFFICER

Yes, and the chippings of the buttery[1] fly after him to scour his gold chain![2]

DUCHESS

Leave us. *Exeunt* [OFFICERS].
[*To* BOSOLA] What do you think of these?

BOSOLA

That these are rogues that in's prosperity,
But to have waited on his fortune, could have wished
His dusty stirrup riveted through their noses,
And followed after's mule like a bear in a ring;[3]
Would have prostituted their daughters to his lust,
Made their first-born intelligencers; thought none happy
But such as were born under his blessed planet
And wore his livery; and do these lice drop off now?
Well, never look to have the like again.
He hath left a sort of flatt'ring rogues behind him;
Their doom must follow. Princes pay flatterers
In their own money. Flatterers dissemble their vices,
And they dissemble their lies – that's justice.
Alas, poor gentleman!

DUCHESS

Poor? He hath amply filled his coffers.

BOSOLA

Sure, he was too honest. Pluto,[4] the god of riches,
When he's sent by Jupiter to any man,
He goes limping, to signify that wealth
That comes in God's name comes slowly; but when he's sent
On the devil's errand he rides post,[5] and comes in by scuttles.[6]
Let me show you what a most unvalued[7] jewel

1 *chippings of the buttery*: parings of bread crust
2 *gold chain*: the steward's chain of office
3 *bear in a ring*: performing bears were a popular London entertainment
4 *Pluto*: this should be Plutus, god of wealth; Pluto was lord of the underworld
5 *rides post*: post-haste, i.e., speedily
6 *scuttles*: short, hurried runs
7 *unvalued*: priceless, but with a pun on unappreciated

You have, in a wanton humour, thrown away
To bless the man shall find him. He was an excellent
Courtier, and most faithful; a soldier that thought it
As beastly to know his own value too little
As devilish to acknowledge it too much.
Both his virtue and form deserved a far better fortune.
His discourse rather delighted to judge itself than show itself.
His breast was filled with all perfection,
And yet it seemed a private, whisp'ring-room,
It made so little noise of't.

DUCHESS

But he was basely descended.

BOSOLA

Will you make yourself a mercenary herald,[1]
Rather to examine men's pedigrees than virtues?
You shall want him;
For know, an honest statesman to a prince
Is like a cedar planted by a spring:
The spring bathes the tree's root; the grateful tree
Rewards it with his shadow. You have not done so.
I would sooner swim to the Bermudas[2] on
Two politicians' rotten bladders, tied
Together with an intelligencer's heart-string,
Than depend on so changeable a prince's favour!
Fare thee well, Antonio, since the malice of the world
Would needs down with thee. It cannot be said yet
That any ill happened unto thee,
Considering thy fall was accompanied with virtue.

DUCHESS

Oh, you render me excellent music!

BOSOLA

Say you?

DUCHESS

This good one that you speak of is my husband.

1 *herald*: the Heralds' Office determined people's ancestry and sold the right to bear a coat of arms and call oneself a gentleman

2 *Bermudas*: islands notoriously associated with tempests and shipwrecks

BOSOLA
Do I not dream? Can this ambitious age
Have so much goodness in't as to prefer
A man merely for worth, without these shadows
Of wealth and painted honours? Possible?

DUCHESS
I have had three children by him.

BOSOLA
Fortunate lady,
For you have made your private nuptial bed
The humble and fair seminary of peace.
No question but many an unbeneficed[1] scholar
Shall pray for you for this deed, and rejoice
That some preferment in the world can yet
Arise from merit. The virgins of your land
That have no dowries shall hope your example
Will raise them to rich husbands. Should you want
Soldiers, 'twould make the very Turks and Moors
Turn Christians, and serve you for this act.
Last, the neglected poets of your time,
In honour of this trophy of a man,
Raised by that curious[2] engine, your white hand,
Shall thank you in your grave for't, and make that
More reverend than all the cabinets
Of living princes. For Antonio,
His fame shall likewise flow from many a pen,
When heralds shall want coats[3] to sell to men.

DUCHESS
As I taste comfort in this friendly speech,
So would I find concealment.

BOSOLA
Oh, the secret of my prince,
Which I will wear on th'inside of my heart!

1 *unbeneficed*: without an ecclesiastical post
2 *curious*: delicate 3 *want coats*: lack a coats of arms

DUCHESS
You shall take charge of all my coin and jewels,
And follow him, for he retires himself
To Ancona.

BOSOLA
So.

DUCHESS
Whither, within few days,
I mean to follow thee.

BOSOLA
Let me think:
I would wish your Grace to feign a pilgrimage
To Our Lady of Loreto, scarce seven leagues
From fair Ancona; so may you depart
Your country with more honour, and your flight
Will seem a princely progress, retaining
Your usual train about you.

DUCHESS
Sir, your direction
Shall lead me by the hand.

CARIOLA
In my opinion,
She were better progress to the baths
At Lucca,[1] or go visit the Spa[2]
In Germany; for, if you will believe me,
I do not like this jesting with religion,
This feigned pilgrimage.

DUCHESS
Thou art a superstitious fool!
Prepare us instantly for our departure.
Past sorrows, let us moderately lament them;
For those to come, seek wisely to prevent them.
Exeunt [DUCHESS *and* CARIOLA].

1 *Lucca*: a town near Pisa, famous for its waters
2 *Spa*: a famous watering place in Belgium

BOSOLA
A politician is the devil's quilted anvil:
He fashions all sins on him, and the blows
Are never heard. He may work in a lady's chamber,
As here for proof. What rests, but I reveal
All to my lord? Oh, this base quality[1]
Of intelligencer! Why, every quality i'th' world
Prefers[2] but gain or commendation.
Now for this act I am certain to be raised,
And men that paint weeds to the life are praised. *Exit.*

ACT 3

Scene 3

[*Enter*] CARDINAL, MALATESTE [*on one side*]. FERDINAND, DELIO, SILVIO, PESCARA [*on the other*].

CARDINAL
Must we turn soldier then?

MALATESTE
The Emperor,
Hearing your worth that way, ere you attained
This reverend garment,[3] joins you in commission
With the right fortunate soldier, the Marquis of Pescara,
And the famous Lannoy.[4]

CARDINAL
He that had the honour
Of taking the French king prisoner?

MALATESTE
The same.
Here's a plot drawn for a new fortification
At Naples.

1 *quality*: profession 2 *Prefers*: facilitates
3 *reverend garment*: the robes of a cardinal
4 *Lannoy*: Charles de Lannoy (1487–1527) defeated Francis I at the Battle of Pavia in 1525

[*They talk apart.*]

FERDINAND

This great Count Malateste, I perceive,
Hath got employment.

DELIO

No employment, my lord:
A marginal note in the muster-book[1] that he is
A voluntary lord.

FERDINAND

He's no soldier?

DELIO

He has worn gunpowder in's hollow tooth
For the toothache.

SILVIO

He comes to the leaguer[2] with a full intent
To eat fresh beef and garlic; means to stay
Till the scent be gone, and straight return to court.

DELIO

He hath read all the late service[3]
As the city chronicle relates it,
And keeps two pewterers going, only to express
Battles in model.

SILVIO

Then he'll fight by the book?[4]

DELIO

By the almanac, I think,
To choose good days and shun the critical.
That's his mistress' scarf?

SILVIO

Yes, he protests
He would do much for that taffeta.

DELIO

I think he would run away from a battle
To save it from taking prisoner.

1 *muster-book*: military register 2 *leaguer*: army camp
3 *service*: military action
4 *by the book*: according to the rules, but also in theory only

SILVIO

He is horribly afraid
Gunpowder will spoil the perfume on't.

DELIO

I saw a Dutchman break his pate[1] once
For calling him 'pot-gun';[2] he made his head
Have a bore[3] in't, like a musket.

SILVIO

I would he had made a touch-hole[4] to't!
He is, indeed, a guarded sumpter-cloth,[5]
Only for the remove of the court.

[*Enter* BOSOLA, *who speaks to the* CARDINAL *and* FERDINAND.]

PESCARA

Bosola arrived? What should be the business?
Some falling-out amongst the cardinals.
These factions amongst great men! They are like
Foxes: when their heads are divided
They carry fire in their tails,[6] and all the country
About them goes to wrack for't.

SILVIO

What's that Bosola?

DELIO

I knew him in Padua: a fantastical scholar, like such who study to know how many knots was in Hercules' club, of what colour Achilles' beard was, or whether Hector were not troubled with the toothache. He hath studied himself half blear-eyed to know the true symmetry of Caesar's nose by a shoeing-horn; and this he did to gain the name of a speculative man.

1 *break his pate*: hit him over the head
2 *'pot-gun'*: a child's toy gun 3 *bore*: hole
4 *touch-hole*: a hole in the breech for igniting the charge
5 *sumpter-cloth*: cloth covering a mule or packhorse, with ornamental trimmings ('guarded')
6 *Foxes . . . tails*: in Judges 15:4 Samson tied pairs of foxes together, attached firebrands to their tails and used them to burn down the Philistines' crops

PESCARA
Mark Prince Ferdinand.
A very salamander[1] lives in's eye,
To mock the eager violence of fire.

SILVIO
That Cardinal hath made more bad faces with his oppression than ever Michelangelo made good ones. He lifts up's nose like a foul porpoise before a storm.

PESCARA
The Lord Ferdinand laughs.

DELIO
Like a deadly cannon,
That lightens ere it smokes.

PESCARA
These are your true pangs of death:
The pangs of life that struggle with great statesmen.

DELIO
In such a deformed silence, witches whisper
Their charms.
[SILVIO, DELIO *and* PESCARA *stand aside.*]

CARDINAL
Doth she make religion her riding-hood
To keep her from the sun and tempest?

FERDINAND
That,
That damns her. Methinks her fault and beauty,
Blended together, show like leprosy:
The whiter, the fouler. I make it a question
Whether her beggarly brats were ever christened.

CARDINAL
I will instantly solicit the state of Ancona
To have them banished.

FERDINAND
You are for Loreto?
I shall not be at your ceremony; fare you well.
[*To* BOSOLA] Write to the Duke of Malfi, my young nephew

1 *salamander*: a lizard supposed to live in fire, symbol of passion

She had by her first husband,[1] and acquaint him
With's mother's honesty.

BOSOLA

I will.

FERDINAND

Antonio!
A slave, that only smelled of ink and counters,[2]
And ne'er in's life looked like a gentleman,
But in the audit-time. Go, go presently.
Draw me out an hundred and fifty of our horse,
And meet me at the fort-bridge. *Exeunt.*

ACT 3

Scene 4

[Enter] Two PILGRIMS *to the Shrine of Our Lady of Loreto.*

FIRST PILGRIM

I have not seen a goodlier shrine than this,
Yet I have visited many.

SECOND PILGRIM

The Cardinal of Aragon
Is this day to resign his cardinal's hat.
His sister Duchess likewise is arrived
To pay her vow of pilgrimage. I expect
A noble ceremony.

FIRST PILGRIM

No question. – They come.

Here the ceremony of the CARDINAL'S *instalment, in the habit [of] a soldier, performed in delivering up his cross, hat, robes and ring at the shrine, and investing him with sword, helmet, shield and spurs. Then* ANTONIO, *the* DUCHESS *and their*

1 *my young nephew . . . first husband*: this is the only reference to this other child. Since he would inherit the Duchess's property, rather than Ferdinand, it seems likely that Webster changed his mind, but forgot to delete this reference
2 *counters*: small discs used in accounting

CHILDREN,[1] *having presented themselves at the shrine, are, by a form of banishment in dumbshow, expressed towards them by the* CARDINAL *and the State of Ancona, banished. During all which ceremony, this ditty is sung, to very solemn music, by divers churchmen and then Exeunt* [*all except the* PILGRIMS].

The Author disclaims this ditty to be his.

CHURCHMEN [*Sing*]

Arms and honours deck thy story,
To thy fame's eternal glory.
Adverse fortune ever fly thee,
No disastrous fate come nigh thee.

I alone will sing thy praises,
Whom to honour virtue raises;
And thy study, that divine is,
Bent to martial discipline is.
Lay aside all those robes lie by thee,
Crown thy arts with arms: they'll beautify thee.

O worthy of worthiest name, adorned in this manner,
Lead bravely thy forces on, under war's warlike banner.
Oh, may'st thou prove fortunate in all martial courses.[2]
Guide thou still by skill, in arts and forces.
Victory attend thee nigh, whilst Fame sings loud thy
powers,
Triumphant conquest crown thy head, and blessings pour
down showers.

FIRST PILGRIM

Here's a strange turn of state. Who would have thought
So great a lady would have matched herself
Unto so mean a person? Yet the Cardinal

1 *CHILDREN*: these are a girl old enough to say her prayers, a small boy and an infant, probably represented by a doll
2 *courses*: encounters

Bears himself much too cruel.

SECOND PILGRIM

They are banished.

FIRST PILGRIM

But I would ask what power hath this state
Of Ancona to determine of a free prince?

SECOND PILGRIM

They are a free state, sir, and her brother showed
How that the Pope, forehearing of her looseness,
Hath seized into th'protection of the Church
The dukedom which she held as dowager.

FIRST PILGRIM

But by what justice?

SECOND PILGRIM

Sure, I think by none –
Only her brother's instigation.

FIRST PILGRIM

What was it, with such violence, he took
Off from her finger?

SECOND PILGRIM

'Twas her wedding ring,
Which he vowed shortly he would sacrifice
To his revenge.

FIRST PILGRIM

Alas, Antonio!
If that a man be thrust into a well,
No matter who sets hand to't, his own weight
Will bring him sooner to th' bottom. Come, let's hence.
Fortune makes this conclusion general:
All things do help th'unhappy man to fall. *Exeunt.*

ACT 3

Scene 5

[*Enter*] ANTONIO, DUCHESS [*and two*] CHILDREN, CARIOLA [*carrying an infant*], SERVANTS.

DUCHESS
Banished Ancona?

ANTONIO
Yes, you see what power
Lightens[1] in great men's breath.

DUCHESS
Is all our train
Shrunk to this poor remainder?

ANTONIO
These poor men,
Which have got little in your service, vow
To take your fortune; but your wiser buntings,[2]
Now they are fledged, are gone.

DUCHESS
They have done wisely.
This puts me in mind of death: physicians thus,
With their hands full of money, use to give o'er
Their patients.

ANTONIO
Right[3] the fashion of the world:
From decayed fortunes every flatterer shrinks;
Men cease to build where the foundation sinks.

DUCHESS
I had a very strange dream tonight.

ANTONIO
What was't?

1 *Lightens*: flashes like lightning
2 *buntings*: small birds, related to the lark 3 *Right*: Just

DUCHESS
Methought I wore my coronet of state,
And on a sudden all the diamonds
Were changed to pearls.

ANTONIO
My interpretation
Is you'll weep shortly; for, to me, the pearls
Do signify your tears.

DUCHESS
The birds that live i'th' field,
On the wild benefit[1] of nature, live
Happier than we, for they may choose their mates,
And carol their sweet pleasures to the spring.
[*Enter* BOSOLA.]

BOSOLA
You are happily o'erta'en.
[*He hands the* DUCHESS *a letter.*]

DUCHESS
From my brother?

BOSOLA
Yes, from the Lord Ferdinand, your brother,
All love and safety.

DUCHESS
Thou dost blanch mischief;
Wouldst make it white. See, see, like to calm weather
At sea, before a tempest, false hearts speak fair
To those they intend most mischief.
[*Reads*] (*A Letter*) 'Send Antonio to me. I want his head in a business.'
A politic equivocation!
He doth not want your counsel, but your head;
That is, he cannot sleep till you be dead.
And here's another pitfall that's strewed o'er
With roses; mark it – 'tis a cunning one.

1 *benefit*: gift

[*Reads*] 'I stand engaged for your husband for several debts at Naples. Let not that trouble him. I had rather have his heart than his money.'
And I believe so too.

BOSOLA

What do you believe?

DUCHESS

That he so much distrusts my husband's love
He will by no means believe his heart is with him
Until he see it. The devil is not cunning enough
To circumvent us in riddles.

BOSOLA

Will you reject that noble and free league
Of amity and love which I present you?

DUCHESS

Their league is like that of some politic kings:
Only to make themselves of strength and power
To be our after-ruin. Tell them so.

BOSOLA [*To* ANTONIO]

And what from you?

ANTONIO

Thus tell him
I will not come.

BOSOLA

And what of this?

ANTONIO

My brothers[1] have dispersed
Bloodhounds abroad, which till I hear are muzzled
No truce, though hatched with ne'er such politic skill,
Is safe that hangs upon our enemies' will.
I'll not come at them.

BOSOLA

This proclaims your breeding.
Every small thing draws a base mind to fear,

1 *brothers*: brothers-in-law

As the adamant[1] draws iron. Fare you well, sir.
You shall shortly hear from's. *Exit.*

DUCHESS

I suspect some ambush;
Therefore, by all my love, I do conjure you
To take your eldest son and fly towards Milan.
Let us not venture all this poor remainder
In one unlucky bottom.[2]

ANTONIO

You counsel safely.
Best of my life, farewell. Since we must part
Heaven hath a hand in't; but no otherwise
Than as some curious artist takes in sunder
A clock or watch when it is out of frame,
To bring't in better order.

DUCHESS

I know not which is best:
To see you dead or part with you. [*To her eldest son*]
Farewell, boy.
Thou art happy that thou hast not understanding
To know thy misery; for all our wit
And reading brings us to a truer sense
Of sorrow. [*To* ANTONIO] In the eternal Church,[3] sir,
I do hope we shall not part thus.

ANTONIO

Oh, be of comfort!
Make patience a noble fortitude,
And think not how unkindly we are used.
Man, like to cassia,[4] is proved best being bruised.

DUCHESS

Must I, like to a slave-born Russian,
Account it praise to suffer tyranny?
And yet, O heaven, thy heavy hand is in't.

1 *adamant*: magnet
2 *venture . . . bottom*: proverbial: 'Venture not all in one bottom'
3 *eternal Church*: among the saved in heaven
4 *cassia*: a kind of cinnamon, the scent released when the bark is rubbed

I have seen my little boy oft scourge his top,[1]
And compared myself to't: naught made me e'er
Go right but heaven's scourge-stick.

ANTONIO

Do not weep.
Heaven fashioned us of nothing, and we strive
To bring ourselves to nothing. Farewell, Cariola,
And thy sweet armful.[2] [*To the* DUCHESS] If I do never see thee more,[3]
Be a good mother to your little ones,
And save them from the tiger. Fare you well.
[*He kisses her.*]

DUCHESS

Let me look upon you once more, for that speech
Came from a dying father. Your kiss is colder
Than that I have seen an holy anchorite[4]
Give to a dead man's skull.

ANTONIO

My heart is turned to a heavy lump of lead
With which I sound my danger.[5] Fare you well.
Exeunt [ANTONIO *and his eldest son*].

DUCHESS

My laurel is all withered.[6]

CARIOLA

Look, madam, what a troop of armèd men
Make toward us.

Enter BOSOLA [*masked*] *with a* GUARD[7] [*wearing vizards*].

1 *scourge his top*: refers to the child's spinning top, made to turn by whipping it with a 'scourge-stick'
2 *sweet armful*: Cariola is carrying their youngest child
3 *never see thee more*: this phrase echoes throughout the play – see 3.2, 4.1 and 5.3
4 *anchorite*: hermit
5 *heavy . . . danger*: like a plummet that measures the depth of water
6 *laurel . . . withered*: laurel proverbially withered at the death of a king
7 *GUARD*: plural here

DUCHESS

Oh, they are very welcome.
When Fortune's wheel is overcharged with princes,
The weight makes it move swift. I would have my ruin
Be sudden. [*To* BOSOLA] I am your adventure,[1] am I not?

BOSOLA

You are. You must see your husband no more.

DUCHESS

What devil art thou that counterfeits heaven's thunder?

BOSOLA

Is that terrible? I would have you tell me
Whether is that note worse that frights the silly[2] birds
Out of the corn, or that which doth allure them
To the nets? You have hearkened to the last too much.

DUCHESS

O misery! Like to a rusty o'ercharged cannon,
Shall I never fly in pieces? Come: to what prison?

BOSOLA

To none.

DUCHESS

Whither then?

BOSOLA

To your palace.

DUCHESS

I have heard that Charon's boat serves to convey
All o'er the dismal lake,[3] but brings none back again.

BOSOLA

Your brothers mean you safety and pity.

DUCHESS

Pity?

With such a pity men preserve alive
Pheasants and quails, when they are not fat enough
To be eaten.

1 *adventure*: target, what you seek 2 *silly*: weak, defenceless
3 *Charon . . . lake*: in classical mythology, Charon conveyed the dead across the river Styx into Hades

BOSOLA
These are your children?
DUCHESS
Yes.
BOSOLA
Can they prattle?
DUCHESS
No,
But I intend, since they were born accursed,
Curses shall be their first language.
BOSOLA
Fie, madam,
Forget this base, low fellow.
DUCHESS
Were I a man,
I'd beat that counterfeit face[1] into thy other.
BOSOLA
One of no birth.
DUCHESS
Say that he was born mean,
Man is most happy when's own actions
Be arguments and examples of his virtue.
BOSOLA
A barren, beggarly virtue.
DUCHESS
I prithee, who is greatest? Can you tell?
Sad tales befit my woe; I'll tell you one.
A salmon, as she swam unto the sea,
Met with a dog-fish, who encounters her
With this rough language: 'Why art thou so bold
To mix thyself with our high state of floods,
Being no eminent courtier, but one
That for the calmest and fresh time o'th' year
Dost live in shallow rivers, rank'st thyself
With silly smelts[2] and shrimps? And darest thou
Pass by our dog-ship without reverence?'

1 *counterfeit face*: mask 2 *smelts*: small fish, related to the salmon

'O,' quoth the salmon, 'sister, be at peace.
Thank Jupiter, we both have passed the net.
Our value never can be truly known,
Till in the fisher's basket we be shown.
I'th' market then my price may be the higher,
Even when I am nearest to the cook and fire.'
So, to great men the moral may be stretched:
Men oft are valued high, when th'are most wretch'd.
But come: whither you please. I am armed 'gainst misery,
Bent to all sways of the oppressor's will.
There's no deep valley, but near some great hill. *Exeunt.*

ACT 4

Scene 1

[*Enter*] FERDINAND, BOSOLA [*and*] SERVANTS [*with torches*].[1]

FERDINAND
How doth our sister Duchess bear herself
In her imprisonment?

BOSOLA
Nobly; I'll describe her:
She's sad, as one long used to't, and she seems
Rather to welcome the end of misery
Than shun it; a behaviour so noble,
As gives a majesty to adversity.
You may discern the shape of loveliness
More perfect in her tears than in her smiles.
She will muse four hours together, and her silence,
Methinks, expresseth more than if she spake.

FERDINAND
Her melancholy seems to be fortified
With a strange disdain.

1 *torches*: indicating that the scene takes place at night

BOSOLA

'Tis so; and this restraint,
Like English mastiffs that grow fierce with tying,
Makes her too passionately apprehend
Those pleasures she's kept from.

FERDINAND

Curse upon her!
I will no longer study in the book
Of another's heart. Inform her what I told you. *Exit.*

[*Enter* DUCHESS *and* CARIOLA.]

BOSOLA

All comfort to your Grace –

DUCHESS

I will have none.
Pray thee, why dost thou wrap thy poisoned pills
In gold and sugar?

BOSOLA

Your elder brother,[1] the Lord Ferdinand,
Is come to visit you, and sends you word
'Cause once he rashly made a solemn vow
Never to see you more, he comes i'th' night;
And prays you, gently, neither torch nor taper
Shine in your chamber. He will kiss your hand
And reconcile himself, but, for his vow,
He dares not see you.

DUCHESS

At his pleasure.
Take hence the lights. [*Exeunt* SERVANTS *with torches.*]

[*Enter* FERDINAND.]

He's come.

FERDINAND

Where are you?

DUCHESS

Here, sir.

1 *elder brother*: since Ferdinand is supposed to be the Duchess's twin, Webster may have made a mistake here; in the source, Ferdinand is the elder brother

FERDINAND

This darkness suits you well.

DUCHESS

I would ask you pardon.

FERDINAND

You have it;
For I account it the honorabl'st revenge,
Where I may kill, to pardon. Where are your cubs?

DUCHESS

Whom?

FERDINAND

Call them your children;
For though our national law distinguish bastards
From true, legitimate issue, compassionate nature
Makes them all equal.

DUCHESS

Do you visit me for this?
You violate a sacrament o'th' Church
Shall make you howl in hell for't.

FERDINAND

It had been well
Could you have lived thus always; for, indeed,
You were too much i'th' light.[1] But no more;
I come to seal my peace with you. Here's a hand,
To which you have vowed much love. The ring upon't
You gave.

[He] gives her a dead man's hand.[2]

DUCHESS

I affectionately kiss it.

FERDINAND

Pray do, and bury the print of it in your heart.
I will leave this ring with you for a love-token,
And the hand, as sure as the ring; and do not doubt
But you shall have the heart too. When you need a friend,

1 *i'th' light*: in the public eye, but also 'light' meaning wanton
2 *dead man's hand*: thought to cure madness

Send it to him that owed it; you shall see
Whether he can aid you.

DUCHESS

You are very cold.
I fear you are not well after your travel.
Ha? Lights! Oh horrible!

FERDINAND

Let her have lights enough. *Exit.*

[*Enter* SERVANTS *with torches.*]

DUCHESS

What witchcraft doth he practise that he hath left
A dead man's hand here?

Here is discovered, behind a traverse,[1] *the artificial figures of* ANTONIO *and his* CHILDREN, *appearing as if they were dead.*[2]

BOSOLA

Look you, here's the piece from which 'twas ta'en.
He doth present you this sad spectacle
That, now you know directly they are dead,
Hereafter you may wisely cease to grieve
For that which cannot be recoverèd.

DUCHESS

There is not between heaven and earth one wish
I stay for after this. It wastes me more
Than were't my picture, fashioned out of wax,
Stuck with a magical needle, and then buried
In some foul dunghill. And yond's an excellent property[3]
For a tyrant, which I would account mercy.

BOSOLA

What's that?

1 *traverse*: a curtain over the discovery space
2 *dead*: if the waxworks were performed by the actors, the audience's first reaction would be that of the Duchess, believing them really to be dead
3 *property*: device

DUCHESS

If they would bind me to that lifeless trunk,[1]
And let me freeze to death.

BOSOLA

Come, you must live.

DUCHESS

That's the greatest torture souls feel in hell:
In hell that they must live, and cannot die.
Portia, I'll new-kindle thy coals again,
And revive the rare and almost dead example
Of a loving wife.[2]

BOSOLA

O fie! Despair? Remember
You are a Christian.

DUCHESS

The Church enjoins fasting:
I'll starve myself to death.

BOSOLA

Leave this vain sorrow.
Things being at the worst begin to mend;
The bee when he hath shot his sting into your hand
May then play with your eyelid.

DUCHESS

Good, comfortable[3] fellow,
Persuade a wretch that's broke upon the wheel[4]
To have all his bones new-set; entreat him live
To be executed again. Who must dispatch me?
I account this world a tedious theatre,
For I do play a part in't 'gainst my will.

BOSOLA

Come, be of comfort; I will save your life.

1 *bind me to that lifeless trunk*: the image of a living person bound to a corpse was traditionally meant to symbolize ill-matched unions; this line may have inspired the final act of Ford's *The Broken Heart*

2 *Portia . . . wife*: Brutus' wife, who committed suicide by swallowing burning coals on hearing of her husband's defeat and death

3 *comfortable*: offering comfort, supportive 4 *wheel*: a method of torture

DUCHESS
Indeed, I have not leisure to tend so small a business.
BOSOLA
Now, by my life, I pity you.
DUCHESS
Thou art a fool then,
To waste thy pity on a thing so wretched
As cannot pity it. I am full of daggers.[1]
Puff! Let me blow these vipers[2] from me.
[*To* SERVANT] What are you?
SERVANT
One that wishes you long life.
DUCHESS
I would thou wert hanged for the horrible curse
Thou hast given me. I shall shortly grow one
Of the miracles of pity. I'll go pray – No,
I'll go curse.
BOSOLA
Oh fie!
DUCHESS
I could curse the stars –
BOSOLA
Oh fearful!
DUCHESS
And those three smiling seasons of the year
Into a Russian winter – nay, the world
To its first chaos.
BOSOLA
Look you, the stars shine still.
DUCHESS
Oh, but you must remember,
My curse hath a great way to go –
Plagues, that make lanes[3] through largest families,
Consume them.

1 *daggers*: sharp pains 2 *vipers*: poisonous thoughts
3 *make lanes*: like a cannonball through troops in a battle

BOSOLA

Fie, lady!

DUCHESS

Let them, like tyrants,
Never be remembered but for the ill they have done.
Let all the zealous prayers of mortified
Churchmen forget them.

BOSOLA

Oh uncharitable!

DUCHESS

Let heaven a little while cease crowning martyrs,
To punish them.
Go, howl them this, and say I long to bleed.
It is some mercy when men kill with speed.

Exeunt [DUCHESS *and* CARIOLA *with* SERVANTS].

[*Enter* FERDINAND.]

FERDINAND

Excellent! As I would wish. She's plagued in art.[1]
These presentations are but framed in wax
By the curious[2] master in that quality,
Vincentio Lauriola,[3] and she takes them
For true, substantial bodies.

BOSOLA

Why do you do this?

FERDINAND

To bring her to despair.

BOSOLA

'Faith, end here,
And go no farther in your cruelty.
Send her a penitential garment to put on
Next to her delicate skin, and furnish her
With beads and prayer-books.

1 *in art*: by artifice 2 *curious*: ingenious

3 *Vincentio Lauriola*: since no reference to him remains, he may be Webster's invention

FERDINAND

Damn her! That body of hers,
While that my blood ran pure in't, was more worth
Than that which thou wouldst comfort, called a soul.
I will send her masques of common courtesans,
Have her meat served up by bawds and ruffians,
And, 'cause she'll needs be mad, I am resolved
To remove forth the common hospital
All the mad-folk and place them near her lodging.
There let them practise together: sing and dance
And act their gambols to the full o'th' moon.
If she can sleep the better for it, let her.
Your work is almost ended.

BOSOLA

Must I see her again?

FERDINAND

Yes.

BOSOLA

Never.

FERDINAND

You must.

BOSOLA

Never in mine own shape;
That's forfeited by my intelligence,[1]
And this last cruel lie. When you send me next,
The business shall be comfort.

FERDINAND

Very likely!
Thy pity is nothing of kin to thee. Antonio
Lurks about Milan. Thou shalt shortly thither
To feed a fire as great as my revenge,
Which ne'er will slack till it have spent his fuel.
Intemperate agues make physicians cruel. *Exeunt.*

1 *intelligence*: spying

ACT 4

Scene 2

[*Enter*] DUCHESS [*and*] CARIOLA.

DUCHESS
What hideous noise was that?
CARIOLA
'Tis the wild consort[1]
Of madmen, lady, which your tyrant brother
Hath placed about your lodging. This tyranny,
I think, was never practised till this hour.
DUCHESS
Indeed, I thank him. Nothing but noise and folly
Can keep me in my right wits, whereas reason
And silence make me stark mad. Sit down;
Discourse to me some dismal tragedy.
CARIOLA
Oh, 'twill increase your melancholy.
DUCHESS
Thou art deceived;
To hear of greater grief would lessen mine.
This is a prison?
CARIOLA
Yes, but you shall live
To shake this durance off.
DUCHESS
Thou art a fool.
The robin redbreast and the nightingale
Never live long in cages.
CARIOLA
Pray, dry your eyes.
What think you of, madam?

1 *consort*: company, often used of a group of musicians

DUCHESS

Of nothing.
When I muse thus, I sleep.

CARIOLA

Like a madman, with your eyes open?

DUCHESS

Dost thou think we shall know one another
In th'other world?

CARIOLA

Yes, out of question.

DUCHESS

Oh, that it were possible we might
But hold some two days' conference with the dead.
From them I should learn somewhat, I am sure
I never shall know here. I'll tell thee a miracle:
I am not mad yet, to my cause of sorrow.
Th' heaven o'er my head seems made of molten brass,
The earth of flaming sulphur,[1] yet I am not mad.
I am acquainted with sad misery,
As the tanned galley-slave is with his oar.
Necessity makes me suffer constantly,
And custom makes it easy. Who do I look like now?

CARIOLA

Like to your picture in the gallery:
A deal of life in show,[2] but none in practice;
Or rather like some reverend monument
Whose ruins are even pitied.

DUCHESS

Very proper;
And Fortune seems only to have her eyesight[3]
To behold my tragedy.

[*Noises of* MADMEN *within.*]

1 *molten brass . . . flaming sulphur*: from Deuteronomy 28:23 and 29:23
2 *in show*: in appearance
3 *Fortune . . . eyesight*: Fortune was proverbially blind

How now,
What noise is that?
[*Enter* SERVANT.]

SERVANT

I am come to tell you
Your brother hath intended you some sport.
A great physician, when the Pope was sick
Of a deep melancholy, presented him
With several sorts of madmen, which wild object,
Being full of change and sport, forced him to laugh
And so th'impostume[1] broke. The self-same cure
The Duke intends on you.

DUCHESS

Let them come in.

SERVANT

There's a mad lawyer and a secular priest;[2]
A doctor that hath forfeited his wits
By jealousy; an astrologian
That in his works said such a day o'th' month
Should be the day of doom, and failing of't
Ran mad; an English tailor, crazed i'th' brain
With the study of new fashion; a gentleman-usher
Quite beside himself with care to keep in mind
The number of his lady's salutations,
Or 'How do you?', she employed him in each morning;
A farmer too, an excellent knave in grain,[3]
Mad 'cause he was hindered transportation;[4]
And let one broker[5] that's mad loose to these,
You'd think the devil were among them.

1 *impostume*: abscess
2 *secular priest*: one not living in monastic seclusion
3 *knave in grain*: both a crooked dealer in grain and one whose villainy is engrained
4 *transportation*: export; in 1613 there had been a prohibition on exporting grain
5 *broker*: dealer, retailer

DUCHESS

Sit, Cariola. [*To* SERVANT] Let them loose when you please,
For I am chained to endure all your tyranny.

[*Enter* MADMEN.]

Here, by a MADMAN, *this song is sung, to a dismal kind of music.*

[MADMAN *sings*] *Oh, let us howl some heavy note,*
Some deadly, doggèd howl,
Sounding, as from the threat'ning throat,
Of beasts and fatal fowl.
As ravens, screech-owls, bulls and bears,
We'll bill[1] *and bawl our parts,*
Till irksome noise have cloyed your ears,
And corrosived[2] *your hearts.*
At last, when as our choir wants breath,
Our bodies being blessed,
We'll sing like swans to welcome death,[3]
And die in love and rest.

MAD ASTROLOGER

Doomsday not come yet? I'll draw it nearer by a perspective,[4] or make a glass[5] that shall set all the world on fire upon an instant. I cannot sleep – my pillow is stuffed with a litter of porcupines.

MAD LAWYER

Hell is a mere glass-house,[6] where the devils are continually blowing up women's souls on hollow irons, and the fire never goes out.

1 *bill*: utter through the beak 2 *corrosived*: corroded
3 *swans . . . death*: swans were thought to sing sweetly only at the moment before death
4 *perspective*: telescope 5 *glass*: magnifying glass
6 *glass-house*: glass factory

MAD PRIEST

I will lie with every woman in my parish the tenth night; I will tithe them over like haycocks.

MAD DOCTOR

Shall my 'pothecary outgo me because I am a cuckold? I have found out his roguery: he makes alum[1] of his wife's urine and sells it to Puritans that have sore throats with over-straining.

MAD ASTROLOGER

I have skill in heraldry.

MAD LAWYER

Hast?

MAD ASTROLOGER

You do give for your crest a woodcock's head,[2] with the brains picked out[3] on't. You are a very ancient gentleman.

MAD PRIEST

Greek is turned Turk;[4] we are only to be saved by the Helvetian translation.[5]

MAD ASTROLOGER [*To the* MAD LAWYER]

Come on, sir, I will lay[6] the law to you.

MAD LAWYER

Oh, rather lay a corrosive – the law will eat to the bone.

MAD PRIEST

He that drinks but to satisfy nature is damned.

MAD DOCTOR

If I had my glass here, I would show a sight should make all the women here call me mad doctor.

MAD ASTROLOGER [*pointing at the* MAD PRIEST]

What's he? A rope-maker?

1 *alum*: a white mineral salt used in medicine
2 *woodcock*: a proverbially stupid bird
3 *picked out*: removed, also embroidered
4 *Greek is turned Turk*: holy language turned heathen
5 *Helvetian translation*: the Genevan Bible of 1560, favoured by Puritans but condemned by James I in 1603 as 'partial' and 'seditious'
6 *lay*: explain, apply as a medicine

MAD LAWYER
No, no, no, a snuffling knave that, while he shows the tombs, will have his hand in a wench's placket.[1]

MAD PRIEST
Woe to the caroche that brought home my wife from the masque at three o'clock in the morning! It had a large featherbed in it.

MAD DOCTOR
I have pared the devil's nails forty times, roasted them in raven's eggs, and cured agues with them.

MAD PRIEST
Get me three hundred milch-bats to make possets[2] to procure sleep.

MAD DOCTOR
All the college may throw their caps at me,[3] I have made a soap-boiler costive.[4] It was my masterpiece.

Here the dance, consisting of eight MADMEN, *with music answerable thereunto, after which* [*they exeunt and*] BOSOLA, [*disguised*] *like an old man, enters.*

DUCHESS [*Indicating* BOSOLA]
Is he mad too?

SERVANT
Pray, question him. I'll leave you. [*Exit.*]

BOSOLA
I am come to make thy tomb.

DUCHESS
Ha? My tomb?
Thou speak'st as if I lay upon my death-bed,
Gasping for breath. Dost thou perceive me sick?

BOSOLA
Yes, and the more dangerously since thy sickness is insensible.[5]

1 *placket*: slit at the top of the skirt
2 *possets*: hot milk with spiced wine or ale
3 *throw . . . me*: a gesture to acknowledge superiority
4 *costive*: constipated. Soap-makers traditionally suffered from diarrhoea
5 *insensible*: unfelt

DUCHESS
Thou art not mad, sure. Dost know me?

BOSOLA
Yes.

DUCHESS
Who am I?

BOSOLA
Thou art a box of worm-seed;[1] at best, but a salvatory[2] of green mummy.[3] What's this flesh? A little crudded[4] milk, fantastical puff-paste.[5] Our bodies are weaker than those paper prisons boys use to keep flies in – more contemptible, since ours is to preserve earthworms. Didst thou ever see a lark in a cage? Such is the soul in the body: this world is like her little turf of grass, and the heaven o'er our heads like her looking-glass, only gives us a miserable knowledge of the small compass of our prison.

DUCHESS
Am not I thy Duchess?

BOSOLA
Thou art some great woman, sure, for riot[6] begins to sit on thy forehead, clad in grey hairs, twenty years sooner than on a merry milkmaid's. Thou sleep'st worse than if a mouse should be forced to take up her lodging in a cat's ear. A little infant that breeds its teeth, should it lie with thee, would cry out, as if thou wert the more unquiet bedfellow.

DUCHESS
I am Duchess of Malfi still.

BOSOLA
That makes thy sleeps so broken.
Glories, like glow-worms, afar off shine bright,
But looked to near, have neither heat nor light.[7]

1 *worm-seed*: a general term for plants whose dried flower heads were used to treat intestinal worms; also food for worms
2 *salvatory*: ointment box
3 *mummy*: medicine from mummified corpses
4 *crudded*: curdled, congealed; also allusion to Job 10:10
5 *puff-paste*: puff pastry 6 *riot*: riotous, extravagant living
7 *Glories . . . light*: this couplet also appears in *The White Devil*, 5.1

DUCHESS
Thou art very plain.

BOSOLA
My trade is to flatter the dead not the living;
I am a tomb-maker.

DUCHESS
And thou com'st to make my tomb?

BOSOLA
Yes.

DUCHESS
Let me be a little merry:
Of what stuff wilt thou make it?

BOSOLA
Nay, resolve me first of what fashion.

DUCHESS
Why, do we grow fantastical in our death-bed?
Do we affect fashion in the grave?

BOSOLA
Most ambitiously. Princes' images on their tombs do not lie, as they were wont, seeming to pray up to heaven, but with their hands under their cheeks, as if they died of the tooth-ache. They are not carved with their eyes fixed upon the stars, but as their minds were wholly bent upon the world – the self-same way they seem to turn their faces.

DUCHESS
Let me know fully, therefore, the effect
Of this thy dismal preparation,
This talk fit for a charnel.

BOSOLA
Now, I shall.

[*Enter* EXECUTIONERS *with*] *a* [*shrouded*] *coffin, cords and a bell.*

Here is a present from your princely brothers,
And may it arrive welcome, for it brings
Last benefit, last sorrow.

DUCHESS

Let me see it.
I have so much obedience in my blood,
I wish it in their veins to do them good.

BOSOLA

This is your last presence-chamber.
[*He reveals the coffin.*]

CARIOLA

O my sweet lady!

DUCHESS

Peace, it affrights not me.

BOSOLA

I am the common bellman,[1]
That usually is sent to condemned persons
The night before they suffer.

DUCHESS

Even now thou said'st
Thou wast a tomb-maker.

BOSOLA

'Twas to bring you
By degrees to mortification.[2] Listen!
[BOSOLA *rings the bell.*]
Hark, now everything is still,
The screech-owl and the whistler[3] *shrill*
Call upon our dame, aloud,
And bid her quickly don her shroud.
Much you had of land and rent,
Your length in clay's now competent.[4]
A long war disturbed your mind,
Here your perfect peace is signed.
Of what is't fools make such vain keeping?
Sin their conception, their birth weeping,
Their life a general mist of error,

1 *bellman*: paid to make speeches urging repentance under the prison window of condemned criminals

2 *mortification*: a spiritual process, leading to the rejection of worldly existence and repentance

3 *whistler*: a bird of ill-omen 4 *competent*: sufficient

Their death a hideous storm of terror.
Strew your hair with powders sweet,[1]
Don clean linen, bathe your feet,
And – the foul fiend more to check –
A crucifix let bless your neck.
'Tis now full tide 'tween night and day;
End your groan and come away.
[*The* EXECUTIONERS *approach.*]

CARIOLA
Hence, villains, tyrants, murderers! Alas,
What will you do with my lady? – Call for help!

DUCHESS
To whom? To our next neighbours? They are mad folks.

BOSOLA
Remove that noise.
[EXECUTIONERS *seize* CARIOLA.]

DUCHESS
Farewell, Cariola.
In my last will, I have not much to give.
A many hungry guests have fed upon me;
Thine will be a poor reversion.[2]

CARIOLA
I will die with her.

DUCHESS
I pray thee, look thou giv'st my little boy
Some syrup for his cold, and let the girl
Say her prayers ere she sleep.
[*Exeunt* EXECUTIONERS *with* CARIOLA.]
Now what you please:
What death?

BOSOLA
Strangling.
[*Re-enter* EXECUTIONERS.]
Here are your executioners.

1 *Strew . . . sweet*: the same advice as given to brides in epithalamia
2 *reversion*: bequest

DUCHESS

I forgive them.
The apoplexy, catarrh or cough o'th' lungs
Would do as much as they do.

BOSOLA

Doth not death fright you?

DUCHESS

Who would be afraid on't,
Knowing to meet such excellent company
In th'other world?

BOSOLA

Yet, methinks
The manner of your death should much afflict you;
This cord should terrify you.

DUCHESS

Not a whit.
What would it pleasure me to have my throat cut
With diamonds, or to be smothered
With cassia, or to be shot to death with pearls?
I know death hath ten thousand several doors
For men to take their exits; and 'tis found
They go on such strange, geometrical hinges,
You may open them both ways.[1] Any way, for heaven' sake,
So I were out of your whispering! Tell my brothers
That I perceive death, now I am well awake,
Best gift is they can give or I can take.
I would fain put off my last woman's fault:[2]
I'd not be tedious to you.

[EXECUTIONERS *place the noose around her neck and hold each end.*]

EXECUTIONER

We are ready.

1 *both ways*: i.e., by pulling or pushing; by suicide or murder
2 *woman's fault*: i.e., being talkative

DUCHESS

Dispose my breath how please you, but my body
Bestow upon my women. Will you?

EXECUTIONER

Yes.

DUCHESS

Pull, and pull strongly, for your able strength
Must pull down heaven upon me.
Yet, stay. Heaven gates are not so highly arched
As princes' palaces; they that enter there
Must go upon their knees. [*Kneels*] Come, violent death,
Serve for mandragora[1] to make me sleep.
Go tell my brothers, when I am laid out[2]
They then may feed in quiet.

They strangle her.

BOSOLA

Where's the waiting-woman?
Fetch her. Some other strangle the children.

[EXECUTIONERS *exeunt and re-enter with* CARIOLA.]

Look you, there sleeps your mistress.

CARIOLA

Oh, you are damned
Perpetually for this! My turn is next;
Is't not so ordered?

BOSOLA

Yes, and I am glad
You are so well prepared for't.

CARIOLA

You are deceived, sir;
I am not prepared for't. I will not die!
I will first come to my answer, and know
How I have offended.

1 *mandragora*: mandrake root, having narcotic properties
2 *laid out*: prepared for burial, waiting in bed as a bride

BOSOLA [*To* EXECUTIONERS]
Come, dispatch her.
[*To* CARIOLA] You kept her counsel, now you shall keep ours.

CARIOLA
I will not die; I must not. I am contracted
To a young gentleman.

EXECUTIONER
Here's your wedding-ring.
[*Showing her the noose*]

CARIOLA
Let me but speak with the Duke: I'll discover
Treason to his person.

BOSOLA
Delays – throttle her!

EXECUTIONER
She bites and scratches.

CARIOLA
If you kill me now
I am damned! I have not been at confession
This two years.

BOSOLA
When?[1]

CARIOLA
I am quick with child.

BOSOLA
Why then,
Your credit's[2] saved.
[EXECUTIONERS *strangle* CARIOLA.]
Bear her into th'next room.
Let this lie still.
[*Exeunt* EXECUTIONERS *with* CARIOLA*'s body.*]
[*Enter* FERDINAND.]

1 *When?*: i.e., when will I be obeyed?
2 *credit*: reputation, i.e., death will prevent the social disgrace of an illegitimate child

FERDINAND

Is she dead?

BOSOLA

She is what
You'd have her. But here begin your pity.
[*He draws a curtain and*] *shows the children strangled.*
Alas, how have these offended?

FERDINAND

The death
Of young wolves is never to be pitied.

BOSOLA [*indicating the* DUCHESS]
Fix your eye here.

FERDINAND

Constantly.

BOSOLA

Do you not weep?
Other sins only speak; murder shrieks out.
The element of water moistens the earth,
But blood flies upwards and bedews the heavens.

FERDINAND
Cover her face. Mine eyes dazzle.[1] She died young.

BOSOLA
I think not so [*covering her face*]; her infelicity
Seemed to have years too many.

FERDINAND

She and I were twins,
And should I die this instant, I had lived
Her time to a minute.

BOSOLA

It seems she was born first.
You have bloodily approved the ancient truth
That kindred commonly do worse agree
Than remote strangers.

1 *dazzle*: the Duchess is consistently associated with light, Ferdinand with darkness; his eyes may also be dazzled because they are filled with tears

FERDINAND

Let me see her face again.

[BOSOLA *uncovers her.*]

Why didst not thou pity her? What an excellent,
Honest man might'st thou have been
If thou hadst borne her to some sanctuary,
Or, bold in a good cause, opposed thyself
With thy advancèd sword above thy head,
Between her innocence and my revenge!
I bade thee, when I was distracted of my wits,
Go kill my dearest friend,[1] and thou hast done't.
For let me but examine well the cause:
What was the meanness of her match to me?
Only, I must confess, I had a hope,
Had she continued widow, to have gained
An infinite mass of treasure by her death,[2]
And that was the main cause: her marriage –
That drew a stream of gall quite through my heart.
For thee – as we observe in tragedies
That a good actor many times is cursed
For playing a villain's part – I hate thee for't,
And, for my sake, say thou hast done much ill well.

BOSOLA

Let me quicken your memory, for I perceive
You are falling into ingratitude. I challenge[3]
The reward due to my service.

FERDINAND

I'll tell thee

What I'll give thee –

BOSOLA

Do.

1 *friend*: companion or lover
2 *I had a hope . . . by her death*: this motive would be contradicted by the existence of a son by her dead husband, perhaps an oversight on Webster's part
3 *challenge*: demand

FERDINAND
I'll give thee a pardon
For this murder.
BOSOLA
Ha?
FERDINAND
Yes, and 'tis
The largest bounty I can study to do thee.
By what authority didst thou execute
This bloody sentence?
BOSOLA
By yours.
FERDINAND
Mine? Was I her judge?
Did any ceremonial form of law
Doom her to not-being? Did a complete jury
Deliver her conviction up i'th' court?
Where shalt thou find this judgement registered
Unless in hell? See, like a bloody fool
Th'hast forfeited thy life, and thou shalt die for't.
BOSOLA
The office of justice is perverted quite
When one thief hangs another. Who shall dare
To reveal this?
FERDINAND
Oh, I'll tell thee:
The wolf shall find her grave, and scrape it up –
Not to devour the corpse, but to discover
The horrid murder.[1]
BOSOLA
You, not I, shall quake for't.
FERDINAND
Leave me.
BOSOLA
I will first receive my pension.

1 *The wolf . . . horrid murder*: echoes *The White Devil*, 5.4

FERDINAND
You are a villain.

BOSOLA
When your ingratitude
Is judge, I am so.

FERDINAND
O horror!
That not the fear of him which binds the devils
Can prescribe man obedience!
Never look upon me more.

BOSOLA
Why, fare thee well.
Your brother and yourself are worthy men;
You have a pair of hearts are hollow graves,
Rotten, and rotting others; and your vengeance,
Like two chained bullets,[1] still goes arm-in-arm.
You may be brothers: for treason, like the plague,
Doth take much in a blood.[2] I stand like one
That long hath ta'en a sweet and golden dream;
I am angry with myself now that I wake.

FERDINAND
Get thee into some unknown part o'th' world
That I may never see thee.

BOSOLA
Let me know
Wherefore I should be thus neglected? Sir,
I served your tyranny, and rather strove
To satisfy yourself than all the world;
And though I loathed the evil, yet I loved
You that did counsel it, and rather sought
To appear a true servant than an honest man.

FERDINAND
I'll go hunt the badger by owl-light[3] –
'Tis a deed of darkness. *Exit.*

1 *chained bullets*: cannonballs linked by chains, mainly used in naval warfare
2 *take much in a blood*: takes hold in families 3 *owl-light*: dusk

BOSOLA

He's much distracted. Off, my painted[1] honour!
While with vain hopes our faculties we tire,
We seem to sweat in ice, and freeze in fire.
What would I do, were this to do again?
I would not change my peace of conscience
For all the wealth of Europe.
[*The* DUCHESS *sighs.*]
She stirs! Here's life!
Return, fair soul, from darkness, and lead mine
Out of this sensible[2] hell. She's warm. She breathes!
Upon thy pale lips I will melt my heart,
To store them with fresh colour.
[*He kisses her.*]
[*Noises offstage*]
Who's there?
Some cordial[3] drink! – Alas, I dare not call;
So pity would destroy pity. Her eye opes,
And heaven in it seems to ope, that late was shut,
To take me up to mercy.

DUCHESS

Antonio?

BOSOLA

Yes, madam, he is living.
The dead bodies you saw were but feigned statues.
He's reconciled to your brothers. The Pope hath wrought
The atonement.

DUCHESS

Mercy. *She dies.*

BOSOLA

Oh, she's gone again. There the cords of life[4] broke.
O sacred Innocence, that sweetly sleeps
On turtles' feathers, whilst a guilty conscience
Is a black register wherein is writ
All our good deeds and bad: a perspective

1 *painted*: false, superficial 2 *sensible*: palpable, living 3 *cordial*: reviving
4 *cords of life*: heartstrings

That shows us hell. That we cannot be suffered
To do good when we have a mind to it!
[*Weeping*] This is manly sorrow:
These tears, I am very certain, never grew
In my mother's milk. My estate is sunk
Below the degree of fear. Where were
These penitent fountains while she was living?
Oh, they were frozen up. Here is a sight
As direful to my soul as is the sword
Unto a wretch hath slain his father.
Come, I'll bear thee hence,
And execute thy last will – that's deliver
Thy body to the reverend dispose
Of some good women; that the cruel tyrant
Shall not deny me. Then I'll post to Milan,
Where somewhat I will speedily enact
Worth my dejection.[1] *Exit* [*carrying the* DUCHESS*'s body.*]

ACT 5

Scene 1

[*Enter*] ANTONIO [*and*] DELIO.

ANTONIO
What think you of my hope of reconcilement
To the Aragonian brethren?

DELIO
I misdoubt it,
For though they have sent their letters of safe conduct
For your repair to Milan, they appear
But nets to entrap you. The Marquis of Pescara,
Under whom you hold certain land in 'cheat,[2]
Much 'gainst his noble nature, hath been moved

1 *dejection*: abasement, also despair
2 *'cheat*: an escheat, i.e., the property reverts to another if the owner is convicted of a felony or treason

To seize those lands, and some of his dependents
Are, at this instant, making it their suit
To be invested in your revenues.
I cannot think they mean well to your life
That do deprive you of your means of life –
Your living.

ANTONIO

You are still an heretic
To any safety I can shape myself.

[*Enter* PESCARA.]

DELIO

Here comes the Marquis. I will make myself
Petitioner for some part of your land
To know whither it is flying.

ANTONIO

I pray, do.

[ANTONIO *stands aside.*]

DELIO

Sir, I have a suit to you.

PESCARA

To me?

DELIO

An easy one.
There is the citadel of St Bennet,[1]
With some demesnes,[2] of late in the possession
Of Antonio Bologna. Please you, bestow them on me.

PESCARA

You are my friend; but this is such a suit
Nor fit for me to give, nor you to take.

DELIO

No, sir?

[*Enter* JULIA.]

PESCARA

I will give you ample reason for't
Soon in private. Here's the Cardinal's mistress.

1 *Bennet*: Benedict 2 *demesnes*: land

JULIA

My lord, I am grown your poor petitioner,
And should be an ill beggar, had I not
A great man's letter here, the Cardinal's,
To court you in my favour.

[*She gives* PESCARA *the letter which he reads.*]

PESCARA

He entreats for you
The citadel of Saint Bennet, that belonged
To the banished Bologna.

JULIA

Yes.

PESCARA

I could not have thought of a friend I could
Rather pleasure with it: 'tis yours.

JULIA

Sir, I thank you;
And he shall know how doubly I am engaged
Both in your gift, and speediness of giving,
Which makes your grant the greater. *Exit.*

ANTONIO [*Aside*]

How they fortify
Themselves with my ruin!

DELIO [*To* PESCARA]

Sir, I am
Little bound to you.

PESCARA

Why?

DELIO

Because you denied this suit to me, and gave't
To such a creature.

PESCARA

Do you know what it was?
It was Antonio's land – not forfeited
By course of law, but ravished from his throat
By the Cardinal's entreaty. It were not fit
I should bestow so main a piece of wrong
Upon my friend; 'tis a gratification

Only due to a strumpet, for it is injustice.
Shall I sprinkle the pure blood of innocents
To make those followers I call my friends
Look ruddier[1] upon me? I am glad
This land, ta'en from the owner by such wrong,
Returns again unto so foul an use
As salary for his lust. Learn, good Delio,
To ask noble things of me, and you shall find
I'll be a noble giver.

DELIO

You instruct me well.

ANTONIO [*Aside*]

Why, here's a man, now, would fright impudence
From sauciest beggars.

PESCARA

Prince Ferdinand's come to Milan
Sick, as they give out, of an apoplexy;
But some say 'tis a frenzy.[2] I am going
To visit him. *Exit.*

ANTONIO [*coming forward*]

'Tis a noble old fellow.

DELIO

What course do you mean to take, Antonio?

ANTONIO

This night I mean to venture all my fortune –
Which is no more than a poor, ling'ring life –
To the Cardinal's worst of malice. I have got
Private access to his chamber, and intend
To visit him about the mid of night,
As once his brother did our noble Duchess.
It may be that the sudden apprehension
Of danger – for I'll go in mine own shape –
When he shall see it fraught with love and duty,
May draw the poison out of him, and work
A friendly reconcilement. If it fail,

1 *ruddier*: more favourably 2 *frenzy*: inflammation of the brain

Yet it shall rid me of this infamous calling;[1]
For better fall once than be ever falling.

DELIO

I'll second you in all danger and, howe'er,[2]
My life keeps rank with yours.

ANTONIO

You are still my loved and best friend. *Exeunt.*

ACT 5

Scene 2

[*Enter*] PESCARA [*and*] *a* DOCTOR.

PESCARA

Now, Doctor, may I visit your patient?

DOCTOR

If't please your lordship, but he's instantly
To take the air here in the gallery,[3]
By my direction.

PESCARA

Pray thee, what's his disease?

DOCTOR

A very pestilent[4] disease, my lord,
They call 'lycanthropia'.

PESCARA

What's that?
I need a dictionary to't.

DOCTOR

I'll tell you:
In those that are possessed with't there o'erflows
Such melancholy humour, they imagine
Themselves to be transformed into wolves:
Steal forth to churchyards in the dead of night,
And dig dead bodies up; as, two nights since,

1 *calling*: position 2 *howe'er*: whatever happens
3 *gallery*: a long room designed for walking 4 *pestilent*: deadly

One met the Duke, 'bout midnight, in a lane
Behind St Mark's church, with the leg of a man
Upon his shoulder; and he howled fearfully,
Said he was a wolf – only the difference
Was a wolf's skin was hairy on the outside,
His on the inside; bade them take their swords,
Rip up his flesh, and try. Straight I was sent for,
And having ministered to him, found his Grace
Very well recovered.

PESCARA

I am glad on't.

DOCTOR

Yet not without some fear of a relapse.
If he grow to his fit again I'll go
A nearer[1] way to work with him than ever
Paracelsus[2] dreamed of. If they'll give me leave,
I'll buffet[3] his madness out of him.
Stand aside. He comes.

[*Enter* FERDINAND, MALATESTE, CARDINAL *and* BOSOLA.]

FERDINAND

Leave me.

MALATESTE

Why doth your lordship love this solitariness?

FERDINAND

Eagles commonly fly alone. They are crows, daws and starlings that flock together. Look, what's that follows me?

MALATESTE

Nothing, my lord.

FERDINAND

Yes.

MALATESTE

'Tis your shadow.

1 *nearer*: more direct
2 *Paracelsus*: (1493–1541) famous Swiss doctor and scientist
3 *buffet*: whip

FERDINAND
Stay it! Let it not haunt me.[1]
MALATESTE
Impossible if you move and the sun shine.
FERDINAND
I will throttle it.
[He throws himself onto the shadow.]
MALATESTE
Oh, my lord, you are angry with nothing!
FERDINAND
You are a fool.
How is't possible I should catch my shadow
Unless I fall upon't? When I go to hell,
I mean to carry a bribe, for look you,
Good gifts ever more make way for the worst persons.
PESCARA
Rise, good my lord.
FERDINAND
I am studying the art of patience.
PESCARA
'Tis a noble virtue.
FERDINAND
To drive six snails before me from this town to Moscow; neither use goad[2] nor whip to them, but let them take their own time – the patient'st man i'th' world match me for an experiment! – and I'll crawl after like a sheep-biter.[3]
CARDINAL
Force him up.
[They get FERDINAND *to his feet.]*
FERDINAND
Use me well, you were best. What I have done, I have done;
I'll confess nothing.[4]

1 *haunt me*: the image of a man afraid of his own shadow was used as an emblem for guilt in Whitney's *Choice of Emblemes* (1586)
2 *goad*: pointed stick used for driving cattle
3 *sheep-biter*: dog that worries sheep
4 *What . . . nothing*: recalls Iago at the end of *Othello*, 5.2.309–10

DOCTOR

Now let me come to him. Are you mad, my lord? Are you out of your princely wits?

FERDINAND

What's he?

PESCARA

Your doctor.

FERDINAND

Let me have his beard sawed off, and his eyebrows filed more civil.[1]

DOCTOR [*Aside*]

I must do mad tricks with him, for that's the only way on't. [*Aloud*] I have brought your grace a salamander's[2] skin to keep you from sun-burning.

FERDINAND

I have cruel sore eyes.

DOCTOR

The white of a cockatrice's[3] egg is present remedy.

FERDINAND

Let it be a new-laid one, you were best. [*To* PESCARA] Hide me from him! Physicians are like kings: they brook no contradiction.

DOCTOR

Now he begins to fear me. Now let me alone with him.

[FERDINAND *starts to undress.*]

CARDINAL

How now, put off your gown?

[*The* CARDINAL *restrains him.*]

DOCTOR

Let me have some forty urinals filled with rose-water. He and I'll go pelt one another with them. Now he begins to fear

1 *Let me . . . more civil*: if the Doctor and Cariola were played by the same boy actor, he may have worn an exaggerated beard and eyebrows to make the distinction

2 *salamander*: a lizard believed to live in fire

3 *cockatrice's egg*: thought to be deadly

me. – Can you fetch a frisk,[1] sir? – Let him go, let him go, upon my peril.

[*The* CARDINAL *releases him.*]

I find by his eye he stands in awe of me; I'll make him as tame as a dormouse.

[FERDINAND *attacks the* DOCTOR.]

FERDINAND

Can you fetch your frisks, sir? I will stamp him into a cullis,[2] flay off his skin to cover one of the anatomies[3] this rogue hath set i'th' cold yonder, in Barber-Chirurgeons' Hall. Hence, hence! You are all of you like beasts for sacrifice; there's nothing left of you but tongue and belly – flattery and lechery. [*Exit.*]

PESCARA

Doctor, he did not fear you throughly.

DOCTOR

True, I was somewhat too forward. [*Exit.*]

BOSOLA [*Aside*]

Mercy upon me, what a fatal judgement
Hath fall'n upon this Ferdinand!

PESCARA

Knows your Grace
What accident hath brought unto the Prince
This strange distraction?

CARDINAL [*Aside*]

I must feign somewhat. [*Aloud*] Thus they say it grew:
You have heard it rumoured for these many years,
None of our family dies but there is seen
The shape of an old woman, which is given
By tradition to us to have been murdered
By her nephews for her riches. Such a figure
One night, as the Prince sat up late at's book,
Appeared to him, when, crying out for help,
The gentlemen of's chamber found his Grace

1 *fetch a frisk*: dance 2 *cullis*: meat broth
3 *anatomies*: skeletons, displayed in the entrance to Barber-Surgeons' Hall, where dissections were performed for medical students

All on a cold sweat, altered much in face
And language; since which apparition,
He hath grown worse and worse, and I much fear
He cannot live.

BOSOLA [*To the* CARDINAL]
Sir, I would speak with you.

PESCARA
We'll leave your Grace,
Wishing to the sick Prince, our noble lord,
All health of mind and body.

CARDINAL
You are most welcome.
[*Exeunt all except* CARDINAL AND BOSOLA.]
[*Aside*] Are you come? So. This fellow must not know
By any means I had intelligence
In our Duchess's death; for, though I counselled it,
The full of all th'engagement[1] seemed to grow
From Ferdinand. [*To* BOSOLA] Now sir, how fares our sister?
I do not think but sorrow makes her look
Like to an oft-dyed garment. She shall now
Taste comfort from me. Why do you look so wildly?
Oh, the fortune of your master here, the Prince,
Dejects you; but be you of happy comfort.
If you'll do one thing for me, I'll entreat,
Though he had a cold tombstone o'er his bones,[2]
I'd make you what you would be.

BOSOLA
Anything.
Give it me in a breath, and let me fly to't.
They that think long, small expedition[3] win,
For musing much o'th' end, cannot begin.
[*Enter* JULIA.]

JULIA
Sir, will you come in to supper?

1 *engagement*: employment (of Bosola)
2 *Though . . . bones*: even if the consequence were his death
3 *expedition*: progress

CARDINAL

I am busy. Leave me.

JULIA [*Aside*]

What an excellent shape hath that fellow! *Exit.*

CARDINAL

'Tis thus: Antonio lurks here in Milan.
Enquire him out and kill him. While he lives
Our sister cannot marry, and I have thought
Of an excellent match for her. Do this, and style me
Thy advancement.[1]

BOSOLA

But by what means shall I find him out?

CARDINAL

There is a gentleman called Delio,
Here in the camp, that hath been long approved
His loyal friend. Set eye upon that fellow,
Follow him to Mass: may be Antonio,
Although he do account religion
But a school-name,[2] for fashion of the world
May accompany him; or else go enquire out
Delio's confessor, and see if you can bribe
Him to reveal it. There are a thousand ways
A man might find to trace him, as to know
What fellows haunt the Jews for taking up[3]
Great sums of money – for sure he's in want;
Or else to go to th'picture-makers and learn
Who bought her picture lately. Some of these
Happily[4] may take.

BOSOLA

Well, I'll not freeze i'th' business.
I would see that wretched thing, Antonio,
Above all sights i'th' world.

1 *style . . . advancement*: name me as a means for your preferment
2 *school-name*: invention of Church fathers
3 *taking up*: borrowing
4 *Happily*: by chance, fortunately

CARDINAL

Do, and be happy. *Exit.*

BOSOLA

This fellow doth breed basilisks in's eyes.
He's nothing else but Murder. Yet he seems
Not to have notice of the Duchess's death.
'Tis his cunning. I must follow his example:
There cannot be a surer way to trace
Than that of an old fox.

[*Enter* JULIA, *pointing a pistol at him.*]

JULIA

So, sir, you are well met.

BOSOLA

How now?

JULIA

Nay, the doors are fast enough.
Now, sir, I will make you confess your treachery.

BOSOLA

Treachery?

JULIA

Yes, confess to me
Which of my women 'twas you hired to put
Love-powder into my drink.

BOSOLA

Love-powder?

JULIA

Yes, when I was at Malfi;
Why should I fall in love with such a face else?
I have already suffered for thee so much pain,
The only remedy to do me good
Is to kill my longing.

BOSOLA

Sure, your pistol holds
Nothing but perfumes or kissing comfits.[1] Excellent lady,
You have a pretty way on't to discover

1 *kissing comfits*: sweets used to freshen the breath

Your longing. Come, come, I'll disarm you,
And arm you thus. [*Embracing her*] Yet this is wondrous
strange!

JULIA
Compare thy form and my eyes together,
You'll find my love no such great miracle.
[*She kisses him.*]
Now you'll say I am wanton. This nice[1] modesty
In ladies is but a troublesome familiar
That haunts them.

BOSOLA
Know you me? I am a blunt soldier.

JULIA
The better;
Sure, there wants[2] fire where there are no lively sparks
Of roughness.

BOSOLA
And I want compliment.[3]

JULIA
Why,
Ignorance in courtship cannot make you do amiss,
If you have a heart to do well.

BOSOLA
You are very fair.

JULIA
Nay, if you lay beauty to my charge,
I must plead unguilty.

BOSOLA
Your bright eyes
Carry a quiver of darts in them, sharper
Than sunbeams.

JULIA
You will mar me with commendation.
Put yourself to the charge of courting me,
Whereas now I woo you.

1 *nice*: fastidious 2 *wants*: lacks
3 *want compliment*: lack courtly manners

BOSOLA [*Aside*]
I have it: I will work upon this creature.
[*To* JULIA] Let us grow most amorously familiar.
If the great Cardinal now should see me thus,
Would he not count me a villain?

JULIA
No, he might count me a wanton,
Not lay a scruple of offence on you;
For if I see and steal a diamond,
The fault is not i'th' stone but in me the thief
That purloins it. I am sudden with you;
We that are great women of pleasure use to cut off
These uncertain wishes and unquiet longings,
And in an instant join the sweet delight
And the pretty excuse together. Had you been in th'street,
Under my chamber window, even there
I should have courted you.

BOSOLA
Oh, you are an excellent lady!

JULIA
Bid me do somewhat for you presently,[1]
To express I love you.

BOSOLA
I will, and if you love me
Fail not to effect it.
The Cardinal is grown wondrous melancholy;
Demand the cause. Let him not put you off
With feigned excuse; discover the main ground on't.

JULIA
Why would you know this?

BOSOLA
I have depended on him,
And I hear that he is fall'n in some disgrace
With the Emperor. If he be, like the mice
That forsake falling houses, I would shift
To other dependence.

1 *presently*: immediately

JULIA
You shall not need follow the wars;
I'll be your maintenance.

BOSOLA
And I your loyal servant;
But I cannot leave my calling.

JULIA
Not leave
An ungrateful general for the love of a sweet lady?
You are like some cannot sleep in featherbeds,
But must have blocks for their pillows.

BOSOLA
Will you do this?

JULIA
Cunningly.

BOSOLA
Tomorrow I'll expect th'intelligence.

JULIA
Tomorrow? Get you into my cabinet;[1]
You shall have it with you. Do not delay me,
No more than I do you. I am like one
That is condemned: I have my pardon promised,
But I would see it sealed. Go, get you in.
You shall see me wind my tongue about his heart
Like a skein of silk.

[BOSOLA *withdraws into the cabinet.*]
[*Enter* CARDINAL.]

CARDINAL
Where are you?

[*Enter* SERVANTS.]

SERVANTS
Here.

1 *cabinet*: private chamber

CARDINAL

Let none, upon your lives,
Have conference with the Prince Ferdinand
Unless I know it. [*Exeunt* SERVANTS.]
[*Aside*] In this distraction
He may reveal the murder.
[*Seeing* JULIA] Yond's my ling'ring consumption.
I am weary of her, and by any means
Would be quit of.

JULIA

How now, my lord,
What ails you?

CARDINAL

Nothing.

JULIA

Oh, you are much altered.
Come, I must be your secretary and remove
This lead from off your bosom. What's the matter?

CARDINAL

I may not tell you.

JULIA

Are you so far in love with sorrow
You cannot part with part of it? Or think you
I cannot love your Grace when you are sad,
As well as merry? Or do you suspect
I, that have been a secret to your heart
These many winters, cannot be the same
Unto your tongue?

CARDINAL

Satisfy thy longing.
The only way to make thee keep my counsel
Is not to tell thee.

JULIA

Tell your echo this,
Or flatterers that, like echoes, still report
What they hear, though most imperfect, and not me.

For, if that you be true unto yourself,[1]
I'll know.

CARDINAL
Will you rack[2] me?

JULIA
No, judgement shall
Draw it from you. It is an equal fault
To tell one's secrets unto all, or none.

CARDINAL
The first argues folly.

JULIA
But the last tyranny.

CARDINAL
Very well. Why, imagine I have committed
Some secret deed, which I desire the world
May never hear of.

JULIA
Therefore may not I know it?
You have concealed for me as great a sin
As adultery. Sir, never was occasion
For perfect trial of my constancy
Till now. Sir, I beseech you.

CARDINAL
You'll repent it.

JULIA
Never.

CARDINAL
It hurries thee to ruin; I'll not tell thee.
Be well advised, and think what danger 'tis
To receive a prince's secrets. They that do
Had need have their breasts hooped with adamant[3]
To contain them. I pray thee, yet be satisfied.
Examine thine own frailty. 'Tis more easy

1 *if . . . yourself*: because Julia is his second self
2 *rack*: torture instrument to elicit confession
3 *adamant*: very hard rock or mineral

To tie knots than unloose them. 'Tis a secret
That, like a ling'ring poison, may chance lie
Spread in thy veins, and kill thee seven year hence.

JULIA
Now you dally with me.

CARDINAL
No more: thou shalt know it.
By my appointment the great Duchess of Malfi
And two of her young children, four nights since,
Were strangled.

JULIA
Oh heaven! Sir, what have you done?

CARDINAL
How now? How settles this?[1] Think you your bosom
Will be a grave dark and obscure enough
For such a secret?

JULIA
You have undone yourself, sir.

CARDINAL
Why?

JULIA
It lies not in me to conceal it.

CARDINAL
No?
Come, I will swear you to't upon this book.

JULIA
Most religiously.

CARDINAL
Kiss it.
[*She kisses the book.*]
Now you shall never utter it. Thy curiosity
Hath undone thee; thou'rt poisoned with that book.
Because I knew thou could'st not keep my counsel,
I have bound thee to't by death.

BOSOLA *emerges from the cabinet.*

1 *How settles this?* What do you mean by this?

BOSOLA
For pity sake, hold!

CARDINAL
Ha, Bosola?

JULIA
I forgive you
This equal piece of justice you have done,
For I betrayed your counsel to that fellow.
He overheard it; that was the cause I said
It lay not in me to conceal it.

BOSOLA
Oh foolish woman,
Could'st not thou have poisoned him?

JULIA
'Tis weakness
Too much to think what should have been done.
I go I know not whither. [*She dies.*]

CARDINAL
Wherefore com'st thou hither?

BOSOLA
That I might find a great man, like yourself,
Not out of his wits as the Lord Ferdinand,
To remember[1] my service.

CARDINAL
I'll have thee hewed in pieces!

BOSOLA
Make not yourself such a promise of that life
Which is not yours to dispose of.

CARDINAL
Who placed thee here?

BOSOLA
Her lust, as she intended.

CARDINAL
Very well,
Now you know me for your fellow murderer.

1 *remember*: reward

BOSOLA

And wherefore should you lay fair marble colours[1]
Upon your rotten purposes to me?
Unless you imitate some that do plot great treasons,
And, when they have done, go hide themselves
I'th' graves of those were actors in't?[2]

CARDINAL

No more, there is a fortune attends thee.

BOSOLA

Shall I go sue to Fortune any longer?
'Tis the fool's pilgrimage.

CARDINAL

I have honours in store for thee.

BOSOLA

There are a many ways that conduct to seeming
Honour – and some of them very dirty ones.

CARDINAL

Throw to the devil
Thy melancholy. The fire burns well.
What need we keep a-stirring of't, and make
A greater smother?[3] Thou wilt kill Antonio?

BOSOLA

Yes.

CARDINAL

Take up that body.

BOSOLA

I think I shall
Shortly grow the common bier[4] for churchyards!

CARDINAL

I will allow thee some dozen of attendants
To aid thee in the murder.

BOSOLA

Oh, by no means.

1 *fair marble colours*: i.e., a good appearance; wood was often painted to resemble marble

2 *graves . . . in't*: i.e., they kill their accomplices

3 *A greater smother*: more stifling smoke

4 *bier*: a stretcher used to carry corpses to the grave

Physicians that apply horse-leeches to any rank swelling use to cut off their tails, that the blood may run through them the faster. Let me have no train when I go to shed blood, lest it make me have a greater when I ride to the gallows.

CARDINAL

Come to me after midnight to help to remove that body to her own lodging. I'll give out she died o'th' plague: 'twill breed the less enquiry after her death.

BOSOLA

Where's Castruccio, her husband?

CARDINAL

He's rode to Naples to take possession
Of Antonio's citadel.

BOSOLA

Believe me, you have done a very happy turn.

CARDINAL

Fail not to come. There is the master-key
Of our lodgings, and by that you may conceive
What trust I plant in you.

BOSOLA

You shall find me ready.

Exit [CARDINAL.]

O poor Antonio! Though nothing be so needful
To thy estate as pity, yet I find
Nothing so dangerous. I must look to my footing:
In such slippery ice-pavements men had need
To be frost-nailed[1] well; they may break their necks else.
The precedent's here afore me: how this man
Bears up in blood,[2] seems fearless! Why, 'tis well:
Security[3] some men call the suburbs of hell –
Only a dead[4] wall between. Well, good Antonio,
I'll seek thee out, and all my care shall be
To put thee into safety from the reach

1 *frost-nailed*: given hobnailed boots
2 *Bears up in blood*: keeps up his courage
3 *Security*: suggesting not enough concern for the state of the soul and its vocation after death
4 *dead*: continuous

Of these most cruel biters that have got
Some of thy blood already.[1] It may be
I'll join with thee in a most just revenge.
The weakest arm is strong enough, that strikes
With the sword of justice. Still, methinks the Duchess
Haunts me.
There, there; 'tis nothing but my melancholy.[2]
O Penitence, let me truly taste thy cup,
That throws men down, only to raise them up.

Exit [*with* JULIA*'s body*].

ACT 5

Scene 3

[*Enter*] ANTONIO, DELIO, [*and*] ECHO *from the Duchess's grave.*[3]

DELIO

Yond's the Cardinal's window. This fortification
Grew from the ruins of an ancient abbey,
And to yond side o'th' river lies a wall,
Piece of a cloister, which in my opinion
Gives the best echo that you ever heard:
So hollow and so dismal,[4] and withal
So plain in the distinction of our words,
That many have supposed it is a spirit
That answers.

ANTONIO

I do love these ancient ruins.
We never tread upon them but we set
Our foot upon some reverend[5] history,
And, questionless, here in this open court,

1 *Some . . . already*: i.e., his children 2 *melancholy*: remorse
3 ECHO: presumably a reminder to the actor speaking the lines offstage, rather than implying an entrance
4 *dismal*: boding ill 5 *reverend*: venerable

Which now lies naked to the injuries
Of stormy weather, some men lie interred
Loved the church so well, and gave so largely to't,
They thought it should have canopied their bones
Till doomsday. But all things have their end:
Churches and cities, which have diseases[1] like to men,
Must have like death that we have.

ECHO
Like death that we have.

DELIO
Now the echo hath caught you.

ANTONIO
It groaned, methought, and gave
A very deadly accent.

ECHO
Deadly accent.

DELIO
I told you 'twas a pretty one. You may make it
A huntsman or a falconer, a musician,
Or a thing of sorrow.

ECHO
A thing of sorrow.

ANTONIO
Ay, sure, that suits it best.

ECHO
That suits it best.

ANTONIO
'Tis very like my wife's voice.

ECHO
Ay, wife's voice.

DELIO
Come, let us walk farther from't:
I would not have you go to th'Cardinal's tonight.
Do not.

ECHO
Do not.

1 *diseases*: disturbances

DELIO
Wisdom doth not more moderate wasting sorrow
Than time. Take time for't; be mindful of thy safety.

ECHO
Be mindful of thy safety.

ANTONIO
Necessity compels me.
Make scrutiny throughout the passes[1]
Of your own life; you'll find it impossible
To fly your fate.

ECHO
Oh, fly your fate!

DELIO
Hark, the dead stones seem to have pity on you
And give you good counsel.

ANTONIO
Echo, I will not talk with thee,
For thou art a dead thing.

ECHO
Thou art a dead thing.

ANTONIO
My Duchess is asleep now,
And her little ones, I hope, sweetly. O heaven,
Shall I never see her more?

ECHO
Never see her more.

ANTONIO
I marked not one repetition of the echo
But that, and on the sudden, a clear light
Presented me a face folded in sorrow.

DELIO
Your fancy, merely.

ANTONIO
Come, I'll be out of this ague;[2]
For to live thus is not indeed to live:
It is a mockery and abuse of life.

1 *passes*: events 2 *ague*: fever

I will not, henceforth, save myself by halves:
Lose all, or nothing.

DELIO

Your own virtue save you.
I'll fetch your eldest son and second you.
It may be that the sight of his[1] own blood,
Spread[2] in so sweet a figure, may beget
The more compassion.

ANTONIO

However,[3] fare you well.
Though in our miseries Fortune have a part,
Yet in our noble suff'rings she hath none.
Contempt of pain – that we may call our own. *Exeunt.*

ACT 5

Scene 4

[*Enter*] CARDINAL, PESCARA, MALATESTE, RODERIGO [*and*] GRISOLAN [*carrying torches*].

CARDINAL

You shall not watch tonight by the sick prince.
His Grace is very well recovered.

MALATESTE

Good my lord, suffer[4] us.

CARDINAL

Oh, by no means.
The noise, and change of object in his eye,
Doth more distract him. I pray, all to bed;
And though you hear him in his violent fit,
Do not rise, I entreat you.

PESCARA

So sir, we shall not.

1 *his*: i.e., the Cardinal's 2 *Spread*: displayed
3 *However*: howsoever 4 *suffer*: allow

CARDINAL
Nay, I must have you promise
Upon your honours; for I was enjoined to't
By himself, and he seemed to urge it sensibly.[1]

PESCARA
Let our honours bind[2] this trifle.

CARDINAL
Nor any of your followers.

MALATESTE
Neither.

CARDINAL
It may be, to make trial of your promise,
When he's asleep, myself will rise and feign
Some of his mad tricks, and cry out for help,
And feign myself in danger.

MALATESTE
If your throat were cutting,
I'd not come at you, now I have protested[3] against it.

CARDINAL
Why, I thank you.
[CARDINAL *stands apart.*]

GRISOLAN
'Twas a foul storm tonight.

RODERIGO
The Lord Ferdinand's chamber shook like an osier.[4]

MALATESTE
'Twas nothing but pure kindness in the devil
To rock his own child.
Exeunt [*all except* CARDINAL].

CARDINAL
The reason why I would not suffer these
About my brother is because at midnight
I may, with better privacy, convey
Julia's body to her own lodging. O my conscience!

1 *sensibly*: passionately 2 *bind*: confirm us
3 *protested*: vowed 4 *osier*: willow tree

I would pray now, but the devil takes away my heart
Fro' having any confidence in prayer.
[*Enter* BOSOLA, *unseen.*]
About this hour I appointed Bosola
To fetch the body. When he hath served my turn,
He dies. *Exit.*

BOSOLA
Ha? 'Twas the Cardinal's voice. I heard him name
Bosola, and my death. Listen, I hear one's footing.[1]
[*Enter* FERDINAND.]

FERDINAND
Strangling is a very quiet death.

BOSOLA [*Aside*]
Nay then, I see I must stand upon my guard.

FERDINAND
What say' to that? Whisper softly: do you agree to't?
So. It must be done i'th' dark. The Cardinal
Would not for a thousand pounds the Doctor should see it.
Exit.

BOSOLA
My death is plotted; here's the consequence of murder.
We value not desert nor Christian breath,
When we know black deeds must be cured with death.
[*Enter* SERVANT *with* ANTONIO.]

SERVANT
Here stay, sir, and be confident, I pray.
I'll fetch you a dark lantern. *Exit.*

ANTONIO
Could I take him
At his prayers, there were hope of pardon.

BOSOLA
Fall right my sword!
I'll not give thee so much leisure as to pray.
[*He stabs* ANTONIO *in the dark.*]

1 *footing*: footsteps

ANTONIO

Oh, I am gone! Thou hast ended a long suit[1]
In a minute.

BOSOLA

What art thou?

ANTONIO

A most wretched thing,
That only have thy benefit[2] in death,
To appear myself.

[*Enter* SERVANT *with a dark lantern.*]

SERVANT

Where are you, sir?

ANTONIO

Very near my home – Bosola?

SERVANT

Oh misfortune!

BOSOLA [*To* SERVANT]

Smother thy pity! Thou art dead else – Antonio!
The man I would have saved 'bove mine own life!
We are merely the stars' tennis-balls, struck and banded[3]
Which way please them. O good Antonio,
I'll whisper one thing in thy dying ear
Shall make thy heart break quickly: thy fair Duchess
And two sweet children –

ANTONIO

Their very names
Kindle a little life in me.

BOSOLA

– are murdered!

ANTONIO

Some men have wished to die
At the hearing of sad tidings. I am glad
That I shall do't in sadness.[4] I would not now
Wish my wounds balmed nor healed, for I have no use
To put my life to. In all our quest of greatness,

1 *suit*: petition, quest 2 *benefit*: assistance
3 *banded*: bandied, hit randomly 4 *sadness*: earnest

Like wanton boys whose pastime is their care,
We follow after bubbles blown in th'air.
Pleasure of life, what is't? Only the good hours
Of an ague; merely a preparative to rest,
To endure vexation. I do not ask
The process of my death. Only commend me
To Delio.

BOSOLA
Break, heart!

ANTONIO
And let my son fly the courts of princes. [*He dies.*]

BOSOLA [*To* SERVANT]
Thou seem'st to have loved Antonio?

SERVANT
I brought him hither
To have reconciled him to the Cardinal.

BOSOLA
I do not ask thee that.
Take him up, if thou tender thine own life,
And bear him where the Lady Julia
Was wont to lodge. [*Aside*] Oh, my fate moves swift!
I have this Cardinal in the forge already.
Now I'll bring him to th'hammer. O direful misprision![1]
I will not imitate things glorious,
No more than base; I'll be mine own example.
[*To* SERVANT] On, on, and look thou represent, for silence,
The thing thou bear'st.[2]
Exeunt [BOSOLA *and* SERVANT *carrying* ANTONIO*'s body*].

1 *misprision*: mistake
2 *represent . . . bear'st*: be as silent as the corpse you carry

ACT 5

Scene 5

[*Enter*] CARDINAL, *with a book.*

CARDINAL
I am puzzled in a question about hell.
He says, in hell there's one material fire,
And yet it shall not burn all men alike.
Lay him by.
[*He puts down the book.*]
How tedious is a guilty conscience!
When I look into the fish-ponds in my garden,
Methinks I see a thing, armed with a rake,
That seems to strike at me.
[*Enter* BOSOLA *and* SERVANT *with* ANTONIO*'s body.*]
Now, art thou come? Thou look'st ghastly.[1]
There sits in thy face some great determination,[2]
Mixed with some fear.

BOSOLA
Thus it lightens into action.
[*He draws his sword.*]
I am come to kill thee.

CARDINAL
Ha? Help! Our guard!

BOSOLA
Thou art deceived: they are out of thy howling.

CARDINAL
Hold, and I will faithfully divide
Revenues with thee.

BOSOLA
Thy prayers and proffers
Are both unseasonable.

1 *ghastly*: fearful 2 *determination*: resolution

CARDINAL [*shouts*]
Raise the watch! We are betrayed!

BOSOLA
I have confined your flight.
I'll suffer your retreat to Julia's chamber,
But no further.

CARDINAL
Help! We are betrayed!

[*Enter above* MALATESTE, RODERIGO, GRISOLAN *and* PESCARA.]

MALATESTE
Listen.

CARDINAL
My dukedom for rescue!

RODERIGO
Fie upon his counterfeiting!

MALATESTE
Why, 'tis not the Cardinal.

RODERIGO
Yes, yes, 'tis he,
But I'll see him hanged ere I'll go down to him.

CARDINAL
Here's a plot upon me. I am assaulted! I am lost
Unless some rescue!

GRISOLAN
He doth this pretty well,
But it will not serve to laugh me out of mine honour.

CARDINAL
The sword's at my throat!

RODERIGO
You would not bawl so loud then.

MALATESTE
Come, come, let's go to bed.
He told us thus much aforehand.

PESCARA
He wished you should not come at him, but, believe't,
The accent of the voice sounds not in jest.

I'll down to him, howsoever, and with engines[1]
Force ope the doors. [*Exit.*]

RODERIGO

Let's follow him aloof,
And note how the Cardinal will laugh at him.
[*Exeunt* MALATESTE, RODERIGO *and* GRISOLAN.]

BOSOLA

There's for you first –
He kills the SERVANT.
'Cause you shall not unbarricade the door
To let in rescue.

CARDINAL

What cause hast thou to pursue my life?

BOSOLA

Look there!

CARDINAL

Antonio?

BOSOLA

Slain by my hand, unwittingly.
Pray, and be sudden. When thou killed'st thy sister,
Thou took'st from Justice her most equal balance,[2]
And left her naught but her sword.

CARDINAL

Oh, mercy!

BOSOLA

Now it seems thy greatness was only outward,
For thou fall'st faster of thyself than calamity
Can drive thee. I'll not waste longer time. There!
[*He stabs the* CARDINAL.]

CARDINAL

Thou hast hurt me!

BOSOLA

Again!
[*Stabs him again.*]

1 *engines*: devices, perhaps a battering ram
2 *equal balance*: Justice was usually depicted holding scales as well as a sword

CARDINAL

Shall I die like a leveret,
Without any resistance? Help, help, help!
I am slain!

[*Enter* FERDINAND.]

FERDINAND

Th'alarum![1] Give me a fresh horse!
Rally the vanguard[2] or the day is lost![3]
[*To the* CARDINAL] Yield, yield! I give you the honour of arms,
Shake my sword over you. Will you yield?

CARDINAL

Help me! I am your brother.

FERDINAND

The devil?
My brother fight upon the adverse party?

He wounds the CARDINAL *and, in the scuffle, gives* BOSOLA *his death-wound.*

There flies your ransom.

CARDINAL

Oh, justice!
I suffer now for what hath former been:
Sorrow is held the eldest child of Sin.

FERDINAND

Now you're brave[4] fellows. Caesar's fortune was harder than Pompey's: Caesar died in the arms of prosperity, Pompey at the feet of disgrace. You both died in the field. The pain's nothing – pain, many times, is taken away with the apprehension of greater, as the toothache with the sight of a barber that comes to pull it out. There's philosophy for you.

1 *alarum*: call to arms on the battlefield

2 *vanguard*: foremost division of the army

3 *Give . . . lost*: the echoes of Shakespeare's *Richard III* ('My kingdom for a horse') would have been reinforced by the fact that the actor playing Ferdinand, Richard Burbage, had also played that king

4 *brave*: splendid

BOSOLA

Now my revenge is perfect.

He kills FERDINAND.

Sink, thou main cause
Of my undoing! The last part of my life
Hath done me best service.

FERDINAND

Give me some wet hay; I am broken-winded.[1]
I do account this world but a dog-kennel.
I will vault credit,[2] and affect[3] high pleasures
Beyond death.

BOSOLA

He seems to come to himself,
Now he's so near the bottom.

FERDINAND

My sister! Oh, my sister! There's the cause on't.
Whether we fall by ambition, blood or lust,
Like diamonds we are cut with our own dust. [*He dies.*]

CARDINAL [*To* BOSOLA]

Thou hast thy payment[4] too.

BOSOLA

Yes, I hold my weary soul in my teeth;
'Tis ready to part from me. I do glory
That thou, which stood'st like a huge pyramid,
Begun upon a large and ample base,
Shalt end in a little point, a kind of nothing.

[*Enter* PESCARA, MALATESTE, RODERIGO *and* GRISOLAN.]

PESCARA

How now, my lord?

MALATESTE

O sad disaster!

1 *wet hay*: a customary cure for broken-winded horses
2 *vault credit*: ignore reputation 3 *affect*: aspire to
4 *payment*: i.e., his death wound

RODERIGO

How comes this?

BOSOLA

Revenge for the Duchess of Malfi, murdered
By th'Aragonian brethren; for Antonio,
Slain by this hand; for lustful Julia,
Poisoned by this man; and lastly, for myself,
That was an actor in the main of all,
Much 'gainst mine own good nature, yet i'th' end
Neglected.

PESCARA

How now, my lord?

CARDINAL

Look to my brother.
He gave us these large wounds as we were struggling
Here i'th' rushes.[1] And now, I pray, let me
Be laid by and never thought of. [*He dies.*]

PESCARA

How fatally, it seems, he did withstand
His own rescue!

MALATESTE

Thou wretched thing of blood,
How came Antonio by his death?

BOSOLA

In a mist – I know not how.
Such a mistake as I have often seen
In a play. Oh, I am gone!
We are only like dead[2] walls, or vaulted graves
That, ruined, yields no echo. Fare you well.
It may be pain, but no harm to me to die
In so good a quarrel. Oh, this gloomy world!
In what a shadow, or deep pit of darkness,
Doth womanish and fearful mankind live!

1 *rushes*: plants used as floor-covering for houses and also the stage
2 *dead*: continuous

Let worthy minds ne'er stagger[1] in distrust
To suffer death or shame for what is just.
Mine is another voyage. [*He dies.*]

PESCARA

The noble Delio, as I came to th'palace,
Told me of Antonio's being here, and showed me
A pretty gentleman: his son and heir.

[*Enter* DELIO *with* ANTONIO*'s eldest son.*]

MALATESTE

Oh sir, you come too late.

DELIO

I heard so, and
Was armed for't ere I came. Let us make noble use
Of this great ruin, and join all our force
To establish this young, hopeful gentleman
In's mother's right.[2] These wretched eminent things
Leave no more fame behind 'em than should one
Fall in a frost, and leave his print in snow;
As soon as the sun shines, it ever melts,
Both form and matter. I have ever thought
Nature doth nothing so great for great men,
As when she's pleased to make them lords of truth.
Integrity of life is fame's best friend,
Which nobly, beyond death, shall crown the end. *Exeunt.*

FINIS.

1 *stagger*: hesitate, waver 2 *right*: inheritance, position

JOHN FORD

THE BROKEN HEART

To the most worthy deserver of the noblest titles in honour, WILLIAM, LORD CRAVEN, *Baron of Hamstead Marshall.*[1]

My lord,

The glory of a great name, acquired by a greater glory of action, hath in all ages lived the truest chronicle to his own memory. In the practice of which argument, your growth to perfection, even in youth, hath appeared so sincere, so unflattering a pen-man, that posterity cannot with more delight read the merit of noble endeavours than noble endeavours merit thanks from posterity to be read with delight. Many nations, many eyes, have been witnesses of your deserts and loved them. Be pleased, then, with the freedom of your own nature, to admit one, amongst all, particularly into the list of such as honour a fair example of nobility. There is a kind of humble ambition, not uncommendable, when the silence of study breaks forth into discourse, coveting rather encouragement than applause; yet herein censure commonly is too severe an auditor, without the moderation of an able patronage. I have ever been slow in courtship of greatness,[2] not ignorant of such defects as are frequent to opinion; but the justice of your inclination to industry emboldens my weakness of confidence to relish an experience of your mercy, as many brave dangers have tasted of your courage. Your lordship strove to be known to the world, when the world knew you least, by voluntary but excellent attempts.[3]

1 *WILLIAM . . . Marshall*: William Craven, Earl of Craven (1608–97), one of the nine wealthiest peers in England and a distinguished soldier, having commanded English troops on behalf of Frederick, the Elector Palatine, in Germany; he provided lifelong support, financial and chivalrous, to the Elector's wife (and James I's daughter) Elizabeth of Bohemia

2 *courtship of greatness*: courting great men as patrons

3 *voluntary . . . attempts*: presumably because he volunteered for military service

Like allowance I plead of being known to your lordship, in this low presumption, by tendering to a favourable entertainment[1] a devotion offered from a heart that can be as truly sensible of any least respect,[3] as ever profess the owner in my best, my readiest services, a lover of your natural love to virtue,

John Ford

1 *entertainment*: reception 3 *least respect*: smallest sign of favour

The Prologue

Our scene is Sparta. He whose best of art
Hath drawn this piece calls it *The Broken Heart.*
The title lends no expectation here
Of apish laughter, or of some lame jeer
At place or persons; no pretended clause
Of jests,[1] fit for a brothel, courts applause
From vulgar admiration. Such low songs,
Tuned to unchaste ears, suit not modest tongues.
The virgin sisters[2] then deserved fresh bays[3]
When innocence and sweetness crowned their lays.[4]
Then vices gasped for breath, whose whole commerce[5]
Was whipped to exile by unblushing verse.
This law we keep in our presentment[6] now:
Not to take freedom more than we allow.
What may be here thought a fiction, when Time's youth
Wanted[7] some riper years was known *A Truth*;[8]
In which, if words have clothed the subject right,
You may partake a pity with delight.

1 *clause of jests*: passage of ribald jokes
2 *virgin sisters*: the nine Muses
3 *bays*: laurel leaves, signs of victory and poetic achievement
4 *lays*: songs 5 *commerce*: trade
6 *presentment*: presentation (of the play) 7 *Wanted*: lacked
8 *A Truth*: the relationship between Sir Philip Sidney and Lady Penelope Devereux may have been one of the sources for the play and part of its audience appeal (see Introduction)

LIST OF CHARACTERS

ORGILUS (angry)[1] *formerly betrothed to Penthea, disguised as a scholar named Aplotes* (simplicity)
CROTOLON (noise) *father of Orgilus, a counsellor to the King*
EUPHRANIA (joy) *sister of Orgilus, later wife to Prophilus*
TECNICUS (artist) *a philosopher, adviser to Orgilus*

PENTHEA (complaint) *formerly betrothed to Orgilus, now wife of Bassanes*
BASSANES (vexation) *Penthea's husband, a wealthy nobleman*
GRAUSIS[2] (old beldam) *Penthea's attendant*
PHULAS (watchful) *Bassanes's servant*

ITHOCLES (honour of loveliness) *twin brother of Penthea, General of the King's army*
ARMOSTES (an appeaser) *uncle to Ithocles and Penthea, a counsellor to the King*
PROPHILUS (dear) *Ithocles's friend, later husband to Euphrania*

AMYCLAS (common to the kings of Laconia) *King of Sparta*
CALANTHA (flower of beauty) *Princess of Sparta, later betrothed to Ithocles*
NEARCHUS (young prince) *Prince of Argos, Calantha's cousin and suitor*
AMELUS (trusty) *friend of Nearchus*
CHRYSTALLA (crystal) *lady-in-waiting to Calantha*

1 *angry*: all the names in the cast list of the 1633 Quarto include these translations of their meaning

2 *GRAUSIS*: spelled GRANSIS throughout the stage directions and speeches and 'Gran' in speech prefixes; however, its meaning suggests this revised spelling, which also appeared in the cast list of some quartos

PHILEMA (a kiss) *lady-in-waiting to Calantha*
LEMOPHIL[1] (glutton) *courtier*
GRONEAS (tavern-haunter) *courtier*

Lords, Courtiers, Officers, Attendants, Servants, Musicians

The Scene: Sparta

1 *lemophil*: consistently spelled HEMOPHIL or HEMOPHILL in stage directions and speeches; however, the name LEMOPHIL is used from 5.2 onwards and better fits the definition 'glutton'

ACT 1

Scene 1

Enter CROTOLON *and* ORGILUS.

CROTOLON
Dally not further. I will know the reason
That speeds thee to this journey.

ORGILUS
Reason? Good sir,
I can yield many.

CROTOLON
Give me one, a good one –
Such I expect, and ere we part must have.
Athens? Pray, why to Athens? You intend not
To kick against the world, turn Cynic, Stoic,[1]
Or read the logic lecture,[2] or become
An Areopagite[3] and judge in causes
Touching the commonwealth? For, as I take it,
The budding of your chin[4] cannot prognosticate
So grave an honour.

ORGILUS
All this I acknowledge.

CROTOLON
You do? Then, son, if books and love of knowledge
Inflame you to this travel, here in Sparta
You may as freely study.

ORGILUS
'Tis not that, sir.

1 *Cynic, Stoic*: schools of Greek philosophy: Cynics reject pleasure and wealth; Stoics renounce the world and patiently endure suffering
2 *read the logic lecture*: study logic
3 *Areopagite*: a member of the uppermost Athenian criminal court
4 *budding of your chin*: youthful facial hair

CROTOLON

Not that, sir? As a father I command thee
To acquaint me with the truth.

ORGILUS

Thus I obey 'ee.
After so many quarrels as dissension,
Fury and rage had broached in blood, and sometimes
With death to such confederates as sided
With now-dead Thrasus[1] and yourself, my lord,
Our present king, Amyclas, reconciled
Your eager swords and sealed a gentle peace.
Friends you professed yourselves; which to confirm,
A resolution for a lasting league
Betwixt your families was entertained,
By joining in a Hymenean bond[2]
Me and the fair Penthea, only daughter
To Thrasus.

CROTOLON

What of this?

ORGILUS

Much, much, dear sir.
A freedom of converse, an interchange
Of holy and chaste love so fixed our souls
In a firm growth of holy union, that no time
Can eat into the pledge. We had enjoyed
The sweets our vows expected, had not cruelty
Prevented all those triumphs[3] we prepared for
By Thrasus his untimely death.

CROTOLON

Most certain.

ORGILUS

From this time sprouted up that poisonous stalk
Of aconite,[4] whose ripened fruit hath ravished

1 *Thrasus*: included in the original cast list as the dead father of Ithocles and Penthea, his name meant 'fierceness'

2 *Hymenean bond*: marriage, Hymen being the god of marriage

3 *triumphs*: marriage celebrations

4 *aconite*: wolfsbane, a poisonous plant

All health, all comfort of a happy life.
For Ithocles her brother, proud of youth
And prouder in his power, nourished closely[1]
The memory of former discontents
To glory in revenge. By cunning partly,
Partly by threats, 'a woos at once and forces
His virtuous sister to admit a marriage
With Bassanes – a nobleman in honour
And riches, I confess, beyond my fortunes.

CROTOLON

All this is no sound reason to importune
My leave for thy departure.

ORGILUS

Now it follows:
Beauteous Penthea, wedded to this torture
By an insulting[2] brother, being secretly
Compelled to yield her virgin freedom up
To him who never can usurp her heart,
Before contracted mine, is now so yoked
To a most barbarous thraldom, misery,
Affliction, that he savours not humanity[3]
Whose sorrow melts not into more than pity
In hearing but her name.

CROTOLON

As how, pray?

ORGILUS

Bassanes,
The man that calls her wife, considers truly
What heaven of perfections he is lord of
By thinking fair Penthea his. This thought
Begets a kind of monster-love, which love
Is nurse unto a fear so strong and servile
As brands all dotage with a jealousy.[4]

1 *closely*: secretly 2 *insulting*: boastful, arrogant
3 *savours not humanity*: is not human
4 *As brands ... jealousy*: makes any innocent admiration of Penthea look suspicious

All eyes who gaze upon that shrine of beauty,
He doth resolve,[1] do homage to the miracle.
Someone, he is assured, may now or then –
If opportunity but sort[2] – prevail.
So much, out of a self-unworthiness,
His fears transport him; not that he finds cause
In her obedience, but his own distrust.

CROTOLON

You spin out your discourse.

ORGILUS

My griefs are violent.
For knowing how the maid was heretofore
Courted by me, his jealousies grow wild
That I should steal again into her favours,
And undermine her virtues – which, the gods
Know, I nor dare nor dream of. Hence, from hence
I undertake a voluntary exile.
First, by my absence to take off the cares
Of jealous Bassanes; but chiefly, sir,
To free Penthea from a hell on earth;
Lastly, to lose the memory of something
Her presence makes to live in me afresh.

CROTOLON

Enough, my Orgilus, enough. To Athens
I give a full consent – alas, good lady!
We shall hear from thee often?

ORGILUS

Often.

Enter EUPHRANIA.

CROTOLON

See,
Thy sister comes to give a farewell.

EUPHRANIA

Brother.

1 *resolve*: conclude 2 *sort*: present itself

ORGILUS
Euphrania, thus upon thy cheeks I print
A brother's kiss, more careful of thine honour,
Thy health and thy well-doing than my life.
[*He kisses her.*]
Before we part, in presence of our father,
I must prefer a suit[1] to 'ee –

EUPHRANIA
You may style it,
My brother, a command.

ORGILUS
– That you will promise
To pass never to any man, however worthy,
Your faith, till, with our father's leave,
I give a free consent.

CROTOLON
An easy motion.[2]
I'll promise for her, Orgilus.

ORGILUS
Your pardon:
Euphrania's oath must yield me satisfaction.

EUPHRANIA
By Vesta's[3] sacred fires, I swear.

CROTOLON
And I,
By great Apollo's[4] beams, join in the vow;
Not without thy allowance to bestow her
On any living.

ORGILUS
Dear Euphrania,
Mistake me not. Far, far 'tis from my thought,
As far from any wish of mine, to hinder
Preferment to an honourable bed
Or fitting fortune. Thou art young and handsome,

1 *prefer a suit*: make a request 2 *motion*: proposal
3 *Vesta*: Roman goddess of the hearth, associated with chastity
4 *Apollo*: god of the sun, but also of poetry and reason

And 'twere injustice – more, a tyranny –
Not to advance thy merit. Trust me, sister,
It shall be my first care to see thee matched
As may become thy choice and our contents.[1]
I have your oath?

EUPHRANIA
You have. But mean you, brother,
To leave us as you say?

CROTOLON
Ay, ay, Euphrania,
He has just grounds direct him. I will prove
A father and a brother to thee.

EUPHRANIA
Heaven
Does look into the secrets of all hearts.
Gods, you have mercy with 'ee, else –

CROTOLON
Doubt[2] nothing;
Thy brother will return in safety to us.

ORGILUS [*Aside*]
Souls sunk in sorrows never are without 'em;
They change fresh airs,[3] but bear their griefs about 'em.

Exeunt.

ACT 1

Scene 2

Flourish. Enter AMYCLAS *the King,* ARMOSTES, PROPHILUS *and* ATTENDANTS.

AMYCLAS
The Spartan gods are gracious. Our humility
Shall bend before their altars, and perfume
Their temples with abundant sacrifice.

1 *contents*: satisfaction 2 *Doubt*: fear 3 *fresh airs*: location

See, lords, Amyclas, your old king, is ent'ring
Into his youth again. I shall shake off
This silver badge of age, and change this snow
For hairs as gay as are Apollo's locks.[1]
Our heart leaps in new vigour.

ARMOSTES

May old time
Run back to double your long life, great sir.

AMYCLAS

It will; it must, Armostes. Thy bold nephew,
Death-braving Ithocles, brings to our gates
Triumphs and peace upon his conquering sword.
Laconia[2] is a monarchy at length;[3]
Hath, in this latter war, trod underfoot
Messene's[4] pride. Messene bows her neck
To Lacedemon's[5] royalty. Oh, 'twas
A glorious victory, and doth deserve
More than a chronicle – a temple, lords,
A temple to the name of Ithocles!
Where didst thou leave him, Prophilus?

PROPHILUS

At Pephnon,[6]
Most gracious sovereign. Twenty of the noblest
Of the Messenians there attend your pleasure,
For such conditions as you shall propose
In settling peace and liberty of life.

AMYCLAS

When comes your friend, the General?

PROPHILUS

He promised
To follow with all speed convenient.

1 *Apollo's locks*: the god was usually depicted with long, golden hair

2 *Laconia*: a region in the south-west of the Peloponnese, its capital city was Sparta

3 *monarchy at length*: finally united under one rule

4 *Messene*: capital city of Messenia, a country bordering Laconia

5 *Lacedemon*: another name for Laconia

6 *Pephnon*: an ancient town on the border between Laconia and Messenia

Enter CROTOLON, CALANTHA, CHRYSTALLA, PHILEMA [*with a garland*] *and* EUPHRANIA.

AMYCLAS

Our daughter! – Dear Calantha, the happy news,
The conquest of Messene, hath already
Enriched thy knowledge?

CALANTHA

With the circumstance
And manner of the fight, related faithfully
By Prophilus himself. – But pray, sir, tell me,
How doth the youthful General demean[1]
His actions in these fortunes?

PROPHILUS

Excellent Princess,
Your own fair eyes may soon report a truth
Unto your judgement, with what moderation,
Calmness of nature, measure, bounds and limits
Of thankfulness and joy 'a doth digest
Such amplitude of his success as would
In others, moulded of a spirit less clear,
Advance 'em to comparison with heaven.
But Ithocles –

CALANTHA

Your friend –

PROPHILUS

He is so, madam,
In which the period of my fate[2] consists.
He, in this firmament of honour, stands
Like a star fixed, not moved with any thunder
Of popular applause, or sudden lightning
Of self-opinion. He hath served his country,
And thinks 'twas but his duty.

CROTOLON

You describe
A miracle of man.

1 *demean*: conduct
2 *period of my fate*: height of my good fortune

AMYCLAS

Such, Crotolon,
On forfeit of a king's word, thou wilt find him.
Flourish.
Hark, warning of his coming! All attend him.

Enter ITHOCLES, LEMOPHIL *and* GRONEAS, *the rest of the* LORDS *ushering him in.*

AMYCLAS

Return into these arms, thy home, thy sanctuary,
Delight of Sparta, treasure of my bosom,
Mine own, own Ithocles!
[AMYCLAS *embraces him.*]

ITHOCLES

Your humblest subject.

ARMOSTES

Proud of the blood I claim an interest in,
As brother to thy mother, I embrace thee,
Right noble nephew.
[ARMOSTES *embraces him.*]

ITHOCLES

Sir, your love's too partial.

CROTOLON

Our country speaks by me, who, by thy valour,
Wisdom and service, shares in this great action,
Returning thee, in part[1] of thy due merits,
A general welcome.
[CROTOLON *embraces him.*]

ITHOCLES

You exceed in bounty.

CALANTHA

Chrystalla, Philema: the chaplet.[2]
[*They hand* CALANTHA *a garland.*]
Ithocles,
Upon the wings of fame the singular
And chosen fortune of an high attempt
Is borne so past the view of common sight

1 *part*: part payment 2 *chaplet*: a wreath for the head

That I myself, with mine own hands, have wrought
To crown thy temples this provincial[1] garland.
Accept, wear and enjoy it as our gift:
Deserved, not purchased.[2]
[*She places the garland on* ITHOCLES*'s head.*]

ITHOCLES
Y'are a royal maid.

AMYCLAS
She is, in all, our daughter.

ITHOCLES
Let me blush,
Acknowledging how poorly I have served,
What nothings I have done, compared with th'honours
Heaped on the issue of a willing mind;
In that lay mine ability, that only.
For who is he so sluggish from his birth,
So little worthy of a name or country,
That owes not out of gratitude for life
A debt of service, in what kind so ever
Safety or counsel of the commonwealth
Requires for payment?

CALANTHA
'A speaks truth.

ITHOCLES
Whom heaven
Is pleased to style victorious, there, to such,
Applause runs madding, like the drunken priests
In Bacchus'[3] sacrifices, without reason,
Voicing the leader-on[4] a demi-god;
When as, indeed, each common soldier's blood
Drops down as current[5] coin in that hard purchase,
As his whose much more delicate condition
Hath sucked the milk of ease. Judgement commands,

1 *provincial*: given to the conqueror of a province
2 *purchased*: acquired through his own action 3 *Bacchus*: god of wine
4 *leader-on*: main priest in an orgiastic rite
5 *current*: in circulation

But resolution executes. I use not,
Before this royal presence, these fit slights[1]
As in contempt of such as can direct.
My speech hath other end: not to attribute
All praise to one man's fortune, which is strengthed
By many hands. For instance, here is Prophilus,
A gentleman – I cannot flatter truth –
Of much desert; and, though in other rank,
Both Lemophil and Groneas were not missing
To wish their country's peace. For, in a word,
All there did strive their best, and 'twas our duty.

AMYCLAS

Courtiers turn soldiers? We vouchsafe our hand.
[LEMOPHIL *and* GRONEAS *kiss* AMYCLAS*'s hand.*]
Observe your great example.[2]

LEMOPHIL

With all diligence.

GRONEAS

Obsequiously and hourly.

AMYCLAS

Some repose
After these toils are needful. We must think on
Conditions for the conquered; they expect[3] 'em.
On! Come, my Ithocles.
[PROPHILUS *offers* EUPHRANIA *his arm.*]

EUPHRANIA

Sir, with your favour,
I need not a supporter.[4]

PROPHILUS

Fate instructs me.

Exeunt, all except LEMOPHIL, GRONEAS, CHRYSTALLA *and* PHILEMA.
LEMOPHIL *stays* CHRYSTALLA. GRONEAS [*stays*] PHILEMA.

1 *fit slights*: appropriate, self-deprecatory remarks
2 *Observe your great example*: i.e., model yourselves on Ithocles
3 *expect*: are waiting for
4 *supporter*: an escort, also physical support by taking her arm

CHRYSTALLA
With me?

PHILEMA
Indeed, I dare not stay.

LEMOPHIL [*To* CHRYSTALLA]
Sweet lady,
Soldiers are blunt. Your lip –
[*He tries to kiss her.*]

CHRYSTALLA
Fie, this is rudeness!
You went not hence such creatures.

GRONEAS
Spirit of valour
Is of a mounting[1] nature.

PHILEMA
It appears so.
Pray, in earnest, how many men apiece
Have you two been the death of?

GRONEAS
'Faith, not many:
We were composed of mercy.

LEMOPHIL
For our daring
You heard the General's approbation
Before the King.

CHRYSTALLA
You 'wished your country's peace':
That showed your charity. Where are your spoils,
Such as the soldier fights for?

PHILEMA
They are coming.

CHRYSTALLA
By the next carrier, are they not?

GRONEAS
Sweet Philema,
When I was in the thickest of mine enemies,

1 *mounting*: aspiring, with a sexual pun

Slashing off one man's head, another's nose,
Another's arms and legs –

PHILEMA

And all together.

GRONEAS

– Then would I with a sigh remember thee,
And cry 'Dear Philema, 'tis for thy sake
I do these deeds of wonder!' Dost not love me
With all thy heart now?

PHILEMA

Now as heretofore.
I have not put my love to use.[1] The principal
Will hardly yield an interest.

GRONEAS

By Mars,[2]
I'll marry thee.

PHILEMA

By Vulcan,[3] y'are forsworn,
Except[4] my mind do alter strangely.

GRONEAS

One word.

CHRYSTALLA

You lie beyond all modesty. Forbear me.

LEMOPHIL

I'll make thee mistress of a city. 'Tis
Mine own by conquest.

CHRYSTALLA

By petition. Sue for't
In forma pauperis.[5] City? Kennel! Gallants,
Off with your feathers. Put on aprons,[6] gallants.

1 *put . . . to use*: loaned it out with interest
2 *Mars*: Roman god of war
3 *Vulcan*: husband of Venus, cuckolded by Mars
4 *Except*: unless 5 *In forma pauperis*: a kind of legal aid
6 *aprons*: working clothes

Learn to reel,[1] thrum,[2] or trim a lady's dog,
And be good, quiet souls of peace. Hobgoblins![3]

LEMOPHIL

Chrystalla!

CHRYSTALLA

Practise to drill[4] hogs in hope
To share in the acorns. Soldiers? Corn-cutters,[5]
But not so valiant: they oft-times draw blood,
Which you durst never do. When you have practised
More wit, or more civility, we'll rank'ee
I'th' list of men; till then, brave things-at-arms,
Dare not to speak to us. Most potent Groneas!
[*She curtsies.*]

PHILEMA

And Lemophil the hardy! [*Curtseying*] At your services.
Exeunt CHRYSTALLA *and* PHILEMA.

GRONEAS

They scorn us as they did before we went.

LEMOPHIL

Hang 'em! Let us scorn them and be revenged.

GRONEAS

Shall we?

LEMOPHIL

We will, and when we slight them thus,
Instead of following them, they'll follow us;
It is a woman's nature.

GRONEAS

'Tis a scurvy one. *Exeunt.*

1 *reel*: to wind wool or silk 2 *thrum*: make tufts in cloth
3 *Hobgoblins*: mischievous sprites, often blamed for domestic misfortunes
4 *drill*: train in military exercises
5 *Corn-cutters*: chiropodists, a notoriously degrading profession

ACT 1

Scene 3

Enter TECNICUS, *a philosopher, and* ORGILUS, *disguised like a scholar of his* [*carrying a book*].

TECNICUS

Tempt not the stars, young man. Thou canst not play
With the severity of fate. This change
Of habit, and disguise in outward view,
Hides not the secrets of thy soul within thee
From their quick-piercing eyes, which dive at all times
Down to thy thoughts. In thy aspect[1] I note
A consequence[2] of danger.

ORGILUS

Give me leave,
Grave Tecnicus, without fore-dooming[3] destiny,
Under thy roof to ease my silent griefs
By applying to my hidden wounds the balm
Of thy oraculous lectures. If my fortune
Run such a crooked by-way as to wrest
My steps to ruin, yet thy learnèd precepts
Shall call me back, and set my footings straight.
I will not court the world.

TECNICUS

Ah, Orgilus,
Neglects in young men of delights and life
Run often to extremities. They care not
For harms to others who contemn[4] their own.

1 *aspect*: horoscope, also face 2 *consequence*: augury, warning
3 *Fore-dooming*: prejudging 4 *contemn*: despise

ORGILUS

But I, most learnèd artist,[1] am not so much
At odds with nature that I grudge the thrift[2]
Of any true deserver; nor doth malice[3]
Of present hopes so check them with despair
As that I yield to thought of more affliction
Than what is incident to frailty;[4] wherefore,
Impute not this retirèd course of living
Some little time to any other cause
Than what I justly render: the information[5]
Of an unsettled mind, as the effect
Must clearly witness.

TECNICUS

Spirit of truth inspire thee!
On these conditions I conceal thy change,
And willingly admit thee for an auditor.
I'll to my study.

ORGILUS

I to contemplations
In these delightful walks. [*Exit* TECNICUS.]
Thus metamorphosed,
I may, without suspicion, hearken after[6]
Penthea's usage and Euphrania's faith.
Love, thou art full of mystery! The deities
Themselves are not secure. In searching out
The secrets of those flames which, hidden, waste
A breast made tributary to[7] the laws
Of beauty, physic yet hath never found
A remedy to cure a lover's wound.

PROPHILUS *passeth over* [*the stage*], *supporting* EUPHRANIA *and whispering.*

Ha? Who are those that cross yon private walk

1 *artist*: philosopher, scholar 2 *thrift*: success
3 *malice*: discouragement
4 *incident to frailty*: necessarily part of the human condition
5 *information*: moulding into a firm shape
6 *hearken after*: hear news of
7 *tributary to*: subject to

Into the shadowing grove, in amorous foldings?[1]
My sister? Oh, my sister! 'Tis Euphrania
With Prophilus, supported too. I would
It were an apparition. Prophilus
Is Ithocles his friend. It strangely puzzles me.

Enter again PROPHILUS *and* EUPHRANIA.

Again? Help me, my book. This scholar's habit
Must stand my privilege.[2] My mind is busy;
Mine eyes and ears are open.

Walk[s] by, reading [then stands aside].

PROPHILUS
Do not waste
The span of this stol'n time, lent by the gods
For precious use, in niceness![3] Bright Euphrania,
Should I repeat old vows, or study new,
For purchase of belief to my desires –

ORGILUS [*Aside*]
Desires?

PROPHILUS
My service, my integrity –

ORGILUS [*Aside*]
That's better.

PROPHILUS
I should but repeat a lesson
Oft conned[4] without a prompter but thine eyes.
My love is honourable –

ORGILUS [*Aside*]
So was mine
To my Penthea, chastely honourable.

PROPHILUS
Nor wants there more addition to my wish
Of happiness than having thee a wife,
Already sure of Ithocles, a friend
Firm and unalterable.

1 *amorous foldings*: embraces 2 *stand my privilege*: justify my being here
2 *niceness*: coyness 4 *conned*: memorized

ORGILUS [*Aside*]
But a brother
More cruel than the grave.

EUPHRANIA
What can you look for
In answer to your noble protestations
From an unskilful[1] maid but language suited
To a divided mind?

ORGILUS [*Aside*]
Hold out, Euphrania.

EUPHRANIA
Know, Prophilus, I never undervalued –
From the first time you mentioned worthy love –
Your merit, means or person. It had been
A fault of judgement in me, and a dullness
In my affections, not to weigh and thank
My better stars that offered me the grace
Of so much blissfulness. For, to speak truth,
The law[2] of my desires kept equal pace
With yours, nor have I left that resolution;
But only, in a word, whatever choice[3]
Lives nearest in my heart must first procure
Consent both from my father and my brother,
Ere he can own me his.

ORGILUS [*Aside*]
She is forsworn else.

PROPHILUS
Leave me that task.

EUPHRANIA
My brother, ere he parted
To Athens, had my oath.

ORGILUS [*Aside*]
Yes, yes, 'a had, sure.

PROPHILUS
I doubt not, with the means the court supplies,
But to prevail at pleasure.

1 *unskilful*: inexperienced 2 *law*: governing power 3 *choice*: chosen lover

ORGILUS [*Aside*]

Very likely.

PROPHILUS

Meantime, best, dearest, I may build my hopes
On the foundation of thy constant suff'rance[1]
In any opposition?

EUPHRANIA

Death shall sooner
Divorce life and the joys I have in living
Than my chaste vows from truth.

PROPHILUS

On thy fair hand
I seal the like.[2]
[*He kisses her hand.*]

ORGILUS [*Aside*]

There is no faith in woman.
Passion, O be contained! My very heartstrings
Are on the tenters.[3]

EUPHRANIA [*startled*]

Sir, we are overheard!
Cupid protect us! 'Twas a stirring, sir,
Of someone near.

PROPHILUS

Your fears are needless, lady.
None have access into these private pleasures,[4]
Except some near in court, or bosom-student
From Tecnicus his oratory,[5] granted
By special favour lately from the King
Unto the grave philosopher.

EUPHRANIA

Methinks
I hear one talking to himself. I see him!

1 *suff'rance*: endurance 2 *seal the like*: vow the same
3 *tenters*: hooks for stretching cloth
4 *pleasures*: pleasure grounds
5 *Tecnicus his oratory*: Tecnicus's school for public speaking

PROPHILUS

'Tis a poor scholar, as I told you, lady.

ORGILUS [*Aside*]

I am discovered. [*Aloud*][1] Say it: is it possible
With a smooth tongue, a leering countenance,
Flattery or force of reason – I come t'ee, sir –
To turn or to appease the raging sea?
Answer to that. – Your art? What art to catch
And hold fast in a net the sun's small atoms?
No, no, they'll out, they'll out. Ye may as easily
Out-run a cloud, driven by a northern blast,
As fiddle-faddle[2] so. Peace, or speak sense.

EUPHRANIA

Call you this thing a scholar? 'Las, he's lunatic.

PROPHILUS

Observe him, sweet; 'tis but his recreation.

ORGILUS

But will you hear a little? You are so tetchy.
You keep no rule in argument. Philosophy
Works not upon impossibilities
But natural conclusions. – Mew![3] Absurd!
The metaphysics are but speculations[4]
Of the celestial bodies, or such accidents
As, not mixed perfectly, in the air engendered,
Appear to us unnatural; that's all.
Prove it. – Yet, with a reverence to your gravity,
I'll balk[5] illiterate[6] sauciness, submitting
My sole opinion to the touch[7] of writers.

[*He consults his book.*]

1 *Aloud*: Orgilus disputes with an imagined companion, uttering scraps of Greek and medieval philosophy, intended to sound old-fashioned to Ford's audience

2 *fiddle-faddle*: fuss, waste your time

3 *Mew!*: an expression of contempt

4 *speculations*: observations of astronomical phenomena

5 *balk*: shun 6 *illiterate*: uninformed

7 *touch*: touchstone

PROPHILUS
Now let us fall in with him.
ORGILUS
Ha, ha, ha!
These apish boys, when they but taste the grammates[1]
And principles of theory, imagine
They can oppose their teachers. Confidence
Leads many into errors.
PROPHILUS [*To* ORGILUS]
By your leave, sir.
EUPHRANIA
Are you a scholar, friend?
ORGILUS
I am, gay creature,
With pardon of your deities, a mushroom
On whom the dew of heaven drops now and then.
The sun shines on me too, I thank his beams.
Sometime I feel their warmth, and eat and sleep.
PROPHILUS
Does Tecnicus read to[2] thee?
ORGILUS
Yes, forsooth,
He is my master, surely. Yonder door
Opens upon his study.
PROPHILUS
Happy creatures!
Such people toil not, sweet, in heats of state,
Nor sink in thaws of greatness. Their affections
Keep order with the limits of their modesty.[3]
Their love is love of virtue. – What's thy name?
ORGILUS
Aplotes, sumptuous master, a poor wretch.

1 *taste the grammates*: acquire the rudiments
2 *read to*: teach 3 *modesty*: modest position in life

EUPHRANIA
Dost thou want[1] anything?
ORGILUS
Books, Venus, books.
PROPHILUS
Lady, a new conceit[2] comes in my thought,
And most available[3] for both our comforts.
EUPHRANIA
My lord?
PROPHILUS
Whiles I endeavour to deserve
Your father's blessing to our loves, this scholar
May daily, at some certain hours, attend
What notice I can write of my success,
Here in this grove, and give it to your hands;
The like from you to me. So can we never,
Barred of our mutual speech, want sure intelligence,[4]
And thus our hearts may talk when our tongues cannot.
EUPHRANIA
Occasion is most favourable; use it.
PROPHILUS
Aplotes, wilt thou wait us twice a day,
At nine i'th' morning and at four at night,
Here in this bower, to convey such letters
As each shall send to other? Do it willingly,
Safely and secretly, and I will furnish
Thy study, or what else thou canst desire.
ORGILUS
Jove make me thankful! Thankful, I beseech thee,
Propitious Jove! I will prove sure and trusty.
You will not fail me books?
PROPHILUS
Nor aught besides
Thy heart can wish. This lady's name's Euphrania,
Mine Prophilus.

1 *want*: lack 2 *conceit*: idea 3 *available*: efficacious
4 *want sure intelligence*: lack reliable information

ORGILUS

I have a pretty[1] memory;
It must prove my best friend. I will not miss
One minute of the hours appointed.

PROPHILUS

Write
The books thou wouldst have bought thee in a note,
Or take thyself some money.

ORGILUS

No, no money.
Money to scholars is a spirit invisible;
We dare not finger it – or books or nothing.

PROPHILUS

Books of what sort thou wilt. Do not forget
Our names.

ORGILUS

I warrant 'ee, I warrant 'ee.

PROPHILUS

Smile, Hymen, on the growth of our desires.
We'll feed thy torches with eternal fires.

Exeunt [PROPHILUS *and* EUPHRANIA].

ORGILUS

Put out thy torches, Hymen, or their light
Shall meet a darkness of eternal night.
Inspire me, Mercury,[2] with swift deceits.
Ingenious fate has leapt into mine arms,
Beyond the compass of my brain. Mortality
Creeps on the dung of earth, and cannot reach[3]
The riddles which are purposed by the gods.
Great acts best write themselves in their own stories;
They die too basely who outlive their glories. *Exit.*

1 *pretty*: skilful, fine 2 *Mercury*: Roman god of eloquence and trickery
3 *reach*: comprehend

ACT 2

Scene 1

Enter BASSANES *and* PHULAS.

BASSANES

I'll have that window next the street dammed up.
It gives too full a prospect to temptation,[1]
And courts a gazer's glances. There's a lust
Committed by the eye that sweats and travails,
Plots, wakes, contrives, till the deformed bear-whelp,
Adultery, be licked into the act,[2]
The very act. That light[3] shall be dammed up –
D'ee hear, sir?

PHULAS

I do hear, my lord. A mason
Shall be provided suddenly.[4]

BASSANES

Some rogue,
Some rogue of your confederacy – factor[5]
For slaves and strumpets – to convey close packets[6]
From this spruce springal[7] and the t'other youngster,
That gaudy earwig,[8] or my lord, your patron,
Whose pensioner[9] you are. I'll tear thy throat out –
Son of a cat, ill-looking hound's-head – rip up
Thy ulcerous maw,[10] if I but scent a paper,
A scroll, but half as big as what can cover
A wart upon thy nose, a spot, a pimple,

1 *prospect to temptation*: outlook onto temptation, but also offering a tempting glimpse of Penthea

2 *licked . . . act*: according to Pliny, bear cubs were licked into shape by their mothers

3 *light*: window 4 *suddenly*: at once 5 *factor*: agent

6 *close packets*: secret (sealed) letters

7 *springal*: youth

8 *earwig*: flatterer (wriggler into the ear)

9 *pensioner*: person who receives a payment

10 *maw*: throat

Directed to my lady. It may prove
A mystical[1] preparative to lewdness.

PHULAS

Care shall be had. I will turn every thread
About me to an eye.[2] [*Aside*] Here's a sweet life!

BASSANES

The city housewives,[3] cunning in the traffic[4]
Of chamber-merchandise, set all at price
By wholesale;[5] yet they wipe their mouths and simper,
Cull,[6] kiss and cry 'Sweetheart!', and stroke the head
Which they have branched,[7] and all is well again.
Dull clods of dirt, who dare not feel the rubs[8]
Stuck on their foreheads!

PHULAS

'Tis a villainous world.
One cannot hold his own in't.

BASSANES

Dames at court,
Who flaunt in riots,[9] run another bias.[10]
Their pleasure heaves[11] the patient ass that suffers[12]
Upon the stilts of office, titles, incomes.
Promotion justifies the shame, and sues for't.
Poor Honour, thou art stabbed and bleed'st to death
By such unlawful hire.[13] The country mistress
Is yet more wary, and in blushes hides

1 *mystical*: secret
2 *I will . . . eye*: in classical mythology, one-hundred-eyed Argos guarded the chastity of Io; he was often depicted wearing a gown covered in eyes
3 *housewives*: hussies
4 *traffic*: trade
5 *set . . . wholesale*: sell sexual favours in large numbers, without making a profit
6 *Cull*: embrace
7 *branched*: horned, made a cuckold
8 *rubs*: bumps, literally uneven terrain in bowling
9 *riots*: debauchery, wanton revels
10 *run another bias*: run from the straight path of virtue, take a different approach to adultery
11 *heaves*: lifts up, raises 12 *ass . . . suffers*: cuckold husband
13 *hire*: advancement at court

Whatever trespass draws her troth to guilt.
But all are false. On this truth I am bold:
No woman but can fall, and doth, or would.
Now for the newest news about the city –
What blab the voices, sirrah?

PHULAS

O my lord,
The rarest, quaintest, strangest, tickling news
That ever –

BASSANES

Hey-day![1] Up and ride me,[2] rascal!
What is't?

PHULAS

Forsooth, they say the King has mewed[3]
All his grey beard, instead of which is budded
Another of a pure carnation[4] colour,
Speckled with green and russet.

BASSANES

Ignorant block!

PHULAS

Yes, truly; and 'tis talked about the streets
That since Lord Ithocles came home, the lions
Never left roaring, at which noise the bears
Have danced their very hearts out.

BASSANES

Dance out thine, too.

PHULAS

Besides, Lord Orgilus is fled to Athens
Upon a fiery dragon,[5] and 'tis thought
'A never can return.

BASSANES

Grant it, Apollo!

1 *Hey-day*: exclamation of surprise or wonder
2 *Up and ride me*: get on with it
3 *mewed*: moulted 48 *carnation*: flesh-coloured
5 *fled . . . dragon*: allusion to the flight of vengeful Medea to Athens, as described by Euripides and Ovid

PHULAS

Moreover, please your lordship, 'tis reported
For certain that whoever is found jealous,
Without apparent proof that's[1] wife is wanton,
Shall be divorced. But this is but she-news:
I had it from a midwife. I have more yet.

BASSANES

Antic,[2] no more! Idiots and stupid fools
Grate[3] my calamities. Why to be fair
Should yield presumption of a faulty soul –
Look to the doors.

PHULAS [*Aside*]

The horn of plenty crest him![4] *Exit* PHULAS.

BASSANES

Swarms of confusion huddle in my thoughts
In rare distemper. Beauty? Oh, it is
An unmatched blessing or a horrid curse.

Enter PENTHEA *and* GRAUSIS, *an old lady.*

She comes, she comes! So shoots the morning forth,
Spangled with pearls of transparent dew!
The way to poverty is to be rich,
As I in her am wealthy; but for her,
In all contents a bankrupt. – Loved Penthea,
How fares my heart's best joy?

GRAUSIS

In sooth, not well;
She is so over-sad.

BASSANES

Leave chattering, magpie.
[*To* PENTHEA] Thy brother is returned, sweet, safe, and honoured
With a triumphant victory. Thou shalt visit him.
We will to court, where, if it be thy pleasure,
Thou shalt appear in such a ravishing lustre
Of jewels above value that the dames

1 *that's*: that his 2 *Antic*: fool 3 *Grate*: exacerbate
4 *The horn . . . him*: may he be cuckolded many times!

Who brave it[1] there, in rage to be outshined,
Shall hide them in their closets,[2] and unseen
Fret in their tears, whiles every wond'ring eye
Shall crave none other brightness but thy presence.
Choose thine own recreations. Be a queen
Of what delights thou fanciest best, what company,
What place, what times. Do anything, do all things
Youth can command, so thou wilt chase these clouds
From the pure firmament of thy fair looks.

GRAUSIS

Now 'tis well said, my lord. What, lady? Laugh!
Be merry! Time is precious.

BASSANES [*Aside to* GRAUSIS]

Furies[3] whip thee!

PENTHEA

Alas, my lord, this language to your handmaid
Sounds as would music to the deaf. I need
No braveries[4] nor cost of art to draw
The whiteness of my name into offence.
Let such – if any such there are – who covet
A curiosity[5] of admiration,
By laying out their plenty to full view,
Appear in gaudy outsides. My attires
Shall suit the inward fashion of my mind;
From which, if your opinion, nobly placed,
Change not the livery[6] your words bestow,
My fortunes with my hopes are at the highest.

BASSANES

This house, methinks, stands somewhat too much inward.[7]
It is too melancholy. We'll remove

1 *brave it*: flaunt themselves 2 *closets*: private chambers
3 *Furies*: female agents of revenge in classical mythology, punished evildoers in hell by whipping
4 *braveries*: extravagancies, fine clothes
5 *Curiosity*: excessive degree
6 *livery*: clothing that displays loyalty and ownership, here an appearance of value
7 *inward*: withdrawn from the street

Nearer the court; or what thinks my Penthea
Of the delightful island we command?
Rule me as thou canst wish.

PENTHEA

I am no mistress.
Whither you please, I must attend. All ways
Are alike pleasant to me.

GRAUSIS

Island? Prison!
A prison is as gaysome. We'll no islands.
Marry, out upon 'em! Whom shall we see there?
Seagulls and porpoises and water-rats
And crabs and mews[1] and dogfish! Goodly gear
For a young lady's dealing, or an old one's.
On no terms, islands; I'll be stewed[2] first.

BASSANES [*Aside*]

Grausis,
You are a juggling[3] bawd. [*To* PENTHEA] This sadness, sweetest,
Becomes not youthful blood. [*Aside to* GRAUSIS] I'll have you pounded![4]
[*To* PENTHEA] For my sake, put on a more cheerful mirth.
Thou'lt mar thy cheeks, and make me old in griefs.
[*Aside to* GRAUSIS] Damnable bitch-fox!

GRAUSIS

I am thick of hearing
Still,[5] when the wind blows southerly. What think 'ee
If your fresh lady breed young bones, my lord?
Would not a chopping[6] boy d'ee good at heart?
But, as you said –

1 *mews*: seagulls 2 *stewed*: confined in narrow quarters, sent to a brothel
3 *juggling*: deceitful 4 *pounded*: put into a pound, like a stray animal
5 *Still*: always 6 *chopping*: strapping

BASSANES [*Aside to* GRAUSIS]
I'll spit thee on a stake,
Or chop thee into collops![1]

GRAUSIS
Pray, speak louder.
Sure, sure, the wind blows south still.

PENTHEA
Thou prat'st madly.

BASSANES
'Tis very hot. I sweat extremely.[2]

Enter PHULAS.

Now?

PHULAS
A herd of lords, sir.

BASSANES
Ha?

PHULAS
A flock of ladies.

BASSANES
Where?

PHULAS
Shoals of horses.

BASSANES
Peasant, how?

PHULAS
Caroches[3]
In drifts – th'one enter, th'other stand without, sir.
And now I vanish. *Exit* PHULAS.

Enter PROPHILUS, LEMOPHIL, GRONEAS, CHRYSTALLA *and* PHILEMA.

PROPHILUS
Noble Bassanes.

1 *collops*: chunks of meat
2 *sweat*: sweating was thought to be one of the physical signs of jealousy
3 *Caroches*: luxurious coaches

BASSANES
Most welcome, Prophilus. Ladies, gentlemen,
To all my heart is open. You all honour me –
[*Aside*] A tympany[1] swells in my head already –
[*Aloud*] Honour me bountifully. [*Aside*] How they flutter,
Wagtails and jays[2] together!

PROPHILUS [*To* PENTHEA]
From your brother,
By virtue of your love to him, I require
Your instant presence, fairest.

PENTHEA
He is well, sir?

PROPHILUS
The gods preserve him ever. Yet, dear beauty,
I find some alteration in him lately,
Since his return to Sparta. – My good lord,
I pray, use no delay.

BASSANES
We had not needed
An invitation if his sister's health
Had not fallen into question. – Haste, Penthea;
Slack not a minute. Lead the way, good Prophilus;
I'll follow step by step.

PROPHILUS
Your arm, fair madam.
Exeunt all except BASSANES *and* GRAUSIS.

BASSANES
One word with your old bawdship. Th'hadst been better
Railed at the sins thou worshipp'st [3] than have thwarted
My will. I'll use thee cursedly.

1 *tympany*: a tumour or swelling, used figuratively of jealousy, perhaps cuckold's horns
2 *Wagtails and jays*: birds often used as symbols of unchaste women
3 *Th'hadst . . . worshipp'st*: you would have done better to blaspheme against the sins you worship

GRAUSIS

You dote.
You are beside yourself. A politician[1]
In jealousy? No, y'are too gross, too vulgar.
Pish, teach not me my trade. I know my cue.
My crossing you sinks me into her trust,
By which I shall know all. My trade's a sure one.

BASSANES

Forgive me, Grausis. 'Twas consideration
I relished not.[2] But have a care now.

GRAUSIS

Fear not,
I am no new-come to't.

BASSANES

Thy life's upon it,
And so is mine. My agonies are infinite! *Exeunt.*

ACT 2

Scene 2

Enter ITHOCLES, *alone.*

ITHOCLES

Ambition? 'Tis of viper's breed: it gnaws
A passage through the womb that gave it motion.[3]
Ambition, like a seelèd dove,[4] mounts upward,
Higher and higher still, to perch on clouds,
But tumbles headlong down with heavier ruin.
So squibs and crackers[5] fly into the air.
Then, only breaking with a noise, they vanish
In stench and smoke. Morality, applied

1 *politician*: schemer
2 *consideration . . . not*: a point I hadn't thought of
3 *viper . . . motion*: Pliny argued that this was how snakes were born
4 *seelèd dove*: with its eyes sewn shut, so it would have no sense of direction and fly upwards
5 *squibs and crackers*: fireworks

To timely practice,[1] keeps the soul in tune,
At whose sweet music all our actions dance.
But this is form of books and school-tradition;
It physics not the sickness of a mind
Broken with griefs. Strong fevers are not eased
With counsel, but with best receipts[2] and means,
Means, speedy means and certain; that's the cure.

Enter ARMOSTES *and* CROTOLON.

ARMOSTES

You stick, Lord Crotolon, upon a point
Too nice[3] and too unnecessary. Prophilus
Is every way desertful. I am confident
Your wisdom is too ripe to need instruction
From your son's tutelage.

CROTOLON

Yet not so ripe,
My lord Armostes, that it dares to dote
Upon the painted meat[4] of smooth persuasion,
Which tempts me to a breach of faith.

ITHOCLES

Not yet
Resolved, my lord? Why, if your son's consent
Be so available,[5] we'll write to Athens
For his repair to Sparta. The King's hand
Will join with our desires. He has been moved to't.

ARMOSTES

Yes, and the King himself importuned Crotolon
For a dispatch.

CROTOLON

Kings may command. Their wills
Are laws not to be questioned.

ITHOCLES

By this marriage
You knit an union so devout, so hearty,

1 *timely practice*: present business 2 *receipts*: recipes for medicine
3 *nice*: pedantic, scrupulous 4 *painted meat*: bait
5 *available*: able to produce a result

Between your loves to me and mine to yours,
As if mine own blood had an interest in it;
For Prophilus is mine, and I am his.

CROTOLON
My lord, my lord –

ITHOCLES
What, good sir? Speak your thought.

CROTOLON
Had this sincerity been real once,
My Orgilus had not been now un-wived,
Nor your lost sister buried in a bride-bed.
Your uncle here, Armostes, knows this truth;
For had your father, Thrasus, lived – but peace
Dwell in his grave. I have done.

ARMOSTES
Y'are bold and bitter.

ITHOCLES
'A presses home the injury; it smarts.
[*To* ARMOSTES] No reprehensions, uncle, I deserve 'em.
[*To* CROTOLON] Yet, gentle sir, consider what the heat
Of an unsteady youth, a giddy brain,
Green indiscretion, flattery of greatness,
Rawness of judgement, wilfulness in folly,
Thoughts vagrant as the wind and as uncertain,
Might lead a boy in years to. 'Twas a fault,
A capital[1] fault. For then I could not dive
Into the secrets of commanding love.
Since when, experience – by the extremities in others –
Hath forced me to collect;[2] and trust me, Crotolon,
I will redeem those wrongs with any service
Your satisfaction can require for current.[3]

ARMOSTES
Thy acknowledgement is satisfaction.
[*To* CROTOLON] What would you more?

1 *capital*: deadly 2 *collect*: reconsider 3 *current*: payment

CROTOLON

I'm conquered. If Euphrania
Herself admit[1] the motion, let it be so.
I doubt not my son's liking.

ITHOCLES

Use my fortunes;
Life, power, sword, and heart, all are your own.

Enter BASSANES, PROPHILUS, CALANTHA, PENTHEA, EUPHRANIA, CHRYSTALLA, PHILEMA *and* GRAUSIS.

ARMOSTES

The Princess, with your sister.

CALANTHA [*leading forward* PENTHEA]

I present 'ee
A stranger here in court, my lord. For did not
Desire of seeing you draw her abroad,
We had not been made happy in her company.

ITHOCLES

You are a gracious princess. – Sister, wedlock
Holds too severe a passion in your nature
Which can engross all duty to your husband,
Without attendance on so dear a mistress.
'Tis not my brother's[2] pleasure, I presume,
T'immure her in a chamber?

BASSANES

'Tis her will.
She governs her own hours. Noble Ithocles,
We thank the gods for your success and welfare.
Our lady has of late been indisposed,
Else we had waited on you with the first.

ITHOCLES

How does Penthea now?

PENTHEA

You best know, brother,
From whom my health and comfort are derived.

1 *admit*: accept 2 *brother*: brother-in-law's

BASSANES [*Aside*]
I like the answer well: 'tis sad[1] and modest.
There may be tricks yet, tricks. – Have an eye, Grausis.

CALANTHA
Now, Crotolon, the suit we joined in must not
Fall by too long demur.[2]

CROTOLON
'Tis granted, Princess,
For my part.

ARMOSTES
With condition that his son
Favour the contract.

CALANTHA
Such delay is easy.
The joys of marriage make thee, Prophilus,
A proud deserver of Euphrania's love,
And her of thy desert.

PROPHILUS [*bowing*]
Most sweetly gracious.

BASSANES
The joys of marriage are the heaven on earth.
Life's paradise, great Princess, the soul's quiet,
Sinews of concord, earthly immortality,
Eternity of pleasures – no restoratives
Like to a constant woman. [*Aside*] But where is she?
'Twould puzzle all the gods but to create
Such a new monster. [*Aloud*] I can speak by proof,
For I rest in Elysium; 'tis my happiness.

CROTOLON
Euphrania, how are you resolved – speak freely –
In your affections to this gentleman?

EUPHRANIA
Nor more nor less than as his love assures me,[3]
Which, if your liking with my brother's warrants,
I cannot but approve in all points worthy.

1 *sad*: grave 2 *demur*: delay
3 *assures me*: makes me confident, also promises me marriage

CROTOLON [*To* PROPHILUS]
So, so, I know your answer.

ITHOCLES
'T had been pity
To sunder hearts so equally consented.

Enter LEMOPHIL.

LEMOPHIL
The King, Lord Ithocles, commands your presence;
And, fairest Princess, yours.

CALANTHA
We will attend him.

Enter GRONEAS.

GRONEAS
Where are the lords? All must unto the King
Without delay. The Prince of Argos[1] –

CALANTHA
Well, sir?

GRONEAS
Is coming to the court, sweet lady.

CALANTHA
How!
The Prince of Argos?

GRONEAS
'Twas my fortune, madam,
T'enjoy the honour of these happy tidings.

ITHOCLES
Penthea.

PENTHEA
Brother?

ITHOCLES
Let me an hour hence
Meet you alone within the palace grove.
I have some secret with you. [*To* PROPHILUS] Prithee, friend,
Conduct her thither, and have special care
The walks be cleared of any to disturb us.

1 *Argos*: territory to the north-east of Laconia

PROPHILUS
I shall.
BASSANES [*Aside*]
How's that?
ITHOCLES
Alone, pray be alone.
[*To* CALANTHA] I am your creature, Princess. – On, my lords!
Exeunt [*all except* BASSANES].
BASSANES
'Alone', 'alone'? What means that word 'alone'?
Why might not I be there? Hum! He's her brother.
Brothers and sisters are but flesh and blood,
And this same whoreson court-ease[1] is temptation
To a rebellion in the veins. Besides,
His fine friend, Prophilus, must be her guardian.
Why may not he dispatch a business[2] nimbly
Before the other come? Or pand'ring, pand'ring
For one another, be't to sister, mother,
Wife, cousin, anything, 'mongst youths of mettle
Is in request.[3] It is so. Stubborn fate!
But if I be a cuckold, and can know it,
I will be fell[4] and fell.
Enter GRONEAS.
GRONEAS
My lord, y'are called for.
BASSANES
Most heartily, I thank ye. Where's my wife, pray?
GRONEAS
Retired amongst the ladies.
BASSANES
Still I thank 'ee.
There's an old waiter[5] with her. Saw you her too?

1 *court-ease*: leisurely life at court
2 *dispatch a business*: make a sexual conquest
3 *in request*: fashionable 4 *fell*: cruel, ruthless 5 *waiter*: attendant

GRONEAS
She sits i'th' presence-lobby[1] fast asleep, sir.
BASSANES
Asleep? Sleep, sir?
GRONEAS
Is your lordship troubled?
You will not to the King?
BASSANES
Your humblest vassal.
GRONEAS
Your servant, my good lord.
BASSANES
I wait[2] your footsteps. *Exeunt.*

ACT 2

Scene 3

[*Enter*] PROPHILUS [*and*] PENTHEA.

PROPHILUS
In this walk, lady, will your brother find you;
And, with your favour, give me leave a little
To work a preparation.[3] In his fashion[4]
I have observed of late some kind of slackness
To such alacrity as nature
And custom took delight in. Sadness grows
Upon his recreations, which he hoards
In such a willing[5] silence, that to question
The grounds will argue little skill in friendship,
And less good manners.

1 *presence-lobby*: the anteroom of a reception chamber
2 *wait*: attend on, follow
3 *work a preparation*: prepare you in advance
4 *fashion*: behaviour 5 *willing*: determined

PENTHEA

Sir, I'm not inquisitive
Of secrecies without an invitation.

PROPHILUS

With pardon, lady, not a syllable
Of mine implies so rude a sense. The drift –

Enter ORGILUS [*disguised as Aplotes*].

[*To* ORGILUS]

Do thy best
To make this lady merry for an hour.

ORGILUS

Your will shall be a law, sir. *Exit* [PROPHILUS].

PENTHEA

Prithee, leave me.
I have some private thoughts I would account with.[1]
Use thou thine own.

ORGILUS

Speak on, fair nymph. Our souls
Can dance as well to music of the spheres[2]
As any's who have feasted with the gods.

PENTHEA

Your school-terms[3] are too troublesome.

ORGILUS

What heaven
Refines mortality from dross of earth,
But such as uncompounded beauty hallows
With glorified perfection?[4]

PENTHEA

Set thy wits
In a less wild proportion.[5]

1 *account with*: occupy myself with
2 *music of the spheres*: the revolution of the planets was thought to produce music, synonymous with harmony and order
3 *school-terms*: language of scholastic philosophy, pedantry
4 *What heaven ... perfection*: must not heaven, which creates man out of earth, also sanctify pure beauty with the name of perfection?
5 *proportion*: order

ORGILUS

Time can never
On the white table of unguilty faith
Write counterfeit dishonour. Turn those eyes,
The arrows of pure love, upon that fire
Which once rose to a flame, perfumed with vows
As sweetly scented as the incense smoking
The holiest altars. Virgin tears, like those
On Vesta's odours, sprinkled dews to feed 'em
And to increase their fervour.[1]

PENTHEA

Be not frantic.

ORGILUS

All pleasures are but mere imagination,
Feeding the hungry appetite with steam
And sight of banquet, whilst the body pines,
Not relishing the real taste of food.
Such is the leanness of a heart divided
From intercourse of troth-contracted loves.
No horror should deface that precious figure,
Sealed with the lively stamp of equal[2] souls.

PENTHEA

Away! Some fury hath bewitched thy tongue.
The breath of ignorance that flies from thence
Ripens a knowledge in me of afflictions
Above all suff'rance. Thing of talk, be gone!
Be gone without reply!

ORGILUS

Be just, Penthea,
In thy commands. When thou send'st forth a doom
Of banishment, know first on whom it lights.
Thus I take off the shroud in which my cares

1 *Virgin . . . fervour*: i.e., virgin tears enhanced the power of their vows, just as the perfume on Vesta's altars is enhanced by the addition of water

2 *equal*: equally consenting

Are folded up from view of common eyes.
[*He removes his disguise.*]
What is thy sentence next?

PENTHEA

Rash man, thou layest
A blemish on mine honour with the hazard
Of thy too-desperate life. Yet I profess,
By all the laws of ceremonious wedlock,
I have not given admittance to one thought
Of female change,[1] since cruelty enforced
Divorce betwixt my body and my heart.
Why would you fall from goodness thus?

ORGILUS

Oh, rather
Examine me how I could live to say
I have been much, much wronged. 'Tis for thy sake
I put on this imposture. Dear Penthea,
If thy soft bosom be not turned to marble,
Thou'lt pity our calamities. My interest[2]
Confirms me thou art mine still.

PENTHEA

Lend your hand.
With both of mine I clasp it thus, thus kiss it,
Thus kneel before ye.
[*She kneels.*]

ORGILUS

You instruct my duty.[3]
[*He kneels.*]

PENTHEA

We may stand up.
[*They rise.*]
Have you aught else to urge
Of new demand? As for the old, forget it.
'Tis buried in an everlasting silence,
And shall be, shall be ever. What more would ye?

1 *change*: inconstancy 2 *interest*: claim, through their former betrothal
3 *instruct my duty*: teach me what I should do

ORGILUS

I would possess my wife! The equity
Of very reason bids me.

PENTHEA

Is that all?

ORGILUS

Why, 'tis the all of me, myself.

PENTHEA

Remove
Your steps some distance from me. At this space
A few words I dare change,[1] but first put on
Your borrowed shape.

[*He resumes his disguise.*]

ORGILUS

You are obeyed; 'tis done.

PENTHEA

How, Orgilus, by promise I was thine
The heavens do witness. They can witness too
A rape done on my truth. How I do love thee
Yet, Orgilus, and yet, must best appear
In tendering[2] thy freedom. For I find
The constant preservation of thy merit
By thy not daring to attempt my fame[3]
With injury of any loose conceit,[4]
Which might give deeper wounds to discontents.
Continue this fair race.[5] Then, though I cannot
Add to thy comfort, yet I shall more often
Remember from what fortune I am fallen,
And pity mine own ruin. Live, live happy –
Happy in thy next choice, that thou may'st people
This barren age[6] with virtues in thy issue.
And oh, when thou art married, think on me
With mercy, not contempt. I hope thy wife,

1 *change*: exchange 2 *tendering*: cherishing
3 *attempt my fame*: endanger my reputation
4 *loose conceit*: improper suggestion
5 *race*: course of action 6 *barren age*: barren in terms of virtue

Hearing my story, will not scorn my fall.
Now let us part.

ORGILUS

Part? Yet advise thee better:
Penthea is the wife to Orgilus,
And ever shall be.

PENTHEA

Never shall nor will.

ORGILUS

How!

PENTHEA

Hear me: in a word I'll tell thee why.
The virgin-dowry which my birth bestowed
Is ravished by another. My true love
Abhors to think that Orgilus deserved
No better favours than a second bed.

ORGILUS

I must not take this reason.

PENTHEA

To confirm it:
Should I outlive my bondage, let me meet
Another worse than this – and less desired –
If, of all the men alive, thou shouldst but touch
My lip or hand again.

ORGILUS

Penthea, now
I tell 'ee you grow wanton in my sufferance.[1]
Come, sweet, th'art mine!
[*He tries to embrace her.*]

PENTHEA

Uncivil sir, forbear,
Or I can turn affection into vengeance!
Your reputation, if you value any,
Lies bleeding at my feet. Unworthy man,
If ever henceforth thou appear in language,

1 *wanton in my sufferance*: reckless or violent in making me suffer or increasing my pain

Message, or letter to betray my frailty,
I'll call thy former protestations lust,
And curse my stars for forfeit of my judgement.[1]
Go thou, fit only for disguise and walks[2]
To hide thy shame. This once I spare thy life.
I laugh at mine own confidence. My sorrows
By thee are made inferior to my fortunes.[3]
If ever thou didst harbour worthy love,
Dare not to answer. My good genius[4] guide me,
That I may never see thee more. Go from me!

ORGILUS

I'll tear my veil of politic frenzy[5] off,
And stand up like a man resolved to do.
Action, not words, shall show me.[6] O Penthea!

Exit ORGILUS.

PENTHEA

'A sighed my name, sure, as he parted from me.
I fear I was too rough. Alas, poor gentleman,
'A looked not like the ruins of his youth,
But like the ruins of those ruins. Honour,
How much we fight with weakness to preserve thee!

Enter BASSANES *and* GRAUSIS.

BASSANES

Fie on thee! Damn thee, rotten maggot, damn thee!
Sleep? Sleep at court? And now? Aches, convulsions,
Impostumes,[7] rheums,[8] gouts, palsies[9] clog thy bones
A dozen years more yet!

GRAUSIS

Now y'are in humours.[10]

1 *forfeit of my judgement*: i.e., in loving Orgilus
2 *walks*: covered walks
3 *My . . . fortunes*: I feel less sorrow than would otherwise be caused by my misfortunes
4 *good genius*: good angel
5 *veil of politic frenzy*: disguise of cunning madness
6 *show me*: demonstrate what I am 7 *Impostumes*: abscesses
8 *rheums*: mucous secretions 9 *palsies*: tremors or paralysis
10 *in humours*: in a disordered state, bad-tempered

BASSANES [*seeing* PENTHEA]
She's by herself. There's hope of that. She's sad, too.
She's in strong contemplation, yes, and fixed.[1]
The signs are wholesome.

GRAUSIS
Very wholesome, truly.

BASSANES
Hold your chops,[2] nightmare! [*To* PENTHEA] Lady, come. Your brother
Is carried to his closet. You must thither.

PENTHEA
Not well, my lord?

BASSANES
A sudden fit, 'twill off –
Some surfeit or disorder. How dost, dearest?

PENTHEA
Your news is none o'th' best.

Enter PROPHILUS.

PROPHILUS
The chief of men,
The excellentest Ithocles, desires
Your presence, madam.

BASSANES
We are hasting to him.

PENTHEA
In vain we labour in this course of life
To piece our journey out at length, or crave
Respite of breath. Our home is in the grave.

BASSANES
Perfect philosophy!

PENTHEA
Then let us care
To live so that our reckonings may fall even
When w'are to make account.

1 *fixed*: abstracted 2 *chops*: tongue, literally jaws

PROPHILUS

He cannot fear
Who builds on noble grounds. Sickness or pain
Is the deserver's exercise,[1] and such
Your virtuous brother to the world is known.
Speak comfort to him, lady; be all gentle.
Stars fall, but in the grossness of our sight,
A good man dying, th'earth doth lose a light.[2] *Exeunt.*

ACT 3

Scene 1

Enter TECNICUS *and* ORGILUS *in his own shape.*[3]

TECNICUS

Be well advised; let not a resolution
Of giddy rashness choke the breath of reason.

ORGILUS

It shall not, most sage master.

TECNICUS

I am jealous;[4]
For if the borrowed shape so late put on
Inferred a consequence, we must conclude
Some violent design of sudden nature
Hath shook that shadow off, to fly upon
A new-hatched execution.[5] Orgilus,
Take heed thou hast not, under our integrity,
Shrouded unlawful plots. Our mortal eyes
Pierce not the secrets of your hearts; the gods
Are only privy to them.

1 *exercise*: discipline
2 *light*: sun or moon, as opposed to the shooting star
3 *in his own shape*: i.e., no longer in disguise
4 *jealous*: suspicious 5 *execution*: scheme

ORGILUS

Learnèd Tecnicus,
Such doubts are causeless; and, to clear the truth
From misconceit,[1] the present state[2] commands me.
The Prince of Argos comes himself in person
In quest of great Calantha for his bride,
Our kingdom's heir. Besides, mine only sister,
Euphrania, is disposed[3] to Prophilus.
Lastly, the King is sending letters for me
To Athens, for my quick repair to court.
Please to accept these reasons.

TECNICUS

Just ones, Orgilus,
Not to be contradicted. Yet beware
Of an unsure foundation. No fair colours
Can fortify a building faintly[4] jointed.
I have observed a growth in thy aspect[5]
Of dangerous extent, sudden, and – look to't –
I might add, certain –

ORGILUS

My aspect? Could art
Run through mine inmost thoughts, it should not sift
An inclination there more than what suited
With justice of mine honour.

TECNICUS

I believe it;
But know then, Orgilus, what honour is.
Honour consists not in a bare opinion
By doing any act that feeds content[6] –
Brave in appearance, 'cause we think it brave.
Such honour comes by accident, not nature,
Proceeding from the vices of our passion,
Which makes our reason drunk. But real honour

1 *misconceit*: misunderstanding 2 *state*: state of affairs
3 *disposed*: betrothed 4 *faintly*: weakly
5 *growth in thy aspect*: change in your appearance, alteration in horoscope
6 *feeds content*: satisfies vanity

Is the reward of virtue, and acquired
By justice or by valour, which for basis
Hath justice to uphold it. He then fails
In honour who, for lucre[1] or revenge,
Commits thefts, murders, treasons and adulteries,
With such like, by entrenching on just laws,
Whose sov'reignty is best preserved by justice.
Thus, as you see how honour must be grounded
On knowledge, not opinion – for opinion
Relies on probability and accident,
But knowledge on necessity and truth –
I leave thee to the fit consideration
Of what becomes the grace of real honour,
Wishing success to all thy virtuous meanings.

ORGILUS

The gods increase thy wisdom, reverend oracle,
And in thy precepts make me ever thrifty.[2]

TECNICUS

I thank thy wish. *Exit* ORGILUS.
Much mystery of fate
Lies hid in that man's fortunes. Curiosity[3]
May lead his actions into rare attempts.[4]
But let the gods be moderators still;
No human power can prevent[5] their will.

Enter ARMOSTES [*with a casket*].

From whence come 'ee?

ARMOSTES

From King Amyclas. Pardon
My interruption of your studies. Here,
In this sealed box, he sends a treasure dear
To him as his crown. 'A prays your gravity
You would examine, ponder, sift and bolt[6]

1 *lucre*: money 2 *thrifty*: careful, prosperous
3 *Curiosity*: intellectual ambition
4 *rare attempts*: exceptional deeds
5 *prevent*: anticipate 6 *bolt*: sieve

The pith and circumstance of every tittle
The scroll within contains.

TECNICUS

What is't, Armostes?

ARMOSTES

It is the health of Sparta, the King's life,
Sinews and safety of the commonwealth –
The sum of what the oracle delivered
When last he visited the prophetic temple
At Delphos.[1] What his reasons are for which,
After so long a silence, he requires
Your counsel now, grave man, his majesty
Will soon himself acquaint you with.

TECNICUS

Apollo
Inspire my intellect! [*Taking the casket*] The Prince of Argos
Is entertained?[2]

ARMOSTES

He is, and has demanded
Our Princess for his wife, which I conceive
One special cause the King importunes you
For resolution[3] of the oracle.

TECNICUS

My duty to the King, good peace to Sparta,
And fair day to Armostes.

ARMOSTES

Like[4] to Tecnicus. *Exeunt.*

1 *Delphos*: a combination of Delphi, the famous site of an oracle, and Delos, the island birthplace of Apollo
2 *entertained*: received as a guest
3 *resolution*: interpretation 4 *Like*: the same

ACT 3

Scene 2

Soft music. A song [within]. During which time, enter PROPHILUS, BASSANES, PENTHEA, GRAUSIS, *passing over the stage.* BASSANES *and* GRAUSIS *enter again softly, stealing to several stands,*[1] *and listen.*

Can you paint a thought or number,
Every fancy in a slumber?
Can you count soft minutes roving
From a dial's point by moving?
Can you grasp a sigh, or, lastly,
Rob a virgin's honour chastely?
No, oh no! Yet you may
Sooner do both that and this,
This and that, and never miss,
Than by any praise display
Beauty's beauty. Such a glory
As beyond all fate, all story,
All arms, all arts,
All loves, all hearts,
Greater than those, or they,
Do, shall and must obey.

BASSANES
All silent, calm, secure. – Grausis, no creaking?
No noise? Dost hear nothing?

GRAUSIS
Not a mouse,
Or whisper of the wind.

BASSANES
The floor is matted.
The bed-posts, sure, are steel or marble. Soldiers
Should not affect, methinks, strains so effeminate.

1 *several stands*: separate positions

Sounds of such delicacy are but fawnings
Upon the sloth of luxury:[1] they heighten
Cinders of covert lust up to a flame.

GRAUSIS

What do you mean, my lord? Speak low. That gabbling
Of yours will but undo us.

BASSANES

Chamber-combats[2]
Are felt not heard.

PROPHILUS [*Within*]

'A wakes.

BASSANES

What's that?

ITHOCLES [*Within*]

Who's there?
Sister? – All quit the room else.

BASSANES

'Tis consented.

Enter PROPHILUS.

PROPHILUS

Lord Bassanes, your brother[3] would be private.
We must forbear; his sleep hath newly left him.
Please 'ee withdraw.

BASSANES

By any means, 'tis fit.

PROPHILUS

Pray, gentlewoman, walk too.

GRAUSIS

Yes, I will, sir. *Exeunt.*

[*Enter*] ITHOCLES *discovered*[4] *in a chair, and* PENTHEA.

ITHOCLES

Sit nearer, sister, to me – nearer yet.
We had one father, in one womb took life,

1 *luxury*: lechery 2 *Chamber-combats*: bedroom encounters
3 *brother*: brother-in-law
4 *discovered*: perhaps a curtain was drawn to reveal him in the discovery space

Were brought up twins together, yet have lived
At distance like two strangers. I could wish
That the first pillow whereon I was cradled
Had proved to me a grave.

PENTHEA

You had been happy;
Then had you never known that sin of life
Which blots all following glories with a vengeance,
For forfeiting the last will of the dead,[1]
From whom you had your being.

ITHOCLES

Sad Penthea,
Thou canst not be too cruel. My rash spleen
Hath, with a violent hand, plucked from thy bosom
A lover-blessed heart to grind it into dust –
For which mine's now a-breaking.

PENTHEA

Not yet, heaven,
I do beseech thee. First, let some wild fires
Scorch, not consume, it. May the heat be cherished
With desires infinite, but hopes impossible.

ITHOCLES

Wronged soul, thy prayers are heard.

PENTHEA

Here, lo, I breathe,
A miserable creature, led to ruin
By an unnatural brother.

ITHOCLES

I consume
In languishing affections for that trespass,
Yet cannot die.

PENTHEA

The handmaid to the wages
Of country toil[2] drinks the untroubled streams,
With leaping kids and with the bleating lambs,

1 *the dead*: i.e., of their father, Thrasus, who wanted her to marry Orgilus
2 *handmaid . . . toil*: country girl

And so allays her thirst secure,[1] whiles I
Quench my hot sighs with fleetings[2] of my tears.

ITHOCLES

The labourer doth eat his coarsest bread,
Earned with his sweat, and lies him down to sleep;
While every bit I touch turns in digestion
To gall, as bitter as Penthea's curse.
Put me to any penance for my tyranny,
And I will call thee merciful.

PENTHEA

Pray, kill me.
Rid me from living with a jealous husband.
Then we will join in friendship, be again
Brother and sister. Kill me, pray – nay, will 'ee?

ITHOCLES

How does thy lord esteem thee?

PENTHEA

Such an one
As only you have made me: a faith-breaker,
A spotted[3] whore! Forgive me; I am one
In act, not in desires, the gods must witness.

ITHOCLES

Thou dost belie thy friend.[4]

PENTHEA

I do not, Ithocles;
For she that's wife to Orgilus, and lives
In known adultery with Bassanes,
Is at the best a whore. Wilt kill me now?
The ashes of our parents will assume
Some dreadful figure and appear, to charge
Thy bloody guilt that hast betrayed their name
To infamy in this reproachful match.

1 *secure*: untroubled 2 *fleetings*: streams, flowings
3 *spotted*: blemished in character
4 *friend*: this could be Bassanes, Orgilus or Ithocles himself

ITHOCLES

After my victories abroad, at home
I meet despair. Ingratitude of nature
Hath made my actions monstrous. Thou shalt stand
A deity, my sister, and be worshipped
For thy resolvèd martyrdom. Wronged maids
And married wives shall to thy hallowed shrine
Offer their orisons,[1] and sacrifice
Pure turtles,[2] crowned with myrtle,[3] if thy pity
Unto a yielding brother's pressure lend
One finger but to ease it.

PENTHEA

Oh, no more!

ITHOCLES

Death waits to waft me to the Stygian banks,[4]
And free me from this chaos of my bondage;
And till thou wilt forgive, I must endure.

PENTHEA

Who is the saint you serve?[5]

ITHOCLES

Friendship or nearness
Of birth to any but my sister durst not
Have moved that question, as a secret, sister,
I dare not murmur to myself.

PENTHEA

Let me –
By your new protestations I conjure 'ee –
Partake her name.

ITHOCLES

Her name? 'Tis – 'tis – I dare not.

1 *orisons*: prayers
2 *turtles*: turtle doves, symbolic of monogamous love
3 *myrtle*: plant sacred to Venus, symbolic of love
4 *Stygian banks*: in classical mythology, the dead had to cross the river Styx before reaching the lands of the dead
5 *saint you serve*: woman you adore

PENTHEA

All your respects[1] are forged!

ITHOCLES

They are not. Peace!
Calantha is the princess, the King's daughter,
Sole heir of Sparta – Me most miserable!
Do I now love thee? For my injuries,[2]
Revenge thyself with bravery,[3] and gossip
My treasons to the King's ears. Do! Calantha
Knows it not yet, nor Prophilus, my nearest.

PENTHEA

Suppose you were contracted to her: would it not
Split even your very soul to see her father
Snatch her out of your arms against her will,
And force her on the Prince of Argos?

ITHOCLES

Trouble not
The fountains of mine eyes with thine own story;
I sweat in blood for't.

PENTHEA

We are reconciled.
Alas, sir, being children, but two branches
Of one stock, 'tis not fit we should divide.
Have comfort; you may find it.

ITHOCLES

Yes, in thee,
Only in thee, Penthea mine.

PENTHEA

If sorrows
Have not too much dulled my infected brain,
I'll cheer invention for an active strain.[4]

ITHOCLES

Madman! Why have I wronged a maid so excellent?

1 *respects*: expressions of respect 2 *injuries*: injuries to you
3 *bravery*: boasting 4 *cheer . . . strain*: try to devise a plan of action

Enter BASSANES *with a poniard,*[1] PROPHILUS, GRONEAS, LEMOPHIL *and* GRAUSIS.

BASSANES
I can forbear no longer! More, I will not.
Keep off your hands, or fall upon my point![2]
Patience is tired, for like a slow-paced ass
Ye ride my easy nature, and proclaim
My sloth-to-vengeance a reproach and property.[3]

ITHOCLES
The meaning of this rudeness?

PROPHILUS
He's distracted.

PENTHEA
O my grieved lord!

GRAUSIS
Sweet lady, come not near him.
He holds his perilous weapon in his hand
To prick 'a cares not whom nor where. See, see, see!

BASSANES [*To* ITHOCLES]
My birth is noble, though the popular blast
Of vanity,[4] as giddy as thy youth,
Hath reared thy name up to bestride a cloud,[5]
Or progress[6] in the chariot of the sun.[7]
I am no clod of trade to lackey[8] Pride,
Nor, like your slave of expectation,[9] wait[10]

1 *poniard*: dagger 2 *point*: blade of the dagger
3 *property*: personal characteristic
4 *popular . . . vanity*: public adulation, the inherently worthless voice of the people
5 *bestride a cloud*: in classical mythology Ixion was deceived by Jupiter when he attempted to seduce Juno, embracing only a cloud
6 *progress*: make a ceremonious journey
7 *chariot of the sun*: Phaeton, son of Apollo, who stole his father's chariot of the sun and was killed; an example of youthful presumption
8 *lackey*: run errands for
9 *slave of expectation*: servant in hopes of reward
10 *wait*: wait outside

The bawdy hinges of your doors, or whistle
For mystical conveyance[1] to your bed-sports.

GRONEAS
Fine humours! They become him.

LEMOPHIL
How 'a stares,
Struts, puffs and sweats. Most admirable[2] lunacy!

ITHOCLES
But that I may conceive the spirit of wine
Has took possession of your soberer custom,
I'd say you were unmannerly.

PENTHEA
Dear brother –

BASSANES
Unmannerly? Mew, kitling![3] Smooth Formality
Is usher to the rankness of the blood,
But Impudence bears up the train. Indeed, sir,
Your fiery mettle or your springal[4] blaze
Of huge renown is no sufficient royalty
To print upon my forehead the scorn 'cuckold'.

ITHOCLES
His jealousy has robbed him of his wits.
'A talks 'a knows not what.

BASSANES
Yes, and 'a knows
To whom 'a talks: to one that franks[5] his lust
In swine-security of bestial incest.

ITHOCLES
Ha, devil?

BASSANES
I will halloo't,[6] though I blush more
To name the filthiness than thou to act it.

1 *mystical conveyance*: secret communication
2 *admirable*: to be wondered at 3 *kitling*: kitten 4 *springal*: youthful
5 *franks*: satisfies; a frank is an enclosure in which boars are fattened
6 *halloo't*: proclaim it

ITHOCLES
Monster!
[*He draws his sword.*]
PROPHILUS
Sir, by our friendship –
PENTHEA
By our bloods,
Will you quite both undo us, brother?
GRAUSIS
Out on him!
These are his megrims,[1] firks[2] and melancholies.
LEMOPHIL
Well said, old touch-hole.[3]
GRONEAS
Kick him out at doors.
PENTHEA
With favour, let me speak. – My lord, what slackness
In my obedience hath deserved this rage?
Except[4] humility and silent duty
Have drawn on your unquiet, my simplicity
Ne'er studied your vexation.[5]
BASSANES
Light of beauty,
Deal not ungently with a desperate wound!
No breach of reason dares make war with her
Whose looks are sovereignty, whose breath is balm.
Oh, that I could preserve thee in fruition[6]
As in devotion!

1 *megrims*: low spirits 2 *firks*: caprices
3 *touch-hole*: bawd; one who infects with venereal disease like the part of a gun through which the charge is ignited
4 *Except*: unless
5 *studied your vexation*: intended to annoy you
6 *preserve thee in fruition*: Bassanes expresses the desire to retain his physical possession of Penthea and to keep her image alive, perhaps by begetting children

PENTHEA

Sir, may every evil
Locked in Pandora's box[1] shower, in your presence,
On my unhappy head, if, since you made me
A partner in your bed, I have been faulty
In one unseemly thought against your honour.

ITHOCLES

Purge not his griefs, Penthea.

BASSANES

Yes, say on,
Excellent creature. [*To* ITHOCLES] Good,[2] be not a hindrance
To peace and praise of virtue. Oh, my senses
Are charmed with sounds celestial! [*To* PENTHEA] On, dear, on!
I never gave you one ill word. Say, did I?
Indeed, I did not.

PENTHEA

Nor, by Juno's forehead,[3]
Was I e'er guilty of a wanton error.

BASSANES

A goddess! Let me kneel.
[*He falls to his knees.*]

GRAUSIS

Alas, kind animal.

ITHOCLES [*sheathing his sword*]

No, but for penance –

BASSANES

Noble sir, what is it?
With gladness I embrace it. Yet, pray, let not
My rashness teach you to be too unmerciful.

ITHOCLES

When you shall show good proof that manly wisdom,

1 *Pandora's box*: in classical mythology Pandora opened a box containing all the world's evils
2 *Good*: good sir
3 *Juno's forehead*: Juno was goddess of marriage; her beauty, as symbolized by her forehead, is also praised in *'Tis Pity She's a Whore*

Not over-swayed by passion or opinion,
Knows how to lead judgement, then this lady –
Your wife, my sister – shall return in safety
Home to be guided by you. But till first
I can, out of clear evidence, approve[1] it,
She shall be my care.

BASSANES
Rip my bosom up;
I'll stand the execution with a constancy.
This torture[2] is insufferable!

ITHOCLES
Well, sir,
I dare not trust her to your fury.

BASSANES
But
Penthea says not so?

PENTHEA
She needs no tongue
To plead excuse, who never purposed wrong.

LEMOPHIL [*To* GRAUSIS]
Virgin of reverence and antiquity,
Stay you behind.

GRONEAS
The court wants not your diligence.
Exeunt all, except BASSANES *and* GRAUSIS.

GRAUSIS
What will you do, my lord? My lady's gone!
I am denied to follow.

BASSANES
I may see her
Or speak to her once more.

GRAUSIS
And feel her too, man.
Be of good cheer. She's your own flesh and bone.

1 *approve*: be certain of 2 *This torture*: i.e., the loss of Penthea

BASSANES
Diseases desperate must find cures alike.
She swore she has been true.

GRAUSIS
True, on my modesty.

BASSANES
Let him want truth[1] who credits not her vows.
Much wrong I did her, but her brother infinite.
Rumour will voice me the contempt of manhood,
Should I run on thus. Some way I must try
To outdo art,[2] and cry a' jealousy.[3] *Exeunt.*

ACT 3

Scene 3

Flourish. Enter AMYCLAS, NEARCHUS *leading* CALANTHA, ARMOSTES, CROTOLON, EUPHRANIA, CHRYSTALLA, PHILEMA *and* AMELUS.

AMYCLAS
Cousin of Argos, what the heavens have pleased,
In their unchanging counsels, to conclude
For both our kingdoms' weal we must submit to;
Nor can we be unthankful to their bounties
Who, when we were even creeping to our grave,
Sent us a daughter, in whose birth our hope
Continues of succession. As you are
In title next, being grandchild to our aunt,
So we in heart desire you may sit nearest
Calantha's love – since we have ever vowed
Not to enforce affection by our will,
But by her own choice to confirm it gladly.

1 *want truth*: not be believed 2 *outdo art*: make the pose into reality
3 *cry a' jealousy*: declaim against jealousy

NEARCHUS

You speak the nature of a right just father.
I come not hither roughly to demand
My cousin's thraldom, but to free mine own.
Report of great Calantha's beauty, virtue,
Sweetness and singular perfections courted
All ears to credit[1] what I find was published[2]
By constant truth; from which, if any service
Of my desert can purchase fair construction,
This lady must command it.

CALANTHA

Princely sir,
So well you know how to profess observance[3]
That you instruct your hearers to become
Practitioners in duty;[4] of which number
I'll study to be chief.

NEARCHUS

Chief, glorious virgin,
In my devotions, as in all men's wonder.

AMYCLAS

Excellent cousin,[5] we deny no liberty;
Use thine own opportunities.

[CALANTHA *and* NEARCHUS *talk apart.*]

Armostes,
We must consult with the philosophers.
The business is of weight.

ARMOSTES

Sir, at your pleasure.

AMYCLAS

You told me, Crotolon, your son's returned
From Athens. Wherefore comes 'a not to court
As we commanded?

1 *credit*: believe 2 *published*: made public
3 *observance*: courteous attention, amorous devotion
4 *duty*: homage
5 *cousin*: used of any kinsman, here meaning 'nephew'

CROTOLON

He shall soon attend
Your royal will, great sir.

AMYCLAS

The marriage
Between young Prophilus and Euphrania
Tastes of too much delay.

CROTOLON

My lord –

AMYCLAS

Some pleasures
At celebration of it would give life
To th'entertainment of the Prince, our kinsman.
Our court wears gravity more than we relish.

ARMOSTES

Yet the heavens smile on all your high attempts,[1]
Without a cloud.

CROTOLON

So may the gods protect us.

[CALANTHA *and* NEARCHUS *come forward.*]

CALANTHA

A prince a subject?

NEARCHUS

Yes, to Beauty's sceptre;
As all hearts kneel, so mine.

CALANTHA

You are too courtly.

[*Enter*] *to them* ITHOCLES, ORGILUS [*and*] PROPHILUS.

ITHOCLES [*To* ORGILUS]

Your safe return to Sparta is most welcome.
I joy to meet you here, and as occasion
Shall grant us privacy, will yield you reasons
Why I should covet to deserve the title
Of your respected friend. For, without compliment,
Believe it, Orgilus, 'tis my ambition.

1 *high attempts*: noble enterprises

ORGILUS

Your lordship may command me, your poor servant.

ITHOCLES [*Aside, observing* CALANTHA]

So amorously close so soon? My heart!

PROPHILUS

What sudden change is next?

ITHOCLES

Life to the King!
To whom I here present this noble gentleman,
New-come from Athens. Royal sir, vouchsafe
Your gracious hand in favour of his merit.

[ORGILUS *kisses* AMYCLAS*'s hand.*]

CROTOLON [*Aside*]

My son preferred[1] by Ithocles?

AMYCLAS

Our bounties
Shall open to thee, Orgilus; for instance, –
Hark in thine ear – if, out of those inventions[2]
Which flow in Athens, thou hast there engrossed[3]
Some rarity of wit to grace the nuptials
Of thy fair sister, and renown[4] our court
In th'eyes of this young prince, we shall be debtor
To thy conceit.[5] Think on't.

ORGILUS

Your Highness honours me.

NEARCHUS

My tongue and heart are twins.

CALANTHA

A noble birth,
Becoming such a father. – Worthy Orgilus,
You are a guest most wished for.

1 *preferred*: put forward for advancement
2 *inventions*: literary compositions, including plays
3 *engrossed*: acquired 4 *renown*: make famous 5 *conceit*: invention

ORGILUS

May my duty
Still[1] rise in your opinion, sacred Princess.

ITHOCLES [*To* NEARCHUS]

Euphrania's brother, sir – a gentleman
Well worthy of your knowledge.

NEARCHUS

We embrace him,
Proud of so dear acquaintance.

AMYCLAS

All prepare
For revels and disport.[2] The joys of Hymen,
Like Phoebus[3] in his lustre, puts to flight
All mists of dullness. Crown the hours with gladness.
No sounds but music; no discourse but mirth.

CALANTHA

Thine arm, I prithee, Ithocles. [*To* NEARCHUS] Nay, good
My lord, keep on your way; I am provided.

NEARCHUS

I dare not disobey.

ITHOCLES

Most heavenly lady! *Exeunt.*

ACT 3

Scene 4

Enter CROTOLON [*and*] ORGILUS.

CROTOLON

The King hath spoke his mind.

ORGILUS

His will he hath;
But were it lawful to hold plea[4] against

1 *Still*: always 2 *disport*: entertainment
3 *Phoebus*: Greek god of the sun (Apollo)
4 *hold plea*: try a legal action

The power of greatness, not the reason, haply
Such under-shrubs as subjects sometimes might
Borrow of nature justice to inform[1]
That licence[2] sovereignty holds without check
Over a meek obedience.

CROTOLON

How resolve you
Touching your sister's marriage? Prophilus
Is a deserving and a hopeful[3] youth.

ORGILUS

I envy not his merit, but applaud it;
Could wish him thrift[4] in all his best desires;
And, with a willingness, enleague our blood
With his for purchase of full growth in friendship.
He never touched on any wrong that maliced[5]
The honour of our house, nor stirred our peace.
Yet, with your favour, let me not forget
Under whose wing he gathers warmth and comfort,
Whose creature he is bound, made, and must live so.

CROTOLON

Son, son, I find in thee a harsh condition.[6]
No courtesy can win it; 'tis too rancorous.

ORGILUS

Good sir, be not severe in your construction.
I am no stranger to such easy calms
As sit in tender bosoms. Lordly Ithocles
Hath graced my entertainment in abundance,
Too humbly hath descended from that height
Of arrogance and spleen which wrought the rape
On grieved Penthea's purity. His scorn
Of my untoward[7] fortunes is reclaimed
Unto a courtship, almost to a fawning.
I'll kiss his foot, since you will have it so.

1 *inform*: control, guide 2 *licence*: authority, scope
3 *hopeful*: promising 4 *thrift*: success 5 *maliced*: threatened
6 *condition*: state of mind 7 *untoward*: declining, unprosperous

CROTOLON

Since I will have it so? Friend, I will have it so,
Without our ruin by your politic plots,
Or wolf of hatred snarling in your breast.
You have a spirit, sir, have ye? A familiar[1]
That posts[2] i'th' air for your intelligence?[3]
Some such hobgoblin hurried you from Athens,
For yet you come unsent for.

ORGILUS

If unwelcome,
I might have found a grave there.

CROTOLON

Sure, your business
Was soon dispatched, or your mind altered quickly.

ORGILUS

'Twas care, sir, of my health cut short my journey;
For there, a general infection[4]
Threatens a desolation.

CROTOLON

And I fear
Thou hast brought back a worse infection with thee:
Infection of thy mind; which, as thou say'st,
Threatens the desolation of our family.

ORGILUS

Forbid it, our dear genius![5] I will rather
Be made a sacrifice on Thrasus' monument,
Or kneel to Ithocles, his son, in dust,
Than woo a father's curse. My sister's marriage
With Prophilus is from my heart confirmed.
May I live hated, may I die despised,
If I omit to further it in all
That can concern me.

1 *familiar*: supernatural assistant of a witch
2 *posts*: travels 3 *intelligence*: secret information 4 *infection*: plague
5 *genius*: guiding spirit

CROTOLON

I have been too rough.
My duty to my king made me so earnest.
Excuse it, Orgilus.

ORGILUS

Dear sir.

[*They embrace.*]

Enter to them PROPHILUS, EUPHRANIA, ITHOCLES, GRONEAS [*and*] LEMOPHIL.

CROTOLON

Here comes
Euphrania, with Prophilus and Ithocles.

ORGILUS

Most honoured, ever famous!

ITHOCLES

Your true friend,
On earth not any truer. With smooth[1] eyes
Look on this worthy couple. Your consent
Can only[2] make them one.

ORGILUS

They have it. – Sister,
Thou pawned'st to me an oath, of which engagement
I never will release thee, if thou aim'st
At any other choice than this.

EUPHRANIA

Dear brother,
At him or none.

CROTOLON

To which my blessing's added.

ORGILUS

Which, till a greater ceremony[3] perfect,
Euphrania, lend thy hand. Here take her, Prophilus.

[*He joins them together.*]

1 *smooth*: kindly 2 *only*: alone
3 *greater ceremony*: the wedding itself

Live long a happy man and wife; and further,
That these in presence may conclude an omen,[1]
Thus for a bridal song I close my wishes:
[*Sings*] *Comforts lasting, loves increasing,*
Like soft hours never ceasing;
Plenty's pleasure, peace complying,
Without jars or tongues envying;
Hearts by holy union wedded,
More than theirs by custom bedded;
Fruitful issues, life so graced,
Not by age to be defaced;
Budding, as the year ensu'th,
Every spring another youth;[2]
All what thought can add beside,
Crown this bridegroom and this bride.

PROPHILUS
You have sealed joy close to my soul. – Euphrania,
Now I may call thee mine.

ITHOCLES
I but exchange
One good friend for another.

ORGILUS [*indicating* GRONEAS *and* LEMOPHIL]
If these gallants
Will please to grace a poor invention,
By joining with me in some slight device,[3]
I'll venture on a strain[4] my younger days
Have studied for delight.

LEMOPHIL
With thankful willingness
I offer my attendance.

GRONEAS
No endeavour
Of mine shall fail to show itself.

1 *conclude an omen*: infer a happy outcome
2 *Every spring . . . youth*: i.e., another son every year
3 *device*: theatrical performance, also cunning stratagem
4 *strain*: literary endeavour

ITHOCLES

We will

All join to wait on thy directions, Orgilus.

ORGILUS

O my good lord, your favours flow towards
A too unworthy worm. But, as you please:
I am what you will shape me.

ITHOCLES

A fast friend.

CROTOLON

I thank thee, son, for this acknowledgement;
It is a sight of gladness.

ORGILUS

But[1] my duty. *Exeunt.*

ACT 3

Scene 5

Enter CALANTHA, PENTHEA [*with a paper*], CHRYSTALLA [*and*] PHILEMA.

CALANTHA

Whoe'er would speak with us, deny his entrance.
Be careful of our charge.

CHRYSTALLA

We shall, madam.

CALANTHA

Except the King himself, give none admittance;
Not any.

PHILEMA

Madam, it shall be our care.

Exeunt [CHRYSTALLA *and* PHILEMA].

1 *But*: no more than

CALANTHA
Being alone, Penthea, you have granted[1]
The opportunity you sought, and might
At all times have commanded.

PENTHEA
'Tis a benefit
Which I shall owe your goodness even in death for.
My glass[2] of life, sweet Princess, hath few minutes
Remaining to run down; the sands are spent.
For by an inward messenger I feel
The summons of departure short[3] and certain.

CALANTHA
You feed too much your melancholy.

PENTHEA
Glories
Of human greatness are but pleasing dreams,
And shadows soon decaying. On the stage
Of my mortality, my youth hath acted
Some scenes of vanity, drawn out at length
By varied pleasures, sweetened in the mixture,
But tragical in issue.[4] Beauty, pomp –
With every sensuality[5] our giddiness
Doth frame an idol – are unconstant friends
When any troubled passion makes assault
On the unguarded castle of the mind.

CALANTHA
Contemn not your condition for the proof
Of bare opinion only.[6] To what end
Reach all these moral texts?

PENTHEA
To place before 'ee
A perfect mirror, wherein you may see
How weary I am of a ling'ring life,
Who count the best a misery.

1 *granted*: been granted 2 *glass*: hourglass 3 *short*: imminent
4 *issue*: conclusion 5 *sensuality*: sensual pleasure
6 *proof . . . opinion*: to prove commonplaces true

CALANTHA

Indeed,
You have no little cause; yet none so great
As to distrust a remedy.

PENTHEA

That remedy
Must be a winding-sheet, a fold of lead,[1]
And some untrod-on corner in the earth.
Not to detain your expectation, Princess,
I have an humble suit.

CALANTHA

Speak, I enjoin it.

PENTHEA

Vouchsafe, then, to be my executrix,
And take that trouble on 'ee to dispose
Such legacies as I bequeath impartially.
I have not much to give; the pains are easy.
Heaven will reward your piety, and thank it
When I am dead. For, sure, I must not live.
I hope I cannot.

CALANTHA [*in tears*]

Now, beshrew thy sadness;
Thou turn'st me too much woman.

PENTHEA [*Aside*]

Her fair eyes
Melt into passion. Then I have assurance
Encouraging my boldness. [*Aloud*] In this paper
My will was charactered,[2] which you, with pardon,
Shall now know from mine own mouth.

CALANTHA

Talk on, prithee;
It is a pretty earnest.[3]

PENTHEA

I have left me
But three poor jewels to bequeath. The first is

1 *fold of lead*: coffin 2 *charactered*: written
3 *earnest*: seriousness, taste of what's to come

My youth, for though I am much old in griefs,
In years I am a child.

CALANTHA

To whom that?

PENTHEA

To virgin wives, such as abuse not wedlock
By freedom of desires, but covet chiefly
The pledges of chaste beds for ties of love,
Rather than ranging of their blood;[1] and next
To married maids, such as prefer the number
Of honourable issue in their virtues,
Before the flattery of delights by marriage:
May those be ever young.

CALANTHA

A second jewel
You mean to part with.

PENTHEA

'Tis my fame – I trust
By scandal yet untouched. This I bequeath
To Memory, and Time's old daughter, Truth.[2]
If ever my unhappy name find mention
When I am fall'n to dust, may it deserve
Beseeming[3] charity without dishonour.

CALANTHA

How handsomely thou play'st with harmless sport
Of mere imagination! Speak the last;
I strangely like thy will.

PENTHEA

This jewel, madam,
Is dearly precious to me. You must use
The best of your discretion to employ
This gift as I intend it.

1 *ranging of their blood*: sexual experience outside marriage
2 *Time . . . Truth*: one of Ford's favourite proverbs is 'Truth is the daughter of Time', also associated with revenge tragedy
3 *Beseeming*: befitting

CALANTHA

Do not doubt me.

PENTHEA

'Tis long ago since first I lost my heart;
Long I have lived without it, else for certain
I should have given that too; but instead
Of it, to great Calantha, Sparta's heir,
By service bound and by affection vowed,
I do bequeath, in holiest rites of love,
Mine only brother, Ithocles.

CALANTHA

What said'st thou?

PENTHEA

Impute not, heaven-blessed lady, to ambition
A faith as humbly perfect as the prayers
Of a devoted suppliant can endow it.
Look on him, Princess, with an eye of pity –
How like the ghost of what he late appeared
'A moves before you.

CALANTHA [*Aside*]

Shall I answer here,
Or lend my ear too grossly?[1]

PENTHEA

First, his heart
Shall fall in cinders, scorched by your disdain,
Ere he will dare, poor man, to ope an eye
On these divine looks, but with low-bent thoughts
Accusing such presumption. As for words,
'A dares not utter any but of service.
Yet this lost creature loves 'ee. Be a princess
In sweetness as in blood. Give him his doom,
Or raise him up to comfort.

CALANTHA

What new change
Appears in my behaviour that thou dar'st
Tempt my displeasure?

1 *grossly*: indelicately

PENTHEA

I must leave the world
To revel in Elysium, and 'tis just
To wish my brother some advantage here.
Yet, by my best hopes, Ithocles is ignorant
Of this pursuit.[1] But if you please to kill him,
Lend him one angry look, or one harsh word,
And you shall soon conclude how strong a power
Your absolute authority holds over
His life and end.

CALANTHA

You have forgot, Penthea,
How still I have a father.

PENTHEA

But remember
I am a sister, though to me this brother
Hath been, you know, unkind. Oh most unkind!

CALANTHA

Chrystalla, Philema, where are 'ee? – Lady,
Your check[2] lies in my silence.

Enter CHRYSTALLA *and* PHILEMA.

BOTH

Madam, here.

CALANTHA

I think 'ee sleep, 'ee drones. Wait on Penthea
Unto her lodging. [*Aside*] Ithocles? Wronged lady!

PENTHEA [*Aside*]

My reckonings are made even.[3] Death or fate
Can now nor strike too soon, nor force too late. *Exeunt.*

1 *pursuit*: request 2 *check*: rebuke
3 *My reckonings are made even*: I have balanced with good deeds any evil I have done

ACT 4

Scene 1

Enter ITHOCLES *and* ARMOSTES.

ITHOCLES

Forbear your inquisition. Curiosity[1]
Is of too subtle and too searching nature;
In fears of love too quick, too slow of credit.
I am not what you doubt me.[2]

ARMOSTES

Nephew, be then
As I would wish. All is not right. Good heaven
Confirm your resolutions for dependence
On worthy ends,[3] which may advance your quiet.

ITHOCLES

I did the noble Orgilus much injury,
But grieved Penthea more. I now repent it.
Now, uncle, now, this 'now' is now too late.
So provident is folly in sad issue,
That after-wit,[4] like bankrupt's debts, stands tallied,
Without[5] all possibilities of payment.
Sure, he's an honest, very honest gentleman;
A man of single[6] meaning.

ARMOSTES

I believe it;
Yet, nephew, 'tis the tongue informs our ears.
Our eyes can never pierce into the thoughts,
For they are lodged too inward – but I question
No truth in Orgilus.

1 *Curiosity*: excessive care 2 *doubt me*: fear me to be
3 *resolutions . . . ends*: i.e., may your decision to trust in Orgilus have a positive outcome
4 *after-wit*: knowledge after the event 5 *Without*: beyond
6 *single*: direct, sincere

Enter NEARCHUS *leading* CALANTHA, AMELUS, CHRYSTALLA [*and*] PHILEMA.

The Princess, sir.

ITHOCLES

The Princess? Ha!

ARMOSTES

With her the Prince of Argos.

NEARCHUS

Great fair one, grace my hopes with any instance
Of livery[1] from the allowance of your favour.
This little spark – [*Pointing to* CALANTHA'*s ring*]

CALANTHA

A toy.

NEARCHUS

Love feasts on toys,
For Cupid is a child. Vouchsafe this bounty;
It cannot be denied.

CALANTHA

You shall not value,
Sweet cousin, at a price what I count cheap;
So cheap that let him take it who dares stoop for't,
And give it at next meeting to a mistress.
She'll thank him for't, perhaps.

Casts it to ITHOCLES [*who picks it up*].

AMELUS

The ring, sir, is
The Princess's. I could have took it up.

ITHOCLES

Learn manners, prithee. [*To* CALANTHA] To the blessed owner,
Upon my knees –

[*He offers her the ring.*]

NEARCHUS

Y'are saucy.

1 *livery*: visual token, signifying loyalty and service

CALANTHA

This is pretty.
I am, belike, a 'mistress'? Wondrous pretty!
Let the man keep his fortune, since he found it.
He's worthy on't. – On, cousin.

ITHOCLES [*To* AMELUS]

Follow, spaniel;
I'll force 'ee to a fawning, else.

AMELUS:

You dare not.

Exeunt all except ITHOCLES *and* ARMOSTES.

ARMOSTES

My lord, you were too forward.

ITHOCLES

Look'ee, uncle,
Some such there are whose liberal contents[1]
Swarm without care in every sort of plenty;
Who, after full repasts, can lay them down
To sleep – and they sleep, uncle – in which silence
Their very dreams present 'em choice of pleasures,
Pleasures – observe me, uncle – of rare object.
Here heaps of gold, there increments of honours,
Now change of garments, then the votes of people,
Anon varieties of beauties,[2] courting
In flatteries of the night, exchange of dalliance;
Yet these are still but dreams. Give me felicity
Of which my senses waking are partakers,
A real, visible, material happiness –
And then, too, when I stagger in expectance
Of the least comfort that can cherish life.
I saw it, sir, I saw it; for it came
From her own hand.

ARMOSTES

The Princess threw it t'ee.

1 *liberal contents*: easygoing contentedness 2 *beauties*: beautiful women

ITHOCLES
True, and she said – well I remember what.
Her cousin prince would beg it.

ARMOSTES
Yes, and parted
In anger at your taking on't.

ITHOCLES [*Aside*]
Penthea!
Oh thou hast pleaded with a powerful language.
I want a fee to gratify thy merit.[1]
But I will do –

ARMOSTES
What is't you say?

ITHOCLES
In anger,
In anger let him part; for could his breath,
Like whirlwinds, toss such servile slaves as lick
The dust his footsteps print into a vapour,
It durst not stir a hair of mine. It should not;
I'd rend it up by th'roots first. To be anything
Calantha smiles on is to be a blessing
More sacred than a petty prince of Argos
Can wish to equal, or[2] in worth or title.

ARMOSTES
Contain yourself, my lord. Ixion, aiming
To embrace Juno, bosomed[3] but a cloud,
And begat centaurs; 'tis an useful moral.
Ambition hatched in clouds of mere opinion
Proves but in birth a prodigy.[4]

ITHOCLES
I thank'ee;
Yet, with your licence, I should seem uncharitable
To gentler fate if, relishing the dainties
Of a soul's settled peace, I were so feeble
Not to digest it.

1 *I want . . . merit*: I lack the means to reward you as you deserve
2 *or*: either 3 *bosomed*: embraced 4 *prodigy*: monster

ARMOSTES

He deserves small trust
Who is not privy counsellor to himself.

Enter NEARCHUS, ORGILUS *and* AMELUS.

NEARCHUS

Brave[1] me?

ORGILUS

Your Excellence mistakes his temper;
For Ithocles in fashion of his mind
Is beautiful, soft, gentle, the clear mirror
Of absolute perfection.

AMELUS

Was't your modesty
Termed any of the Prince his servants 'spaniel'?
Your nurse, sure, taught you other language.

ITHOCLES

Language?

NEARCHUS

A gallant man-at-arms is here, a doctor[2]
In feats of chivalry, blunt and rough-spoken,
Vouchsafing not the fustian[3] of civility,
Which rash spirits style good manners.

ITHOCLES

Manners?

ORGILUS

No more, illustrious sir; 'tis matchless Ithocles.

NEARCHUS

You might have understood who I am.

ITHOCLES

Yes,
I did, else – but the presence[4] calmed th'affront.
Y'are cousin to the Princess.

1 *Brave*: challenge, defy 2 *doctor*: expert 3 *fustian*: bombast
4 *presence*: i.e., the royal presence

NEARCHUS

To the King too –
A certain instrument that lent supportance
To your colossic greatness. To that King too,
You might have added.

ITHOCLES

There is more divinity
In beauty than in majesty.

ARMOSTES

Oh, fie, fie!

NEARCHUS

This odd youth's pride turns heretic in loyalty.
Sirrah, low mushrooms[1] never rival cedars.

Exeunt NEARCHUS *and* AMELUS.

ITHOCLES

Come back! What pitiful, dull thing am I
So to be tamely scolded at! Come back!
Let him come back and echo once again
That scornful sound of 'mushroom'. Painted colts,[2]
Like heralds' coats gilt o'er with crowns and sceptres,
May bait a muzzled lion.[3]

ARMOSTES

Cousin, cousin,
Thy tongue is not thy friend.

ORGILUS

In point of honour
Discretion knows no bounds. Amelus told me
'Twas all about a little ring.

ITHOCLES

A ring
The Princess threw away and I took up.
Admit she threw't to me, what arm of brass
Can snatch it hence? No, could 'a grind the hoop

1 *low mushrooms*: upstarts, as opposed to kings (cedars)

2 *Painted colts*: decorated young horses, synonymous with headstrong will and folly

3 *lion*: it was believed that lions were afraid of royal blood and might be deceived by the herald's coat adorned with royal emblems

To powder, 'a might sooner reach my heart
Than steal and wear one dust on't. – Orgilus,
I am extremely wronged.

ORGILUS

A lady's favour
Is not to be so slighted.

ITHOCLES

Slighted?

ARMOSTES

Quiet
These vain, unruly passions, which will render ye
Into a madness.

ORGILUS

Griefs will have their vent.

Enter TECNICUS [*with a scroll*].

ARMOSTES

Welcome. Thou com'st in season, reverend man,
To pour the balsam of a suppling[1] patience
Into the festering wound of ill-spent fury.

ORGILUS [*Aside*]

What makes he here?

TECNICUS

The hurts are yet but mortal,[2]
Which shortly will prove deadly. To the King,
Armostes, see in safety thou deliver
This sealed-up counsel. Bid him with a constancy
Peruse the secrets of the gods. O Sparta!
O Lacedemon! Double-named, but one
In fate. When kingdoms reel – mark well my saw[3] –
Their heads must needs be giddy. Tell the King
That henceforth he no more must enquire after
My agèd head – Apollo wills it so.
I am for Delphos.

1 *suppling*: softening
2 *but mortal*: i.e., dangerous but not yet fatal 3 *saw*: proverbial saying

ARMOSTES

Not without some conference
With our great master.

TECNICUS

Never more to see him.
A greater prince[1] commands me. – Ithocles,
'*When youth is ripe, and age from time doth part,*
The lifeless trunk shall wed the broken heart.'

ITHOCLES

What's this, if understood?

TECNICUS

List, Orgilus;
Remember what I told thee long before –
These tears shall be my witness.

ARMOSTES

'Las, good man.

TECNICUS

'*Let craft with courtesy a while confer;*
Revenge proves its own executioner.'

ORGILUS

Dark sentences are for Apollo's priests;
I am not Oedipus.[2]

TECNICUS

My hour is come.
Cheer up the King. Farewell to all. O Sparta!
O Lacedemon! *Exit* TECNICUS.

ARMOSTES

If prophetic fire
Have warmed this old man's bosom, we might construe
His words to fatal sense.

1 *A greater prince*: i.e., Apollo
2 *Oedipus*: mythological figure famous for solving the riddle of the Sphinx

ITHOCLES

Leave to the powers
Above us the effects of their decrees;
My burden lies within me. Servile fears
Prevent[1] no great effects. [*Aside*] Divine Calantha!

ARMOSTES

The gods be still propitious!

Exeunt all except ORGILUS.

ORGILUS

Something oddly
The book-man prated; yet 'a talked it weeping.
'*Let craft with courtesy a while confer;*
Revenge proves its own executioner.'
Con[2] it again. For what? It shall not puzzle me;
'Tis dotage of a withered brain. Penthea
Forbade me not her presence. I may see her,
And gaze my fill. Why, see her then I may;
When if I faint to speak I must be silent. *Exit* ORGILUS.

ACT 4

Scene 2

Enter BASSANES, GRAUSIS *and* PHULAS.

BASSANES

Pray, use your recreations. All the service
I will expect is quietness amongst 'ee.
Take liberty at home, abroad, at all times,
And in your charities appease the gods,
Whom I, with my distractions, have offended.

GRAUSIS

Fair blessings on thy heart!

1 *Prevent*: anticipate, foretell 2 *Con*: study, memorize

PHULAS [*Aside*]

Here's a rare change!
My lord, to cure the itch, is surely gelded.
The cuckold, in conceit,[1] hath cast his horns.

BASSANES

Betake 'ee to your several occasions,[2]
And wherein I have heretofore been faulty,
Let your constructions mildly pass it over.
Henceforth, I'll study reformation. More
I have not for employment.

GRAUSIS

O sweet man,
Thou art the very 'Honeycomb of Honesty'.

PHULAS

The 'Garland of Goodwill'.[3] Old lady, hold up
Thy reverend snout and trot behind me softly,
As it becomes a moil[4] of ancient carriage.

Exeunt [*except for* BASSANES].

BASSANES

Beasts, only capable of sense,[5] enjoy
The benefit of food and ease with thankfulness.
Such silly creatures, with a grudging, kick not
Against the portion nature hath bestowed;
But men, endowed with reason and the use
Of reason, to distinguish from the chaff
Of abject scarcity[6] the quintessence,
Soul and elixir of the earth's abundance,
The treasures of the sea, the air, nay, heaven,
Repining at these glories of creation
Are verier beasts than beasts; and of those beasts
The worst am I. I, who was made a monarch

1 *in conceit*: in his own imagination
2 *several occasions*: various activities
3 *Honeycomb . . . Goodwill*: perhaps both are titles of popular ballad collections; *A Garland of Goodwill* was published in 1593 and 1631
4 *moil*: mule
5 *capable of sense*: responsive only to sense impressions, i.e., not rational
6 *chaff . . . scarcity*: poor sustenance of the poor

Of what a heart could wish for – a chaste wife –
Endeavoured what in me lay to pull down
That temple, built for adoration only,
And level't in the dust of causeless scandal.
But to redeem a sacrilege so impious,
Humility shall pour, before the deities
I have incensed, a largesse of more patience
Than their displeasèd altars can require.
No tempests of commotion shall disquiet
The calms of my composure.

Enter ORGILUS.

ORGILUS

I have found thee,
Thou patron of more horrors than the bulk
Of manhood, hooped about with ribs of iron,
Can cram within thy breast. Penthea, Bassanes,
Cursed by thy jealousies – more, by thy dotage –
Is left a prey to words.[1]

BASSANES

Exercise
Your trials[2] for addition to my penance;
I am resolved.

ORGILUS

Play not with misery
Past cure. Some angry minister of fate hath
Deposed the empress of her soul, her reason,
From its most proper throne; but – what's the miracle
More new – I, I have seen it, and yet live!

BASSANES

You may delude my senses, not my judgement.
'Tis anchored into a firm resolution.
Dalliance of mirth or wit can ne'er unfix it.
Practise yet further.[3]

1 *words*: scandal, defamation 2 *trials*: tests of endurance
3 *Practise yet further*: try harder to deceive or distress me

ORGILUS

May thy death-of-love to her
Damn all thy comforts to a lasting fast
From every joy of life. Thou barren rock,
By thee we have been split in ken[1] of harbour.

Enter ITHOCLES, PENTHEA, *her hair about her ears,*[2] PHILEMA, CHRYSTALLA [ARMOSTES *and* CROTOLON].

ITHOCLES

Sister, look up! Your Ithocles, your brother,
Speaks t'ee. Why do you weep? Dear, turn not from me –
Here is a killing sight! Lo, Bassanes,
A lamentable object.

ORGILUS

Man, dost see't?
Sports are more gamesome. Am I yet in merriment?
Why dost not laugh?

BASSANES

Divine and best of ladies,
Please to forget my outrage. Mercy ever
Cannot but lodge under a roof so excellent.
I have cast off that cruelty of frenzy
Which once appeared imposterous,[3] and then juggled[4]
To cheat my sleeps of rest.

ORGILUS

Was I in earnest?

PENTHEA

Sure, if we were all sirens[5] we should sing pitifully;
And 'twere a comely music, when in parts[6]
One sung another's knell. The turtle[7] sighs
When he hath lost his mate; and yet some say

1 *ken*: sight
2 *her hair about her ears*: a theatre convention for madness, though early modern brides also wore their hair loose
3 *imposterous*: seemed to be practising an imposture on me
4 *juggled*: tricked me
5 *sirens*: mythological creatures, part-woman, part-bird, whose song lured sailors to their deaths
6 *in parts*: taking different parts 7 *turtle*: turtle dove

'A must be dead first. 'Tis a fine deceit
To pass away in a dream. Indeed, I've slept
With mine eyes open a great while. No falsehood
Equals a broken faith. There's not a hair
Sticks on my head but, like a leaden plummet,
It sinks me to the grave. I must creep thither;
The journey is not long.

ITHOCLES

But thou, Penthea,
Hast many years, I hope, to number yet,
Ere thou canst travel that way.

BASSANES

Let the sun first
Be wrapped up in an everlasting darkness,
Before the light of nature, chiefly formed
For the whole world's delight, feel an eclipse
So universal.

ORGILUS

Wisdom, look'ee, begins
To rave! [*To* BASSANES] Art thou mad too, Antiquity?[1]

PENTHEA

Since I was first a wife, I might have been
Mother to many pretty, prattling babes.
They would have smiled when I smiled; and, for certain,
I should have cried when they cried. – Truly, brother,
My father would have picked me out a husband,
And then my little ones had been no bastards.
But 'tis too late for me to marry now;
I am past child-bearing. 'Tis not my fault.

BASSANES

Fall on me, if there be a burning Etna,[2]
And bury me in flames! Sweats, hot as sulphur,
Boil through my pores! Affliction hath in store
No torture like to this.

1 *Antiquity*: suggesting that Bassanes is an old man
2 *Etna*: volcano in north-east Sicily

ORGILUS

Behold a patience![1]
Lay by thy whining, grey Dissimulation.
Do something worth a chronicle. Show justice
Upon the author of this mischief! Dig out
The jealousies that hatched this thraldom first
With thine own poniard. Every antic rapture[2]
Can roar as thine does.

ITHOCLES

Orgilus, forbear!

BASSANES

Disturb him not. It is a talking motion[3]
Provided for my torment. What a fool am I
To bawdy[4] passion! Ere I'll speak a word,
I will look on and burst.

PENTHEA [*To* ORGILUS]

I loved you once.

ORGILUS

Thou didst, wronged creature, in despite of malice;
For it, I love thee ever.

PENTHEA

Spare[5] your hand.
Believe me, I'll not hurt it.
[ORGILUS *offers his hand.*]

ORGILUS

Pain my heart too.

PENTHEA

Complain not, though I wring it hard. I'll kiss it.
Oh, 'tis a fine, soft palm. Hark in thine ear:
Like whom do I look, prithee? Nay, no whispering.
Goodness, we had been happy! Too much happiness
Will make folk proud, they say. But that is he (*points at* ITHOCLES) –

1 *Behold a patience*: Orgilus is being sarcastic
2 *antic rapture*: actor's onstage passion
3 *motion*: puppet show, entertainment 4 *bawdy*: cheapen
5 *Spare*: give me

And yet he paid for't home.[1] Alas, his heart
Is crept into the cabinet[2] of the Princess.
We shall have points and bride-laces.[3] Remember
When we last gathered roses in the garden?
I found my wits, but truly you lost yours.
[*Pointing again at* ITHOCLES] That's he, and still 'tis he.

ITHOCLES

Poor soul, how idly[4]
Her fancies guide her tongue.

BASSANES [*Aside*]

Keep in, vexation,
And break not into clamour.

ORGILUS [*Aside*]

She has tutored me.
Some powerful inspiration checks[5] my laziness.
[*To* PENTHEA] Now let me kiss your hand, grieved beauty.

PENTHEA

Kiss it.

[ORGILUS *kisses her hand.*]

Alack, alack, his lips be wondrous cold!
Dear soul, h'as lost his colour. Have 'ee seen
A straying heart? All crannies![6] Every drop
Of blood is turned to an amethyst,[7]
Which married bachelors hang in their ears.

ORGILUS

Peace usher her into Elysium!
[*Aside*] If this be madness, madness is an oracle.[8]

Exit ORGILUS.

1 *he paid for't home*: he suffered for it
2 *cabinet*: private chamber, jewel box
3 *points and bride-laces*: wedding favours, respectively lacework and pieces of gold, silk or lace to tie up sprigs of rosemary
4 *idly*: madly, pointlessly
5 *checks*: reproaches
6 *crannies*: holes, fissures
7 *amethyst*: supposed to have the power to prevent intoxication, so inhibiting revenge, also a weak purple colour
8 *an oracle*: i.e., a source of instruction

ITHOCLES
Chrystalla, Philema, when slept my sister?
Her ravings are so wild.
CHRYSTALLA
Sir, not these ten days.
PHILEMA
We watch by her continually. Besides,
We cannot any way pray her to eat.
BASSANES
Oh, misery of miseries!
PENTHEA
Take comfort:
You may live well, and die a good old man.
[*To* CROTOLON] By yea and nay[1] – an oath not to be broken –
If you had joined our hands once in the temple –
'Twas since my father died, for had he lived
He would have done't – I must have called you father.
O my wracked honour, ruined by those tyrants:
A cruel brother and a desperate dotage!
There is no peace left for a ravished wife,
Widowed by lawless marriage. To all memory,
Penthea's, poor Penthea's name is strumpeted!
But since her blood was seasoned, by the forfeit
Of noble shame, with mixtures of pollution,
Her blood – 'tis just – be henceforth never heightened
With taste of sustenance. Starve. Let that fullness
Whose pleurisy[2] hath severed faith and modesty –
Forgive me – Oh, I faint.
ARMOSTES
Be not so wilful,
Sweet niece, to work thine own destruction.
ITHOCLES
Nature
Will call her daughter monster. What? Not eat?
Refuse the only ordinary means

1 *By yea and nay*: a mild Puritan oath 2 *pleurisy*: excess

Which are ordained for life? Be not, my sister,
A murderess to thyself. – Hear'st thou this, Bassanes?

BASSANES

Foh! I am busy; for I have not thoughts
Enough to think. All shall be well anon.
'Tis tumbling in my head. There is a mastery[1]
In art to fatten and keep smooth the outside;
Yes, and to comfort up the vital spirits
Without the help of food. Fumes or perfumes,
Perfumes or fumes – Let her alone. I'll search out
The trick on't.

PENTHEA

Lead me gently. Heavens reward ye.
Griefs are sure friends; they leave, without control,
Nor cure nor comforts for a leprous soul.

Exeunt the maids [CHRYSTALLA *and* PHILEMA] *supporting* PENTHEA.

BASSANES

I grant t'ee; and will put in practice instantly
What you shall still admire.[2] 'Tis wonderful,
'Tis super-singular, not to be matched!
Yet when I've done't, I've done't; ye shall all thank me.

Exit BASSANES.

ARMOSTES

The sight is full of terror.

ITHOCLES

On my soul
Lies such an infinite clog[3] of massy dullness,
As that I have not sense enough to feel it.

Enter NEARCHUS *and* AMELUS.

See, uncle, th'angry thing returns again.
Shall's welcome him with thunder? We are haunted,
And must use exorcism to conjure down
This spirit of malevolence.

1 *mastery*: skill 2 *admire*: wonder at
3 *clog*: heavy piece of wood used to prevent escape

ARMOSTES

Mildly, nephew.

NEARCHUS

I come not, sir, to chide your late disorder,[1]
Admitting that th'inurement to a roughness
In soldiers of your years and fortunes, chiefly
So lately prosperous, hath not yet shook off
The custom of the war in hours of leisure.
Nor shall you need excuse, since y'are to render
Account to that fair excellence, the Princess,
Who in her private gallery expects it
From your own mouth alone. I am a messenger
But to her pleasure.

ITHOCLES

Excellent Nearchus,
Be prince still[2] of my services, and conquer
Without the combat of dispute. [*Kneeling*] I honour 'ee.

NEARCHUS

The King is on a sudden indisposed.
Physicians are called for. 'Twere fit, Armostes,
You should be near him.

ARMOSTES

Sir, I kiss your hands.

Exeunt all except NEARCHUS *and* AMELUS.

NEARCHUS

Amelus, I perceive Calantha's bosom
Is warmed with other fires than such as can
Take strength from any fuel of the love
I might address to her. Young Ithocles,
Or ever[3] I mistake, is lord ascendant[4]
Of her devotions; one, to speak him truly,
In every disposition nobly fashioned.

1 *disorder*: unmannerly conduct 2 *still*: always 3 *Or ever*: unless
4 *lord ascendant*: an astrological term, referring to the planet within the house of the ascendant, i.e., influential

AMELUS
But can your Highness brook to be so rivalled,
Considering th'inequality of the persons?

NEARCHUS
I can, Amelus; for affections injured
By tyranny or rigour of compulsion,
Like tempest-threatened trees unfirmly rooted,
Ne'er spring to timely growth. Observe, for instance,
Life-spent Penthea and unhappy Orgilus.

AMELUS
How does your Grace determine?

NEARCHUS
To be jealous
In public of what privately I'll further;
And though they shall not know, yet they shall find it.
Exeunt.

ACT 4

Scene 3

Enter LEMOPHIL *and* GRONEAS *leading* AMYCLAS, *and placing him in a chair, followed by* ARMOSTES [*with a casket*], CROTOLON *and* PROPHILUS.

AMYCLAS
Our daughter is not near?

ARMOSTES
She is retired, sir,
Into her gallery.

AMYCLAS
Where's the Prince, our cousin?

PROPHILUS
New walked into the grove, my lord.

AMYCLAS
All leave us,
Except Armostes, and you, Crotolon;
We would be private.

PROPHILUS

Health unto your Majesty!

Exeunt PROPHILUS, LEMOPHIL *and* GRONEAS.

AMYCLAS

What, Tecnicus is gone?

ARMOSTES

He is, to Delphos;
And to your royal hands presents this box.

AMYCLAS

Unseal it, good Armostes. Therein lies
The secrets of the oracle. Out with it.
Apollo live our patron! Read, Armostes.

ARMOSTES [*Reads*]

'The plot in which the vine takes root,
Begins to dry from head to foot.
The stock soon withering, want of sap
Doth cause to quail[1] *the budding grape.*
But from the neighbouring elm a dew
Shall drop, and feed the plot anew.'

AMYCLAS

That is the oracle. What exposition
Makes the philosopher?

ARMOSTES

This brief one only:
'The plot is Sparta; the dried vine the King;
The quailing grape his daughter; but the thing
Of most importance, not to be revealed,
Is a near prince, the elm; the rest concealed.
Tecnicus.'

AMYCLAS

Enough. Although the opening[2] of this riddle
Be but itself a riddle, yet we construe
How near our labouring age draws to a rest.
But must Calantha quail too? That young grape
Untimely budded? I could mourn for her;

1 *quail*: dry up, fade 2 *opening*: interpretation

Her tenderness hath yet deserved no rigour,
So to be crossed by fate.

ARMOSTES

You misapply, sir –
With favour let me speak it – what Apollo
Hath clouded in hid sense. I here conjecture
Her marriage with some neighb'ring prince, the dew
Of which befriending elm shall ever strengthen
Your subjects with a sovereignty of power.

CROTOLON

Besides, most gracious lord, the pith of oracles
Is to be then digested when th'events
Expound their truth, not brought as soon to light
As uttered. Truth is child of Time; and herein
I find no scruple,[1] rather cause of comfort,
With unity of kingdoms.

AMYCLAS

May it prove so,
For weal[2] of this dear nation. Where is Ithocles?
Armostes, Crotolon, when this withered vine
Of my frail carcass on the funeral pile
Is fired into its ashes, let that young man
Be hedged about still with your cares and loves.
Much owe I to his worth, much to his service.
Let such as wait come in now.

ARMOSTES

All attend here!

Enter ITHOCLES, CALANTHA, PROPHILUS, ORGILUS, EUPHRANIA, LEMOPHIL *and* GRONEAS.

CALANTHA

Dear sir, king, father!

ITHOCLES

O my royal master!

AMYCLAS

Cleave not my heart, sweet twins of my life's solace,
With your fore-judging fears. There is no physic[3]

1 *scruple*: cause for anxiety 2 *weal*: prosperity 3 *physic*: medicine

So cunningly restorative to cherish
The fall of age, or call back youth and vigour,
As your consents in duty. I will shake off
This languishing disease of time, to quicken
Fresh pleasures in these drooping hours of sadness.
Is fair Euphrania married yet to Prophilus?

CROTOLON

This morning, gracious lord.

ORGILUS

This very morning,
Which, with your Highness' leave, you may observe too.
Our sister looks, methinks, mirthful and sprightly,
As if her chaster fancy could already
Expound the riddle of her gain in losing
A trifle maids know only that they know not.
[*To* EUPHRANIA] Pish! Prithee, blush not. 'Tis but honest change
Of fashion in the garment: loose for straight;[1]
And so the modest maid is made a wife.
Shrewd[2] business, is't not, sister?

EUPHRANIA

You are pleasant.

AMYCLAS

We thank thee, Orgilus; this mirth becomes thee.
But wherefore sits the court in such a silence?
A wedding without revels is not seemly.

CALANTHA

Your late indisposition, sir, forbade it.

AMYCLAS

Be it thy charge, Calantha, to set forward
The bridal-sports, to which I will be present;
If not, at least consenting. – Mine own Ithocles,
I have done little for thee yet.

1 *loose for straight*: the loose gown of pregnancy, but also sexual experience as opposed to the 'strait' state of virginity
2 *Shrewd*: cunning

ITHOCLES

Y'have built me
To the full height I stand in.

CALANTHA [*Aside*]

Now or never –
[*Aloud*] May I propose a suit?

AMYCLAS

Demand and have it.

[AMYCLAS *takes* CALANTHA *and* ITHOCLES *to one side.* ORGILUS *listens in.*][1]

CALANTHA

Pray, sir, give me this young man, and no further
Account him yours than he deserves in all things
To be thought worthy mine. I will esteem him
According to his merit.

AMYCLAS

Still th'art my daughter,
Still grow'st upon my heart. [*To* ITHOCLES] Give me thine hand.
Calantha, take thine own.

[*He joins their hands together.*]

In noble actions
Thou'lt find him firm and absolute.[2] – I would not
Have parted with thee, Ithocles, to any
But to a mistress who is all what I am.

ITHOCLES

A change, great king, most wished for, 'cause the same.

CALANTHA [*To* ITHOCLES]

Th'art mine. Have I now kept my word?

ITHOCLES [*To* CALANTHA]

Divinely.

1 AMYCLAS *takes* ... ORGILUS *listens in*: a stage direction separating off this part of the action seems to be required by the fact that Nearchus is later surprised to learn of Calantha's betrothal to Ithocles

2 *absolute*: without imperfection

ORGILUS
Rich fortunes – guard to favour of a princess –
Rock thee, brave man, in ever-crownèd plenty.
Y'are minion[1] of the time; be thankful for it.
[*Aside*] Ho, here's a swinge[2] in destiny! Apparent,[3]
The youth is up on tiptoe, yet may stumble.
[AMYCLAS, CALANTHA *and* ITHOCLES *rejoin the others.*]

AMYCLAS
On to your recreations! Now convey me
Unto my bedchamber. None on his forehead
Wear a distempered look.

ALL
The gods preserve 'ee!

CALANTHA [*Aside to* ITHOCLES]
Sweet, be not from my sight.

ITHOCLES [*Aside to* CALANTHA]
My whole felicity!

Exeunt, carrying out of the KING. ORGILUS *stays*[4] ITHOCLES.

ORGILUS
Shall I be bold, my lord?

ITHOCLES
Thou canst not, Orgilus.
Call me thine own, for Prophilus must henceforth
Be all thy sister's. Friendship, though it cease not
In marriage, yet is oft at less command
Than when a single freedom can dispose it.

ORGILUS
Most right, my most good lord, my most great lord,
My gracious, princely lord – I might add 'royal'.

ITHOCLES
Royal? A subject royal?

1 *minion*: favourite
2 *swinge*: whirling movement, like that of Fortune's wheel
3 *Apparent*: obviously 4 *stays*: stops

ORGILUS

Why not, pray, sir?
The sovereignty of kingdoms, in their nonage,[1]
Stooped to desert, not birth. There's as much merit
In clearness of affection[2] as in puddle
Of generation.[3] You have conquered love
Even in the loveliest. If I greatly err not,
The son of Venus hath bequeathed his quiver
To Ithocles his manage,[4] by whose arrows
Calantha's breast is opened.

ITHOCLES

Can't be possible?

ORGILUS

I was myself a piece of suitor once,
And forward in preferment too; so forward
That, speaking truth, I may without offence, sir,
Presume to whisper that my hopes, and – hark 'ee –
My certainty of marriage stood assured
With as firm footing, by your leave, as any's
Now at this very instant, but –

ITHOCLES

'Tis granted;
And for a league of privacy between us,
Read o'er my bosom and partake a secret:
The Princess is contracted mine.

ORGILUS

Still,[5] why not?
I now applaud her wisdom. When your kingdom
Stands seated in your will, secure and settled,
I dare pronounce you will be a just monarch.
Greece must admire, and tremble.

1 *nonage*: early stages of their history
2 *clearness of affection*: purity of love
3 *puddle of generation*: dark or compromised heredity
4 *Ithocles his manage*: into the hands of Ithocles
5 *Still*: even so

ITHOCLES

Then the sweetness
Of so imparadised a comfort, Orgilus!
It is to banquet with the gods.

ORGILUS

The glory
Of numerous children, potency of nobles,
Bent knees, hearts paved to tread on!

ITHOCLES

With a friendship
So dear, so fast as thine.

ORGILUS

I am unfitting
For office; but for service –

ITHOCLES

We'll distinguish
Our fortunes merely in the title: partners
In all respects else but the bed –

ORGILUS

The bed?
Forfend[1] it Jove's own jealousy – till lastly
We slip down in the common earth together,
And there our beds are equal, save some monument
To show this was the king, and this the subject.
Soft sad music.
List, what sad sounds are these? Extremely sad ones.

ITHOCLES

Sure, from Penthea's lodgings.

ORGILUS

Hark, a voice too!
A Song [within][2]
Oh, no more, no more, too late
Sighs are spent. The burning tapers

1 *Forfend*: forbid
2 *A Song*: later said to have been sung by Philema

Of a life as chaste as fate,
Pure as are unwritten papers,
Are burnt out. No heat, no light
Now remains. 'Tis ever night.
Love is dead. Let lovers' eyes,
Locked in endless dreams,
Th'extremes of all extremes,
Ope no more, for now Love dies,
Now Love dies, implying
Love's martyrs must be ever, ever dying.

ITHOCLES

Oh, my misgiving heart!

ORGILUS

A horrid stillness
Succeeds this deathful air. Let's know the reason.
Tread softly: there is mystery[1] in mourning. *Exeunt.*

ACT 4

Scene 4

Enter CHRYSTALLA *and* PHILEMA, *bringing in* PENTHEA *in a chair, veiled. Two other* SERVANTS *placing two chairs, one on the one side, and the other with an engine*[2] *on the other. The maids* [CHRYSTALLA *and* PHILEMA] *sit down at her feet, mourning. The* SERVANTS *go out; meet them* ITHOCLES *and* ORGILUS.

SERVANT [*Aside to* ORGILUS]

'Tis done; that on her right hand.

ORGILUS [*Aside to* SERVANT]

Good. Be gone.
[*Exeunt* SERVANTS.]

1 *mystery*: a divine secret that resists human understanding

2 *engine*: mechanism; a chair capable of entrapping the sitter's arms was also used in Barnabe Barnes's play *The Devil's Charter* (1607)

ITHOCLES
Soft peace enrich this room.

ORGILUS
How fares the lady?

PHILEMA
Dead.

CHRYSTALLA
Dead!

PHILEMA
Starved.

CHRYSTALLA
Starved!

ITHOCLES
Me miserable!

ORGILUS
Tell us
How parted she from life?

PHILEMA
She called for music,
And begged some gentle voice to tune a farewell
To life and griefs. Chrystalla touched the lute;
I wept the funeral song.

CHRYSTALLA
Which scarce was ended,
But her last breath sealed up these hollow sounds:
'O cruel Ithocles, and injured Orgilus!'
So down she drew her veil, so died.

ITHOCLES
So died?

ORGILUS
Up! You are messengers of death; go from us.
Here's woe enough to court without a prompter.
Away! And hark ye: till you see us next,
No syllable that she is dead. Away!
Keep a smooth brow. *Exeunt* PHILEMA *and* CHRYSTALLA.
My lord –

ITHOCLES

Mine only sister!
Another is not left me.

ORGILUS

Take that chair;
I'll seat me here in this. Between us sits
The object of our sorrows. Some few tears
We'll part among us. I, perhaps, can mix
One lamentable story to prepare 'em.
There, there, sit there, my lord.

ITHOCLES

Yes, as you please.

ITHOCLES *sits down and is caught in the engine.*

What means this treachery?

ORGILUS

Caught! You are caught,
Young master! 'Tis thy throne of coronation,
Thou fool of greatness. See, I take this veil off.
[*He reveals* PENTHEA*'s face.*]
Survey a beauty withered by the flames
Of an insulting[1] Phaeton,[2] her brother.

ITHOCLES

Thou mean'st to kill me basely?

ORGILUS

I foreknew
The last act of her life, and trained[3] thee hither
To sacrifice a tyrant to a turtle.[4]
You dreamt of kingdoms, did 'ee? How to bosom[5]
The delicacies of a youngling princess;
How with this nod to grace that subtle courtier;
How with that frown to make this noble tremble;
And so forth – whiles Penthea's groans and tortures,
Her agonies, her miseries, afflictions,

1 *insulting*: arrogant
2 *Phaeton*: son of Apollo, who stole his father's chariot of the sun and was killed; an example of youthful presumption
3 *trained*: lured 4 *turtle*: turtle dove 5 *bosom*: embrace

Ne'er touched upon your thought. As for my injuries,
Alas, they were beneath your royal pity;
But yet they lived, thou proud man, to confound thee!
Behold thy fate: this steel.
[*He draws his sword.*]

ITHOCLES

Strike home! A courage
As keen as thy revenge shall give it welcome.
But, prithee, faint not. If the wound close up,
Tent[1] it with double force, and search it deeply.
Thou look'st that I should whine and beg compassion,
As loath to leave the vainness of my glories?
A statelier resolution arms my confidence:
To cozen[2] thee of honour. Neither could I,
With equal trial of unequal fortune,
By hazard of a duel – 'twere a bravery[3]
Too mighty for a slave intending murder.
On to the execution, and inherit
A conflict with thy horrors.

ORGILUS

By Apollo,
Thou talk'st a goodly language. For requital,
I will report thee to thy mistress richly,
And take this peace along:[4] some few short minutes
Determined,[5] my resolves shall quickly follow
Thy wrathful ghost.[6] Then, if we tug for mastery,
Penthea's sacred eyes shall lend new courage.
Give me thy hand. Be healthful in thy parting
From lost mortality. Thus, thus, I free it.
[*Stabs*] *him.*

ITHOCLES

Yet, yet, I scorn to shrink.

1 *Tent*: probe 2 *cozen*: cheat 3 *a bravery*: act of bravado
4 *take . . . along*: take this consolation into death
5 *Determined*: having elapsed
6 *my resolves . . . ghost*: i.e., Orgilus will commit suicide

ORGILUS

Keep up thy spirit.
I will be gentle even in blood. To linger
Pain, which I strive to cure, were to be cruel.
[*Stabs him again.*]

ITHOCLES

Nimble in vengeance, I forgive thee. Follow
Safety, with best success. O may it prosper!
Penthea, by thy side thy brother bleeds –
The earnest[1] of his wrongs to thy forced faith.
Thoughts of ambition, or delicious banquet,
With beauty, youth, and love, together perish
In my last breath, which on the sacred altar
Of a long-looked-for peace now moves to heaven. *He dies.*

ORGILUS

Farewell, fair spring of manhood. Henceforth welcome
Best expectation of a noble suff'rance.
I'll lock the bodies safe, till what must follow
Shall be approved.[2] Sweet twins, shine stars forever.
In vain they build their hopes whose life is shame;
No monument lasts but a happy name.
Exit ORGILUS [*with the bodies*].

ACT 5

Scene 1

Enter BASSANES *alone.*

BASSANES

Athens, to Athens I have sent – the nursery
Of Greece for learning, and the fount of knowledge –
For here in Sparta there's not left amongst us
One wise man to direct; we're all turned madcaps.
'Tis said Apollo is the god of herbs;
Then certainly he knows the virtue of 'em.

1 *earnest*: payment 2 *approved*: made good

To Delphos I have sent, too. If there can be
A help for nature, we are sure yet.
Enter ORGILUS.

ORGILUS

Honour
Attend thy counsels ever!

BASSANES

I beseech thee
With all my heart, let me go from thee quietly.
I will not aught to do with thee, of all men.
The doubles[1] of a hare, or, in a morning,
Salutes from a splay-footed[2] witch, to drop
Three drops of blood at th'nose,[3] just and no more,
Croaking of ravens or the screech of owls,[4]
Are not so boding mischief as thy crossing
My private meditations. Shun me, prithee;
And if I cannot love thee heartily,
I'll love thee as well as I can.

ORGILUS

Noble Bassanes,
Mistake me not –

BASSANES

Phew![5] Then we shall be troubled.
Thou wert ordained my plague. Heaven make me thankful,
And give me patience too, heaven, I beseech thee.

ORGILUS

Accept a league of amity; for henceforth
I vow, by my best genius,[6] in a syllable
Never to speak vexation. I will study

1 *doubles*: sharp turns made when being pursued
2 *splay-footed*: thought to be one of the distinguishing marks of a witch
3 *drops . . . nose*: thought to foretell the victim's death (see Antonio in *The Duchess of Malfi*); three was especially unlucky
4 *doubles . . . owls*: all bad omens
5 *Phew*: an expression of weariness or disgust
6 *genius*: guiding spirit

Service and friendship, with a zealous sorrow
For my past incivility towards 'ee.

BASSANES

Hey-day! Good words, good words! I must believe 'em,
And be a coxcomb for my labour.

ORGILUS

Use not
So hard a language. Your misdoubt[1] is causeless.
For instance, if you promise to put on
A constancy of patience – such a patience
As chronicle or history ne'er mentioned,
As follows not example,[2] but shall stand
A wonder and a theme for imitation,
The first, the index[3] pointing to a second –
I will acquaint'ee with an unmatched secret,
Whose knowledge to your griefs shall set a period.

BASSANES

Thou canst not, Orgilus; 'tis in the power
Of the gods only. Yet, for satisfaction,
Because I note an earnest in thine utterance,
Unforced and naturally free, be resolute
The virgin bays shall not withstand the lightning
With a more careless danger[4] than my constancy
The full of thy relation.[5] Could it move
Distraction in a senseless marble statue,
It should find me a rock. I do expect now
Some truth of unheard moment.[6]

1 *misdoubt*: mistrust
2 *follows not example*: has no precedent
3 *index*: pointing hand included in the margin of early modern books to draw attention to something
4 *a more careless danger*: greater disregard for danger; bay trees were thought to be resistant to lightning
5 *full . . . relation*: full disclosure of your secret
6 *unheard moment*: unprecedented significance

ORGILUS

To your patience
You must add privacy, as strong in silence
As mysteries locked up in Jove's own bosom.

BASSANES

A skull hid in the earth a treble age
Shall sooner prate.

ORGILUS

Lastly, to such direction
As the severity of a glorious action
Deserves to lead your wisdom and your judgement,
You ought to yield obedience.

BASSANES

With assurance
Of will and thankfulness.

ORGILUS

With manly courage
Please then to follow me.

BASSANES

Where'er, I fear not. *Exeunt.*

ACT 5

Scene 2

Loud music. Enter GRONEAS *and* LEMOPHIL *leading* EUPHRANIA; CHRYSTALLA *and* PHILEMA *leading* PROPHILUS; NEARCHUS *supporting* CALANTHA; CROTOLON *and* AMELUS [*and* ATTENDANTS]. *Cease loud music. All make a stand.*[1]

CALANTHA

We miss our servant, Ithocles, and Orgilus.
On whom attend they?

1 *make a stand*: come to a halt

CROTOLON

My son, gracious Princess,
Whispered some new device,[1] to which these revels
Should be but usher; wherein I conceive
Lord Ithocles and he himself are actors.

CALANTHA

A fair excuse for absence; as for Bassanes,
Delights to him are troublesome. Armostes
Is with the King?

CROTOLON

He is.

CALANTHA

On to the dance.
[*To* NEARCHUS] Dear cousin, hand you[2] the bride. The bridegroom must be
Entrusted to my courtship. – Be not jealous,
Euphrania; I shall scarcely prove a temptress.
Fall to our dance!

Music.

NEARCHUS *dance*[*s*] *with* EUPHRANIA, PROPHILUS *with* CALANTHA, CHRYSTALLA *with* LEMOPHIL, PHILEMA *with* GRONEAS. *Dance the first change,*[3] *during which enter* ARMOSTES.

ARMOSTES (*In* CALANTHA*'s ear*)

The King your father's dead.

CALANTHA

To the other change.

ARMOSTES

Is't possible?
[*He stands aside.*]

Dance again. Enter BASSANES.

1 *device*: performance 2 *hand you*: conduct
3 *change*: a figure or set of steps in dancing

BASSANES
Oh, madam!
Penthea, poor Penthea's starved.

CALANTHA
Beshrew thee!
Lead to the next.

BASSANES
Amazement dulls my senses.
[*He stands aside.*]
Dance again. Enter ORGILUS.

ORGILUS
Brave Ithocles is murdered, murdered cruelly!

CALANTHA
How dull this music sounds! Strike up more sprightly!
Our footings[1] are not active like our heart,
Which treads the nimbler measure.

ORGILUS
I am thunder-struck.
[*He stands aside.*]
Last change. Cease music.

CALANTHA
So, let us breathe a while. Hath not this motion
Raised fresher colour on your cheeks?

NEARCHUS
Sweet Princess,
A perfect purity of blood enamels
The beauty of your white.

CALANTHA
We all look cheerfully;
And, cousin, 'tis, methinks, a rare presumption
In any who prefers our lawful pleasures
Before their own sour censure to interrupt
The custom of this ceremony bluntly.

1 *footings*: steps

NEARCHUS

None dares, lady.

CALANTHA

Yes, yes; some hollow voice delivered to me
How that the King was dead.

ARMOSTES

The King is dead.
That fatal news was mine; for in mine arms
He breathed his last, and with his crown bequeathed 'ee
Your mother's wedding ring, which here I tender.

[*Presents the ring to* CALANTHA.]

CROTOLON

Most strange!

CALANTHA

Peace crown his ashes! We are queen then.

NEARCHUS

Long live Calantha, Sparta's sovereign queen!

ALL

Long live the Queen!

CALANTHA

What whispered Bassanes?

BASSANES

That my Penthea, miserable soul,
Was starved to death.

CALANTHA

She's happy; she hath finished
A long and painful progress. A third murmur
Pierced mine unwilling ears.

ORGILUS

That Ithocles
Was murdered – rather butchered, had not bravery
Of an undaunted spirit, conquering terror,
Proclaimed his last act triumph over ruin.

ARMOSTES

How? Murdered?

CALANTHA

By whose hand?

ORGILUS

By mine. This weapon
[*Showing his sword*] Was instrument to my revenge. The reasons
Are just and known. Quit him of these, and then
Never lived gentleman of greater merit,
Hope or abiliment[1] to steer a kingdom.

CROTOLON

Fie, Orgilus!

EUPHRANIA

Fie, brother!

CALANTHA

You have done it?

BASSANES

How it was done let him report, the forfeit
Of whose allegiance to our laws doth covet
Rigour of justice; but that done it is,
Mine eyes have been an evidence of credit
Too sure to be convinced.[2] Armostes, rend not
Thine arteries with hearing the bare circumstances
Of these calamities. Thou'st lost a nephew,
A niece, and I a wife. Continue man still.
Make me the pattern of digesting evils,
Who can outlive my mighty ones, not shrinking
At such a pressure as would sink a soul
Into what's most of death, the worst of horrors.
But I have sealed a covenant with sadness,
And entered into bonds without condition
To stand these tempests calmly. Mark me, nobles:
I do not shed a tear, not for Penthea.
Excellent misery!

CALANTHA

We begin our reign
With a first act of justice. Thy confession,
Unhappy Orgilus, dooms thee a sentence;
But yet thy father's or thy sister's presence

1 *abiliment*: capability 2 *convinced*: refuted

Shall be excused. Give, Crotolon, a blessing
To thy lost son. Euphrania, take a farewell,
And both be gone.

CROTOLON [*To* ORGILUS]

Confirm thee, noble sorrow,
In worthy resolution.

EUPHRANIA

Could my tears speak,
My griefs were slight.

ORGILUS

All goodness dwell amongst ye.
Enjoy my sister, Prophilus. My vengeance
Aimed never at thy prejudice.[1]

CALANTHA

Now withdraw.

Exeunt CROTOLON, PROPHILUS *and* EUPHRANIA.

[*To* ORGILUS] Bloody relater of thy stains in blood,
For that thou hast reported him – whose fortunes
And life by thee are both at once snatched from him –
With honourable mention, make thy choice
Of what death likes thee best. There's all our bounty.
[*To* NEARCHUS] But to excuse[2] delays, let me, dear cousin,
Entreat you and these lords see execution
Instant before 'ee part.

NEARCHUS

Your will commands us.

ORGILUS

One suit, just Queen: my last. Vouchsafe your clemency
That by no common hand I be divided
From this, my humble frailty.[3]

CALANTHA

To their wisdoms
Who are to be spectators of thine end
I make the reference.[4] Those that are dead
Are dead. Had they not now died, of necessity

1 *at thy prejudice*: at injuring you 2 *excuse*: obviate
3 *humble frailty*: mortal life 4 *make the reference*: defer the judgement

They must have paid the debt they owed to nature
One time or other. Use dispatch, my lords.
We'll suddenly[1] prepare our coronation.
Exeunt CALANTHA, PHILEMA [*and*] CHRYSTALLA.

ARMOSTES
'Tis strange these tragedies should never touch on
Her female pity.

BASSANES
She has a masculine spirit.
And wherefore should I pule[2] and, like a girl,
Put finger in the eye? Let's be all toughness,
Without distinction betwixt sex and sex.

NEARCHUS
Now, Orgilus, thy choice.

ORGILUS
To bleed to death.[3]

ARMOSTES
The executioner?

ORGILUS
Myself; no surgeon.
I am well skilled in letting blood. Bind fast
This arm, that so the pipes[4] may from their conduits[5]
Convey a full stream. Here's a skilful instrument.
[*Showing his sword*]
Only I am a beggar to some charity
To speed me in this execution,
By lending th'other prick to th' tother arm,
When this is bubbling life out.

BASSANES
I am for 'ee.
It most concerns my art, my care, my credit.
Quick, fillet[6] both his arms.
[SERVANTS *bind him.*][7]

1 *suddenly*: immediately 2 *pule*: whine
3 *bleed to death*: a method of suicide favoured by the Stoics
4 *pipes*: veins 5 *conduits*: arteries
6 *fillet*: bind with a narrow strip of cloth
7 SERVANTS *bind him*: or alternatively Lemophil, Groneas or Nearchus

ORGILUS

Gramercy,[1] friendship;
Such courtesies are real which flow cheerfully
Without an expectation of requital.
Reach me a staff in this hand.
[BASSANES *gives him a staff to support himself.*]
If a proneness
Or custom in my nature, from my cradle,
Had been inclined to fierce and eager bloodshed,
A coward guilt, hid in a coward quaking,
Would have betrayed fame[2] to ignoble flight,
And vagabond pursuit of dreadful[3] safety.
But look upon my steadiness, and scorn not
The sickness of my fortune, which, since Bassanes
Was husband to Penthea, had lain bed-rid.
We trifle time in words. Thus I show cunning[4]
In opening of a vein too full, too lively.
[*He cuts an artery in his own arm.*]

ARMOSTES

Desperate courage!

NEARCHUS

Honourable infamy!

LEMOPHIL

I tremble at the sight.

GRONEAS

Would I were loose![5]

BASSANES

It sparkles like a lusty wine, new-broached.
The vessel must be sound from which it issues.
Grasp hard this other stick.
[*He gives* ORGILUS *another staff.*]
I'll be as nimble.
But, prithee, look not pale. Have at 'ee; stretch out
Thine arm with vigour and unshook virtue.
[*He opens an artery in* ORGILUS*'s other arm.*]

1 *Gramercy*: thank you 2 *fame*: reputation 3 *dreadful*: fearful, cowardly
4 *cunning*: skill 5 *loose*: free to leave

Good. Oh, I envy not a rival, fitted
To conquer in extremities. This pastime
Appears majestical. Some high-tuned poem
Hereafter shall deliver to posterity
The writer's glory, and his subject's triumph.
How is't, man? Droop not yet.

ORGILUS

I feel no palsies.
On a pair-royal[1] do I wait in death:
My sovereign, as his liegeman; on my mistress,
As a devoted servant; and on Ithocles,
As if no brave, yet no unworthy enemy.
Nor did I use an engine to entrap
His life out of a slavish fear to combat
Youth, strength or cunning, but for that I durst not
Engage[2] the goodness of a cause on fortune,
By which his name might have out-faced my vengeance.
O Tecnicus, inspired with Phoebus' fire,
I call to mind thy augury; 'twas perfect:
'*Revenge proves its own executioner.*'
When feeble man is bending to his mother,[3]
The dust 'a was first framed on, thus he totters.
[ORGILUS *collapses.*]

BASSANES

Life's fountain is dried up.

ORGILUS

So falls the standard[4]
Of my prerogative[5] in being a creature.
A mist hangs o'er mine eyes.[6] The sun's bright splendour
Is clouded in an everlasting shadow.

1 *pair-royal*: three of a kind in a card game, i.e., Penthea, Ithocles and Amyclas
2 *Engage*: stake 3 *mother*: Mother Earth
4 *standard*: flag raised as the sign of a king or military commander, sign of excellence
5 *prerogative*: distinguishing quality, privilege i.e., Orgilus has been defined by his Stoic endurance or uprightness and now falls
6 *A mist . . . eyes*: perhaps borrowed from Flaminio's death speech in *The White Devil*

Welcome, thou ice that sit'st about my heart;
No heat can ever thaw thee. *[He] dies.*

NEARCHUS

Speech hath left him.

BASSANES

'A has shook hands with time. His funeral urn
Shall be my charge. Remove the bloodless body.
The coronation must require attendance.
That past, my few days can be but one mourning. *Exeunt.*

ACT 5

Scene 3

An altar covered with white; two lights of virgin[1] *wax, during which music of recorders. Enter four bearing* ITHOCLES *on a hearse, or in a chair, in a rich robe, and a crown on his head. [They] place him on one side of the altar. After him enter* CALANTHA *in a white robe and crowned,* EUPHRANIA, PHILEMA, CHRYSTALLA *in white;* NEARCHUS, ARMOSTES, CROTOLON, PROPHILUS, AMELUS, BASSANES, LEMOPHIL *and* GRONEAS. CALANTHA *goes and kneels before the altar. The rest stand off, the women kneeling behind. Cease recorders during her devotions. Soft music.* CALANTHA *and the rest rise, doing obeisance to the altar.*

CALANTHA

Our orisons[2] are heard: the gods are merciful.
Now tell me, you whose loyalties pays tribute
To us, your lawful sovereign, how unskilful[3]
Your duties or obedience is to render
Subjection to the sceptre of a virgin,
Who have been ever fortunate in princes

1 *virgin*: candles were made from a special purified bees wax
2 *orisons*: prayers 3 *unskilful*: unwise

Of masculine and stirring composition?[1]
A woman has enough to govern wisely
Her own demeanours, passions, and divisions.[2]
A nation warlike, and inured to practice
Of policy and labour, cannot brook
A feminate authority. We therefore
Command your counsel, how you may advise us
In choosing of a husband whose abilities
Can better guide this kingdom.

NEARCHUS

Royal lady,
Your law is in your will.

ARMOSTES

We have seen tokens
Of constancy too lately to mistrust it.

CROTOLON

Yet, if your highness settle on a choice
By your own judgement both allowed and liked of,
Sparta may grow in power, and proceed
To an increasing height.

CALANTHA

Hold you the same mind?

BASSANES

Alas, great mistress, reason is so clouded
With the thick darkness of my infinite woes
That I forecast nor dangers, hopes, or safety.
Give me some corner of the world to wear out
The remnant of the minutes I must number,
Where I may hear no sounds but sad complaints
Of virgins who have lost contracted partners;
Of husbands howling that their wives were ravished
By some untimely fate; of friends divided
By churlish opposition; or of fathers
Weeping upon their children's slaughtered carcasses;

1 *how unskilful ... composition*: this is ironic, given how successfully England had been ruled by Elizabeth I
2 *divisions*: conflicts

Or daughters groaning o'er their fathers' hearses,
And I can dwell there, and with these keep consort[1]
As musical as theirs. What can you look for
From an old, foolish, peevish, doting man,
But craziness of age?

CALANTHA

Cousin of Argos –

NEARCHUS

Madam.

CALANTHA

Were I presently
To choose you for my lord, I'll open freely
What articles I would propose to treat on[2]
Before our marriage.

NEARCHUS

Name them, virtuous lady.

CALANTHA

I would presume you would retain the royalty
Of Sparta in her own bounds. Then in Argos
Armostes might be viceroy; in Messene
Might Crotolon bear sway; and Bassanes –

BASSANES

I, Queen? Alas, what I?

CALANTHA

Be Sparta's marshal.
The multitudes of high employments could not
But set a peace to private griefs. These gentlemen,
Groneas and Lemophil, with worthy pensions
Should wait upon your person in your chamber.
I would bestow Chrystalla on Amelus –
She'll prove a constant wife – and Philema
Should into Vesta's temple.[3]

BASSANES [*Aside*]

This is a testament;
It sounds not like conditions on a marriage.

1 *consort*: fellowship, harmony 2 *treat on*: negotiate
3 *Vesta's temple*: i.e., become a Vestal virgin

NEARCHUS
All this should be performed.
CALANTHA
Lastly, for Prophilus,
He should be, cousin, solemnly invested
In all those honours, titles and preferments
Which his dear friend, and my neglected husband,
Too short a time enjoyed.
PROPHILUS
I am unworthy
To live in your remembrance.
EUPHRANIA
Excellent lady!
NEARCHUS
Madam, what means that word 'neglected husband'?
CALANTHA
Forgive me. [*To* ITHOCLES'*s body*] Now I turn to thee, thou shadow
Of my contracted lord. Bear witness all,
I put my mother's wedding ring upon
His finger; 'twas my father's last bequest.
Thus I new-marry him whose wife I am;
Death shall not separate us. O my lords,
I but deceived your eyes with antic[1] gesture.
When one news straight came huddling on another,
Of death, and death, and death, still I danced forward,
But it struck home, and here [*pointing to her heart*], and in an instant.
Be such mere women, who with shrieks and outcries,
Can vow a present end to all their sorrows,
Yet live to vow new pleasures,[2] and outlive them.
They are the silent griefs which cut the heart-strings;[3]
Let me die smiling.

1 *antic*: grotesque, also theatrical 2 *vow new pleasures*: remarry
3 *They . . . heart-strings*: a translation of Seneca's *Hippolytus*, 607

NEARCHUS

'Tis a truth too ominous.

CALANTHA

One kiss on these cold lips, my last.
[*She kisses* ITHOCLES*'s corpse.*]
Crack, crack!
Argos now's Sparta's king. Command the voices
Which wait at th'altar now to sing the song
I fitted for my end.

NEARCHUS

Sirs, the song.

A Song.

ALL *Glories, pleasures, pomps, delights and ease*
Can but please
Th'outward senses, when the mind
Is or[1] *untroubled, or by peace*[2] *refined.*
1[3] *Crowns may flourish and decay;*
Beauties shine, but fade away.
2 *Youth may revel, yet it must*
Lie down in a bed of dust.
3 *Earthly honours flow and waste;*
Time alone doth change and last.
ALL *Sorrows mingled with contents prepare*
Rest for care.
Love only reigns in death, though art
Can find no comfort for a broken heart.
[CALANTHA *dies.*]

ARMOSTES

Look to the Queen!

1 *or*: either 2 *peace*: i.e, of approaching death
3 *1*: numbers suggest that the song was sung in parts

BASSANES

Her heart is broke indeed.
O royal maid, would thou had'st missed this part;
Yet 'twas a brave one. I must weep to see
Her smile in death.

ARMOSTES

Wise Tecnicus, thus said he:
'*When youth is ripe, and age from time doth part,*
The lifeless trunk shall wed the broken heart.'
'Tis here fulfilled.

NEARCHUS

I am your king.

ALL

Long live
Nearchus, King of Sparta!

NEARCHUS

Her last will
Shall never be digressed from. Wait in order
Upon these faithful lovers, as becomes us.
The counsels[1] of the gods are never known,
Till men can call th'effects of them their own. [*Exeunt*].

FINIS.

The Epilogue

Where noble judgements and clear eyes are fixed
To grace endeavour, there sits truth, not mixed
With ignorance. Those censures[2] may command
Belief which talk not till they understand.
Let some say 'This was flat'; some 'Here the scene
Fell from its height'; another that 'The mean[3]
Was ill observed in such a growing passion,
As it transcended either state or fashion.'
Some few may cry ' 'Twas pretty well', or 'So,

1 *counsels*: secret designs 2 *censures*: opinions
3 *The mean*: necessary artistic restraint

But – ', and there shrug in silence. Yet we know
Our writer's aim was in the whole addressed
Well to deserve of all, but please the best;
Which granted, by th'allowance of this strain,[1]
The Broken Heart may be pieced up again.

FINIS.

1 *allowance of this strain*: approval of this offspring

JOHN FORD

'TIS PITY SHE'S A WHORE

LIST OF CHARACTERS

GIOVANNI *brother of Annabella*
ANNABELLA *sister of Giovanni*
FRIAR *Bonaventura, tutor and confessor to Giovanni*
PUTTANA[1] *tutoress to Annabella*
FLORIO *a citizen of Parma, father of Giovanni and Annabella*

Lord SORANZO *a nobleman, later husband of Annabella*
VASQUEZ[2] *servant to Soranzo, a Spaniard*

DONADO *a citizen of Parma, uncle of Bergetto*
BERGETTO *nephew of Donado, suitor of Annabella and later Philotis*
POGGIO *servant of Bergetto*

RICHARDETTO *husband of Hippolita, believed dead; disguised as a doctor*
HIPPOLITA *wife of Richardetto, formerly mistress of Soranzo*
PHILOTIS *niece of Richardetto*

GRIMALDI *a Roman gentleman and soldier, suitor to Annabella*
The CARDINAL *Nuncio to the Pope*
SERVANT *to the Cardinal*
BANDITTI

Officers of the Watch, Ladies, Attendants

1 *PUTTANA*: spelled PUTANA in Q, but corrected here to the contemporary Italian spelling
2 *VASQUEZ*: spelled VASQUES in Q, but corrected here to the contemporary Spanish spelling

To the truly noble JOHN, EARL OF PETERBOROUGH,
Lord Mordaunt, Baron of Turvey.[1]

My lord,

Where a truth of merit hath a general warrant,[2] there love is but a debt, acknowledgement a justice. Greatness cannot often claim virtue by inheritance; yet in this, yours appears most eminent, for that you are not more rightly heir to your fortunes, than glory shall be to your memory. Sweetness of disposition ennobles a freedom[3] of birth; in both, your lawful interest adds honour to your own name and mercy to my presumption. Your noble allowance[4] of these first fruits of my leisure in the action[5] emboldens my confidence of your as noble construction[6] in this presentment;[7] especially since my service must ever owe particular duty to your favours, by a particular engagement.[8] The gravity of the subject may easily excuse the lightness[9] of the title. Otherwise, I had been a severe judge against mine own guilt. Princes have vouchsafed grace to trifles, offered from a purity of devotion. Your lordship may likewise please to admit into your good opinion, with these weak endeavours, the constancy of affection from the sincere lover of your deserts in honour,

John Ford

1 *JOHN . . . Turvey*: (1599–1643) came from a Catholic family and his father was arrested over the Gunpowder Plot (1605); he nevertheless became a favourite with James I and converted to Protestantism in 1625
2 *hath . . . warrant*: is generally acknowledged
3 *freedom*: distinction 4 *allowance*: appraisal
5 *action*: performance, i.e., Mordaunt must have already seen the play on stage
6 *construction*: judgement
7 *this presentment*: the published text and, specifically, the dedication
8 *particular engagement*: it is not known what Ford means here
9 *lightness*: triviality, but also 'light', meaning 'unchaste'

To my Friend, the Author.

With admiration I beheld this whore,
Adorned with beauty, such as might restore
(If ever being as thy Muse[1] hath famed)
Her Giovanni, in his love unblamed.
The ready Graces[2] lent their willing aid.
Pallas[3] herself now played the chambermaid,
And helped to put her dressings on. Secure
Rest thou that thy name herein shall endure
To th'end of age; and Annabella be
Gloriously fair, even in her infamy.

Thomas Ellice.[4]

1 *Muse*: nine goddesses presiding over the Arts in classical mythology
2 *Graces*: three daughters of Zeus, symbolizing beauty, kindness and grace
3 *Pallas*: goddess of wisdom and war, also associated with the Arts
4 *Thomas Ellice*: (b. 1607) was a member of Gray's Inn and part of Ford's literary circle; Ford's *The Lover's Melancholy* is dedicated to his brother Robert, among others

ACT 1

Scene 1

Enter FRIAR *and* GIOVANNI.

FRIAR

Dispute no more in this; for know, young man,[1]
These are no school-points.[2] Nice[3] philosophy
May tolerate unlikely arguments,
But heaven admits[4] no jest. Wits[5] that presumed
On wit too much, by striving how to prove
There was no God, with foolish grounds of art[6]
Discovered first the nearest way to hell,
And filled the world with devilish atheism.
Such questions, youth, are fond;[7] for better 'tis
To bless the sun than reason why it shines –
Yet He thou talk'st of is above the sun.
No more! I may not hear it.

GIOVANNI

Gentle father,
To you I have unclasped my burdened soul,
Emptied the store-house of my thoughts and heart,
Made myself poor of secrets, have not left
Another word untold which hath not spoke
All what I ever durst or think or know;
And yet is here the comfort I shall have?
Must I not do what all men else may: love?

1 *young man*: the literal translation of 'giovane' in Italian
2 *school-points*: arguments raised in a university debate
3 *Nice*: abstract, subtle 4 *admits*: allows
5 *Wits*: intellectuals, particularly university students
6 *grounds of art*: scholarly proofs 7 *fond*: foolish

FRIAR

Yes, you may love, fair son.

GIOVANNI

Must I not praise
That beauty which, if framed anew, the gods
Would make a god of, if they had it there,
And kneel to it, as I do kneel to them?

FRIAR

Why, foolish madman!

GIOVANNI

Shall a peevish[1] sound,
A customary form from man to man,[2]
Of brother and of sister, be a bar
'Twixt my perpetual happiness and me?
Say that we had one father, say one womb –
Curse to my joys! – gave both us life and birth;
Are we not therefore each to other bound
So much the more by nature, by the links
Of blood, of reason – nay, if you will have't,
Even of religion – to be ever one?
One soul, one flesh,[3] one love, one heart, one all.

FRIAR

Have done, unhappy[4] youth, for thou art lost!

GIOVANNI

Shall then, for that[5] I am her brother born,
My joys be ever banished from her bed?
No, father, in your eyes I see the change
Of pity and compassion. From your age,
As from a sacred oracle, distils
The life of counsel. Tell me, holy man,
What cure shall give me ease in these extremes?

1 *peevish*: senseless, spiteful
2 *customary … man*: i.e., not divinely prohibited, but outlawed merely by social custom
3 *one flesh*: recalls the terms of the marriage ceremony
4 *unhappy*: ill-fated 5 *for that*: because

FRIAR

Repentance, son, and sorrow for this sin;
For thou hast moved a majesty above
With thy unrangèd[1] almost blasphemy.

GIOVANNI

Oh, do not speak of that, dear confessor.

FRIAR

Art thou, my son, that miracle of wit
Who once, within these three months, wert esteemed
A wonder of thine age throughout Bologna?[2]
How did the university applaud
Thy government,[3] behaviour, learning, speech,
Sweetness, and all that could make up a man!
I was proud of my tutelage, and chose
Rather to leave my books than part with thee.
I did so; but the fruits of all my hopes
Are lost in thee, as thou art in thyself.
O Giovanni, hast thou left the schools
Of knowledge to converse with Lust and Death?
For Death waits[4] on thy lust. Look through the world,
And thou shalt see a thousand faces shine
More glorious than this idol thou ador'st.
Leave her, and take thy choice; 'tis much less sin,
Though in such games as those they lose that win.[5]

GIOVANNI

It were more ease to stop the ocean
From floats and ebbs[6] than to dissuade my vows.

FRIAR

Then I have done, and in thy wilful flames
Already see thy ruin. Heaven is just –
Yet hear my counsel.

1 *unrangèd*: limitless, uncontrolled
2 *Bologna*: the location of Italy's oldest university, with a reputation for blasphemous free-thinking
3 *government*: self-discipline, temperance 4 *waits*: attends, follows
5 *less sin . . . win*: the Friar condemns sex outside marriage, but views it as a lesser sin than incest
6 *floats and ebbs*: high and low tides

GIOVANNI

As a voice of life.

FRIAR

Hie[1] to thy father's house. There lock thee fast
Alone within thy chamber, then fall down
On both thy knees and grovel on the ground.
Cry to thy heart, wash every word thou utter'st
In tears – and if't be possible – of blood.
Beg heaven to cleanse the leprosy of lust
That rots thy soul. Acknowledge what thou art:
A wretch, a worm, a nothing. Weep, sigh, pray
Three times a day, and three times every night.
For seven days' space do this; then, if thou find'st
No change in thy desires, return to me.
I'll think on remedy. Pray for thyself
At home, whilst I pray for thee here. Away!
My blessing with thee; we have need to pray.

GIOVANNI

All this I'll do to free me from the rod
Of vengeance; else I'll swear my fate's my god. *Exeunt.*

ACT 1

Scene 2

Enter GRIMALDI, *and* VASQUEZ, *ready to fight.*[2]

VASQUEZ

Come, sir, stand to your tackling.[3] If you prove craven,[4] I'll make you run quickly.

GRIMALDI

Thou art no equal[5] match for me.

1 *Hie*: go immediately 2 *ready to fight*: only Vasquez has his sword drawn
3 *tackling*: weapons, i.e., prepare to fight 4 *craven*: cowardly
5 *no equal*: because Vasquez is only a servant

VASQUEZ

Indeed, I never went to the wars to bring home news; nor cannot play the mountebank[1] for a meal's meat, and swear I got my wounds in the field. See you these grey hairs? They'll not flinch for a bloody nose. Wilt thou to this gear?[2]

GRIMALDI

Why, slave, think'st thou I'll balance my reputation with a cast-suit?[3] Call thy master; he shall know that I dare –

VASQUEZ

Scold like a cotquean[4] – that's your profession, thou poor shadow of a soldier. I will make thee know my master keeps servants thy betters in quality and performance. Com'st thou to fight or prate?[5]

GRIMALDI

Neither with thee. I am a Roman[6] and a gentleman, one that have got mine honour with expense of blood.

VASQUEZ

You are a lying coward and a fool. Fight, or by these hilts I'll kill thee –

[GRIMALDI *draws his sword.*]

Brave my lord, you'll fight!

GRIMALDI

Provoke me not, for if thou dost –

VASQUEZ

Have at you!

They fight. GRIMALDI *hath the worst.*

Enter FLORIO, DONADO [*and*], SORANZO.

FLORIO

What mean these sudden broils[7] so near my doors?
Have you not other places but my house
To vent the spleen[6] of your disordered bloods?

1 *mountebank*: a travelling medicine man, charlatan
2 *gear*: the matter at hand, i.e., the fight
3 *cast-suit*: someone reliant on cast-off clothing, characteristic of a servant
4 *cotquean*: low-born housewife, harlot 5 *prate*: chatter
6 *Roman*: of ancient Italian descent 7 *broils*: quarrels
6 *spleen*: violent temper, associated with an imbalance of the blood

Must I be haunted still with such unrest,
As not to eat or sleep in peace at home?
Is this your love, Grimaldi? Fie, 'tis naught.

DONADO

And, Vasquez, I may tell thee 'tis not well
To broach these quarrels. You are ever forward
In seconding contentions.

Enter above[1] ANNABELLA *and* PUTTANA.

FLORIO

What's the ground?[2]

SORANZO

That, with your patience, signors, I'll resolve:[3]
This gentleman, whom fame reports a soldier –
For else I know not[4] – rivals me in love
To Signor Florio's daughter, to whose ears
He still prefers[5] his suit to my disgrace,
Thinking the way to recommend himself
Is to disparage me in his report.
But know, Grimaldi, though may be thou art
My equal in thy blood, yet this bewrays[6]
A lowness in thy mind, which, wert thou noble,
Thou wouldst as much disdain as I do thee
For this unworthiness. [*To* FLORIO] And on this ground
I willed my servant to correct this tongue,
Holding a man so base no match for me.

VASQUEZ

And had not your sudden coming prevented us, I had let my gentleman blood under the gills.[7] [*To* GRIMALDI] I should have wormed you, sir, for running mad.[8]

GRIMALDI

I'll be revenged, Soranzo.

1 *above*: on the stage balcony 2 *ground*: cause of the argument
3 *resolve*: explain 4 *For . . . not*: he has seen no evidence of it himself
5 *prefers*: puts forward 6 *bewrays*: reveals
7 *let . . . gills*: have cut Grimaldi's throat
8 *wormed*: to prevent rabies, dogs had a ligament under their tongues cut, called the 'worm'

VASQUEZ

On a dish of warm broth to stay your stomach?[1] Do, honest Innocence, do! Spoon-meat[2] is a wholesomer diet than a Spanish blade.

GRIMALDI

Remember this.

SORANZO

I fear thee not, Grimaldi. *Exit* GRIMALDI.

FLORIO

My lord Soranzo, this is strange to me,
Why you should storm, having my word[3] engaged.
Owing[4] her heart, what need you doubt her ear?
Losers may talk, by law of any game.[5]

VASQUEZ

Yet the villainy of words, Signor Florio, may be such as would make any unspleened[6] dove choleric. Blame not my lord in this.

FLORIO

Be you more silent!
I would not, for my wealth, my daughter's love
Should cause the spilling of one drop of blood.
Vasquez, put up.[7] Let's end this fray in wine.

Exeunt [FLORIO, DONADO, SORANZO *and* VASQUEZ].

PUTTANA

How like you this, child? Here's threatening, challenging, quarrelling and fighting on every side, and all is for your sake. You had need look to yourself, charge, you'll be stolen away sleeping else, shortly.

1 *stay your stomach*: satisfy your appetite
2 *Spoon-meat*: liquid food eaten by infants, invalids and the very old
3 *word*: consent 4 *Owing*: possessing
5 *Losers . . . game*: it is natural for losers to complain, but not for the winner
6 *unspleened dove*: doves' spleens were not thought to produce choler, the humour which made people aggressive
7 *put up*: sheathe your sword

ANNABELLA

But, tut'ress, such a life gives no content
To me. My thoughts are fixed on other ends.
Would you would leave me.

PUTTANA

Leave you? No marvel else![1] Leave me no leaving, charge; this is love outright. Indeed, I blame you not. You have choice fit for the best lady in Italy.

ANNABELLA

Pray, do not talk so much.

PUTTANA

Take the worst with the best. There's Grimaldi the soldier: a very well-timbered[2] fellow. They say he is a Roman, nephew to the Duke Monferrato. They say he did good service in the wars against the Milanese. But 'faith, charge, I do not like him, an't be for nothing but for being a soldier. One amongst twenty of your skirmishing captains but have some privy maim[3] or other that mars their standing upright.[4] I like him the worse; he crinkles so much in the hams.[5] Though he might serve if there were no more men, yet he's not the man I would choose.

ANNABELLA

Fie, how thou prat'st!

PUTTANA

As I am a very woman, I like Signor Soranzo well. He is wise; and, what is more, rich; and, what is more than that, kind; and, what is more than all this, a nobleman. Such a one, were I the fair Annabella myself, I would wish and pray for. Then he is bountiful; besides he is handsome; and, by my troth, I think wholesome[6] – and that's news in a gallant of

1 *No marvel else*: it's no wonder you want me to
2 *well-timbered*: well-built
3 *privy maim*: hidden wound
4 *standing upright*: also ability to maintain an erection
5 *crinkles . . . hams*: bows obsequiously or shrinks from sex
6 *wholesome*: not suffering from venereal disease

three-and-twenty! Liberal,[1] that I know; loving, that you know; and a man,[2] sure, else he could never ha' purchased such a good name with Hippolita, the lusty widow, in her husband's lifetime. An 'twere but for that report, sweetheart, would 'a were thine! Commend a man for his qualities, but take a husband as he is a plain-sufficient,[3] naked man. Such a one is for your bed, and such a one is Signor Soranzo, my life for't!

ANNABELLA

Sure, the woman took her morning's draught[4] too soon!

Enter BERGETTO *and* POGGIO.

PUTTANA

But look, sweetheart, look, what thing comes now. Here's another of your ciphers[5] to fill up the number. O brave old ape in a silken coat![6] Observe.

BERGETTO

Didst thou think, Poggio, that I would spoil my new clothes and leave my dinner to fight?[7]

POGGIO

No, sir, I did not take you for so arrant a baby.

BERGETTO

I am wiser than so; for I hope, Poggio, thou never heard'st of an elder brother that was a coxcomb,[8] didst, Poggio?

POGGIO

Never, indeed, sir, as long as they had either land or money left them to inherit.

1 *Liberal*: generous with money, perhaps implying Soranzo has bribed Puttana for access to Annabella
2 *a man*: i.e., sexually capable
3 *plain-sufficient*: adequate
4 *morning's draught*: usually a drink of beer or wine
5 *ciphers*: nonentities
6 *brave . . . coat*: from the proverb, an ape is an ape though clad in fine ('brave') clothing
7 *leave my dinner*: unlike Florio and the others whose meal was interrupted by the fighting, Bergetto stayed behind to finish
8 *coxcomb*: fool

BERGETTO

Is it possible, Poggio? Oh, monstrous! Why, I'll undertake with a handful of silver to buy a headful of wit at any time. But, sirrah, I have another purchase in hand. I shall have the wench, mine uncle says. I will but wash my face, and shift[1] socks, and then have at her, i'faith! Mark my pace, Poggio.

[*He puts on an exaggerated walk.*]

POGGIO

Sir, I have seen an ass and a mule trot the Spanish pavan[2] with a better grace, I know not how often.

Exeunt [BERGETTO *and* POGGIO].

ANNABELLA

This idiot haunts me too.

PUTTANA

Ay, ay, he needs no description. The rich magnifico[3] that is below with your father, charge, Signor Donado his uncle, for that he means to make this his cousin a golden calf, thinks that you will be a right Israelite and fall down[4] to him presently;[5] but I hope I have tutored you better. They say a fool's bauble[6] is a lady's playfellow. Yet you, having wealth enough, you need not cast upon the dearth of flesh[7] at any rate. Hang him! Innocent!

Enter GIOVANNI.

ANNABELLA

But see, Puttana, see what blessèd shape
Of some celestial creature now appears!
What man is he, that with such sad aspect
Walks careless of himself?

PUTTANA

Where?

1 *shift*: change 2 *pavan*: slow, stately dance
3 *magnifico*: wealthy and influential citizen
4 *Israelite . . . down*: an allusion to Exodus 32 in which the Israelites worship the golden calf, with a sexual pun on 'fall down'
5 *presently*: immediately
6 *bauble*: the professional fool's carved stick, also penis
7 *cast . . . flesh*: take decisions based on a shortage of suitors ('flesh' also alluding to penises)

ANNABELLA

Look below.

PUTTANA

Oh, 'tis your brother, sweet.

ANNABELLA

Ha?

PUTTANA

'Tis your brother.

ANNABELLA

Sure, 'tis not he. This is some woeful thing
Wrapped up in grief, some shadow of a man.
Alas, he beats his breast, and wipes his eyes
Drowned all in tears. Methinks I hear him sigh.
Let's down, Puttana, and partake the cause.
I know my brother, in the love he bears me,
Will not deny me partage[1] in his sadness.
My soul is full of heaviness and fear.

Exeunt [ANNABELLA *and* PUTTANA].

GIOVANNI

Lost, I am lost! My fates have doomed my death.
The more I strive, I love; the more I love,
The less I hope. I see my ruin, certain.
What judgement or endeavours could apply
To my incurable and restless wounds
I throughly[2] have examined, but in vain.
Oh, that it were not in religion sin
To make our love a god and worship it!
I have even wearied heaven with prayers, dried up
The spring of my continual tears, even starved
My veins with daily fasts. What wit[3] or art
Could counsel I have practised. But, alas,
I find all these but dreams and old men's tales
To fright unsteady youth. I'm still the same;
Or[4] I must speak or burst. 'Tis not, I know,
My lust, but 'tis my fate that leads me on.

1 *partage*: a share 2 *throughly*: thoroughly 3 *wit*: wisdom
4 *Or*: either

Keep fear, and low, faint-hearted shame with slaves![1]
I'll tell her that I love her, though my heart
Were rated at the price of that attempt.[2]

Enter ANNABELLA *and* PUTTANA.

O me! She comes.

ANNABELLA

Brother –

GIOVANNI [*Aside*]

If such a thing
As courage dwell in men, ye heavenly powers,
Now double all that virtue in my tongue.

ANNABELLA

Why, brother, will you not speak to me?

GIOVANNI

Yes; how d'ee, sister?

ANNABELLA

Howsoever I am, methinks you are not well.

PUTTANA

Bless us, why are you so sad, sir?

GIOVANNI

Let me entreat you leave us a while, Puttana.
Sister, I would be private with you.

ANNABELLA

Withdraw, Puttana.

PUTTANA

I will. [*Aside*] If this were any other company for her, I should think my absence an office of some credit;[3] but I will leave them together. *Exit* PUTTANA.

GIOVANNI

Come, sister, lend your hand. Let's walk together.
I hope you need not blush to walk with me;
Here's none but you and I.

1 *Keep ... slaves*: may fear and ... shame dwell with slaves.
2 *though ... attempt*: though the attempt should cost me my heart
3 *credit*: reward, i.e., other people would have to bribe Puttana for this opportunity

ANNABELLA
How's this?
GIOVANNI
'Faith, I mean no harm.
ANNABELLA
Harm?
GIOVANNI
No, good faith. How is't with'ee?
ANNABELLA [*Aside*]
I trust he be not frantic.[1]
[*Aloud*] I am very well, brother.
GIOVANNI
Trust me, but I am sick. I fear, so sick
'Twill cost my life.
ANNABELLA
Mercy forbid it! 'Tis not so, I hope.
GIOVANNI
I think you love me, sister.
ANNABELLA
Yes, you know I do.
GIOVANNI
I know't, indeed. – Y'are very fair.
ANNABELLA
Nay, then, I see you have a merry sickness.
GIOVANNI
That's as it proves. The poets feign, I read,
That Juno[2] for her forehead did exceed
All other goddesses, but I durst swear
Your forehead exceeds hers, as hers did theirs.
ANNABELLA
Troth, this is pretty.

1 *frantic*: insane
2 *Juno*: goddess of marriage, both twin sister and wife to Jupiter

GIOVANNI

Such a pair of stars
As are thine eyes would, like Promethean fire,[1]
If gently glanced,[2] give life to senseless stones.

ANNABELLA

Fie upon'ee!

GIOVANNI

The lily and the rose, most sweetly strange,[3]
Upon your dimpled cheeks do strive for 'change.[4]
Such lips would tempt a saint; such hands as those
Would make an anchorite[5] lascivious.

ANNABELLA

D'ee mock me or flatter me?

GIOVANNI

If you would see a beauty more exact
Than Art can counterfeit or Nature frame,
Look in your glass, and there behold your own.

ANNABELLA

Oh, you are a trim[6] youth!

GIOVANNI

Here.

[*He*] *offers his dagger to her.*

ANNABELLA

What to do?

GIOVANNI

And here's my breast. Strike home!
Rip up my bosom! There thou shalt behold
A heart in which is writ the truth I speak.
Why stand'ee?[7]

1 *Promethean fire*: in classical mythology Prometheus stole fire from the gods and used it to animate mankind
2 *glanced*: looked at, struck to produce sparks
3 *strange*: opposite to one another
4 *lily and the rose . . . 'change*: i.e., Annabella is alternately pale and blushing
5 *anchorite*: a religious recluse, by definition celibate
6 *trim*: proper, because flattering
7 *Why stand'ee?*: Why do you hesitate?

ANNABELLA

Are you earnest?

GIOVANNI

Yes, most earnest.
You cannot love?

ANNABELLA

Whom?

GIOVANNI

Me! My tortured soul
Hath felt affliction in the heat of death.[1]
O Annabella, I am quite undone!
The love of thee, my sister, and the view
Of thy immortal beauty hath untuned
All harmony, both of my rest and life.
Why d'ee not strike?

ANNABELLA

Forbid it, my just[2] fears!
If this be true, 'twere fitter I were dead.

GIOVANNI

True, Annabella? 'Tis no time to jest.
I have too long suppressed the hidden flames
That almost have consumed me. I have spent
Many a silent night in sighs and groans,
Ran over all my thoughts, despised my fate,
Reasoned against the reasons of my love,
Done all that smooth-cheeked[3] Virtue could advise,
But found all bootless.[4] 'Tis my destiny
That you must either love, or I must die.

ANNABELLA

Comes this in sadness[5] from you?

GIOVANNI

Let some mischief
Befall me soon if I dissemble aught.

1 *affliction . . . death*: has suffered the fires of hell
2 *just*: well-founded
3 *smooth-cheeked*: beardless, i.e., youthful, sexually inexperienced
4 *bootless*: in vain 5 *in sadness*: sincerely

ANNABELLA
You are my brother, Giovanni.
GIOVANNI
You
My sister, Annabella. I know this,
And could afford you instance why to love
So much the more for this, to which intent
Wise Nature first in your creation meant
To make you mine; else't had been sin and foul
To share one beauty to a double soul.
Nearness in birth or blood doth but persuade
A nearer nearness in affection.
I have asked counsel of the holy Church,
Who tells me I may love you; and 'tis just,
That since I may, I should and will, yes, will.
Must I now live, or die?
ANNABELLA
Live. Thou hast won
The field and never fought. What thou hast urged
My captive heart had long ago resolved.
I blush to tell thee – but I'll tell thee now –
For every sigh that thou hast spent for me,
I have sighed ten; for every tear, shed twenty;
And not so much for that I loved, as that
I durst not say I loved, nor scarcely think it.
GIOVANNI
Let not this music be a dream, ye gods,
For pity's sake, I beg'ee!
ANNABELLA
On my knees,
She kneels.
Brother, even by our mother's dust I charge you,
Do not betray me to your mirth or hate:
Love me, or kill me, brother.
GIOVANNI
On my knees,
He kneels.

Sister, even by my mother's dust I charge you,
Do not betray me to your mirth or hate:
Love me, or kill me, sister.

ANNABELLA
You mean good sooth,[1] then?

GIOVANNI
In good troth, I do;
And so do you, I hope. Say I'm in earnest.[2]

ANNABELLA
I'll swear't – and I.[3]

GIOVANNI
And I, and by this kiss –
Kisses her.
Once more. [*Kisses her.*] Yet once more. [*Kisses her.*] Now let's rise, by this.
[*He kisses her and they stand up together.*]
I would not change[4] this minute for Elysium.[5]
What must we now do?

ANNABELLA
What you will.

GIOVANNI
Come, then;
After so many tears as we have wept,
Let's learn to court in smiles, to kiss and sleep. *Exeunt.*

1 *good sooth*: truthfully
2 *Say . . . earnest*: i.e., that you believe me to be sincere
3 *and I*: I mean it too 4 *change*: exchange
5 *Elysium*: a pagan version of heaven

ACT 1

Scene 3

Enter FLORIO *and* DONADO.

FLORIO
Signor Donado, you have said enough.
I understand you, but would have you know
I will not force my daughter 'gainst her will.
You see I have but two: a son and her –
And he is so devoted to his book
As, I must tell you true, I doubt[1] his health.
Should he miscarry,[2] all my hopes rely
Upon my girl. As for worldly fortune,
I am, I thank my stars, blessed with enough.
My care is how to match her to her liking.
I would not have her marry wealth but love;
And if she like your nephew, let him have her.
Here's all that I can say.

DONADO
Sir, you say well,
Like a true father; and for my part, I,
If the young folks can like – 'twixt you and me –
Will promise to assure my nephew presently[3]
Three thousand florins yearly during life,[4]
And, after I am dead, my whole estate.

FLORIO
'Tis a fair proffer, sir. Meantime, your nephew
Shall have free passage to commence his suit.
If he can thrive, he shall have my consent.
So for this time I'll leave you, signor. *Exit.*

DONADO
Well,

1 *doubt*: fear 2 *miscarry*: die before having produced an heir
3 *presently*: now
4 *Three thousand florins*: equivalent to £250, not lavish as incomes went

Here's hope yet, if my nephew would have wit.
But he is such another dunce, I fear
He'll never win the wench. When I was young
I could have done't, i'faith, and so shall he
If he will learn of me –

Enter BERGETTO *and* POGGIO.

and in good time
He comes himself.
How now, Bergetto, whither away so fast?

BERGETTO

O uncle, I have heard the strangest news that ever came out of the mint[1] – have I not, Poggio?

POGGIO

Yes, indeed, sir.

DONADO

What news, Bergetto?

BERGETTO

Why, look ye, uncle, my barber told me just now that there is a fellow come to town who undertakes to make a mill go without the mortal help of any water or wind, only with sandbags! And this fellow hath a strange horse – a most excellent beast, I'll assure you, uncle, my barber says – whose head, to the wonder of all Christian people, stands just behind where his tail is.[2] Is't not true, Poggio?

POGGIO

So the barber[3] swore, forsooth.

DONADO

And you are running thither?

BERGETTO

Ay, forsooth, uncle.

DONADO

Wilt thou be a fool still? Come, sir, you shall not go. You have more mind of a puppet play[4] than on the business I told ye.

1 *mint*: i.e., the newest news, freshly minted
2 *strange horse*: a popular fairground trick
3 *barber*: a profession notorious for spreading lies
4 *puppet play*: another fairground entertainment

Why, thou great baby, wilt never have wit? Wilt make thyself a May-game[1] to all the world?

POGGIO

Answer for yourself, master.

BERGETTO

Why, uncle, should I sit at home still, and not go abroad to see fashions like other gallants?

DONADO

To see hobby-horses![2] What wise talk, I pray, had you with Annabella when you were at Signor Florio's house?

BERGETTO

Oh, the wench! Uds sa' me,[3] uncle, I tickled her with a rare speech, that I made her almost burst her belly with laughing.

DONADO

Nay, I think so; and what speech was't?

BERGETTO

What did I say, Poggio?

POGGIO

Forsooth, my master said that he loved her almost as well as he loved Parmesan,[4] and swore – I'll be sworn for him – that she wanted but such a nose as his was to be as pretty a young woman as any was in Parma.

DONADO

Oh, gross!

BERGETTO

Nay, uncle, then she asked me whether my father had any more children than myself, and I said, 'No, 'twere better he should have had his brains knocked out first.'

DONADO

This is intolerable.

BERGETTO

Then said she, 'Will Signor Donado, your uncle, leave you all his wealth?'

1 *May-game*: i.e., a laughing stock

2 *hobby-horses*: a horse costume worn in Morris dances and stage entertainments, but also a term for prostitutes

3 *Uds sa' me*: God save me

4 *Parmesan*: either the hard Italian cheese or a style of drinking

DONADO

Ha! That was good. Did she harp upon that string?

BERGETTO

Did she harp upon that string? Ay, that she did. I answered, 'Leave me all his wealth? Why, woman, he hath no other wit.[1] If he had, he should hear on't to his everlasting glory[2] and confusion. I know,' quoth I, 'I am his white boy,[3] and will not be gulled.'[4] And with that she fell into a great smile, and went away. Nay, I did fit her.[5]

DONADO

Ah, sirrah, then I see there is no changing of nature. Well, Bergetto, I fear thou wilt be a very ass still.

BERGETTO

I should be sorry for that, uncle.

DONADO

Come, come you home with me. Since you are no better a speaker, I'll have you write to her after some courtly manner, and enclose some rich jewel in the letter.

BERGETTO

Ay, marry, that will be excellent.

DONADO

Peace, innocent!
Once in my time I'll set my wits to school.
If all fail, 'tis but the fortune of a fool.

BERGETTO

Poggio, 'twill do, Poggio. *Exeunt.*

1 *wit*: thought
2 *glory*: a malapropism – he means 'shame'
3 *white boy*: favourite child 4 *gulled*: cheated
5 *fit her*: answer her aptly

ACT 2

Scene 1

Enter GIOVANNI *and* ANNABELLA, *as from their chamber.*

GIOVANNI

Come, Annabella; no more sister now,
But love – a name more gracious. Do not blush,
Beauty's sweet wonder, but be proud to know
That, yielding,[1] thou hast conquered and enflamed
A heart whose tribute[2] is thy brother's life.

ANNABELLA

And mine is his. Oh, how these stol'n contents[3]
Would print a modest crimson on my cheeks,
Had any but my heart's delight prevailed!

GIOVANNI

I marvel why the chaster of your sex
Should think this pretty toy[4] called maidenhead
So strange a loss, when, being lost, 'tis nothing,[5]
And you are still the same.

ANNABELLA

'Tis well for you;
Now you can talk.

GIOVANNI

Music as well consists
In th'ear as in the playing.[6]

ANNABELLA

Oh, y'are wanton!
Tell on't, y'are best, do.

1 *yielding*: giving up her virginity 2 *tribute*: tax or homage
3 *contents*: pleasures 4 *toy*: trivial thing
5 *nothing*: of no importance, also 'vagina'
6 *Music . . . playing*: i.e., the pleasure of sex is partly in talking about it; also that to take the passive (feminine) role of the ear, receiving music, is as pleasurable as the active (masculine) part

GIOVANNI

Thou wilt chide me, then.
Kiss me. [*They kiss*] So. Thus hung Jove on Leda's neck,[1]
And sucked divine ambrosia from her lips.
I envy not the mightiest man alive,
But hold myself, in being king of thee,
More great than were I king of all the world.
But I shall lose you, sweetheart.

ANNABELLA

But you shall not.

GIOVANNI

You must be married, mistress.

ANNABELLA

Yes? To whom?

GIOVANNI

Someone must have you.

ANNABELLA

You must.

GIOVANNI

Nay, some other.

ANNABELLA

Now, prithee, do not speak so without jesting;
You'll make me weep in earnest.

GIOVANNI

What? You will not.
But tell me, sweet, canst thou be dared to swear
That thou wilt live to me,[2] and to no other?

ANNABELLA

By both our loves, I dare; for didst thou know,
My Giovanni, how all suitors seem
To my eyes hateful, thou wouldst trust me then.

GIOVANNI

Enough, I take thy word. Sweet, we must part.
Remember what thou vow'st: keep well my heart.

1 *Leda*: in classical mythology the god Jove, disguised as a swan, seduced or raped Leda
2 *live to*: be faithful to

ANNABELLA

Will you be gone?

GIOVANNI

I must.

ANNABELLA

When to return?

GIOVANNI

Soon.

ANNABELLA

Look you do.

GIOVANNI

Farewell. *Exit.*

ANNABELLA

Go where thou wilt, in mind I'll keep thee here;
And where thou art, I know I shall be there.
[*Calls*] Guardian!

Enter PUTTANA.

PUTTANA

Child, how is't, child? Well, thank heaven, ha?

ANNABELLA

O guardian, what a paradise of joy
Have I passed over![1]

PUTTANA

Nay, what a paradise of joy have you passed under![2] Why, now I commend thee, charge. Fear nothing, sweetheart. What, though he be your brother? Your brother's a man, I hope; and I say still, if a young wench feel the fit[3] upon her, let her take anybody: father or brother, all is one.

ANNABELLA

I would not have it known for all the world.

PUTTANA

Nor I, indeed, for the speech of the people;[4] else 'twere nothing.

1 *passed over*: experienced
2 *under*: referring to her sexual position under Giovanni
3 *fit*: sexual desire, like a sickness
4 *speech of the people*: vulgar gossip

FLORIO (*Within*)
Daughter Annabella!

ANNABELLA
O me, my father! – Here, sir! [*To* PUTTANA] Reach my work.

[PUTTANA *gives her a piece of needlework.*]

FLORIO (*Within*)
What are you doing?

ANNABELLA [*To* PUTTANA]
So, let him come now.

Enter FLORIO, RICHARDETTO [*disguised*] *like a doctor of physic,*[1] *and* PHILOTIS *with a lute in her hand.*

FLORIO
So hard at work? That's well; you lose[2] no time.
Look, I have brought you company. Here's one,
A learned doctor, lately come from Padova,[3]
Much skilled in physic; and for that I see
You have of late been sickly,[4] I entreated
This reverend man to visit you some time.

ANNABELLA
Y'are very welcome, sir.

RICHARDETTO
I thank you, mistress.
Loud fame in large[5] report hath spoke your praise,
As well for virtue as perfection;[6]
For which I have been bold to bring with me
A kinswoman of mine, a maid, for song
And music. One, perhaps, will give content.
Please you to know her?

1 *physic*: medicine 2 *lose*: waste

3 *Padova*: city in the north-east of Italy, famous for its medical school so an appropriate part of Richardetto's cover story

4 *sickly*: perhaps because Annabella is already pregnant

5 *large*: generous, ubiquitous

6 *perfection*: beauty and graceful accomplishments

ANNABELLA

They are parts[1] I love,
And she for them most welcome.

PHILOTIS

Thank you, lady.

FLORIO

Sir, now you know my house, pray make not strange;[2]
And if you find my daughter need your art,[3]
I'll be your pay-master.

RICHARDETTO

Sir, what I am
She shall command.

FLORIO

You shall bind me to you.
Daughter, I must have conference with you
About some matters that concerns us both.
Good master Doctor, please you but walk in;
We'll crave a little of your cousin's[4] cunning.[5]
I think my girl hath not quite forgot
To touch an instrument;[6] she could have done't.[7]
We'll hear them both.

RICHARDETTO

I'll wait upon you, sir. *Exeunt.*

1 *parts*: skills, with a pun on musical parts
2 *make not strange*: don't be a stranger 3 *art*: medical skill
4 *cousin*: niece 5 *cunning*: skill
6 *instrument*: also a euphemism for penis, alluding unconsciously to Annabella's loss of virginity
7 *could have done't*: used to be able to

ACT 2

Scene 2

Enter SORANZO *in his study, reading a book.*

SORANZO

'Love's measure is extreme; the comfort, pain;
The life, unrest; and the reward, disdain.'
What's here? Look't o'er again. 'Tis so, so writes
This smooth, licentious poet in his rhymes.
But, Sannazar,[1] thou liest; for had thy bosom
Felt such oppression as is laid on mine,
Thou wouldst have kissed the rod that made the smart.
To work then, happy Muse,[2] and contradict
What Sannazar hath, in his envy, writ:
[*Writes*] 'Love's measure is the mean,[3] sweet his annoys,[4]
His pleasures life, and his reward all joys.'
Had Annabella lived when Sannazar
Did in his brief encomium celebrate
Venice, that queen of cities, he had left[5]
That verse, which gained him such a sum of gold,
And for one only look from Annabel
Had writ of her, and her diviner cheeks.
Oh, how my thoughts are –

VASQUEZ (*Within*)

Pray, forbear! In rules of civility, let me give notice on't. I shall be taxed of[6] my neglect of duty and service.

1 *Sannazar*: Neapolitan poet Jacopo Sannazaro (1457–1530), author of a Latin eulogy of Venice (1535), for which the city awarded him 600 crowns
2 *Muse*: perhaps Erato, the Muse of love poetry
3 *mean*: happy medium 4 *annoys*: troubles
5 *left*: abandoned 6 *taxed of*: blamed for

SORANZO
What rude intrusion interrupts my peace?
Can I be nowhere private?
VASQUEZ (*Within*)
Troth, you wrong your modesty.
SORANZO
What's the matter, Vasquez? Who is't?
Enter HIPPOLITA [*dressed in mourning*] *and* VASQUEZ.
HIPPOLITA
'Tis I;
Do you know me now?[1] Look, perjured man, on her
Whom thou and thy distracted lust have wronged.
Thy sensual rage of blood[2] hath made my youth
A scorn to men and angels; and shall I
Be now a foil to thy unsated change?[3]
Thou know'st, false wanton, when my modest fame[4]
Stood free from stain or scandal, all the charms
Of hell or sorcery could not prevail
Against the honour of my chaster bosom.
Thine eyes did plead in tears, thy tongue in oaths,
Such and so many that a heart of steel
Would have been wrought to pity, as was mine.
And shall the conquest of my lawful bed,
My husband's death urged on by his disgrace,[5]
My loss of womanhood,[6] be ill rewarded
With hatred and contempt? No, know Soranzo,
I have a spirit doth as much distaste
The slavery of fearing thee, as thou
Dost loathe the memory of what hath passed.

1 *Do . . . now*: perhaps Hippolita is wearing a mourning veil, which she lifts up
2 *blood*: lustful frenzy
3 *unsated*: still unsatisfied; Soranzo uses Hippolita as a 'foil' or contrast to set off the attractions of Annabella
4 *modest fame*: reputation for modesty
5 *disgrace*: Hippolita implies he partly died from shame at being cuckolded
6 *womanhood*: here defined as marital chastity

SORANZO

Nay, dear Hippolita –

HIPPOLITA

Call me not 'dear',
Nor think with supple words to smooth the grossness
Of my abuses. 'Tis not your new mistress,
Your goodly Madam Merchant, shall triumph
On my dejection. Tell her thus from me:
My birth was nobler, and by much more free.[1]

SORANZO

You are too violent.

HIPPOLITA

You are too double[2]
In your dissimulation. See'st thou this,
This habit, these black mourning-weeds[3] of care?
'Tis thou art cause of this, and hast divorced
My husband from his life and me from him,
And made me widow in my widowhood.[4]

SORANZO

Will you yet hear?

HIPPOLITA

More of thy perjuries?
Thy soul is drowned too deeply in those sins;
Thou need'st not add to th'number.

SORANZO

Then I'll leave you;
You are past all rules of sense.

HIPPOLITA

And thou of grace.

VASQUEZ

Fie, mistress, you are not near the limits of reason. If my lord had a resolution as noble as virtue itself, you take the course to unedge[5] it all. [*To* SORANZO] Sir, I beseech you, do not

1 *free*: honourable, well-bred 2 *double*: duplicitous 3 *weeds*: clothes
4 *widow . . . widowhood*: Soranzo's abandonment makes her a widow for the second time; widows were notoriously lustful, which Soranzo's seduction appears to confirm
5 *unedge*: make blunt

perplex[1] her. Griefs, alas, will have a vent. I dare undertake
Madam Hippolita will now freely hear you.

SORANZO

Talk to a woman frantic? Are these the fruits of your love?

HIPPOLITA

They are the fruits of thy untruth, false man.
Didst thou not swear whilst yet my husband lived,
That thou wouldst wish no happiness on earth
More than to call me wife? Didst thou not vow,
When he should die, to marry me? For which
The devil in my blood, and thy protests,[2]
Caused me to counsel him to undertake
A voyage to Leghorn,[3] for that we heard
His brother there was dead, and left a daughter
Young and unfriended, who with much ado
I wished him to bring hither. He did so,
And went, and, as thou know'st, died on the way.
Unhappy man to buy his death so dear
With my advice! Yet thou, for whom I did it,
Forget'st thy vows, and leav'st me to my shame.

SORANZO

Who could help this?

HIPPOLITA

Who, perjured man? Thou could'st,
If thou hadst faith or love.

SORANZO

You are deceived:
The vows I made, if you remember well,
Were wicked and unlawful. 'Twere more sin
To keep them than to break them. As for me,
I cannot mask my penitence. Think thou
How much thou hast digressed from honest shame
In bringing of a gentleman to death
Who was thy husband; such a one as he,

1 *perplex*: torment 2 *protests*: promises (to marry her)
3 *Leghorn*: coastal town of Livorno, reached from Parma only through dangerous mountain regions, notorious for outlaws and highwaymen

So noble in his quality,[1] condition,
Learning, behaviour, entertainment,[2] love,
As Parma could not show a braver[3] man.

VASQUEZ
You do not well; this was not your promise.

SORANZO
I care not; let her know her monstrous life.
Ere I'll be servile to so black a sin,
I'll be a corpse. [*To* HIPPOLITA] Woman, come here no more.
Learn to repent and die; for, by my honour,
I hate thee and thy lust. You have been too foul.
[*Exit* SORANZO.]

VASQUEZ
This part has been scurvily played.

HIPPOLITA
How foolishly this beast contemns his fate,
And shuns the use of that which I more scorn
Than I once loved: his love. But let him go.
My vengeance shall give comfort to his woe.[4]
She offers to go away.

VASQUEZ [*following after her*]
Mistress, mistress! Madam Hippolita!
Pray, a word or two.

HIPPOLITA
With me, sir?

VASQUEZ
With you, if you please.

HIPPOLITA
What is't?

VASQUEZ
I know you are infinitely moved now, and you think you have cause. Some, I confess, you have, but, sure, not so much as you imagine.

1 *quality*: social standing 2 *entertainment*: hospitality 3 *braver*: finer
4 *woe*: the misery he has caused her

HIPPOLITA

Indeed?

VASQUEZ

Oh, you were miserably bitter, which you followed even to the last syllable. 'Faith, you were somewhat too shrewd.[1] By my life, you could not have took my lord in a worse time since I first knew him. Tomorrow you shall find him a new man.

HIPPOLITA

Well, I shall wait his leisure.

VASQUEZ

Fie, this is not a hearty[2] patience; it comes sourly from you. Troth, let me persuade you for once.

HIPPOLITA [*Aside*]

I have it, and it shall be so. Thanks, Opportunity.
[*Aloud*] Persuade me to what?

VASQUEZ

Visit him in some milder temper. Oh, if you could but master a little your female spleen,[3] how might you win him!

HIPPOLITA

He will never love me. Vasquez, thou hast been a too trusty servant to such a master, and I believe thy reward in the end will fall out like mine.

VASQUEZ

So, perhaps, too.

HIPPOLITA

Resolve thyself, it will. Had I one so true, so truly honest, so secret to my counsels, as thou hast been to him and his,[4] I should think it a slight acquittance[5] not only to make him master of all I have, but even of myself.[6]

VASQUEZ

Oh, you are a noble gentlewoman!

1 *shrewd*: malicious 2 *hearty*: heartfelt 3 *spleen*: anger, rage
4 *his*: Soranzo's father 5 *acquittance*: repayment of debt
6 *of myself*: i.e., by marrying him

HIPPOLITA
Wilt thou feed always upon hopes? Well, I know thou art wise, and seest the reward of an old servant daily what it is.

VASQUEZ
Beggary and neglect.

HIPPOLITA
True, but Vasquez, wert thou mine, and wouldst be private to me and my designs, I here protest, myself, and all what I can else call mine, should be at thy dispose.[1]

VASQUEZ [*Aside*]
Work you that way, old mole?[2] Then I have the wind of you.[3] [*Aloud*] I were not worthy of it, by any desert that could lie within my compass. If I could –

HIPPOLITA
What then?

VASQUEZ
I should then hope to live, in these my old years, with rest and security.

HIPPOLITA
Give me thy hand. Now promise but thy silence,
And help to bring to pass a plot I have,
And here in sight of heaven, that being done,
I make thee lord of me and mine estate.

VASQUEZ
Come, you are merry![4] This is such a happiness that I can neither think or believe.

HIPPOLITA
Promise thy secrecy, and 'tis confirmed.

VASQUEZ
Then here I call our good genii[5] for witnesses whatsoever your designs are, or against whomsoever, I will not only be a special actor therein, but never disclose it till it be effected.

1 *dispose*: disposal
2 *old mole*: because the mole works underground, but also because Hippolyta is blind to Vasquez's true nature
3 *have the wind of you*: like a predator upwind of its prey, he has her scent
4 *merry*: only joking 5 *genii*: a pagan version of guardian angels

HIPPOLITA
I take thy word, and with that, thee for mine.
Come, then, let's more confer of this anon.
On this delicious bane[1] my thoughts shall banquet;
Revenge shall sweeten what my griefs have tasted. *Exeunt.*

ACT 2

Scene 3

Enter RICHARDETTO *[in disguise as the Doctor]* *and* PHILOTIS.

RICHARDETTO
Thou seest, my lovely niece, these strange mishaps;
How all my fortunes turn to my disgrace,
Wherein I am but as a looker-on,
Whiles others act my shame, and I am silent.

PHILOTIS
But, uncle, wherein can this borrowed shape
Give you content?

RICHARDETTO
I'll tell thee, gentle niece:
Thy wanton aunt in her lascivious riots
Lives now secure;[2] thinks I am surely dead
In my late journey to Leghorn for you,
As I have caused it to be rumoured out.
Now would I see with what an impudence
She gives scope to her loose adultery,
And how the common voice[3] allows hereof:
Thus far I have prevailed.

PHILOTIS
Alas, I fear
You mean some strange revenge.

1 *bane*: poison 2 *secure*: unsuspecting 3 *common voice*: popular opinion

RICHARDETTO

Oh, be not troubled;
Your ignorance shall plead for you in all.
But to our business: what, you learnt for certain
How[1] Signor Florio means to give his daughter
In marriage to Soranzo?

PHILOTIS

Yes, for certain.

RICHARDETTO

But how find you young Annabella's love
Inclined to him?

PHILOTIS

For aught I could perceive,
She neither fancies him or any else.

RICHARDETTO

There's mystery in that which time must show.
She used[2] you kindly?

PHILOTIS

Yes.

RICHARDETTO

And craved your company?

PHILOTIS

Often.

RICHARDETTO

'Tis well; it goes as I could wish.
I am the doctor now, and, as for you,
None knows you. If all fail not, we shall thrive.
But who comes here?

Enter GRIMALDI.

I know him. 'Tis Grimaldi:
A Roman and a soldier, near allied
Unto the Duke of Monferrato, one
Attending on the Nuncio[3] of the Pope

1 *How*: that 2 *used*: treated
3 *Nuncio*: representative of the Pope at a foreign court, possessing ecclesiastical and political powers

That now resides in Parma, by which means[1]
He hopes to get the love of Annabella.

GRIMALDI
Save you,[2] sir.

RICHARDETTO
And you, sir.

GRIMALDI
I have heard
Of your approvèd skill, which through the city
Is freely talked of, and would crave your aid.

RICHARDETTO
For what, sir?

GRIMALDI
Marry, sir, for this –
But I would speak in private.

RICHARDETTO
Leave us, cousin.[3]
Exit PHILOTIS.

GRIMALDI
I love fair Annabella, and would know
Whether in arts[4] there may not be receipts[5]
To move affection.

RICHARDETTO
Sir, perhaps there may,
But these will nothing profit you.

GRIMALDI
Not me?

RICHARDETTO
Unless I be mistook, you are a man
Greatly in favour with the Cardinal.

GRIMALDI
What of that?

1 *means*: connection 2 *Save you*: God save you
3 *cousin*: also used to mean 'niece'
4 *arts*: medical science 5 *receipts*: recipes (for love potions)

RICHARDETTO
In duty to his grace,
I will be bold to tell you, if you seek
To marry Florio's daughter, you must first
Remove a bar 'twixt you and her.

GRIMALDI
Who's that?

RICHARDETTO
Soranzo is the man that hath her heart,
And while he lives, be sure you cannot speed.[1]

GRIMALDI
Soranzo? What, mine enemy, is't he?

RICHARDETTO
Is he your enemy?

GRIMALDI
The man I hate
Worse than confusion.[2] I'll kill him straight.

RICHARDETTO
Nay, then, take mine advice:
Even for his grace's sake, the Cardinal,
I'll find a time when he and she do meet,
Of which I'll give you notice; and to be sure
He shall not 'scape you, I'll provide a poison
To dip your rapier's point in. If he had
As many heads as Hydra[3] had, he dies.

GRIMALDI
But shall I trust thee, Doctor?

RICHARDETTO
As yourself;
Doubt not in aught. [*Aside*] Thus shall the Fates decree:
By me Soranzo falls, that ruined me. *Exeunt.*

1 *speed*: succeed 2 *confusion*: perdition, ruin
3 *Hydra*: in classical mythology a many-headed monster that grew two heads for every one that was cut off

ACT 2

Scene 4

Enter DONADO [*with a letter*], BERGETTO *and* POGGIO.

DONADO

Well, sir, I must be content to be both your secretary[1] and your messenger myself. I cannot tell what this letter may work, but, as sure as I am alive, if thou come once to talk with her, I fear thou wilt mar whatsoever I make.

BERGETTO

You make, uncle? Why, am not I big enough to carry mine own letter, I pray?

DONADO

Ay, ay, carry a fool's head o'thy own. Why, thou dunce, wouldst thou write a letter and carry it thyself?

BERGETTO

Yes, that I would, and read it to her with my own mouth; for you must think, if she will not believe me myself when she hears me speak, she will not believe another's handwriting. Oh, you think I am a blockhead, uncle! No, sir, Poggio knows I have indited[2] a letter myself, so I have.

POGGIO

Yes, truly, sir. I have it in my pocket.

DONADO

A sweet one, no doubt. Pray, let's see't.

[POGGIO *hands* BERGETTO *the letter.*]

BERGETTO

I cannot read my own hand very well, Poggio. Read it, Poggio.

DONADO

Begin.

POGGIO (*Reads*)

'Most dainty and honey-sweet mistress, I could call you fair, and lie as fast[3] as any that loves you; but my uncle, being the

1 *secretary*: because he has written the letter 2 *indited*: written
3 *fast*: easily, absolutely

elder man, I leave it to him as more fit for his age and the colour of his beard.[1] I am wise enough to tell you I can board[2] where I see occasion; or, if you like my uncle's wit better than mine, you shall marry me. If you like mine better than his, I will marry you in spite of your teeth.[3] So, commending my best parts[4] to you, I rest

Yours upwards and downwards, or you may choose,
Bergetto.'

BERGETTO
Ah ha! Here's stuff, uncle!

DONADO
Here's stuff, indeed, to shame us all. Pray, whose advice did you take in this learnèd letter?

POGGIO
None, upon my word, but mine own.

BERGETTO
And mine, uncle. Believe it, nobody's else. 'Twas mine own brain, I thank a good wit for't.

DONADO
Get you home, sir, and look you keep within doors till I return.

BERGETTO
How? That were a jest, indeed. I scorn it, i'faith.

DONADO
What, you do not?
[*He threatens to strike him.*]

BERGETTO
Judge me, but I do now.

POGGIO
Indeed, sir, 'tis very unhealthy.

1 *colour of his beard*: presumably white, denoting his gravity
2 *board*: make sexual advances
3 *in spite of your teeth*: whether you like it or not; an unflattering reference to her beauty, like that to her nose
4 *parts*: accomplishments, genitals

DONADO

Well, sir, if I hear any of your apish[1] running to motions[2] and fopperies till I come back, you were as good no.[3] Look to't!

Exit.

BERGETTO

Poggio, shall's steal[4] to see this horse with the head in's tail?

POGGIO

Ay, but you must take heed of whipping.

BERGETTO

Dost take me for a child, Poggio? Come, honest Poggio.

Exeunt.

ACT 2

Scene 5

Enter FRIAR *and* GIOVANNI.

FRIAR

Peace! Thou hast told a tale whose every word
Threatens eternal slaughter to the soul.
I'm sorry I have heard it. Would mine ears
Had been one minute deaf before the hour
That thou cam'st to me! O young man, cast away
By the religious number[5] of mine order,
I day and night have waked my agèd eyes,
Above my strength to weep on thy behalf.
But heaven is angry, and, be thou resolved,
Thou art a man remarked[6] to taste a mischief.
Look for't; though it come late, it will come sure.

GIOVANNI

Father, in this you are uncharitable.[6]
What I have done I'll prove both fit and good.

1 *apish*: foolish 2 *motions*: puppet shows
3 *as good no*: it would be better you hadn't 4 *steal*: sneak away
5 *number*: members 6 *remarked*: marked out
6 *uncharitable*: lacking in Christian love

It is a principle, which you have taught
When I was yet your scholar, that the frame
And composition of the mind doth follow
The frame and composition of the body;
So where the body's furniture[1] is beauty,
The mind's must needs be virtue; which allowed,
Virtue itself is Reason but refined,
And Love the quintessence[2] of that. This proves
My sister's beauty, being rarely fair,
Is rarely virtuous; chiefly in her love,
And chiefly in that love, her love to me.
If hers to me, then so is mine to her,
Since in like causes are effects alike.

FRIAR

O ignorance in knowledge! Long ago
How often have I warned thee this before!
Indeed, if we were sure there were no deity,
Nor heaven nor hell, then to be led alone
By nature's light – as were philosophers
Of elder times – might instance some defence;
But 'tis not so. Then, madman, thou wilt find
That nature is in heaven's positions blind.[3]

GIOVANNI

Your age o'er-rules you; had you youth like mine,
You'd make her love your heaven, and her divine.

FRIAR

Nay, then, I see th'art too far sold to hell;
It lies not in the compass of my prayers
To call thee back. Yet let me counsel thee:
Persuade thy sister to some marriage.

GIOVANNI

Marriage? Why, that's to damn her; that's to prove
Her greedy of variety of lust.

1 *furniture*: equipment, trappings 2 *quintessence*: purest manifestation
3 *nature ... blind*: i.e., Nature is ignorant about the 'positions', or rather absolutes, decreed by God

FRIAR

O fearful! If thou wilt not, give me leave
To shrive her,[1] lest she should die unabsolved.

GIOVANNI

At your best leisure, father; then she'll tell you
How dearly she doth prize my matchless love.
Then you will know what pity 'twere we two
Should have been sundered from each other's arms.
View well her face, and in that little round,
You may observe a world of variety:
For colour, lips; for sweet perfumes, her breath;
For jewels, eyes; for threads of purest gold,
Hair; for delicious choice of flowers, cheeks;
Wonder in every portion of that throne.
Hear her but speak, and you will swear the spheres
Make music to the citizens in heaven;[2]
But father, what is else for pleasure framed,[3]
Lest I offend your ears shall go unnamed.

FRIAR

The more I hear, I pity thee the more –
That one so excellent should give those parts[4]
All to a second death![5] What I can do
Is but to pray; and yet I could advise thee,
Wouldst thou be ruled.

GIOVANNI

In what?

FRIAR

Why, leave her yet.
The throne of mercy is above your trespass.
Yet time is left you both –

1 *shrive her*: hear her confession and absolve her of her sins
2 *spheres . . . music*: it was argued in Ptolemaic cosmology that the movement of the planets around the earth produced music
3 *else . . . framed*: her genitals, here unchristianly associated with pleasure and not procreation
4 *parts*: abilities 5 *second death*: damnation

GIOVANNI

To embrace each other;
Else let all time be struck quite out of number.[1]
She is like me, and I like her, resolved.

FRIAR

No more; I'll visit her. This grieves me most:
Things being thus, a pair of souls are lost. *Exeunt.*

ACT 2

Scene 6

Enter FLORIO, DONADO, ANNABELLA [*and*], PUTTANA.

FLORIO

Where's Giovanni?

ANNABELLA

Newly walked abroad,
And, as I heard him say, gone to the Friar,
His reverend tutor.

FLORIO

That's a blessèd man,
A man made up of holiness. I hope
He'll teach him how to gain another world.

DONADO

Fair gentlewoman, here's a letter sent
To you from my young cousin. I dare swear
He loves you in his soul. Would you could hear
Sometimes what I see daily: sighs and tears,
As if his breast were prison to his heart.
[*He holds out the letter.*]

FLORIO

Receive it, Annabella.

ANNABELLA

Alas, good man.
[*She takes the letter.*]

1 *number*: sequence

DONADO

What's that she said?

PUTTANA

An't please you, sir, she said, 'Alas, good man'. [*Aside to* DONADO] Truly, I do commend him to her every night before her first sleep,[1] because I would have her dream of him, and she hearkens to that most religiously.[2]

DONADO [*Aside to* PUTTANA]

Say'st so? Godamercy,[3] Puttana, there's something for thee [*gives her money*]. And, prithee, do what thou canst on his behalf. Sha' not be lost labour, take my word for't.

PUTTANA [*Aside to* DONADO]

Thank you most heartily, sir. Now I have a feeling[4] of your mind, let me alone to work.

ANNABELLA

Guardian!

PUTTANA

Did you call?

ANNABELLA

Keep this letter.

DONADO

Signor Florio, in any case bid her read it instantly.

FLORIO

Keep it for what? Pray, read it me here right.[5]

ANNABELLA

I shall, sir.

She reads.

DONADO

How d'ee find her inclined, signor?

FLORIO

Troth, sir, I know not how; not all so well
As I could wish.

1 *first sleep*: early part of sleep, associated with erotic dreams
2 *religiously*: fervently 3 *Godamercy*: thank you
4 *feeling*: understanding 5 *right*: straightaway

ANNABELLA
Sir, I am bound to rest your cousin's debtor.
The jewel I'll return; for if he love,
I'll count that love a jewel.
DONADO [*Aside to* FLORIO]
Mark you that?
[*Aloud*] Nay, keep them both, sweet maid.
ANNABELLA
You must excuse me;
Indeed, I will not keep it.
FLORIO
Where's the ring –
That which your mother in her will bequeathed,
And charged you on her blessing not to give't
To any but your husband? Send back that.
ANNABELLA
I have it not.
FLORIO
Ha? 'Have it not'? Where is't?
ANNABELLA
My brother in the morning took it from me;
Said he would wear't today.
FLORIO
Well, what do you say
To young Bergetto's love? Are you content
To match[1] with him? Speak.
DONADO
There's the point, indeed.
ANNABELLA [*Aside*]
What shall I do? I must say something now.
FLORIO
What say? Why d'ee not speak?
ANNABELLA
Sir, with your leave;
Please you to give me freedom?

1 *match*: marry

FLORIO

Yes, you have't.

ANNABELLA

Signor Donado, if your nephew mean
To raise his better fortunes in his match,
The hope of me will hinder such a hope.
Sir, if you love him, as I know you do,
Find one more worthy of his choice than me.
In short, I'm sure I sha' not be his wife.

DONADO

Why, here's plain dealing; I commend thee for't,
And all the worst I wish thee is heaven bless thee!
Your father yet and I will still be friends,
Shall we not, Signor Florio?

FLORIO

Yes, why not?

Enter BERGETTO [*with his head bandaged*] *and* POGGIO.

Look, here your cousin comes.

DONADO [*Aside*]

O coxcomb, what doth he make here?

BERGETTO

Where's my uncle, sirs?

DONADO

What's the news now?

BERGETTO

Save you,[1] uncle, save you. You must not think I come for nothing, masters. [*To* ANNABELLA] And how and how is't? What, you have read my letter? Ah, there I tickled you, i'faith.

POGGIO [*Aside*]

But 'twere better you had tickled her in another place.

BERGETTO

Sirrah sweetheart, I'll tell thee a good jest, and riddle[2] what 'tis.

ANNABELLA

You say you'd tell me.

1 *Save you*: God save you 2 *riddle*: guess

BERGETTO

As I was walking just now in the street, I met a swaggering fellow would needs take the wall of me;[1] and because he did thrust me, I very valiantly called him rogue. He hereupon bade me draw. I told him I had more wit than so; but when he saw that I would not, he did so maul me with the hilts of his rapier, that my head sung whilst my feet capered in the kennel.

DONADO [*Aside*]

Was ever the like ass seen?

ANNABELLA

And what did you all this while?

BERGETTO

Laugh at him for a gull,[2] till I see the blood run about mine ears, and then I could not choose but find in my heart to cry, till a fellow with a broad beard[3] – they say he is a new-come doctor – called me into his house, and gave me a plaster. Look you, here 'tis. And, sir, there was a young wench washed my face and hands most excellently. I'faith, I shall love her as long as I live for't. Did she not, Poggio?

POGGIO

Yes, and kissed him too.

BERGETTO

Why, la, now, you think I tell a lie, uncle, I warrant.

DONADO

Would he that beat thy blood out of thy head had beaten some wit into it, for I fear thou never wilt have any.

BERGETTO

O uncle, but there was a wench would have done a man's heart good to have looked on her. By this light, she had a face, methinks, worth twenty of you, Mistress Annabella.

DONADO [*Aside*]

Was ever such a fool born?

1 *take the wall of me*: it was preferable to walk close to the wall in Caroline England because of the gutter ('kennel') that ran down the centre of the street; Bergetto's assailant has aggressively pushed between him and the wall, perhaps because he assumes himself to be of higher social status

2 *gull*: fool 3 *broad beard*: perhaps part of Richardetto's disguise

ANNABELLA
I am glad she liked[1] you, sir.

BERGETTO
Are you so? By my troth, I thank you, forsooth.

FLORIO
Sure 'twas the Doctor's niece, that was last day with us here.

BERGETTO
'Twas she, 'twas she!

DONADO
How do you know that, Simplicity?

BERGETTO
Why, does not he say so? If I should have said no, I should have given him the lie,[2] uncle, and so have deserved a dry[3] beating again. I'll none of that.

FLORIO
A very modest, well-behaved young maid
As I have seen.

DONADO
Is she indeed?

FLORIO
Indeed
She is, if I have any judgement.

DONADO
Well, sir, now you are free. You need not care for sending letters now; you are dismissed. Your mistress here will none of you.

BERGETTO
No? Why, what care I for that? I can have wenches enough in Parma for half-a-crown apiece, cannot I, Poggio?

POGGIO
I'll warrant you, sir.

1 *liked*: pleased
2 *given him the lie*: told him he was lying – a serious insult
3 *dry*: severe

DONADO

Signor Florio, I thank you for your free recourse[1] you gave for my admittance; and to you, fair maid, that jewel I will give you 'gainst[2] your marriage. [*To* BERGETTO] Come, will you go, sir?

BERGETTO

Ay, marry, will I. Mistress, farewell, mistress. I'll come again tomorrow. Farewell, mistress.

Exeunt DONADO, BERGETTO *and* POGGIO.

Enter GIOVANNI.

FLORIO

Son, where have you been? What, alone, alone, still, still?
I would not have it so. You must forsake
This over-bookish humour.[3] Well, your sister
Hath shook the fool off.

GIOVANNI

'Twas no match for her.

FLORIO

'Twas not, indeed; I meant it nothing less.
Soranzo is the man I only like.[4]
Look on him, Annabella. Come, 'tis supper-time,
And it grows late. *Exit* FLORIO.

GIOVANNI

Whose jewel's that?

ANNABELLA

Some sweetheart's.

GIOVANNI

So I think.

ANNABELLA

A lusty youth, Signor Donado, gave it me
To wear against my marriage.

GIOVANNI

But you shall not wear it.
Send it him back again.

1 *recourse*: access 2 *'gainst*: in anticipation of
3 *humour*: personality trait 4 *the man I only like*: my preferred suitor

ANNABELLA

What, you are jealous?

GIOVANNI

That you shall know anon, at better leisure.
Welcome, sweet Night! The evening crowns the day.

Exeunt.

ACT 3

Scene 1

Enter BERGETTO *and* POGGIO.

BERGETTO

Does my uncle think to make me a baby still? No, Poggio, he shall know I have a sconce[1] now.

POGGIO

Ay, let him not bob you off[2] like an ape with an apple.[3]

BERGETTO

'Sfoot,[4] I will have the wench, if he were ten uncles, in despite of his nose, Poggio.

POGGIO

Hold him to the grindstone, and give not a jot of ground. She hath, in a manner, promised you already.

BERGETTO

True, Poggio, and her uncle the Doctor swore I should marry her.

POGGIO

He swore, I remember.

BERGETTO

And I will have her, that's more. Didst see the codpiece-point[5] she gave me, and the box of marmalade?[6]

1 *sconce*: head 2 *bob you off*: distract you with a toy
3 *ape . . . apple*: apes were thought to be lecherous, apples an aphrodisiac
4 *S'foot*: by God's foot 5 *codpiece-point*: lace for fastening a codpiece
6 *marmalade*: any fruit preserve

POGGIO

Very well, and kissed you that my chops[1] watered at the sight on't. There's no way but to clap up[2] a marriage in hugger-mugger.[3]

BERGETTO

I will do't; for I tell thee, Poggio, I begin to grow valiant, methinks, and my courage begins to rise.[4]

POGGIO

Should you be afraid of your uncle?

BERGETTO

Hang him, old doting rascal, no! I say I will have her.

POGGIO

Lose no time, then.

BERGETTO

I will beget a race of wise men, and constables[5] that shall cart whores[6] at their own charges, and break the duke's peace ere I have done myself. Come, away!

Exeunt.

ACT 3

Scene 2

Enter FLORIO, GIOVANNI, SORANZO, ANNABELLA, PUTTANA *and* VASQUEZ.

FLORIO

My lord Soranzo, though I must confess
The proffers that are made me have been great
In marriage of my daughter, yet the hope
Of your still-rising honours have prevailed

1 *chops*: mouth 2 *clap up*: hastily arrange 3 *hugger-mugger*: secret
4 *to rise*: with a pun on getting an erection
5 *constables*: local officers of justice, proverbially dim-witted
6 *cart whores*: prostitutes were often punished by being driven in a cart through the streets; to pay for this out of his own purse would be a sign of wealth and public-spiritedness

Above all other jointures.[1] Here she is.
She knows my mind. Speak for yourself to her;
And hear you, daughter, see you use him nobly.
For any private speech, I'll give you time.
Come, son, and you the rest. Let them alone,
Agree as they may.

SORANZO
I thank you, sir.

GIOVANNI [*Aside to* ANNABELLA]
Sister, be not all woman.[2] Think on me.

SORANZO
Vasquez!

VASQUEZ
My lord?

SORANZO
Attend me without.[3]

Exeunt all but SORANZO *and* ANNABELLA.

ANNABELLA
Sir, what's your will with me?

SORANZO
Do you not know what I should tell you?

ANNABELLA
Yes,
You'll say you love me.

SORANZO
And I'll swear it too.
Will you believe it?

ANNABELLA
'Tis not point of faith.[4]

Enter GIOVANNI *above.*

SORANZO
Have you not will to love?

1 *jointures*: gifts of property given by a fiancé to his intended bride, here offered by Annabella's suitors
2 *all woman*: i.e., inconstant 3 *without*: outside
4 *not point of faith*: not an article of faith necessary for salvation, i.e., I don't have to believe you

ANNABELLA
Not you.
SORANZO
Whom then?
ANNABELLA
That's as the Fates infer.[1]
GIOVANNI [*Aside*]
Of those I'm regent now.
SORANZO
What mean you, sweet?
ANNABELLA
To live and die a maid.
SORANZO
Oh, that's unfit.
GIOVANNI [*Aside*]
Here's one can say that's but a woman's note.[2]
SORANZO
Did you but see my heart, then would you swear –
ANNABELLA
That you were dead.
GIOVANNI [*Aside*]
That's true, or somewhat near it.
SORANZO
See you these true love's tears?
ANNABELLA
No.
GIOVANNI [*Aside*]
Now she winks.[3]
SORANZO
They plead to you for grace.
ANNABELLA
Yet nothing speak.
SORANZO
Oh, grant my suit!

1 *infer*: determine
2 *a woman's note*: i.e., a lie, given that Annabella has lost her virginity
3 *winks*: closes her eyes

ANNABELLA

What is't?

SORANZO

To let me live –

ANNABELLA

Take it.

SORANZO

– still yours.

ANNABELLA

That is not mine to give.

GIOVANNI [*Aside*]

One such another word would kill his hopes.

SORANZO

Mistress, to leave those fruitless strifes of wit,
I know I have loved you long, and loved you truly.
Not hope of what you have, but what you are
Have drawn me on; then let me not in vain
Still feel the rigour of your chaste disdain.
I'm sick, and sick to th'heart.

ANNABELLA

Help! Aqua-vitae![1]

SORANZO

What mean you?

ANNABELLA

Why, I thought you had been sick!

SORANZO

Do you mock my love?

GIOVANNI [*Aside*]

There, sir, she was too nimble.[2]

SORANZO [*Aside*]

'Tis plain; she laughs at me.
[*To* ANNABELLA] These scornful taunts
Neither become your modesty or years.

1 *Aqua-vitae*: medicinal beverage 2 *nimble*: quick-witted

ANNABELLA

You are no looking-glass, or, if you were,
I'd dress my language by you.[1]

GIOVANNI [*Aside*]

I'm confirmed!

ANNABELLA

To put you out of doubt, my lord, methinks
Your common sense should make you understand
That if I loved you, or desired your love,
Some way I should have given you better taste;[2]
But since you are a nobleman, and one
I would not wish should spend his youth in hopes,[3]
Let me advise you here to forbear[4] your suit;
And think I wish you well I tell you this.

SORANZO

Is't you speak this?

ANNABELLA

Yes, I myself. Yet know –
Thus far I give you comfort – if mine eyes
Could have picked out a man, amongst all those
That sued to me, to make a husband of,
You should have been that man. Let this suffice.
Be noble in your secrecy, and wise.

GIOVANNI [*Aside*]

Why, now I see she loves me.

ANNABELLA

One word more:
As ever virtue lived within your mind,
As ever noble courses were your guide,
As ever you would have me know you loved me,
Let not my father know hereof by you.
If I hereafter find that I must marry,
It shall be you or none.

1 *no looking-glass . . . you*: i.e., if Soranzo were a better role model as lover (looking glass) Annabella would imitate his behaviour

2 *given you better taste*: been nicer to you

3 *hopes*: vain hopes 4 *forbear*: cease

SORANZO

I take that promise.

ANNABELLA

Oh, oh, my head!

SORANZO

What's the matter? Not well?

ANNABELLA

Oh, I begin to sicken.

GIOVANNI [*Aside*]

Heaven forbid!

Exit from above.

SORANZO

Help, help, within there! Ho!

Enter FLORIO, GIOVANNI, [*and*] PUTTANA.

Look to your daughter, Signor Florio.

FLORIO

Hold her up! She swoons.

[GIOVANNI *takes her in his arms.*]

GIOVANNI

Sister, how d'ee?

ANNABELLA

Sick! Brother, are you there?

FLORIO

Convey her to her bed instantly, whilst I send for a physician. Quickly, I say.

PUTTANA

Alas, poor child! *Exeunt all but* SORANZO.

Enter VASQUEZ.

VASQUEZ

My lord.

SORANZO

O Vasquez, now I doubly am undone,
Both in my present and my future hopes.
She plainly told me that she could not love,
And thereupon soon sickened, and I fear
Her life's in danger.

VASQUEZ [*Aside*]

By'r Lady, sir, and so is yours, if you knew all. [*Aloud*] 'Las, sir, I am sorry for that. Maybe 'tis but the maid's sickness[1] – an overflux of youth – and then, sir, there is no such present[2] remedy as present marriage. But hath she given you an absolute denial?

SORANZO

She hath, and she hath not. I'm full of grief –
But what she said, I'll tell thee as we go. *Exeunt.*

ACT 3

Scene 3

Enter GIOVANNI *and* PUTTANA.

PUTTANA

O sir, we are all undone, quite undone, utterly undone and shamed forever! Your sister, O your sister!

GIOVANNI

What of her? For heaven's sake, speak! How does she?

PUTTANA

Oh, that ever I was born to see this day!

GIOVANNI

She is not dead, ha? Is she?

PUTTANA

Dead? No, she is quick![3] 'Tis worse, she is with child. You know what you have done, heaven forgive'ee! 'Tis too late to repent now, heaven help us!

GIOVANNI

With child? How dost thou know't?

1 *maid's sickness*: believed to be cured by sexual intercourse
2 *present*: immediate 3 *quick*: alive, but also pregnant

PUTTANA

How do I know't? Am I, at these years,[1] ignorant what the meanings of qualms[2] and water-pangs[3] be, of changing of colours, queasiness of stomachs, pukings, and another thing that I could name?[4] Do not, for her and your credit's[5] sake, spend the time in asking how and which way 'tis so. She is quick, upon my word. If you let a physician see her water[6] y'are undone.

GIOVANNI

But in what case[7] is she?

PUTTANA

Prettily amended; 'twas but a fit, which I soon espied, and she must look for often henceforward.

GIOVANNI

Commend me to her. Bid her take no care.[8]
Let not the Doctor visit her, I charge you.
Make some excuse till I return. [*Aside*] O me,
I have a world of business[9] in my head!
[*Aloud*] Do not discomfort her. [*Aside*] How do this news perplex me!
[*Aloud*] If my father come to her, Tell him she's recovered well.
Say 'twas but some Ill diet.[10] D'ee hear, woman?
Look you to't.

PUTTANA

I will, sir. *Exeunt.*

1 *at these years*: at my age 2 *qualms*: fainting
3 *water-pangs*: needing to urinate frequently
4 *another thing*: i.e., that Annabella has stopped menstruating
5 *credit's*: reputation's 6 *water*: urine 7 *case*: condition
8 *take no care*: not to worry 9 *business*: cares, distress
10 *Ill diet*: food poisoning

ACT 3

Scene 4

Enter FLORIO *and* RICHARDETTO [*disguised*].

FLORIO
And how d'ee find her, sir?

RICHARDETTO
Indifferent[1] well.
I see no danger, scarce perceive she's sick,
But that she told me she had lately eaten
Melons and, as she thought, those disagreed
With her young stomach.

FLORIO
Did you give her aught?

RICHARDETTO
An easy surfeit-water,[2] nothing else.
You need not doubt her health; I rather think
Her sickness is a fullness of her blood[3] –
You understand me?

FLORIO
I do – you counsel well –
And once within these few days will so order't
She shall be married, ere she know the time.[4]

RICHARDETTO
Yet let not haste, sir, make unworthy choice;
That were dishonour.

FLORIO
Master Doctor, no,
I will not do so neither. In plain words,
My lord Soranzo is the man I mean.

1 *Indifferent*: moderately
2 *surfeit-water*: mild indigestion remedy
3 *fullness of her blood*: i.e., maid's sickness, to be cured by sex
4 *ere she know the time*: before she knows it, with a pun on 'the time' as the period of confinement before labour

RICHARDETTO
A noble and a virtuous gentleman.
FLORIO
As any is in Parma. Not far hence
Dwells Father Bonaventure, a grave friar,
Once tutor to my son; now at his cell
I'll have 'em married.
RICHARDETTO
You have plotted wisely.
FLORIO
I'll send one straight to speak with him tonight.
RICHARDETTO
Soranzo's wise; he will delay no time.
FLORIO
It shall be so.

Enter FRIAR *and* GIOVANNI.

FRIAR
Good peace be here and love.
FLORIO
Welcome, religious[1] friar, you are one
That still[2] bring blessing to the place you come to.
GIOVANNI
Sir, with what speed I could, I did my best
To draw this holy man from forth his cell
To visit my sick sister, that with words
Of ghostly[3] comfort in this time of need
He might absolve her, whether she live or die.
FLORIO
'Twas well done, Giovanni: thou herein
Hast showed a Christian's care, a brother's love.
[*To the* FRIAR] Come, father, I'll conduct you to her chamber,
And one thing would entreat you –
FRIAR
Say on, sir.

1 *religious*: holy 2 *still*: always 3 *ghostly*: spiritual

FLORIO

I have a father's dear impression,[1]
And wish, before I fall into my grave,
That I might see her married, as 'tis fit.
A word from you, grave man, will win her more
Than all our best persuasions.

FRIAR

Gentle sir,
All this I'll say, that heaven may prosper her. *Exeunt.*

ACT 3

Scene 5

Enter GRIMALDI.

GRIMALDI

Now if the Doctor keep his word, Soranzo,
Twenty-to-one you miss your bride. I know
'Tis an un-noble act, and not becomes
A soldier's valour; but in terms of love,
Where merit cannot sway, policy[2] must.
I am resolved: if this physician
Play not on both hands[3] then Soranzo falls.

Enter RICHARDETTO [*disguised, with a box*].

RICHARDETTO

You are come as I could wish. This very night
Soranzo, 'tis ordained, must be affied[4]
To Annabella, and, for aught I know,
Married.

GRIMALDI

How!

1 *a father's dear impression*: loving notion typical of fathers, but also Annabella is the 'impression' or replication of her father, whom he is ambitious to have make further copies

2 *policy*: cunning

3 *Play not on both hands*: doesn't behave duplicitously

4 *affied*: betrothed

RICHARDETTO

Yet your patience.
The place? 'Tis Friar Bonaventure's cell.
Now I would wish you to bestow[1] this night
In watching thereabouts. 'Tis but a night.
If you miss now, tomorrow I'll know all.

GRIMALDI

Have you the poison?

RICHARDETTO

Here 'tis in this box.
[*He hands* GRIMALDI *the poison.*]
Doubt nothing, this will do't. In any case,
As you respect your life, be quick and sure.

GRIMALDI

I'll speed him.[2]

RICHARDETTO

Do. Away, for 'tis not safe
You should be seen much here. Ever my love.

GRIMALDI

And mine to you. *Exit* GRIMALDI.

RICHARDETTO

So, if this hit,[3] I'll laugh and hug revenge;
And they that now dream of a wedding-feast
May chance to mourn the lusty bridegroom's ruin.
But to my other business:
Niece Philotis!

Enter PHILOTIS.

PHILOTIS

Uncle?

RICHARDETTO

My lovely niece,
You have bethought 'ee?[4]

1 *bestow*: spend
2 *speed him*: send him on his journey to death, i.e., kill him
3 *hit*: succeed 4 *bethought 'ee*: considered what to do

PHILOTIS

Yes, and, as you counselled,
Fashioned my heart to love him; but he swears
He will tonight be married, for he fears
His uncle else, if he should know the drift,
Will hinder all, and call his coz to shrift.[1]

RICHARDETTO

Tonight? Why, best of all. But let me see:
I – ha – yes – so it shall be: in disguise
We'll early to the Friar's, I have thought on't.

Enter BERGETTO *and* POGGIO.

PHILOTIS

Uncle, he comes.

RICHARDETTO

Welcome, my worthy coz.

BERGETTO

Lass, pretty lass, come buss,[2] lass!

[*He kisses her.*]

Aha, Poggio!

POGGIO

There's hope of this yet.

RICHARDETTO

You shall have time enough. Withdraw a little:
We must confer at large.[3]

BERGETTO

Have you not sweetmeats or dainty devices[4] for me?

PHILOTIS

You shall enough, sweetheart.

BERGETTO

'Sweetheart'? Mark that, Poggio! [*To* PHILOTIS] By my troth, I cannot choose but kiss thee once more for that word 'sweetheart'.

[*Kisses her.*]

1 *call his coz to shrift*: make his kinsman (Bergetto) repent
2 *buss*: kiss 3 *at large*: at length
4 *dainty devices*: fanciful presents

Poggio, I have a monstrous swelling[1] about my stomach, whatsoever the matter be.

POGGIO

You shall have physic[2] for't, sir.

RICHARDETTO

Time runs apace.

BERGETTO

Time's a blockhead.
[*Kisses her.*]

RICHARDETTO

Be ruled! When we have done what's fit to do,
Then you may kiss your fill, and bed her too. *Exeunt.*

ACT 3

Scene 6

Enter the FRIAR *in his study, sitting in a chair,* ANNABELLA *kneeling and whispering to him, a table before them and wax-lights.*[3] *She weeps and wrings her hands.*

FRIAR

I am glad to see this penance; for, believe me,
You have unripped[4] a soul so foul and guilty
As, I must tell you true, I marvel how
The earth hath borne you up! But weep, weep on:
These tears may do you good. Weep faster yet,
Whiles I do read a lecture.[5]

ANNABELLA

Wretched creature!

FRIAR

Ay, you are wretched, miserably wretched,
Almost condemned alive. There is a place –

1 *swelling*: courage, also an erection
2 *physic*: remedy, here referring to the sexual intercourse following marriage
3 *wax-lights*: candles or tapers 4 *unripped*: disclosed in confession
5 *read a lecture*: deliver an admonitory speech

List,[1] daughter! – in a black and hollow vault,
Where day is never seen. There shines no sun,
But flaming horror of consuming fires,
A lightless sulphur, choked with smoky fogs
Of an infected darkness. In this place
Dwell many thousand, thousand sundry sorts
Of never-dying deaths. There damnèd souls
Roar without pity; there are gluttons fed
With toads and adders; there is burning oil
Poured down the drunkard's throat; the usurer
Is forced to sup whole draughts[2] of molten gold;
There is the murderer forever stabbed,
Yet can he never die; there lies the wanton
On racks of burning steel, whiles in his soul
He feels the torment of his raging lust.

ANNABELLA

Mercy, oh mercy!

FRIAR

There stands these wretched things,
Who have dreamt out whole years in lawless sheets[3]
And secret incests,[4] cursing one another.
Then you will wish each kiss your brother gave
Had been a dagger's point. Then you shall hear
How he will cry 'Oh, would my wicked sister
Had first been damned when she did yield to lust!'
But soft, methinks I see repentance work
New motions[5] in your heart. Say, how is't with you?

ANNABELLA

Is there no way left to redeem my miseries?

FRIAR

There is: despair not. Heaven is merciful
And offers grace, even now. 'Tis thus agreed:
First, for your honour's safety, that you marry

1 *List*: Listen 2 *draughts*: liquid drunk down in one go
3 *lawless sheets*: illicit sexual relationships
4 *incests*: the first time that the word is used in the play
5 *motions*: impulses, emotions

The Lord Soranzo; next, to save your soul,
Leave off this life, and henceforth live to him.[1]

ANNABELLA
Ay me!

FRIAR
Sigh not. I know the baits of sin
Are hard to leave. Oh, 'tis a death to do't!
Remember what must come.[2] Are you content?

ANNABELLA
I am.

FRIAR
I like it well. We'll take the time.[3]
[*Sounds of approach.*]
Who's near us there?

Enter FLORIO [*and*], GIOVANNI.

FLORIO
Did you call, father?

FRIAR
Is Lord Soranzo come?

FLORIO
He stays below.[4]

FRIAR
Have you acquainted him at full?

FLORIO
I have,
And he is overjoyed.

FRIAR
And so are we.
Bid him come near.

GIOVANNI [*Aside*]
My sister weeping, ha?
I fear this friar's falsehood. [*Aloud*] I will call him. *Exit.*

1 *live to him*: be a faithful wife to him
2 *what must come*: i.e., hell
3 *the time*: the present opportunity (to get Soranzo and Annabella betrothed)
4 *stays below*: waits downstairs

FLORIO
Daughter, are you resolved?
ANNABELLA
Father, I am.

Enter GIOVANNI, SORANZO *and* VASQUEZ.

FLORIO
My lord Soranzo, here
Give me your hand; for that I give you this.
[*He joins* SORANZO *and* ANNABELLA*'s hands.*][1]
SORANZO
Lady, say you so too?
ANNABELLA
I do, and vow
To live with you and yours.
FRIAR
Timely resolved;
My blessing rest on both. More to be done,[2]
You may perform it on the morning sun. *Exeunt.*

ACT 3

Scene 7

Enter GRIMALDI, *with his rapier drawn, and a dark lantern.*[3]

GRIMALDI
'Tis early night as yet, and yet too soon
To finish such a work. Here I will lie
To listen who comes next.
He lies down.

1 *joins . . . hands*: a crucial part of the betrothal ritual, also called 'handfasting'
2 *More to be done*: i.e., the wedding ceremony
3 *dark lantern*: a lantern with a slide or shutter that allows the light to be concealed, often associated with villainy

Enter BERGETTO *and* PHILOTIS *disguised,*[1] *and after* RICHARDETTO [*disguised*] *and* POGGIO.

BERGETTO
We are almost at the place, I hope, sweetheart.

GRIMALDI [*Aside*]
I hear them near, and heard one say 'Sweetheart'.
'Tis he! Now guide my hand, some angry Justice,
Home to his bosom. [*Aloud*] Now, have at you, sir!
Strikes BERGETTO *and exits.*

BERGETTO
Oh help, help! Here's a stitch fallen[2] in my guts. Oh, for a flesh-tailor[3] quickly! Poggio!

PHILOTIS
What ails my love?

BERGETTO
I am sure I cannot piss forward and backward, and yet I am wet before and behind. Lights, lights! Ho, lights!

PHILOTIS
Alas, some villain here has slain my love!

RICHARDETTO
Oh heaven forbid it! Raise up the next neighbours instantly, Poggio, and bring lights.

Exit POGGIO.

How is't, Bergetto? Slain? It cannot be. Are you sure y'are hurt?

BERGETTO
Oh, my belly seethes like a porridge-pot. Some cold water! I shall boil over else. My whole body is in a sweat, that you may wring my shirt. Feel here! – Why, Poggio!

Enter POGGIO *with* OFFICERS, *and lights and halberds.*[4]

1 *disguised*: perhaps masked
2 *stitch fallen*: a clothing metaphor, referring to a burst seam
3 *flesh-tailor*: surgeon
4 *halberds*: military weapon, resembling a battle axe combined with a spear

POGGIO

Here! Alas, how do you?

RICHARDETTO

Give me a light! What's here? All blood! O sirs,
Signor Donado's nephew now is slain!
Follow the murderer with all the haste
Up to the city;[1] he cannot be far hence.
Follow, I beseech you!

OFFICERS

Follow, follow, follow!

Exeunt OFFICERS.

RICHARDETTO [*To* PHILOTIS]

Tear off thy linen,[2] coz, to stop his wounds.
[*To* BERGETTO] Be of good comfort, man.

BERGETTO

Is all this mine own blood? Nay, then, goodnight with me. Poggio, commend me to my uncle, dost hear? Bid him, for my sake, make much of this wench. Oh, I am going the wrong way, sure! My belly aches so. Oh, farewell, Poggio! Oh, oh! [*He*] *dies.*

PHILOTIS

Oh, he is dead!

POGGIO

How? Dead?

RICHARDETTO

He's dead, indeed.
'Tis now too late to weep. Let's have him home,
And, with what speed we may, find out the murderer.

POGGIO

O my master, my master, my master! *Exeunt.*

1 *city*: the central administrative district
2 *linen*: petticoats

ACT 3

Scene 8

Enter VASQUEZ *and* HIPPOLITA.

HIPPOLITA
Betrothed?

VASQUEZ
I saw it.

HIPPOLITA
And when's the marriage-day?

VASQUEZ
Some two days hence.

HIPPOLITA
Two days? Why, man, I would but wish two hours
To send him to his last and lasting sleep;[1]
And, Vasquez, thou shalt see, I'll do it bravely.

VASQUEZ
I do not doubt your wisdom, nor, I trust, you my secrecy. I am infinitely yours.

HIPPOLITA
I will be thine in spite of my disgrace.[2]
So soon? O wicked man, I durst be sworn
He'd laugh to see me weep.

VASQUEZ
And that's a villainous fault in him.

HIPPOLITA
No, let him laugh. I'm armed in my resolves.
Be thou still true.

VASQUEZ
I should get little by treachery against[3] so hopeful a preferment as I am like to climb to.

1 *last . . . sleep*: death
2 *my disgrace*: presumably the disgrace of marrying a servant
3 *against*: compared with

HIPPOLITA

Even to my bosom, Vasquez. Let my youth[1]
Revel in these new pleasures. If we thrive,
He now hath but a pair of days to live. *Exeunt.*

ACT 3

Scene 9

Enter FLORIO, DONADO [*weeping*], RICHARDETTO [*disguised*], POGGIO *and* OFFICERS.

FLORIO

'Tis bootless[2] now to show yourself a child,[3]
Signor Donado. What is done, is done.
Spend not the time in tears, but seek for justice.

RICHARDETTO

I must confess, somewhat I was in fault,
That had not first acquainted you what love
Passed 'twixt him and my niece; but, as I live,
His fortune grieves me as it were mine own.

DONADO

Alas, poor creature! He meant no man harm,
That I am sure of.

FLORIO

I believe that too.
But stay, my masters, are you sure you saw
The murderer pass here?

OFFICER

And it please you, sir, we are sure we saw a ruffian, with a naked[4] weapon in his hand, all bloody, get into my Lord Cardinal's grace's gate, that we are sure of; but for fear of his grace – bless us! – we durst go no further.

DONADO

Know you what manner of man he was?

1 *my youth*: Soranzo 2 *bootless*: pointless 3 *a child*: i.e., by weeping
4 *naked*: unsheathed

OFFICER
Yes, sure, I know the man. They say 'a is a soldier. [*To* FLORIO]
He that loved your daughter, sir, an't please ye. 'Twas he, for certain.

FLORIO
Grimaldi, on my life!

OFFICER
Ay, ay, the same.

RICHARDETTO
The Cardinal is noble; he, no doubt,
Will give true justice.

DONADO
Knock someone at the gate!

POGGIO
I'll knock, sir.

POGGIO *knocks.*

SERVANT (*Within*):
What would'ee?

FLORIO
We require speech with the Lord Cardinal
About some present[1] business. Pray, inform
His grace that we are here.

Enter CARDINAL *and* GRIMALDI.

CARDINAL
Why, how now, friends? What saucy mates[2] are you
That know nor duty nor civility?
Are we a person fit to be your host?
Or is our house become your common inn,
To beat our doors at pleasure? What such haste
Is yours, as that it cannot wait fit times?[3]
Are you the masters of this commonwealth
And know no more discretion? [*Sees* DONADO] Oh, your news
Is here before you. You have lost a nephew,
Donado, last night by Grimaldi slain.
Is that your business? Well, sir, we have knowledge on't.

1 *present*: urgent 2 *saucy mates*: rude fellows 3 *fit times*: i.e., until morning

Let that suffice.

GRIMALDI [*Kneels.*]

In presence of your grace,[1]
In thought[2] I never meant Bergetto harm;
But, Florio, you can tell with how much scorn
Soranzo, backed with his confederates,
Hath often wronged me. I, to be revenged,
For that I could not win him else[3] to fight,
Had thought by way of ambush to have killed him,
But was unluckily therein mistook,
Else he had felt what late Bergetto did.
And though my fault to him were merely chance,
Yet humbly I submit me to your grace,
To do with me as you please.

CARDINAL

Rise up, Grimaldi.

[GRIMALDI *stands.*]

You citizens of Parma, if you seek
For justice, know, as Nuncio from the Pope,
For this offence I here receive Grimaldi
Into his Holiness's protection.
He is no common man, but nobly born,
Of prince's blood, though you, Sir Florio,
Thought him too mean[4] a husband for your daughter.
If more you seek for, you must go to Rome,
For he shall thither. Learn more wit,[5] for shame.
Bury your dead. Away, Grimaldi; leave 'em.

Exeunt CARDINAL *and* GRIMALDI.

DONADO

Is this a churchman's voice? Dwells Justice here?

FLORIO

Justice is fled to heaven[6] and comes no nearer.

1 *In . . . grace*: i.e., and therefore speaking truthfully
2 *thought*: intention 3 *else*: by any other means
4 *mean*: lowly 5 *wit*: judgement
6 *Justice is fled to heaven*: in classical mythology Astraea, the goddess of justice, abandoned the earth at the beginning of the Iron Age, partly because of human crimes like murder

Soranzo? Was't for him? Oh, impudence!
Had he the face to speak it, and not blush?
Come, come, Donado, there's no help in this,
When cardinals think murder's not amiss.
Great men may do their wills; we must obey.
But heaven will judge them for't another day. *Exeunt.*

ACT 4

Scene 1

A banquet. Hautboys.[1]

Enter the FRIAR, GIOVANNI, ANNABELLA [*as a bride*], PHILOTIS, SORANZO, DONADO, FLORIO, RICHARDETTO [*disguised*], PUTTANA *and* VASQUEZ.

FRIAR
These holy rites performed, now take your times
To spend the remnant of the day in feast.
Such fit repasts[2] are pleasing to the saints
Who are your guests, though not with mortal eyes
To be beheld. Long prosper in this day,
You happy couple, to each other's joy!

SORANZO
Father, your prayer is heard. The hand of goodness[3]
Hath been a shield for me against my death;
And, more to bless me, hath enriched my life
With this most precious jewel [*indicating* ANNABELLA] – such a prize
As earth hath not another like to this.
Cheer up, my love – and gentlemen, my friends,
Rejoice with me in mirth. This day we'll crown
With lusty[4] cups to Annabella's health.

1 *Hautboys*: wind instruments, resembling the oboe 2 *repasts*: meals
3 *hand of goodness*: divine providence 4 *lusty*: merry

GIOVANNI (*Aside*)

Oh, torture! Were[1] the marriage yet undone!
Ere I'd endure this sight – to see my love
Clipped[2] by another – I would dare confusion,[3]
And stand the horror of ten thousand deaths.

VASQUEZ

Are you not well, sir?

GIOVANNI

Prithee, fellow, wait.[4]
I need not thy officious diligence.

FLORIO

Signor Donado, come. You must forget
Your late mishaps, and drown your cares in wine.

SORANZO

Vasquez?

VASQUEZ

My lord.

SORANZO

Reach me that weighty bowl.[5]
[VASQUEZ *hands him the cup.*]
Here, brother Giovanni, here's to you.
Your turn comes next, though now a bachelor.
Here's to your sister's happiness and mine.
[SORANZO *drinks and offers* GIOVANNI *the cup.*]

GIOVANNI

I cannot drink.

SORANZO

What?

GIOVANNI

'Twill indeed offend[6] me.

ANNABELLA

Pray, do not urge him if he be not willing.
[*Sounds are heard offstage.*]

1 *were*: if only 2 *Clipped*: embraced 3 *confusion*: damnation
4 *wait*: attend to the other guests 5 *bowl*: goblet
6 *offend*: cause me physical discomfort

FLORIO

How now, what noise is this?

VASQUEZ

O sir, I had forgot to tell you: certain young maidens of Parma, in honour to Madam Annabella's marriage, have sent their loves to her in a masque,[1] for which they humbly crave your patience and silence.

SORANZO

We are much bound to them, so much the more
As it comes unexpected. Guide them in. [*Exit* VASQUEZ.]

Hautboys. Enter HIPPOLITA *and* LADIES [*masked*] *in white robes with garlands of willows* [*led in by* VASQUEZ].[2] *Music and a dance.*

SORANZO

Thanks, lovely virgins. Now, might we but know
To whom we have been beholding for this love,
We shall acknowledge it.

HIPPOLITA

Yes, you shall know.
[*She removes her mask.*]
What think you now?

ALL

Hippolita?

HIPPOLITA

'Tis she,
Be not amazed – nor blush, young lovely bride.
I come not to defraud you of your man.
[*To* SORANZO] 'Tis now no time to reckon up[3] the talk,
What Parma long hath rumoured of us both.
Let rash report[4] run on; the breath that vents it
Will, like a bubble, break itself at last.
[*To* ANNABELLA] But now to you, sweet creature, lend's
your hand.

1 *masque*: an entertainment featuring music and dance by masked performers, often performed at weddings
2 *willow*: symbolic of unrequited love
3 *reckon up*: go over in detail 4 *report*: gossip

[*She takes* ANNABELLA*'s hand.*]
Perhaps it hath been said that I would claim
Some interest in Soranzo, now your lord?[1]
What I have right to do, his soul knows best;
But in my duty to your noble worth,
Sweet Annabella, and my care of you,
Here take, Soranzo, take this hand from me.
I'll once more join what, by the holy Church,
Is finished and allowed.[2]
[*She joins their hands together.*]
Have I done well?

SORANZO
You have too much engaged us.[3]

HIPPOLITA
One thing more:
That you may know my single charity,[4]
Freely I here remit[5] all interest
I e'er could claim, and give you back your vows;
And to confirm't – [*To* VASQUEZ] Reach me a cup of wine.
My lord Soranzo, in this draught I drink
Long rest t'ee. [*Aside*] Look to it, Vasquez!

VASQUEZ [*Aside to* HIPPOLITA]
Fear nothing.

He gives her a poisoned cup. She drinks.

SORANZO
Hippolita, I thank you, and will pledge[6]
This happy union as another life. [*To* VASQUEZ] Wine there!

VASQUEZ
You shall have none; neither shall you pledge her.

HIPPOLITA
How?

1 *lord*: husband 2 *allowed*: approved
3 *engaged us*: placed us in your debt
4 *single charity*: special kindness 5 *remit*: renounce
6 *pledge*: drink a toast to

VASQUEZ

Know now, Mistress She-Devil, your own mischievous treachery hath killed you. I must not marry you.

HIPPOLITA

Villain!

ALL

What's the matter?

VASQUEZ

Foolish woman, thou art now like a firebrand that hath kindled others and burnt thyself. *Troppo sperar inganna*:[1] thy vain hope hath deceived thee. Thou art but[2] dead. If thou hast any grace, pray.

HIPPOLITA

Monster!

VASQUEZ

Die in charity,[3] for shame. [*To the others*] This thing of malice, this woman, had privately corrupted me with promise of marriage, under this politic[4] reconciliation to poison my lord, whiles she might laugh at his confusion[5] on his marriage-day. I promised her fair,[6] but I knew what my reward should have been,[7] and would willingly have spared her life, but that I was acquainted with the danger of her disposition, and now have fitted her a just payment in her own coin. There she is; she hath yet – [*To* HIPPOLITA] –[8] and end thy days in peace, vile woman. As for life, there's no hope; think not on't.

ALL

Wonderful justice!

RICHARDETTO

Heaven, thou art righteous!

1 *Troppo sperar inganna*: 'to hope too much deceives'

2 *but*: as good as 3 *in charity*: i.e., by speaking well of others

4 *politic*: cunningly expedient 5 *confusion*: ruin

6 *promised her fair*: encouraged her

7 *my reward . . . been*: perhaps assuming that she would have broken her promise and pinned the murder on him

8 – [*To* HIPPOLITA] – : dashes here indicate gaps in the text where the printer found the copy illegible

HIPPOLITA

Oh, 'tis true,
I feel my minute[1] coming. Had that slave
Kept promise – Oh, my torment! – thou this hour
Hadst died, Soranzo – Heat above hell-fire! –
Yet, ere I pass away – cruel, cruel flames! –
Take here my curse amongst you: may thy bed
Of marriage be a rack unto thy heart. –
Burn, blood, and boil in vengeance. Oh, my heart!
My flame's intolerable! – May'st thou live
To father bastards; may her womb bring forth
Monsters; and die together in your sins,
Hated, scorned and unpitied! – Oh! Oh! [*She*] *dies.*

FLORIO

Was e'er so vile a creature?

RICHARDETTO

Here's the end
Of lust and pride.

ANNABELLA

It is a fearful sight!

SORANZO

Vasquez, I know thee now a trusty servant,
And never will forget thee. [*To* ANNABELLA] Come, my love,
We'll home, and thank the heavens for this escape.
Father and friends, we must break up this mirth;
It is too sad a feast.

DONADO [*To* VASQUEZ]

Bear hence the body.

FRIAR [*Aside to* GIOVANNI]

Here's an ominous change!
Mark this, my Giovanni, and take heed.

1 *minute*: moment of death

I fear the event:[1] that marriage seldom's good,
Where the bride-banquet[2] so begins in blood.
Exeunt [*with the body*].

ACT 4

Scene 2

Enter RICHARDETTO *and* PHILOTIS.

RICHARDETTO
My wretched wife – more wretched in her shame
Than in her wrongs to me – hath paid too soon
The forfeit of her modesty and life.[3]
And I am sure, my niece, though vengeance hover,
Keeping aloof yet from Soranzo's fall,
Yet he will fall, and sink with his own weight.
I need not – now my heart persuades me so –
To further his confusion;[4] there is one
Above begins to work. For, as I hear,
Debates[5] already 'twixt his wife and him
Thicken and run to head.[6] She, as 'tis said,
Slightens[7] his love, and he abandons hers;
Much talk I hear. Since things go thus, my niece,
In tender love and pity of your youth,
My counsel is that you should free your years[8]
From hazard of these woes by flying hence
To fair Cremona,[9] there to vow your soul
In holiness a holy votaress.[10]

1 *the event*: consequences for Soranzo and Annabella
2 *bride-banquet*: wedding breakfast
3 *life*: spiritual life, health of the soul 4 *confusion*: damnation
5 *Debates*: quarrels
6 *run to head*: move to a climax 7 *Slightens*: scorns, treats contemptuously
8 *years*: youth
9 *Cremona*: neighbouring town, notable for its many nunneries
10 *holy votaress*: nun

Leave me to see the end of these extremes.[1]
All human worldly courses are uneven;[2]
No life is blessèd but the way to heaven.

PHILOTIS
Uncle, shall I resolve to be a nun?

RICHARDETTO
Ay, gentle niece, and in your hourly prayers
Remember me, your poor unhappy uncle.
Hie[3] to Cremona now, as Fortune leads;
Your home your cloister, your best friends your beads.[4]
Your chaste and single life shall crown your birth:
Who dies a virgin lives a saint on earth.

PHILOTIS
Then farewell, world, and worldly thoughts, adieu.
Welcome, chaste vows; myself I yield to you. *Exeunt.*

ACT 4

Scene 3

Enter SORANZO *unbraced,*[5] *[with his sword drawn,] and* ANNABELLA *dragged in.*

SORANZO
Come, strumpet, famous[6] whore! Were every drop
Of blood that runs in thy adulterous veins
A life, this sword – dost see't? – should in one blow
Confound[7] them all. Harlot, rare, notable harlot,
That with thy brazen face maintain'st[8] thy sin,
Was there no man in Parma to be bawd[9]
To your loose, cunning whoredom else but I?

1 *extremes*: dire events, tragedies
2 *uneven*: morally irregular 3 *Hie*: go quickly
4 *beads*: rosary beads used by Catholics to count prayers
5 *unbraced*: with his clothes unfastened, often a sign of madness on stage
6 *famous*: infamous 7 *Confound*: destroy 8 *maintain'st*: defends
9 *bawd*: brothel-keeper or pimp

Must your hot itch and pleurisy[1] of lust,
The heyday of your luxury,[2] be fed
Up to a surfeit? And could none but I
Be picked out to be cloak[3] to your close tricks,[4]
Your belly-sports? Now I must be the dad
To all that gallimaufry[5] that's stuffed
In thy corrupted, bastard-bearing womb?
Say, must I?

ANNABELLA

Beastly man! Why, 'tis thy fate:
I sued not to thee, for – but that I thought
Your over-loving lordship would have run
Mad on denial[6] – had ye lent me time,
I would have told 'ee in what case[7] I was,
But you would needs be doing.[8]

SORANZO

Whore of whores!
Dar'st thou tell me this?

ANNABELLA

Oh yes! Why not?
You were deceived in me; 'twas not for love
I chose you, but for honour.[9] Yet know this:
Would you be patient yet, and hide your shame,
I'd see whether I could love you.

SORANZO

Excellent quean![10]
Why, art thou not with child?

ANNABELLA

What needs all this,
When 'tis superfluous? I confess I am.

1 *pleurisy*: excess, also a feverish disease
2 *heyday of your luxury*: climax of your lust 3 *cloak*: disguise
4 *close tricks*: secret liaisons
5 *gallimaufry*: patchwork of materials, i.e., a bastard
6 *on denial*: at being denied 7 *case*: condition
8 *doing*: making a match, with a sexual pun
9 *honour*: reputation 10 *quean*: prostitute

SORANZO
Tell me by whom.

ANNABELLA
Soft, sir, 'twas not in my bargain.[1]
Yet somewhat, sir, to stay your longing stomach[2]
I'm content t'acquaint you with. The man,
The more than man, that got this sprightly boy –
For 'tis a boy, that's for your glory, sir:
Your heir shall be a son.

SORANZO
Damnable monster!

ANNABELLA
Nay, and you will not hear, I'll speak no more.

SORANZO
Yes, speak, and speak thy last.

ANNABELLA
A match, a match.[3]
This noble creature was in every part
So angel-like, so glorious, that a woman
Who had not been but human, as was I,
Would have kneeled to him, and have begged for love.
You? Why, you are not worthy once to name
His name without true worship, or, indeed,
Unless you kneeled, to hear another name him.

SORANZO
What was he called?

ANNABELLA
We are not come to that.
Let it suffice that you shall have the glory
To father what so brave[4] a father got.
In brief, had not this chance fall'n out as't doth,
I never had been troubled with a thought

1 *not in my bargain*: not part of our agreement
2 *stay . . . stomach*: satisfy your appetite (like a pregnancy craving)
3 *match*: deal 4 *brave*: excellent

That you had been a creature;[1] but for marriage,
I scarce dream yet of that.

SORANZO
Tell me his name.

ANNABELLA
Alas, alas, there's all.
Will you believe?

SORANZO
What?

ANNABELLA
You shall never know.

SORANZO
How!

ANNABELLA
Never; if you do, let me be cursed.

SORANZO
Not know it, strumpet? I'll rip up thy heart
And find it there.

ANNABELLA
Do, do!

SORANZO
And with my teeth
Tear the prodigious[2] lecher joint by joint!

ANNABELLA
Ha, ha, ha! The man's merry.

SORANZO
Dost thou laugh?
Come, whore, tell me your lover, or by truth
I'll hew thy flesh to shreds. Who is't?

ANNABELLA (*sings*)
Che morte più dolce che morire per amore?[3]

SORANZO [*grabbing* ANNABELLA]
Thus will I pull thy hair, and thus I'll drag

1 *That you had been a creature*: that you existed
2 *prodigious*: monstrous
3 *Che morte . . . per amore?*: 'What death is sweeter than to die for love?'

Thy lust-belepered[1] body through the dust.
Yet tell his name.

ANNABELLA (*sings*)

Morendo in grazia a lui, morirei senza dolore.[2]

SORANZO

Dost thou triumph? The treasure of the earth
Shall not redeem[3] thee. Were there kneeling kings
Did beg thy life, or angels did come down
To plead in tears, yet should not all prevail
Against my rage.
[*He points his sword at her heart.*]
Dost thou not tremble yet?

ANNABELLA

At what? To die? No, be a gallant hangman.[4]
I dare thee to the worst: strike, and strike home.
I leave revenge behind, and thou shalt feel't.

SORANZO

Yet tell me ere thou diest, and tell me truly:
Knows thy old father this?

ANNABELLA

No, by my life.

SORANZO

Wilt thou confess, and I will spare thy life?

ANNABELLA

My life? I will not buy my life so dear.

SORANZO

I will not slack[5] my vengeance.

Enter VASQUEZ.

VASQUEZ

What d'ee mean, sir?
[*He gets between* ANNABELLA *and* SORANZO*'s sword.*]

1 *lust-belepered*: made leprous through lust
2 *Morendo . . . senza dolore*: 'Dying in favour with him, I would die without pain'
3 *redeem*: ransom
4 *hangman*: a shameful occupation, well beneath Soranzo's rank
5 *slack*: delay

SORANZO
Forbear, Vasquez! Such a damnèd whore
Deserves no pity.

VASQUEZ
Now the gods forfend![1]

And would you be her executioner, and kill her in your rage too? Oh, 'twere most unmanlike! She is your wife. What faults hath been done by her before she married you, were not against you. Alas, poor lady, what hath she committed which any lady in Italy, in the like case, would not? Sir, you must be ruled by your reason and not by your fury – that were unhuman and beastly.

SORANZO
She shall not live.

VASQUEZ
Come, she must. You would have her confess the authors of her present misfortunes, I warrant 'ee. 'Tis an unconscionable demand, and she should lose the estimation that I, for my part, hold of her worth if she had done it. Why, sir, you ought not, of all men living, to know it. Good sir, be reconciled. Alas, good gentlewoman!

ANNABELLA
Pish, do not beg for me. I prize my life
As nothing. If the man will needs be mad,
Why, let him take it.

SORANZO
Vasquez, hear'st thou this?

VASQUEZ
Yes, and commend her for it. In this she shows the nobleness of a gallant spirit, and beshrew[2] my heart but it becomes her rarely. [*Aside to* SORANZO] Sir, in any case smother your revenge. Leave the scenting-out your wrongs to me. Be ruled, as you respect your honour, or you mar all. [*Aloud*] Sir, if ever my service were of any credit with you, be not so violent in your distractions.[3] You are married now. What a triumph

1 *forfend*: forbid 2 *beshrew*: may evil befall 3 *distractions*: mad ravings

might the report of this give to other neglected suitors! 'Tis as manlike to bear extremities,[1] as godlike to forgive.

SORANZO

O Vasquez, Vasquez, in this piece of flesh,
This faithless face of hers, had I laid up
The treasure of my heart! [*To* ANNABELLA] Hadst thou been virtuous,
Fair, wicked woman, not the matchless joys
Of life itself had made me wish to live
With any saint but thee. Deceitful creature,
How hast thou mocked my hopes, and in the shame
Of thy lewd womb even buried me alive!
I did too dearly love thee.

VASQUEZ (*Aside* [*to* SORANZO])

This is well.
Follow this temper[2] with some passion; be brief and moving – 'tis for the purpose.

SORANZO [*To* ANNABELLA]

Be witness to my words thy soul and thoughts,
And tell me: didst not think that in my heart
I did too superstitiously[3] adore thee?

ANNABELLA

I must confess, I know you loved me well.

SORANZO

And wouldst thou use me thus? O Annabella,
Be thou assured, whatsoe'er the villain was
That thus hath tempted thee to this disgrace,
Well he might lust, but never loved like me.
He doted on the picture that hung out
Upon thy cheeks, to please his humorous[4] eye,
Not on the part I loved which was thy heart,
And, as I thought, thy virtues.

1 *extremities*: injuries 2 *temper*: composure
3 *superstitiously*: idolatrously 4 *humorous*: fanciful, changeable

ANNABELLA

O my lord,
These words wound deeper than your sword could do.

VASQUEZ

Let me not ever take comfort, but I begin to weep myself, so much I pity him. Why, madam, I knew when his rage was overpassed what it would come to.

SORANZO [*Sheathing his sword*]

Forgive me, Annabella. Though thy youth
Hath tempted thee above thy strength to folly,
Yet will not I forget what I should be,
And what I am: a husband. In that name
Is hid divinity. If I do find
That thou wilt yet be true, here I remit[1]
All former faults, and take thee to my bosom.

VASQUEZ

By my troth, and that's a point of noble charity.

ANNABELLA [*Kneeling*]

Sir, on my knees –

SORANZO

Rise up; you shall not kneel.
Get you to your chamber; see you make no show
Of alteration.[2] I'll be with you straight.
My reason tells me now that 'tis as common
To err in frailty as to be a woman.
Go to your chamber. *Exit* ANNABELLA.

VASQUEZ

So, this was somewhat to the matter. What do you think of your heaven of happiness now, sir?

SORANZO

I carry hell about me. All my blood
Is fired in swift revenge.

1 *remit*: pardon

2 *show of alteration*: sign of disturbance, evidence of backsliding

VASQUEZ

That may be, but know you how, or on whom? Alas, to marry a great[1] woman, being made great in the stock[2] to your hand, is a usual sport in these days; but to know what ferret it was that haunted[3] your cunny-berry,[4] there's the cunning.

SORANZO

I'll make her tell herself, or –

VASQUEZ

Or what? You must not do so. Let me yet persuade your sufferance a little while. Go to her; use her mildly; win her, if it be possible, to a voluntary,[5] to a weeping tune. For the rest, if all hit,[6] I will not miss my mark. Pray, sir, go in. The next news I tell you shall be wonders.

SORANZO

Delay in vengeance gives a heavier blow. *Exit.*

VASQUEZ

Ah, sirrah, here's work for the nonce![7] I had a suspicion of a bad matter in my head a pretty whiles ago, but after my madam's scurvy looks here at home, her waspish perverseness and loud fault-finding, then I remembered the proverb that 'Where hens crow, and cocks hold their peace, there are sorry houses.'[8] Sfoot, if the lower parts of a she-tailor's[9] cunning can cover such a swelling in the stomach, I'll never blame a false stitch in a shoe whiles I live again. Up,[10] and up so quick? And so quickly too? 'Twere a fine policy to learn by whom; this must be known.

Enter PUTTANA [*weeping*].

And I have thought on't – here's the way or none. [*To* PUTTANA] What, crying, old mistress? Alas, alas, I cannot

1 *great*: well born, pregnant 2 *stock*: body, line of descent
3 *haunted*: frequently resorted 4 *cunny-berry*: rabbit burrow, also vagina
5 *voluntary*: improvised part of a musical performance
6 *if all hit*: if everything comes off 7 *nonce*: present occasion
8 *Where ... houses*: proverb, meaning that where the wife rules the husband there is domestic strife
9 *she-tailor*: women's dressmaker 10 *Up*: pregnant

blame 'ee. We have a lord, heaven help us, is so mad[1] as the devil himself, the more shame for him.

PUTTANA

O Vasquez, that ever I was born to see this day! Doth he use thee so too sometimes, Vasquez?

VASQUEZ

Me? Why, he makes a dog of me; but if some were of my mind, I know what we would do. As sure as I am an honest man, he will go near to kill my lady with unkindness. Say she be with child: is that such a matter for a young woman of her years to be blamed for?

PUTTANA

Alas, good heart; it is against her will full sore.

VASQUEZ

I durst be sworn, all his madness is for that she will not confess whose 'tis, which he will know; and when he doth know it, I am so well acquainted with his humour[2] that he will forget all straight. Well, I could wish she would in plain terms tell all, for that's the way indeed.

PUTTANA

Do you think so?

VASQUEZ

Foh, I know't, provided that he did not win her to't by force.[3] He was once in a mind, that you could tell, and meant to have wrung it out of you, but I somewhat pacified him for that. Yet, sure, you know a great deal –

PUTTANA

Heaven forgive us all, I know a little, Vasquez.

VASQUEZ

Why should you not? Who else should? Upon my conscience, she loves you dearly, and you would not betray her to any affliction[4] for the world.

PUTTANA

Not for all the world, by my faith and troth, Vasquez.

1 *mad*: furious 2 *humour*: temperament

3 *not . . . by force*: if her confession were not extracted by violence

4 *betray . . . affliction*: expose her to suffering

VASQUEZ
'Twere pity of your life if you should; but in this you should both relieve her present discomforts, pacify my lord, and gain yourself everlasting love and preferment.

PUTTANA
Dost think so, Vasquez?

VASQUEZ
Nay, I know't. Sure, 'twas some near and entire[1] friend.

PUTTANA
'Twas a dear friend, indeed, but –

VASQUEZ
But what? Fear not to name him – my life between you and danger! 'Faith, I think 'twas no base fellow.

PUTTANA
Thou wilt stand between me and harm?

VASQUEZ
Ud's pity,[2] what else?[3] You shall be rewarded too, trust me.

PUTTANA
'Twas even no worse than her own brother.

VASQUEZ
Her brother Giovanni, I warrant 'ee?

PUTTANA
Even he, Vasquez: as brave[4] a gentleman as ever kissed fair lady. Oh, they love most perpetually.

VASQUEZ
A brave gentleman, indeed. Why, therein I commend her choice. [*Aside*] Better and better! [*Aloud*] You are sure 'twas he?

PUTTANA
Sure; and you shall see he will not be long from her, too.

VASQUEZ
He were to blame if he would. But may I believe thee?

1 *entire*: intimate 2 *Ud's pity*: by God's pity 3 *what else?*: of course
4 *brave*: fine

PUTTANA

Believe me? Why, dost think I am a Turk or a Jew?[1] No, Vasquez, I have known their dealings too long to belie them now.

VASQUEZ

Where are you? There within, sirs!

Enter BANDITTI.[2]

PUTTANA

How now? What are these?

VASQUEZ

You shall know presently.[3] Come, sirs, take me this old, damnable hag, gag her instantly, and put out her eyes! Quickly, quickly!

[*The* BANDITTI *seize* PUTTANA.]

PUTTANA

Vasquez, Vasquez!

VASQUEZ

Gag her, I say! 'Sfoot, d'ee suffer her to prate? What, d'ee fumble about? Let me come to her. I'll help your old gums, you toad-bellied bitch!

[*He gags* PUTTANA.]

Sirs, carry her closely[4] into the coal-house, and put out her eyes instantly. If she roars, slit her nose. D'ee hear? Be speedy and sure.

Exeunt [BANDITTI] *with* PUTTANA.

Why, this is excellent and above expectation! Her own brother? Oh, horrible! To what a height of liberty[5] in damnation hath the devil trained[6] our age! Her brother? Well, there's yet but a beginning. I must to my lord, and tutor him better in his points of vengeance. Now I see how a smooth tale goes beyond a smooth tail.[7]

Enter GIOVANNI.

1 *a Turk or a Jew*: proverbially untrustworthy
2 BANDITTI: a gang of Italian outlaws and robbers
3 *presently*: immediately 4 *closely*: secretly
5 *liberty*: licentiousness 6 *trained*: led, tutored
7 *how . . . tail*: how persuasive flattery overcomes a wanton woman

But soft, what thing comes next? Giovanni, as I would wish.
My belief is strengthened; 'tis as firm as winter and summer.

GIOVANNI

Where's my sister?

VASQUEZ

Troubled with a new sickness, my lord; she's somewhat ill.

GIOVANNI

Took too much of the flesh,[1] I believe.

VASQUEZ

Troth, sir, and you, I think, have e'en hit it.[2] But my virtuous lady!

GIOVANNI

Where's she?

VASQUEZ

In her chamber. Please you visit her? She is alone. [GIOVANNI *gives him money.*] Your liberality hath doubly made me your servant, and ever shall, ever!

Exit GIOVANNI.

Enter SORANZO.

Sir, I am made a man. I have plied my cue[3] with cunning and success. I beseech you, let's be private.

SORANZO

My lady's brother's come; now he'll know all.

VASQUEZ

Let him know't. I have made some of them fast[4] enough.
How have you dealt with my lady?

SORANZO

Gently, as thou hast counselled. Oh, my soul
Runs circular[5] in sorrow for revenge,
But, Vasquez, thou shalt know –

1 *Took . . . flesh*: ate too much meat, had too much sex
2 *hit it*: made the right diagnosis 3 *plied my cue*: played my part
4 *fast*: secure
5 *Runs circular*: moves but makes no progress, like an animal tied to a stake

VASQUEZ

Nay, I will know no more, for now comes your turn to know. I would not talk so openly[1] with you. Let my young master take time enough, and go at pleasure. He is sold to death, and the devil shall not ransom him. Sir, I beseech you – your privacy.

SORANZO

No conquest can gain glory of my fear.[2] *Exeunt.*

ACT 5

Scene 1

Enter ANNABELLA *above* [*with a letter*].

ANNABELLA

Pleasures, farewell, and all ye thriftless[3] minutes
Wherein false joys have spun a weary life;
To these, my fortunes, now I take my leave.
Thou precious Time, that swiftly rid'st in post[4]
Over the world to finish up the race
Of my last fate, here stay thy restless course,
And bear to ages that are yet unborn
A wretched, woeful woman's tragedy.
My conscience now stands up against my lust[5]
With depositions[6] charactered in guilt,[7]

Enter FRIAR [*below*].

And tells me I am lost. Now I confess,
Beauty that clothes the outside of the face
Is cursèd if it be not clothed with grace.

1 *openly*: publicly
2 *No . . . fear*: perhaps 'No revelation will make me afraid' or 'Whatever defeat I suffer I will not show fear'
3 *thriftless*: profitless 4 *in post*: as a messenger, in haste
5 *stands up . . . lust*: i.e., in court 6 *depositions*: written testimony
7 *charactered in guilt*: written in guilty terms, with a pun on 'gilt' (gold)

Here, like a turtle,[1] mewed up[2] in a cage,
Unmated,[3] I converse with air and walls,
And descant on my vile unhappiness.
O Giovanni, that hast had the spoil[4]
Of thine own virtues and my modest fame;
Would thou hadst been less subject to those stars
That luckless reigned at my nativity!
Oh, would the scourge due to my black offence
Might pass from thee, that I alone might feel
The torment of an uncontrollèd flame.[5]

FRIAR [*Aside*]
What's this I hear?

ANNABELLA
That man, that blessèd friar,
Who joined in ceremonial knot my hand
To him whose wife I now am, told me oft
I trod the path to death, and showed me how.
But they who sleep in lethargies of lust
Hug their confusion, making heaven unjust,[6]
And so did I.

FRIAR [*Aside*]
Here's music to the soul.

ANNABELLA
Forgive me, my good genius,[7] and this once
Be helpful to my ends.[8] Let some good man
Pass this way, to whose trust I may commit
This paper, double-lined with tears and blood;
Which, being granted, here I sadly[9] vow

1 *turtle*: turtle dove, proverbially loyal to its mate
2 *mewed up*: confined 3 *Unmated*: without a mate
4 *had the spoil*: plundered, destroyed
5 *uncontrollèd flame*: i.e., in hell
6 *making heaven unjust*: insisting that heaven is unjust to prohibit their desires
7 *good genius*: guardian angel
8 *ends*: purposes 9 *sadly*: solemnly

Repentance, and a leaving of that life
I long have died in.

FRIAR [*coming forward*]
Lady, heaven hath heard you,
And hath by providence ordained that I
Should be his minister for your behoof.[1]

ANNABELLA
Ha, what are you?

FRIAR
Your brother's friend, the friar,
Glad in my soul that I have lived to hear
This free confession 'twixt your peace and you.
What would you, or to whom? Fear not to speak.

ANNABELLA
Is heaven so bountiful? Then I have found
More favour than I hoped. Here, holy man,
[*She*] *throws* [*down*] *a letter.* [*The* FRIAR *takes it up.*]
Commend me to my brother. Give him that,
That letter. Bid him read it and repent.
Tell him that I – imprisoned in my chamber,
Barred of all company, even of my guardian,[2]
Who[3] gives me cause of much suspect[4] – have time
To blush at what hath passed. Bid him be wise,
And not believe the friendship of my lord.
I fear much more than I can speak. Good father,
The place is dangerous, and spies are busy;
I must break off. You'll do't?

FRIAR
Be sure I will,
And fly with speed. My blessing ever rest
With thee, my daughter. Live to die more blessed. *Exit* FRIAR.

ANNABELLA
Thanks to the heavens, who have prolonged my breath
To this good use. Now I can welcome death. *Exit.*

1 *for your behoof*: on your behalf 2 *my guardian*: Puttana
3 *Who*: the absence of whom 4 *suspect*: suspicion

ACT 5

Scene 2

Enter SORANZO *and* VASQUEZ.

VASQUEZ
Am I to be believed now? First, marry a strumpet, that cast herself away upon you but to laugh at your horns,[1] to feast on your disgrace, riot[2] in your vexations, cuckold you in your bride-bed, waste your estate upon panders and bawds –

SORANZO
No more, I say no more!

VASQUEZ
A cuckold is a goodly, tame beast,[3] my lord.

SORANZO
I am resolved! Urge not another word.
My thoughts are great,[4] and all as resolute
As thunder. In meantime, I'll cause our lady
To deck herself in all her bridal robes,
Kiss her, and fold her gently in my arms.
Be gone. Yet hear you, are the banditti ready
To wait in ambush?

VASQUEZ
Good sir, trouble not yourself about other business than your own resolution. Remember that time lost cannot be recalled.

SORANZO
With all the cunning words thou canst, invite
The states[5] of Parma to my birthday's feast.
Haste to my brother-rival and his father;
Entreat them gently; bid them not to fail.
Be speedy and return.

1 *horns*: signs of his being a cuckold or sexually betrayed husband
2 *riot*: revel 3 *beast*: monster
4 *great*: pregnant, full of matter 5 *states*: dignitaries

VASQUEZ

Let not your pity betray you till my coming back:
Think upon incest and cuckoldry.

SORANZO

Revenge is all the ambition I aspire;[1]
To that I'll climb or fall. My blood's on fire! *Exeunt.*

ACT 5

Scene 3

Enter GIOVANNI.

GIOVANNI

Busy opinion[2] is an idle fool,
That, as a school-rod[3] keeps a child in awe,
Frights the unexperienced temper of the mind.
So did it me, who, ere my precious sister
Was married, thought all taste of love would die
In such a contract; but I find no change
Of pleasure in this formal law of sports.[4]
She is still one[5] to me, and every kiss
As sweet and as delicious as the first
I reaped, when yet the privilege of youth
Entitled her a virgin. Oh, the glory
Of two united hearts like hers and mine!
Let poring bookmen dream of other worlds;
My world, and all of happiness, is here,
And I'd not change it for the best to come.
A life of pleasure is Elysium.

Enter FRIAR.

1 *aspire*: wish for
2 *Busy opinion*: interfering public opinion, conventional thinking
3 *school-rod*: birch twigs used for corporal punishment
4 *formal law of sports*: the legalization of Annabella's sexual activity through marriage
5 *one*: the same

Father, you enter on the jubilee[1]
Of my retired[2] delights. Now I can tell you,
The hell you oft have prompted[3] is nought else
But slavish and fond, superstitious fear,
And I could prove it too –

FRIAR

Thy blindness slays thee!
Look there; 'tis writ to thee.

Gives [him] the letter.

GIOVANNI

From whom?

FRIAR

Unrip the seals and see.
[GIOVANNI *reads the letter.*]
The blood's yet seething-hot that will anon
Be frozen harder than congealed coral.[4]
Why d'ee change colour, son?

GIOVANNI

'Fore heaven, you make
Some petty devil factor[5] 'twixt my love
And your religion-maskèd sorceries.
Where had you this?

FRIAR

Thy conscience, youth, is seared,[6]
Else thou wouldst stoop[7] to warning.

GIOVANNI

'Tis her hand,
I know't; and 'tis all written in her blood.
She writes I know not what. 'Death'? I'll not fear
An armèd thunderbolt aimed at my heart.
She writes we are discovered. Pox on dreams
Of low, faint-hearted cowardice! 'Discovered'?
The devil we are! Which way is't possible?

1 *jubilee*: time of celebration 2 *retired*: private
3 *prompted*: spoken of
4 *congealed coral*: thought to harden on contact with the air
5 *factor*: intermediary 6 *seared*: cauterized
7 *stoop to*: submit to, obey

Are we grown traitors to our own delights?
Confusion take such dotage;[1] 'tis but forged.
This is your peevish chattering, weak old man.

Enter VASQUEZ.

Now, sir, what news bring you?

VASQUEZ

My lord, according to his yearly custom keeping this day a feast in honour of his birthday, by me invites you thither. Your worthy father, with the Pope's reverend Nuncio and other magnificos of Parma, have promised their presence. Wilt please you to be of the number?

GIOVANNI

Yes, tell them I dare come.

VASQUEZ

Dare come?

GIOVANNI

So I said; and tell him more, I will come.

VASQUEZ

These words are strange to me.

GIOVANNI

Say I will come.

VASQUEZ

You will not miss?[2]

GIOVANNI

Yet more? I'll come. Sir, are you answered?

VASQUEZ

So I'll say. My service to you. *Exit* VASQUEZ.

FRIAR

You will not go, I trust.

GIOVANNI

Not go? For what?

FRIAR

Oh, do not go! This feast, I'll gage[3] my life,
Is but a plot to train[4] you to your ruin.
Be ruled, you sha' not go.

1 *dotage*: stupidity 2 *miss*: fail to attend 3 *gage*: wager 4 *train*: lure

GIOVANNI

Not go? Stood Death
Threat'ning his armies of confounding plagues,
With hosts of dangers, hot as blazing stars,[1]
I would be there. Not go? Yes, and resolve
To strike as deep in slaughter as they all,
For I will go.

FRIAR

Go where thou wilt. I see
The wildness of thy fate draws to an end,
To a bad, fearful end. I must not stay
To know thy fall. Back to Bologna I
With speed will haste, and shun this coming blow.
Parma, farewell! Would I had never known thee,
Or aught[2] of thine! Well, young man, since no prayer
Can make thee safe, I leave thee to despair. *Exit* FRIAR.

GIOVANNI

Despair or tortures of a thousand hells –
All's one to me: I have set up my rest.[3]
Now, now, work serious thoughts on baneful[4] plots.
Be all a man, my soul! Let not the curse
Of old prescription[5] rend from me the gall[6]
Of courage, which enrols[7] a glorious death.
If I must totter like a well-grown oak,
Some under-shrubs shall in my weighty fall
Be crushed to splits;[8] with me they all shall perish. *Exit.*

1 *blazing stars*: comets, thought to be a bad omen
2 *aught*: any, i.e., Giovanni
3 *set up my rest*: staked everything, as in a card game
4 *baneful*: destructive 5 *prescription*: custom
6 *gall*: bodily fluid thought to produce aggression, also a secretion from the oak tree used to make ink
7 *enrols*: writes down in the annals of history 8 *splits*: splinters

ACT 5

Scene 4

Enter SORANZO, VASQUEZ *and* BANDITTI.

SORANZO

You will not fail, or shrink in the attempt?

VASQUEZ

I will undertake for[1] their parts. [*To the* BANDITTI] Be sure, my masters, to be bloody enough, and as unmerciful as if you were preying upon a rich booty[2] on the very mountains of Liguria.[3] For your pardons,[4] trust to my lord; but for reward you shall trust none but your own pockets.

ALL THE BANDITTI

We'll make a murder!

SORANZO

Here's gold [*giving them money*]; here's more; want[5]
nothing. What you do
Is noble and an act of brave revenge.
I'll make ye rich banditti, and all free.

ALL

Liberty, liberty!

VASQUEZ

Hold! Take every man a vizard.[6]

[*The* BANDITTI *put on masks.*]

When ye are withdrawn, keep as much silence as you can possibly. You know the watchword, till which be spoken move not; but when you hear that, rush in like a stormy flood. I need not instruct ye in your own profession.

ALL

No, no, no.

1 *undertake for*: guarantee they will fulfil their parts
2 *booty*: plunder associated with robbers
3 *Liguria*: a mountainous region of north-west Italy
4 *pardons*: banditti were often assumed to be outlaws
5 *want*: lack
6 *vizard*: mask

VASQUEZ

In, then. Your ends are profit and preferment. Away!

Exeunt BANDITTI.

SORANZO

The guests will all come, Vasquez?

VASQUEZ

Yes, sir, and now let me a little edge[1] your resolution. You see nothing is unready to this great work but a great mind in you. Call to your remembrance your disgraces, your loss of honour, Hippolita's blood, and arm your courage in your own wrongs. So shall you best right those wrongs in vengeance which you may truly call your own.

SORANZO

'Tis well. The less I speak, the more I burn,
And blood shall quench that flame.

VASQUEZ

Now you begin to turn Italian![2] This beside: when my young incest-monger comes, he will be sharp set on his old bit.[3] Give him time enough; let him have your chamber and bed at liberty. Let my hot hare[4] have law[5] ere he be hunted to his death, that if it be possible, he may post[6] to hell in the very act of his damnation.

Enter GIOVANNI.

SORANZO

It shall be so; and see, as we would wish,
He comes himself first. [*To* GIOVANNI] Welcome, my
much-loved brother.
Now I perceive you honour me; y'are welcome.
But where's my father?[7]

1 *edge*: sharpen

2 *Italian*: assumed to be hot-tempered and prone to outbursts of jealousy and revenge

3 *set on his old bit*: keen for sex with his usual lover

4 *hare*: associated with lust 5 *law*: a head-start

6 *post to*: ride swiftly 7 *my father*: father-in-law

GIOVANNI

With the other states,
Attending on the Nuncio of the Pope
To wait upon him hither. How's my sister?

SORANZO

Like a good housewife – scarcely ready yet.
Y'are best walk to her chamber.

GIOVANNI

If you will.

SORANZO

I must expect[1] my honourable friends.
Good brother, get her forth.

GIOVANNI

You are busy, sir. *Exit* GIOVANNI.

VASQUEZ

Even as the great devil himself would have it! Let him go and glut himself in his own destruction.

Flourish.

Hark, the Nuncio is at hand. Good sir, be ready to receive him.

Enter CARDINAL, FLORIO, DONADO, RICHARDETTO [*disguised*] *and* ATTENDANTS.

SORANZO [*To the* CARDINAL]

Most reverend lord, this grace[2] hath made me proud:
That you vouchsafe[3] my house. I ever rest
Your humble servant for this noble favour.

CARDINAL

You are our friend, my lord. His Holiness
Shall understand how zealously you honour
Saint Peter's vicar[4] in his substitute.
Our special love to you.

SORANZO

Signors, to you
My welcome, and my ever best of thanks

1 *expect*: await 2 *grace*: honour
3 *vouchsafe*: deign to visit
4 *Saint Peter's vicar*: thought to be the first Pope

For this so memorable courtesy.
Pleaseth your grace to walk near?

CARDINAL

My lord, we come
To celebrate your feast with civil mirth,
As ancient custom teacheth. We will go.

SORANZO [*To* ATTENDANTS]

Attend his grace, there! [*To his guests*] Signors, keep your way.[1] *Exeunt.*

ACT 5

Scene 5

Enter GIOVANNI *and* ANNABELLA, *lying on a bed.*

GIOVANNI

What, changed[2] so soon? Hath your new, sprightly lord
Found out a trick in night-games[3] more than we
Could know in our simplicity? Ha, is't so?
Or does the fit[4] come on you to prove treacherous
To your past vows and oaths?

ANNABELLA

Why should you jest
At my calamity, without all sense
Of the approaching dangers you are in?

GIOVANNI

What danger's half so great as thy revolt?
Thou art a faithless sister, else, thou know'st,
Malice, or any treachery beside,
Would stoop to my bent brows.[5] Why, I hold fate
Clasped in my fist, and could command the course
Of time's eternal motion hadst thou been

1 *keep your way*: carry on in the same direction
2 *changed*: alluding to Annabella's repentance
3 *Hath ... night-games*: i.e., is Soranzo a more sophisticated, experienced lover?
4 *fit*: impulse 5 *stoop ... brows*: submit on seeing me frown

One thought more steady than an ebbing sea.
And what? You'll now be honest? That's resolved?

ANNABELLA

Brother, dear brother, know what I have been,
And know that now there's but a dying-time
'Twixt us and our confusion.[1] Let's not waste
These precious hours in vain and useless speech.
Alas, these gay attires[2] were not put on
But to some end; this sudden, solemn[3] feast
Was not ordained to riot in expense:[4]
I, that have now been chambered here alone,
Barred of my guardian, or of any else,
Am not for nothing at an instant freed
To fresh access.[5] Be not deceived, my brother:
This banquet is an harbinger of death
To you and me. Resolve yourself it is,
And be prepared to welcome it.

GIOVANNI

Well then,
The schoolmen[6] teach that all this globe of earth
Shall be consumed to ashes in a minute.

ANNABELLA

So I have read too.

GIOVANNI

But 'twere somewhat strange
To see the waters burn. Could I believe
This might be true, I could believe as well
There might be hell or heaven.

ANNABELLA

That's most certain.

GIOVANNI

A dream, a dream; else in this other world
We should know one another.

1 *confusion*: damnation
2 *gay attires*: Annabella is wearing her bridal clothes
3 *solemn*: ceremonious 4 *to riot in expense*: to waste money
5 *fresh access*: to receive visitors
6 *schoolmen*: scholars, scholastic philosophers

ANNABELLA

So we shall.

GIOVANNI

Have you heard so?

ANNABELLA

For certain.

GIOVANNI

But d'ee think,
That I shall see you there, you look on me?
May we kiss one another, prate[1] or laugh,
Or do as we do here?

ANNABELLA

I know not that;
But, good,[2] for the present, what d'ee mean
To free yourself from danger? Some way think
How to escape. I'm sure the guests are come.

GIOVANNI

Look up, look here: what see you in my face?

ANNABELLA

Distraction and a troubled countenance.

GIOVANNI

Death and a swift, repining[3] wrath! Yet look:
What see you in mine eyes?

ANNABELLA

Methinks you weep.

GIOVANNI

I do, indeed. These are the funeral tears
Shed on your grave; these furrowed up my cheeks
When first I loved and knew not how to woo.
Fair Annabella, should I here repeat
The story of my life, we might lose time.
Be record, all the spirits of the air,
And all things else that are, that day and night,
Early and late, the tribute which my heart
Hath paid to Annabella's sacred love
Hath been these tears, which are her mourners now.

1 *prate*: chatter 2 *good*: dear one 3 *repining*: discontented

Never till now did Nature do her best
To show a matchless beauty to the world,
Which, in an instant, ere it scarce was seen,
The jealous Destinies[1] require again.
Pray, Annabella, pray. Since we must part,
Go thou, white in thy soul, to fill a throne
Of innocence and sanctity in heaven.
Pray, pray, my sister.

ANNABELLA

Then I see your drift.[2]
Ye blessed angels, guard me!

GIOVANNI

So say I.
Kiss me.
[*They kiss.*]
If ever after-times should hear
Of our fast-knit affections, though perhaps
The laws of conscience and of civil use[3]
May justly blame us, yet when they but know
Our loves, that love will wipe away that rigour[4]
Which would in other incests be abhorred.
Give me your hand. How sweetly life doth run
In these well-coloured veins! How constantly
These palms do promise health! But I could chide
With Nature for this cunning flattery.[5]
Kiss me again.
[*They kiss.*]
Forgive me.

ANNABELLA

With my heart.

GIOVANNI

Farewell.

1 *Destinies*: three goddesses in classical mythology who dictated the course and span of a man's life

2 *drift*: intention 3 *civil use*: social custom 4 *rigour*: passionate extremity

5 *cunning flattery*: dissimulation, because Annabella is on the point of death

ANNABELLA

Will you be gone?

GIOVANNI

Be dark, bright sun,
And make this midday night, that thy gilt rays
May not behold a deed will turn their splendour
More sooty than the poets feign their Styx.[1]
One other kiss, my sister.
[*He draws a dagger.*]

ANNABELLA

What means this?

GIOVANNI

To save thy fame,[2] and kill thee in a kiss.
Stabs her [*as they kiss*].
Thus die, and die by me, and by my hand.
Revenge is mine;[3] honour doth love command.

ANNABELLA

O brother, by your hand?

GIOVANNI

When thou art dead
I'll give my reasons for't; for to dispute
With thy – even in thy death – most lovely beauty
Would make me stagger[4] to perform this act
Which I most glory in.

ANNABELLA

Forgive him, heaven,
And me my sins. Farewell, brother unkind,[5] unkind.
Mercy, great heaven! Oh, oh! [*She*] *dies.*

1 *Styx*: a black and poisonous river in the classical underworld

2 *fame*: reputation

3 *Revenge is mine*: an echo of Romans 12:19, where revenge belongs exclusively to God, often quoted in revenge tragedy, for example Kyd's *The Spanish Tragedy* (*c.*1587)

4 *stagger*: hesitate 5 *unkind*: cruel, unnatural, unkinlike

GIOVANNI

She's dead. Alas, good soul. The hapless[1] fruit
That in her womb received its life from me,
Hath had from me a cradle and a grave.
I must not dally. This sad marriage-bed,
In all her best, bore her alive and dead.
Soranzo, thou hast missed thy aim in this;
I have prevented now thy reaching[2] plots
And killed a love for whose each drop of blood
I would have pawned my heart. Fair Annabella,
How over-glorious[3] art thou in thy wounds,
Triumphing over infamy and hate!
Shrink not, courageous hand. Stand up, my heart,
And boldly act my last and greater part!

Exit with the body.

ACT 5

Scene 6

A banquet.

Enter CARDINAL, FLORIO, DONADO, SORANZO, RICHARDETTO [*disguised*], VASQUEZ *and* ATTENDANTS. *They take their places* [*at the table*].

VASQUEZ [*Aside to* SORANZO]

Remember, sir, what you have to do. Be wise and resolute.

SORANZO [*Aside to* VASQUEZ]

Enough! My heart is fixed. [*To the* CARDINAL] Pleaseth your grace
To taste these coarse confections?[4] Though the use
Of such set[5] entertainments more consists
In custom than in cause,[6] yet, reverend sir,
I am still made your servant by your presence.

1 *hapless*: unfortunate 2 *reaching*: far-sighted
3 *over-glorious*: superlatively beautiful
4 *coarse confections*: humble dishes 5 *set*: formal 6 *cause*: reason

CARDINAL
And we your friend.

SORANZO
But where's my brother, Giovanni?

Enter GIOVANNI, *with a heart upon his dagger.*

GIOVANNI
Here, here, Soranzo, trimmed[1] in reeking[2] blood
That triumphs over death; proud in the spoil
Of love and vengeance![3] Fate, or all the powers
That guide the motions of immortal souls,
Could not prevent me.

CARDINAL
What means this?

FLORIO
Son Giovanni?

SORANZO [*Aside*]
Shall I be forestalled?

GIOVANNI
Be not amazed. If your misgiving[4] hearts
Shrink at an idle[5] sight, what bloodless fear
Of coward passion would have seized your senses,
Had you beheld the rape[6] of life and beauty
Which I have acted? My sister, O my sister!

FLORIO
Ha! What of her?

GIOVANNI
The glory of my deed
Darkened the midday sun, made noon as night.
You came to feast, my lords, with dainty fare.
I came to feast too, but I digged for food
In a much richer mine than gold or stone[5]

1 *trimmed*: decorated
2 *reeking*: steaming hot
3 *spoil of love and vengeance*: the destruction of his love and Soranzo's vengeance, but also suggesting that the heart is the plunder taken by Love and Vengeance
4 *misgiving*: fearful 5 *idle*: mere 6 *rape*: violent theft
5 *stone*: precious stones

Of any value balanced.[1] 'Tis a heart,
A heart, my lords, in which is mine entombed.
Look well upon't. D'ee know't?

VASQUEZ
What strange riddle's this?

GIOVANNI
'Tis Annabella's heart, 'tis! Why d'ee startle?[2]
I vow 'tis hers. This dagger's point ploughed up
Her fruitful womb, and left to me the fame
Of a most glorious executioner.

FLORIO
Why, madman, art thyself?

GIOVANNI
Yes, father, and that times to come may know
How, as my fate, I honoured my revenge,
List, father: to your ears I will yield up
How much I have deserved to be your son.[3]

FLORIO
What is't thou say'st?

GIOVANNI
Nine moons have had their changes
Since I first throughly[4] viewed and truly loved
Your daughter and my sister.

FLORIO
How? Alas,
My lords, he's a frantic madman!

GIOVANNI
Father, no.
For nine months' space, in secret I enjoyed
Sweet Annabella's sheets; nine months I lived
A happy monarch of her heart and her.
Soranzo, thou know'st this; thy paler cheek
Bears the confounding print of thy disgrace.

1 *balanced*: calculated 2 *startle*: start
3 *son*: with an allusion to his being Florio's son-in-law
4 *throughly*: thoroughly

For her too fruitful womb too soon bewrayed[1]
The happy passage[2] of our stol'n delights,
And made her mother to a child unborn.

CARDINAL

Incestuous villain!

FLORIO

Oh, his rage[3] belies him![4]

GIOVANNI

It does not. 'Tis the oracle of truth –
I vow it is so.

SORANZO

I shall burst with fury!
[*To* VASQUEZ] Bring the strumpet forth!

VASQUEZ

I shall, sir.

GIOVANNI

Do, sir. *Exit* VASQUEZ.
Have you all no faith
To credit yet my triumphs? Here I swear,
By all that you call sacred, by the love
I bore my Annabella whilst she lived,
These hands have from her bosom ripped this heart.

Enter VASQUEZ.

Is't true or no, sir?

VASQUEZ

'Tis most strangely true.

FLORIO

Cursèd man, have I lived to – [*He*] *dies.*

CARDINAL

Hold up, Florio!
[*To* GIOVANNI] Monster of children, see what thou hast
done:

1 *bewrayed*: betrayed 2 *passage*: sequence of events
3 *rage*: frenzy 4 *belies him*: makes him lie

Broke thy old father's heart! [*To the others*] Is none of you
Dares venture on him?[1]

GIOVANNI

Let 'em! O my father!
How well his death becomes him in his griefs!
Why, this was done with courage. Now survives
None of our house but I, gilt[2] in the blood
Of a fair sister and a hapless father.

SORANZO

Inhuman scorn of men, hast thou a thought
T'outlive thy murders?

GIOVANNI

Yes, I tell thee, yes;
For in my fists I bear the twists of life.[3]
Soranzo, see this heart which was thy wife's:
Thus I exchange it royally[4] for thine,[5]
[*He stabs* SORANZO.]
And thus and thus! [*Stabs him again.*] Now brave revenge is mine.

VASQUEZ

I cannot hold any longer. You, sir, are you grown insolent in your butcheries? Have at you!

GIOVANNI

Come, I am armed to meet thee!
[VASQUEZ *and* GIOVANNI] *fight.* [VASQUEZ *wounds* GIOVANNI.]

VASQUEZ

No? Will it[6] not be yet? If this will not, another shall.
[*He stabs* GIOVANNI *again.*]

1 *venture on him*: take him on 2 *gilt*: gilded, but also guilty

3 *twists of life*: in classical mythology human life is represented by threads which the three Fates spin out, weave and finally cut

4 *royally*: generously

5 *exchange . . . thine*: it is not clear how this is staged; perhaps Giovanni stabs Soranzo with the dagger still bearing the heart or he might remove the heart and give it to Soranzo before stabbing him

6 *it*: i.e., Giovanni's death

Not yet? I shall fit you[1] anon. [*Shouts*] Vengeance![2]

Enter BANDITTI [*masked, with weapons drawn*].

GIOVANNI

Welcome! Come more of you; whate'er you be,
I dare your worst –

[*They fight.* GIOVANNI *is wounded.*]

Oh, I can stand no longer. Feeble arms,
Have you so soon lost strength?

VASQUEZ

Now, you are welcome, sir. [*To the* BANDITTI] Away, my masters! All is done. Shift for yourselves[3] – your reward is your own – shift for yourselves!

BANDITTI

Away, away! *Exeunt* BANDITTI.

VASQUEZ [*To* SORANZO]

How d'ee, my lord? See you this? How is't?

SORANZO

Dead, but in death well pleased that I have lived
To see my wrongs revenged on that black devil.
O Vasquez, to thy bosom let me give
My last of breath.[4] Let not that lecher live – Oh! [*He*] *dies.*

VASQUEZ

The reward of peace and rest be with him, my ever-dearest lord and master.

GIOVANNI

Whose hand gave me this wound?

VASQUEZ

Mine, sir; I was your first man. Have you enough?

GIOVANNI

I thank thee. Thou hast done for me
But what I would have else done on myself.
Art sure thy lord is dead?

1 *fit you*: impose an apt punishment on you
2 *Vengeance*: the code word agreed on with the Banditti
3 *Shift for yourselves*: look to your own safety
4 *last of breath*: dying words

VASQUEZ

O impudent slave,
As sure as I am sure to see thee die!

CARDINAL

Think on thy life and end, and call for mercy.

GIOVANNI

Mercy? Why, I have found it in this justice.

CARDINAL

Strive yet to cry to heaven.

GIOVANNI

Oh, I bleed fast.
Death, thou art a guest long looked-for; I embrace
Thee and thy wounds. Oh, my last minute comes.
Where'er I go, let me enjoy this grace:
Freely to view my Annabella's face. [*He*] *dies.*

DONADO

Strange miracle of justice!

CARDINAL

Raise up the city! We shall be murdered all!

VASQUEZ

You need not fear. You shall not. This strange task being ended, I have paid the duty to the son which I have vowed to the father.

CARDINAL

Speak, wretched villain, what incarnate fiend
Hath led thee on to this?

VASQUEZ

Honesty, and pity of my master's wrongs. For know, my lord, I am by birth a Spaniard,[1] brought forth my country in my youth by Lord Soranzo's father, whom, whilst he lived, I served faithfully; since whose death I have been to this man, as I was to him. What I have done was duty, and I repent nothing but that the loss of my life had not ransomed his.

1 *Spaniard*: conventionally thought to hide malice behind an appearance of friendliness

CARDINAL

Say, fellow, know'st thou any yet unnamed
Of counsel[1] in this incest?

VASQUEZ

Yes, an old woman, sometimes[2] guardian to this murdered lady.

CARDINAL

And what's become of her?

VASQUEZ

Within this room she is, whose eyes, after her confession, I caused to be put out, but kept alive to confirm what from Giovanni's own mouth you have heard. Now, my lord, what I have done you may judge of, and let your own wisdom be a judge in your own reason.

CARDINAL

Peace! First, this woman,[3] chief in these effects:
My sentence is that forthwith she be ta'en
Out of the city, for example's sake,
There to be burnt to ashes.

DONADO

'Tis most just.

CARDINAL

Be it your charge, Donado: see it done.

DONADO

I shall.

VASQUEZ

What for me? If death, 'tis welcome. I have been honest to the son, as I was to the father.

CARDINAL

Fellow, for thee, since what thou didst was done
Not for thyself, being no Italian,
We banish thee forever, to depart

1 *Of counsel*: complicit 2 *sometimes*: formerly
3 *this woman*: Puttana or Annabella

Within three days. In this we do dispense[1]
With grounds of reason,[2] not of thine offence.[3]

VASQUEZ

'Tis well. This conquest is mine, and I rejoice that a Spaniard outwent an Italian in revenge. *Exit* VASQUEZ.

CARDINAL

Take up these slaughtered bodies, see them buried;
And all the gold and jewels, or whatsoever,
Confiscate by the canons of the Church,
We seize upon to the Pope's proper[4] use.

RICHARDETTO [*removing his disguise*]

Your Grace's pardon. Thus long I lived disguised
To see the effect of pride and lust at once
Brought both to shameful ends.

CARDINAL

What, Richardetto, whom we thought for dead?

DONADO

Sir, was it you –

RICHARDETTO

Your friend.

CARDINAL

We shall have time
To talk at large[5] of all; but never yet
Incest and murder have so strangely met.
Of one so young, so rich in Nature's store,[5]
Who could not say, ''Tis pity she's a whore'?[6]

Exeunt [*with the bodies*].

FINIS.

1 *dispense*: offer a dispensation by commuting the punishment from execution to banishment
2 *reason*: motive
3 *not of thine offence*: not ignoring the seriousness of his crime
4 *proper*: personal 5 *at large*: in full 6 *store*: gifts
7 *'Tis pity she's a whore*: the fact that this line is italicized in the quarto might suggest the phrase was already familiar

[PRINTER'S AFTERWORD]

The general commendation deserved by the actors, in their presentment[1] of this tragedy, may easily excuse such few faults as are escaped in the printing. A common charity may allow him the ability of spelling, whom a secure confidence assures that he cannot ignorantly err in the application of sense.[2]

1 *presentment*: performance
2 *A common . . . sense*: it is only fair to assume that a person who understands the meaning of the words he uses also knows how to spell them

Textual Variants

The White Devil

To the Reader
'liven [Edd] life'n
1.1.6 swoop [Edd] swope
19 you [Edd] you, you
1.2.22 whereas [Edd] where a
66 your [Edd] you
79 lyam [Edd] Leon
183 mark [Edd] make
227 'crostics [This edn] crosse-sticks
264 with [Edd] not in Q
266 than [Edd] not in Q
271 leave [Edd] leaves
289 his [Edd] this
2.1.3 such a [Edd] a such
27 that have [Edd] have
51 prey [Edd] pery
86 and 94 SP FRANCISCO [Edd] *Flan.*
90 prowling [Edd] proling
144 Lodovic [Edd] *Lodowicke*
226 heart [Edd] heare
227 Q's SD includes CAMILLO, here delayed until 279
265 *repostum* [Edd] *repositum*
305 Anthony's fire [Edd] *Anthony* fire
321 gallows [Edd] gallouses
322 another's [Edd] another
336 needs [Edd] neede
379 Lodovic [Edd] *Lodowicke*
2.2.8 necromancer [Edd] Nigromancer
32 Lodovic [Edd] *Lodowicke*
35 fate [Edd] face
46 SP BRACCIANO [Edd] *Mar.*
3.1.48 on [Edd] Or
3.2.0 SD Q includes ISABELLA
10 SP LAWYER [Edd] missing in Q
100 brings [Edd] bring
124 cunning [Q] conning
192 he [Edd] her
208 a feast [This edn] feast
228 long [Edd] louing
248 balladed [Edd] ballated
262 princes. Here's [Edd] Princes heares;
263 Q adds SP *Vit.*
274 maw [Edd] mawes
323.5 SP GIOVANNI [Edd] missing in Q
3.3.21 Yon [Edd] You
25 victual under the line [Edd] vittel vnder the liue
50–1 a sawpit [Edd] saw-pit
77 gentle [Edd] gentile
86 rogue [Edd] gue
4.1.89 in so [Edd] so in
4.2.81 hawks [Edd] hawke
94 Ye'd [Edd] Yee'ld

218 breeds [Edd] breds
4.3.17 Lodovic [Edd] *Lodowicke*
60–1 *Concedimus . . . peccatorum* [Edd] missing in this version of Q; added in press correction
80 SP MONTICELSO [Edd] missing in Q
89.5 SP MONTICELSO [Edd] attributed to *Lod.* in Q
137 wills [Edd] will
150 now to [Edd] now. Now to
5.1.31 Q has SD *Enter Duke Brachiano*
60 SP BRACCIANO [Edd] missing in Q
168 diners [Edd] *Diuers*
177 morality [Edd] mortality
200 two [Edd] 10
208, 218, 223 SP FRANCISCO [Edd] *Fla.*
5.2.24 wider [Edd] wilder
5.3.115 orris [Edd] Arras
156 copperas [Edd] copperesse
175, 185, 195, 202, 214 SP FRANCISCO [Edd] *Flo.*
193 feat [Edd] seat
233.5 SP FRANCISCO [Edd] *Fla.*
5.4.60 SP FRANCISCO [Edd] not in Q
71.5 SP LADY [Edd] *Wom.*
5.6.16 They [Edd] the
18 scare [Edd] scarre
27 they [Edd] the
31 worldly [Edd] wordly
140 stinking [Edd] sinking
chimney is [Edd] chimneis
174 safety [Edd] sasty
177 precedent [Edd] president
198 grieves's [Edd] greeu's
263 wives' [Edd] wides

The Duchess of Malfi

1.1.0 SD [*Enter*] ANTONIO *and* DELIO [Edd] ANTONIO *and* DELIO, BOSOLA, CARDINALL
56 died [Edd] did
pardon [Edd] pleadon
57 when [Edd] and, when
64 like [Edd] likes
70 Foix [Edd] Foux
1.2.0 SD [*Enter*] CASTRUCHIO, SILVIO, RODERIGO *and* GRISOLAN [Edd] ANTONIO, DELIO, FERDINAND, CARDINALL, DUTCHESSE, CASTRUCHIO, SILUIO, RODOCICO, GRISOLAN, BOSOLA, IULIA, CARIOLA
33 SP FERDINAND [Edd] missing in Q
Jennet [Edd] Gennit
36 ballasted [Edd] ballass'd
75 flatterers [Edd] Flatters
94 shrewd [Edd] shewed
101 your [Edd] you
131 are [Edd] missing in Q
133 leaguer [Edd] Leagues
134.5 SP DUCHESS [Edd] *Ferd.*
158.5 SP FERDINAND [Edd] *Berd.*
178 to [Edd] missing in Q
182 on't [Edd] out

188 o'er [Edd] are
vile [Edd] vild
275 these [Edd] this
294 you [Edd] yon
300 couple [Edd] cople
301 St Winifred [Edd] St *Winfrid*
332 visitants [Edd] visitans
351 woo . . . woo [Edd] woe . . . woe
386 *de presenti* [Edd] *presenti*
2.1 SD [*Enter*] BOSOLA [*and*] CASTRUCHIO [Edd] BOSOLA, CASTRUCHIO, An OLD LADY, ANTONIO, DELIO, DUCHESSE, RODORICO, GRISOLAN
27 flayed [Edd] Flead
31 but [Edd] but you call
37 children's [Edd] children
ordure [Edd] ordures
42 high-priced [This edn] high-prized
61 couple [Edd] cople
96 cousin-german [Edd] Cosen German
113 lemon [Edd] Lymmon
114 swoon [Edd] sound
116 courtiers [Edd] Courties
119 SP DUCHESS [Edd] missing in Q
126 Methought [Edd] My thought
2.2.0 SD [*Enter*] BOSOLA [*and*] OLD LADY [Edd] BOSOLA, OLD LADY, ANTONIO, RODORIGO, GRISOLAN: SERVANTS, DELIO, CARIOLA
1 tetchiness [Edd] teatchiues
1–2 vulturous [Edd] vulterous
13 bears [Edd] beare
32–62 SPs [1ST] OFFICER/ OFFICERS/[2ND] OFFICER [This edn] Seruant/ Seru./Ser./2.Ser.
48 officers [Edd] Offices
70 looks [Edd] looke
2.3.0 SD [*Enter*] BOSOLA [*with a dark lantern*] [Edd] BOSOLA, ANTONIO.
10 Who's [Edd] whose
52 quit [Edd] quite
65 eighth [Edd] eight
Caetera [Edd] *Caeteta*
70 cased-up [Edd] caside-vp
2.4.0 SD [*Enter*] CARDINAL *and* JULIA [Edd] CARDINALL, *and* JULIA, SERUANT, *and* DELIO
12 turnings [Edd] turning
29 Bore [Edd] Boare
30 thee [Edd] the
38 liver [Edd] liuour
41 moves [Edd] moones
47 you are [Edd] your
66 seethe't [Edd] seeth's
2.5.2 prodigy [Edd] progedy
3 damned [Edd] dampn'd
30 mother's [Edd] mother
44 one o'th [Edd] one th'
3.1.0 SD [*Enter*] ANTONIO *and* DELIO [Edd] ANTONIO, *and* DELIO, DUCHESSE, FERDINAND, BOSOLA
16 insensibly [Edd] inseucibly
27 be [Edd] he
37 of [Edd] off
39 bespeak [Edd] be be-speak
51 of [Edd] off
54 were [Edd] where
57 coulters [Edd] cultures

78 blood [Edd] bood
3.2.0 SD [*Enter*] DUCHESS, ANTONIO [*and*] CARIOLA [Edd] DUTCHESS, ANTONIO, CARIOLA, FERDINAND, BOSOLA, OFFICERS
60 orris [Edd] Arras
79 us [This edn] missing in Q
89 confederacy [Edd] consideracy
90 thee [Edd] the
screech-owl [Edd] Schrech-Owle
96 damn [Edd] dampe
115.5 SP FERDINAND [Edd] *Ford.*
135 shook [Edd] shooked
202 As loath [Edd] A-loth
233 first-born intelligencers [Edd] first-borne and Intelligencers
242 coffers [Edd] cofers
246 in God's [Edd] on god's
246–7 sent On [Edd] sent One
266 Bermudas [Edd] *Bermoothes*
267 tied [Edd] tide
304 Whither [Edd] Whether
3.3.0 SD [*Enter*] CARDINAL, MALATESTE [*on one side*]. FERDINAND, DELIO, SILVIO, PESCARA [*on the other*] [Edd] CARDINALL, FERDINAND, MALLATESTE, PESCARA, SILUIO, DELIO, BOSOLA
17 scent [Edd] sent
20 keeps [Edd] keepe
31 bore [Edd] boare
45 symmetry [Edd] semitry
53 porpoise [Edd] Por-pisse
72 counters [Edd] coumpters
73 life [Edd] like
75 hundred [Edd] hundreth
3.4.36 Off [Edd] Of
3.5.0 SD [*Enter*] ANTONIO, DUCHESS [*and two*] CHILDREN, CARIOLA [*carrying an infant*], SERVANTS [Edd] ANTONIO, DUCHESSE, CHILDREN, CARIOLA, SERUANTS, BOSOLA, SOULDIERS, *with Vizards*
103 o'er-charged [Edd] ore-char'd
105 Whither [Edd] Whether
130 smelts [Edd] Smylts
140 whither [Edd] whether
4.1.0 SD [*Enter*] FERDINAND, BOSOLA [*and*] SERVANTS [*with torches*] [Edd] FERDINAND, BOSOLA, DUTCHESSE, CARIOLA, SERUANTS
4.2.0 SD [*Enter*] DUCHESS [*and*] CARIOLA [Edd] DUCHESSE, CARIOLA, SERUANT, MAD-MEN, BOSOLA, EXECUTIONERS, FERDINAND
67 irksome [Edd] yerk some
73 SP MAD ASTROLOGER [This edn] I. *Mad-man*
77 SP MAD LAWYER [This edn] 2. *Mad.*
80 SP MAD PRIEST [This edn] 3. *Mad.*
82 SP MAD DOCTOR [This edn] 4. *Mad.*
267 done't [Edd] don't
336 mercy [Edd] merry

5.1.0 SD [*Enter*] ANTONIO [*and*] DELIO [Edd] ANTONIO, DELIO, PESCARA, IULIA
6 'cheat [Edd] Cheit
17 whither [Edd] whether
69 fraught [Edd] fraight
74 howe'er [Edd] how ere
5.2.0 SD [*Enter*] PESCARA [*and*] *a* DOCTOR [Edd] PESCARA, A DOCTOR, FERDINAND, CARDINALL, MALATESTE, BOSOLA, IULIA
77 flay [Edd] flea
110 oft-dyed [Edd] oft-di'd
114 one [Edd] on
140 bought [Edd] brought
179 woo [Edd] woe
276 thee [Edd] the
285 whither [Edd] whether
307 smother [Edd] smoother
309 bier [Edd] Beare
313 off [Edd] of
5.3.26 Ay [Edd] I
27 Ay [Edd] I
28 let us [Edd] let's us
36 SP ECHO [Edd] missing in Q
55.5 SP ANTONIO [Edd] missing in Q
5.4.0 SD [*Enter*] CARDINAL, PESCARA, MALATESTE, RODERIGO [*and*] GRISOLAN [*carrying torches*] [Edd] CARDINALL, PESCARA, MALATESTE, RODERIGO, GRISOLAN, BOSOLA, FERDINAND, ANTONIO, SERUANT
11 our [Edd] out
29 Fro' [This edn] For
34 quiet [Edd] quiein
56 struck [Edd] strooke
76 hither [Edd] hether
5.5.0 SD [*Enter*] CARDINAL, *with a book* [Edd] CARDINALL (*with a Booke*) BOSOLA, PESCARA, MALATESTE, RODORIGO, FERDINAND, DELIO, SERUANT *with* ANTONIO's *body.*
29 let's [Edd] lets's
59 fellows [Edd] followes
83 this [Edd] his

The Broken Heart

Dedication
censure [Edd] *Censore*
1.1.18 broached [Edd] brauch't
31 holy union [uncorrected Q] union
1.2.20 Pephnon [Edd] *Pephon*
111 you [Edd] yon
133 feathers [Edd] Fathers
1.3.20 grudge [Edd] grutch
183 acts [Edd] Arts
2.1.4 travails [Edd] trauels
16 ulcerous [Edd] vlterous
29 their [Edd] the
45 Hey-day! [Edd] Hey da
130 Shoals [Edd] Shoalds
145 Haste [Edd] Hast
2.3.9 little [Edd] not in Q
31 altars [Edd] Artars
124 I'll [Edd] I'e
frenzy [Edd] French

134 rheums [Edd] rhemes
149.5 SP PENTHEA Then let us . . . account [Edd] Attributed to BASSANES in Q
3.1.39 basis [Edd] Bases
41 or [Edd] of
58 human [Edd] humane
72 Your [Edd] You
3.2.27 heard [Edd] hard
56 Of country toil drinks the untroubled streams [Edd] The vntroubled of Country toyle, drinkes streames
62 While [Edd] Which
digestion [Edd] disgestion
72 act [Edd] art
94 nearness [Edd] not in Q
160 silent [Edd] sinlent
3.3.5 grave [Edd] graves
51 close [Edd] close close
3.5.14 human [Edd] humane
35 enjoin [Edd] enioy
36 SP PENTHEA [Edd] missing in Q
72 ago [Edd] agone
96 in [Edd] missing in Q
4.1.12 stands [Edd] stand
25 be denied [Edd] beny'd
118 suppling [Edd] supplying
4.2.36 largesse [Edd] largenesse
57 been [Edd] bee
65 roof [Edd] root
67 imposterous [Edd] Impostors
81 sun [Edd] Swan
111 too [Edd] to
112 SP PENTHEA [Edd] missing in Q
143 done't [Edd] don't
161 Enough [Edd] Enow
173 done't . . . done't [Edd] don't . . . don't
177 th'angry [Edd] th'augury
4.3.89 fortunes [Edd] fortuness
96 Wear [Edd] Were
5.1.7 too [Edd] to
12 doubles [Edd] doublers
5.2.55 rend [Edd] rent
75 goodness [Edd] gooddesse
110 his [Edd] this
112 expectation [Edd] expection
124.5 SP NEARCHUS [Edd] *Org.*
151 standard [Edd] Standards
5.3.23 infinite [Edd] infinites
64 mother's [Edd] mother
83 Th'outward [Edd] outward
84 Is or [Edd] Is not

'Tis Pity She's a Whore

1.1.31 the links [Edd] the the links
49 Bologna [Edd] *Bononia*
1.2.21 mean [Edd] meaned
44 not [Edd] missing in Q
56 villainy [Edd] villaine
76 Monferrato [Edd] *Mount Ferratto*
77 Milanese [Edd] *Millanoys*
78 an't be [Edd] and be
115 pavan [Edd] pauin
118 Ay, ay [Edd] I, I
123 bauble [Edd] bable
186 The [Edd] they
221 smooth-cheeked [Edd] smooth'd-cheeke
1.3.29 SP DONADO [Edd] SP *Pog.*

whither [Edd] whether
42 thither [Edd] hither
43 Ay [Edd] I
46 wilt . . . Wilt [Edd] wu't . . . wu't
49 should [Edd] shu'd
58 Parmesan [Edd] Parmasent
2.2.1 SP SORANZO [Edd] not in Q
13 encomium [Edd] *Euconium*
56 thy [Edd] the
73 Leghorn [Edd] *Ligorne*
96 corpse [Edd] Curse
134 Wilt [Edd] Wu't
153 for witnesses [Edd] foe-witnesses
2.3.9 Leghorn [Edd] *Ligorne*
31 Nuncio [Edd] *Nuntio*
48 Who's [Edd] Whose
53 kill [Edd] tell
63 ruined [Edd] min'd
2.4.4 wilt [Edd] wu't
26 choose [Edd] chose
34 you . . . you [Edd] you . . . yon
2.5.8 my [Edd] Thy
15 frame [Edd] Fame
17 of the body [Edd] of *Body*
2.6.12 An't please [Edd] And please
43 have't [Edd] haue
78 his [Edd] this
3.1.8 SP BERGETTO [Edd] SP *Pog.*
3.2.65 SP SORANZO [Edd] SP *Gio.*
66 swoons [Edd] sounes
3.5.12 Friar [Edd] Fryars
31, 35 coz [Edd] Couze
37.5 SP POGGIO [Edd] SP *Phi.*
3.9.38 Let [Edd] Le
4.1.1 rites [Edd] rights
71 *inganna* [Edd] *niganna*
77 marriage [Edd] malice
4.2.28 lives [Edd] liue
4.3.15 Say [Edd] Shey
32 that's for your glory [Edd] that for glory
59 *Che morte più dolce che morire per amore?* [Edd] *Che morte pluis dolce morire per amore*
63 *Morendo in grazia a lui, morirei senza dolore* [Edd] *Morendo in gratia Lei morirere senza dolore*
122 thou [Edd] thus
154 ferret [Edd] *Secret*
5.1.10 depositions [Edd] dispositions
5.3.66 Bologna [Edd] *Bononia*
71 SP GIOVANNI [Edd] missing in Q
75 rend [Edd] rent
5.6.7 SD *a heart* [Edd] *at heart*

THE STORY OF PENGUIN CLASSICS

Before 1946 ... 'Classics' are mainly the domain of academics and students; readable editions for everyone else are almost unheard of. This all changes when a little-known classicist, E. V. Rieu, presents Penguin founder Allen Lane with the translation of Homer's *Odyssey* that he has been working on in his spare time.

1946 Penguin Classics debuts with *The Odyssey*, which promptly sells three million copies. Suddenly, classics are no longer for the privileged few.

1950s Rieu, now series editor, turns to professional writers for the best modern, readable translations, including Dorothy L. Sayers's *Inferno* and Robert Graves's unexpurgated *Twelve Caesars*.

1960s The Classics are given the distinctive black covers that have remained a constant throughout the life of the series. Rieu retires in 1964, hailing the Penguin Classics list as 'the greatest educative force of the twentieth century.'

1970s A new generation of translators swells the Penguin Classics ranks, introducing readers of English to classics of world literature from more than twenty languages. The list grows to encompass more history, philosophy, science, religion and politics.

1980s The Penguin American Library launches with titles such as *Uncle Tom's Cabin*, and joins forces with Penguin Classics to provide the most comprehensive library of world literature available from any paperback publisher.

1990s The launch of Penguin Audiobooks brings the classics to a listening audience for the first time, and in 1999 the worldwide launch of the Penguin Classics website extends their reach to the global online community.

The 21st Century Penguin Classics are completely redesigned for the first time in nearly twenty years. This world-famous series now consists of more than 1300 titles, making the widest range of the best books ever written available to millions – and constantly redefining what makes a 'classic'.

The Odyssey continues ...

The best books ever written

PENGUIN CLASSICS

SINCE 1946

Find out more at www.penguinclassics.com